W9-BXL-299

FREUDIANISM AND THE LITERARY MIND

Freudianism and the literary mind

FREDERICK J. HOFFMAN

Second Edition

LOUISIANA STATE UNIVERSITY PRESS

Baton Rouge, Louisiana 1957

Copyright 1945, 1957 Louisiana State University Press
Library of Congress Card Catalogue Number: 57–11542
Printed in the United States of America by the
J. H. Furst Company, Baltimore. Second edition.

809.04
H 69
1957

To EC and CE

38952

PREFACE

This book is an exposition and an appraisal of Freudian psychology as it relates to modern literature. I have sought to throw light on several matters of importance: the beginnings of Freud's theories, the career of their influence in Western culture, and their specific effects upon the creative activity of a number of writers, principally writers of fiction.

Freud's discoveries and teachings have elicited a bewildering variety of responses. Editorials, sermons, lectures, letters to the editor, and personal reminiscences throughout the twenties and the thirties in the United States enable us to gauge something of the first impact of psychoanalysis. Literary criticism and creative work were affected rapidly and deeply. In the self-conscious Bohemia of metropolitan America, Freud was attacked as a charlatan and revered as a saint; he was put forward, at once, as the master therapist of the modern psyche and accused for sanctioning and fortifying the psyche in its disorder. The clinical method with which he had worked painstakingly for years became a kind of parlor game.

The task of relating Freud's work to the habits and tendencies of his age is most complex. But it is true that complexity is, to some extent, the concomitant of immediacy and intimacy of association, a temporary character which will be dissolved, and its errors righted, by the passing of time. Thus, perhaps we can hope for only a tentative estimate of Freud's importance, though even now his theories have been sufficiently tested to convince us of their basic soundness. I have been constantly aware, nonetheless, of the need for sober judgment in my assessment of Freudianism as it bears upon the aesthetic of our century.

In this new edition of *Freudianism and the Literary Mind*, I have chosen to preserve the substance of the original book, since I believe that it still constitutes a reasonably full and accurate account of its subject. I have amplified my treatment of topics wherever necessary; in some instances I have cut, especially where the evidence seemed to be needlessly multiplied. Throughout I have reviewed the documentation and brought it up to date; at many points I have refined the language and, in general, have attempted to strengthen the book in content and in manner of presentation.

Chapter I mainly summarizes the theories and practices of psychoanalysis. A selective summary, it has been written with the hope of pointing out those aspects of Freud's theory which meant most to the literary experiment of our times. What appear to be *omissions* in this summary *are* exactly that, and deliberately so. I have, however, expanded and elaborated upon certain portions of Freud's work—such as the important study of the habits and eccentricities of dreams—because, in my opinion, writers were more easily attracted to them.

In the second and third chapters I have tried to give a selective tenth or twentieth of the varied responses to Freud's writings—and, incidentally, to describe in some measure the prejudice, the reserve, in some cases the hostility or offensive calm which characterized the reception of Freudian theory, made of it indeed a new thing altogether. In some such way as I have indicated in these chapters, a body of philosophic theory of psychological discovery is altered and modified—sometimes distorted so that it enters the consciousness of an age considerably changed. Assimilation of it is scarcely ever direct. The simple metaphors of science and the discreet terminologies of philosophy are adapted to the aesthetic imagination.

The fourth chapter deals more specifically with the problem

of influence. Here influence is considered and evaluated, and the sociology and ideology of the age are discussed in their relationship with the actual and immediate problem of creation itself. The concluding pages of this chapter summarize what I think are the principal suggestions which Freudianism has provided for literary exploitation.

There follow a number of individual studies. In the course of them, the influence of Freud will, I hope, be shown for what it is—a very complex and very provocative influence, resulting in a great variety of experiments and in the formation of a number of attitudes. (Here I would draw attention to the new detailed examination of F. Scott Fitzgerald's *Tender Is the Night*, unfortunately neglected in the first edition.) If it appears that most of the important writers considered resist entire absorption in psychoanalytic influences, that is because I have tried to show that there is always a margin of freedom in a writer's reaction to any major influence. Those who have not demonstrated that freedom or maintained that resistance are often only of documentary interest. I am sure that a careful reading of this book will reveal that its major concerns are to testify to Freud's great importance to modern writing but also to demonstrate that the artist does insist on a basic independence from a discipline that has a manner of discourse similar to and yet different from his own.

In the final chapter I have tried to alter or modify a reaction which seems an almost inevitable result of a study of this kind. In brief, I do not want to leave the impression that Freud was the only, or even the principal, influence upon the thought of our time. For this reason I have considered very briefly some few men of the nineteenth century whose influence was also a determining factor—whose thought served to make the response to Freud a very complex and surely a confusing phenomenon.

As an appendix, I have included a paper read to the English Institute in September of 1956; it was subsequently distributed to the members of the Modern Language Association (thanks to Leonard Manheim), and has been published in the *Kenyon Review*. This paper will give its readers an idea of the expansion in literary theory possible in a consideration of the Freudian contribution.

I am indebted especially to Doctor Ernst Kris, whose book, *Psychoanalytic Explorations in Art* (International Universities Press, 1952) seems to me the most intelligent study of the complex relationship of psychoanalysis to art. Several of the statements crucial to my thesis in this paper were prompted by my reading of it. Dr. Kris also reminds me that I can profitably clarify what I conceive to be the scope and aim of this book. In his generous review (reprinted in *Psychoanalytic Explorations*) of the original edition of my book, he rightly points out the omission of a number of Continental writers who might well have been included. I would only comment that I have deliberately focused my survey of Freudian influence on the American and British scene. This was done in order that I might treat certain writers more amply and satisfactorily. For this reason, I believe that my inclusion of Mann and Kafka is justified, though I have had to sacrifice Hermann Hesse and Robert Musil.

Once again I should like to acknowledge my debt of gratitude to Eleanor C. Hoffman and to all those who gave me encouragement and made invaluable suggestions when I first undertook this project some years ago: Harlan H. Hatcher, President of the University of Michigan; Leonard B. Beach, Dean of the Graduate School, Vanderbilt University; Harold R. Walley, and Francis L. Utley, of the Department of English, the Ohio State University; and Professor Robert B. Heilman, of the Department of English, University of Washington; also William Sutton, of the Ohio State University, who originally supplied me with important information about Sherwood Anderson; and Miss Carolyn F. Ulrich, now retired from her position as Chief of the Periodicals Division of the New York Public Library, who opened up for me the vast resources of her department, so that I might study the little magazines of our century.

F. J. H.

Madison, Wisconsin
August, 1957

CONTENTS

chapter I

FREUDIAN
THEORY

---

i

Since the death of Freud in September, 1939, we have been abundantly supplied with information about his theories, about the controversies waged over debatable issues in his psychology, and about the role his school of psychoanalysis has had in many related fields. Concerning the problem of influence much has been said; but the problem has not in itself been either solved or clarified. Any serious effort to determine the nature and extent of influence reveals a complicated and confusing pattern, not easily defined or labeled. The confusion results from three conditions: the transference of disciplines, the difficulties of translation, and the nature of the subject matter itself.

The psychology of Freud was to suffer from all three. The shift from psychology to literature altered the use of terms and concepts; for the most part, once they were used in literature, they acquired new meanings, or shades of meaning. The literary Freudian was in no strict sense a psychoanalyst; certain irremovable barriers prevented the psychologist and the artist from collaborating closely or intelligently. Similarly, the artist who consulted translations of Freud lost the advantage of precision which the original might have given him. In many cases he brought to psychoanalysis his own interpretations of human behavior. One may say that, though there was often a great sympathy of interest, the artist allowed psychoanalysis to supplement, but almost never to supplant, his independent judgment.

The principal source of discrepancy lay in the subject matter itself. Since the turn of the century at least, writers have tried in many ways to represent " the irrational." So far as the philosophers of the nineteenth century have directed the interest in this problem (for it must be remembered that philosophers do not by any means always direct the intellectual interests of their contemporaries or successors), four men have been responsible—Schopenhauer, Nietzsche, Bergson, and Freud.

In the nineteenth century skepticism grew concerning the adequacy of reason in explaining all ethical and aesthetic facts. This distrust may be called a part of the " Romantic Protest " of the century, but its roots are deeper than that. The " irrationalists " of the nineteenth century may be divided into two groups: those who, like Kant and Fichte, suggested that reason is not hindered but rather extended by a spiritually stimulated ethical imperative; and those, who with Schopenhauer and Nietzsche, believed that the will worked in opposition to the reason, whether blindly or no, to the detriment of rational structures and in defiance of rationalist limits. Once Kant had fixed the *limits* of reason, there was room for endless speculation about what force caused man to act *contrary* to reason—either in direct opposition to its dictates, or in infinite extension of its possibilities.

Much of the controversy over Freud's theories (discussed in Chapter III)—and much of the enthusiastic welcome they received as well—was due to his being catalogued as an irrationalist. But the term " irrationalist " lends itself to almost as many separate meanings as does the term " romanticist." It may simply suggest a prejudicial attitude, opposed, for example, to the neat simplifications of the reasoning mind. It may stand only for anti-intellectualism, offering opposition chiefly to analysis and preferring intuitive synthesis to a rather tedious and ineffective rational process. Finally, the irrationalist may be preoccupied with limiting and defining certain areas of knowledge and certain methods of knowing which are apparently beyond the reach of ordinary cognition. In all of these cases, the accepted rationalistic approaches to knowledge are threatened, if not with abandonment, at least with radical revision.

In a sense, Freud is himself responsible for the ambiguous role which psychoanalysis played in the literary world of our time. He was at once a physiologist, a psychologist, and a man of letters. His interest in the humanities prevented his being a scientist of pure matter, turned his attention away from inanimate nature and toward problems of human conduct. In his autobiography Freud denied his having at any time wanted the career of a physician. " I was moved, rather, by a sort of curiosity, which was, however, directed more towards human concerns than towards natural objects: . . . " The three original guides he accepted in his earliest career were the Bible, Goethe's essay on Nature, and the theories of Darwin. From 1873 to 1885, his interests were largely in anatomy and physiology; his early publications had to do with such subjects as " the spinal cord of one of the lowest of the fishes." The venture into neuropathology was taken for an admittedly material reason: " with an eye to material considerations, I began to study nervous diseases. . . . In the distance glimmered the great name of Charcot; so I formed a plan of first obtaining an appointment as Lecturer on Nervous Diseases in Vienna and of then going to Paris to continue my studies." [1]

These early steps are important; they show Freud changing, for one reason or another, from the study of minor species to the study of human behavior; and it is well also to note that his interests as a physician were directed very early to mental rather than to physical diseases.

In Paris, where he went in 1885, Freud took the first step which was to bring him fame and notoriety. Dissatisfied with the purely anatomical diagnoses of neurotics, he sought eagerly for another explanation. Under Jean Martin Charcot, he began to see the possibilities of a new approach to the problem of neuroses.

[1] *An Autobiographical Study*, tr. James Strachey (London, 1936), 13, 14, 17, 18–19.

Among the facts insufficiently regarded by his contemporaries, he noted ". . . the genuineness of hysterical phenomena and their conformity to laws, . . . the frequent occurrence of hysteria in men,[2] the production of hysterical paralyses, and contractures by hypnotic suggestion." [3]

Though he brought only suggestions back to Vienna with him, they explained clearly to him why medical practitioners had often to give up neurotics as incurable. Indeed, when he presented his findings to the Society of Medicine in Vienna, they were received with incredulity and distaste. He therefore withdrew from the learned societies, determined to carry these suggestions further.

Freud thus stood, in 1886, at the threshold of psychoanalysis; as yet, both the hints of a new theory of mental life and the technique needed to get at the facts were obscure. Further, since he suspected that "anatomical facts" were inadequate for the task, he was bound to cause displeasure among his colleagues. His problem was this: since neuroses are but poorly treated through the channels of ordinary medical research, their causes must have been inadequately sought. There must be *other causes*, which medical research had as yet been unable to determine. It was a good possibility that some other means would come closer to discovering these causes. At any rate, it was worth the risk. But what other means, then known, were available? How could one reach beyond the surface appearance of a neurosis? One could not discover the cause by taking the pulse count, or examining the blood.

Two methods occurred to Freud: electrotherapy and hypnosis. The first he dismissed as worthless chicanery; the second, which he had seen in operation, was apparently successful. His problem was "to find out something from the patient that the doctor did not know." [4] Perhaps the memory of the patient, once one had access to it, would reveal something. Apparently the best access to the patient's memory was through hypnosis. With Josef

---

[2] Hysteria had been regarded up to that time as a distress peculiar to women.
[3] *An Autobiographical Study*, 21.
[4] Sigmund Freud, *The Origin and Development of Psychoanalysis*, in *An Outline of Psychoanalysis*, ed. J. S. Van Teslaar (New York, 1924), 35.

Breuer, therefore, Freud worked in an effort to discover more of the patient's past and to relate that past with the present illness. Their first important experiment was with a girl of twenty-one years, who had developed "a series of physical and mental disturbances which well deserved to be taken seriously." [5] Through hypnosis, Breuer was able to find the causes of her mental paralyses and to cure her by informing her of these causes. The symptoms vanished, once their causes were made conscious and clear to her.

In 1895 Freud and Breuer published the results of their collaboration in *Studies of Hysteria*. In theory, this book represented a great advance over previous studies of neuroses. It emphasized the "importance of distinguishing between mental acts which are unconscious and those which are conscious (or rather capable of being conscious) ; it introduced a dynamic factor by supposing that a symptom arises through the damming-up of an affect, and an economic factor, by regarding that same symptom as the product . . . of a quantity of energy which would otherwise have been employed in some other way." [6]

Looked at from the perspective of later years, these conclusions have the character of mere beginnings. Some facts were divulged; the nature of mental illness was more than merely suspected; the area in which the source of illness could be found was at least surveyed; and a few of the surveying instruments were tentatively fashioned. From this point Freud was to work independently of Breuer, who was unwilling to go with him and hesitated to accept many of the conclusions that Freud thought inevitable. First of all, Breuer was satisfied that the induced hypnotic state was sufficient to push the "unassimilated foreign bodies" into the "waking consciousness" and thus dispel the source of the symptom. This was what was termed the *cathartic method*, a direct and arbitrary means of getting at the symptoms, which often worked, but neglected a great number of important facts about the original development of the patient's repression. [7]

---

[5] *Ibid.*, 22.
[6] *An Autobiographical Study*, 38.
[7] Sigmund Freud, *The History of the Psychoanalytic Movement*, in *The Basic Writings of Sigmund Freud*, ed. and tr. A. A. Brill (New York, 1938) , 935-36.

Freud's suggestion that many of these states have a sexual origin and development also repelled Breuer, as it had Charcot before him.[8] But more than a mere difference of opinion acted to separate Freud from Breuer at this time. Freud was dissatisfied with the technique of hypnosis; its success was not regular or predictable, and very often not permanent even in those cases upon which it seemed to operate successfully. The patient-doctor relationship was difficult and uncertain in hypnosis.[9] It occurred to Freud that the "memory" revealed in the hypnotic state must also be present in the nonhypnotic state, and that there might be some other method of gaining access to it. The characteristics of the patient's repression seemed to warrant a more thorough study of its sources. (1) The patient seemed to have forgotten entirely the cause of his distress, and this "forgetting" seemed to be "dynamic"—that is, it usually took the form of a positive antipathy to the forgotten material. (2) It could be assumed, therefore, that the forgotten cause was painful, and therefore "resisted" any effort to recall it. (3) If this was the case, then it might be suggested that the patient did not *forget* at all, but that the material known as forgotten was actually *repressed* and had to appear in disguised form. (4) The problem was to allow the "forgotten" material to reappear in *consciousness* and in its original form. (5) Often there was a hint that the "forgotten" material might be traced to a very early period of the patient's life.

Of the importance of these facts Freud was sure; he needed to find a method or technique which would best describe to the physician the path the forgotten, or repressed, materials took in their development. Freud sought some means by which the patient could reconstruct that past without the aid of an induced hypnotic state. At first sight the problem was almost insuperable: it was an attempt to discover information which apparently neither the doctor nor the patient knew.[10] Taking a suggestion from Bernheim, whom he had watched at Nancy, he reinforced the doctor-patient relationship by aiding the patient in his effort to

[8] *Ibid.*, 937.

[9] *An Autobiographical Study*, 47. Cf. Fritz Wittels, *Sigmund Freud*, tr. Eden and Cedar Paul (New York, 1924), 40.

[10] *The Origin and Development of Psychoanalysis*, 35.

"remember." His patient was asked to lie down on a sofa and to relax completely; he seated himself at the patient's head so that the patient could not see him. At the beginning of the treatment, Freud recommended that the following be said to the patient:

> Before I can say anything to you, I must know a great deal about you; please tell me what you know about yourself. . . . One thing more, before you begin. Your talk with me must differ in one respect from an ordinary conversation. Whereas usually you rightly try to keep the threads of your story together and to exclude all intruding associations and side-issues, so as not to wander too far from the point, here you must proceed differently. You will notice that as you relate things various ideas will occur to you which you feel inclined to put aside with certain criticisms and objections. You will be tempted to say to yourself: "This or that has no connection here, . . . or it is nonsensical, so it cannot be necessary to mention it." Never give in to these objections, but mention it even if you feel a disinclination against it, or indeed just because of this. Later on you will perceive and learn to understand the reason for this injunction, which is really the only one you have to follow. So say whatever goes through your mind. Act as if you were sitting at the window of a railway train and describing to some one behind you the changing views you see outside. Finally, never forget that you have promised absolute honesty, and never leave anything unsaid because for any reason it is unpleasant to say it.[11]

This, simply enough stated, is the method of "free association." Since it puts a certain responsibility upon the patient, and since the patient is often unable to assume that responsibility, it was necessary to supplement this method with various kinds of interpretation and suggestion. For, if the patient were to follow the advice absolutely and unreservedly, he would not have been a patient in the first place; he is ill precisely because of the difficulties which stand in the way of free association. This is, of

[11] Sigmund Freud, "Further Recommendations in the Technique of Psycho-analysis: on Beginning the Treatment . . . ," in *The Collected Papers of Sigmund Freud* (London, 1924), II, 355–56.

course, anticipated by the analyst. He must not hope for a coherent story, or even for a sensible one; but he can develop a method of interpretation which will avail itself of the clues which the patient's behavior, or misbehavior, elicits.[12] The very difficulties which both the doctor and the patient meet, and which were absent in hypnosis, convinced Freud that he was right in his suspicions about the mechanism of repression. Beginning, therefore, with the patient who is about to submit to an analysis, we can describe in fairly intelligible outline the nature of these difficulties.

The extent to which the analyst was obliged to alter the procedure of free association, to redirect it, and to note apparently unintelligible gaps in the patient's story seemed to add up to the patient's *resistance* to a straightforward and honest exposition and to indicate the way in which this resistance might be met. Forgetting was an important characteristic of this resistance. The forces which now prevent the emergence of the forgotten material must also have caused the forgetting in the first place. What were these forces?

> In all [pathogenic] experiences it had happened that a wish had been aroused, which was in sharp opposition to the other desires of the individual and was not capable of being reconciled with the ethical, aesthetic, and personal pretensions of the patient's personality. . . . The incompatibility of the idea in question [i. e., the wish] with the " ego " of the patient was the motive of the repression, the ethical and other pretensions of the individual were the repressing force.

The psychic disturbance which has led to illness, far from being a result of either physical injury or mental inadequacy, must have come from a certain conflict of opposing mental forces.

---

[12] The problem of the analyst's qualification for this difficult position has been taken up at some length in various of Freud's works. See Sigmund Freud, " Recommendations for Physicians on the Psychoanalytic Method of Treatment," in *The Collected Papers of Sigmund Freud*, II, 323–33. The analyst must, certainly, be of such character and mind, and must understand his own mental nature so well, that he will not confuse the investigation by his own " complexes " or preconceptions about the patient's case. He must furthermore refrain from any " analytical activity " which might hurry the patient along an ostensibly easy path to recovery. Associated with all of this are the numerous problems of the clinical arrangement, which will be discussed later.

Freud insisted, moreover, that no repressed wish was entirely shut out; "the wish still exists in the unconscious," and it eventually succeeds "in sending into consciousness, instead of the repressed idea, a disguised and unrecognizable surrogate creation, to which the same painful sensations associate themselves that the patient thought he was rid of through his repression."[13] The analyst's task is, then, to bring the repressed idea to light—that is, to transfer it from the unconscious to the patient's consciousness. This is all that Freud wishes the analyst to do.[14]

> Either the personality of the patient may be convinced that he has been wrong in rejecting the pathogenic wish, and he may be made to accept it either wholly or in part; or this wish may itself be directed to a higher goal which is free from objection, by what is called sublimation; or the rejection may be recognized as rightly motivated, and the automatic and therefore insufficient mechanism of repression be reinforced by the higher, more characteristically human mental faculties: one succeeds in mastering his wishes by conscious thought.[15]

We have seen that the psychic life of man is a complicated one, made so by the displacement and diffusion of psychic energies, disturbed by the inability of the organism to pursue a single line of gratification in accordance with the "pleasure principle." The redirection of energies, turned aside from their original paths by conflict with reality and the establishment of set patterns of adjustment to community life, in most cases results in a normal life; but severity of repression causes states of extreme psychic distress,

---

[13] *The Origin and Development of Psychoanalysis*, 36–37, 40.

[14] Freud at first rejected the idea that the physician should act in an advisory capacity, claiming that a conscious knowledge of the repressed source of the neurosis was sufficient. Later, he admitted that the analyst would have to use, but with caution, his position in order to advise in some cases. See Sigmund Freud, "Turnings in the Ways of Psychoanalytic Therapy," in *The Collected Papers of Sigmund Freud*, II, 397–99. ". . . the patient should be educated to liberate and fulfil his own nature, and not to resemble ourselves." *Ibid.*, 399.

[15] *The Origin and Development of Psychoanalysis*, 41. Freud has had constantly to answer the critics who maintain that the psychoanalyst counsels a life of license as a means of conquering repressions. That this is not the case is obvious from the above quotation; that psychoanalysis has been linked with acts of depravity in its brief history cannot be ascribed to any moral looseness in Freud's own thinking or to any untoward suggestions he may have made. This is an important aspect of the history of misinterpretation, especially as it relates to the fight both church and school conducted against the spread of psychoanalytic practice.

in which the energies, not by any means quieted but still very active in the unconscious, conduct the repressed wish along secret and disguised pathways which lead to peculiarities of behavior. Hence even normal life has developed in the same manner. The dividing line between normality and abnormality consists chiefly in the intensity of repression and the violence with which the repressed wish seeks to re-express itself in the face of the ego's opposition.[16] It is possible, therefore, to examine the phenomena of the repressed wish in practically all expressions of daily life, even the most common and most obvious.

Freud supplemented his clinical procedure in various ways. Free association revealed peculiar mannerisms and expressions which were not much different from the psychic " lapses " observable in normal living. To these latter he gave considerable attention in *Psychopathology of Everyday Life*.[17] From his analysis of the absurdity in dreams, and from his discoveries about the significance of word-relationships in the dream, he found material for an ingenious treatment of wit and humor, which he incorporated in *Wit and Its Relation to the Unconscious*.[18]

But the most important aid to clinical procedure was the interpretation of dreams. This interesting world of psychic expression was one of Freud's earliest concerns; and *The Interpretation of Dreams* [19] remains one of the most widely read of Freud's works, and the basis of more than one theory of poetry and the imagination. The advantage of the dream over the active but conscious association of ideas in the analyst's office should be obvious. Freud early claimed that the interpretation of dreams was " the *via*

[16] *An Autobiographical Study*, 86.

[17] First published, Berlin, 1901. See also *A General Introduction to Psychoanalysis*, tr. G. S. Hall (New York, 1920), 1–58. Although *Psychopathology of Everyday Life* is of considerable significance for the study of normal behavior, its influence was relatively slight, and it will be unnecessary to offer any extended summary of it here.

[18] First published, Leipzig and Vienna, 1905. Wit " makes possible the gratification of a craving (lewd or hostile) despite a hindrance which stands in the way . . . *wit affords us the means of surmounting restrictions and of opening up otherwise inaccessible pleasure sources.*" *Wit and Its Relation to the Unconscious*, tr. A. A. Brill (New York, 1916), 696, 698.

[19] Written, 1896–1899; first published, Leipzig and Vienna, 1900. See Frederick Clarke Prescott, *The Poetic Mind* (New York, 1922); Christopher Caudwell [Christopher S. J. Sprigge], *Illusion and Reality: a Study of the Sources of Poetry* (London, 1937); Kenneth Burke, *The Philosophy of Literary Form* (Baton Rouge, 1941).

regia to the interpretation of the unconscious, the surest ground of psychoanalysis and a field in which every worker must win his convictions and gain his education." [20] Why should this be so? Because the dream state illustrates clearly, and without the usual handicaps to its expression, " the processes occurring in the deeper, unconscious layers of the mind, which differ considerably from the familiar normal processes of thought." [21] The function of the dream is to induce and to prolong sleep. It is a condition in which the psychic self renounces the external world, and the principle of reality which dominates it. It follows that the dream will express in some form the wishes that in normal life remain opposed by the conscious world. It is also true that the censor is considerably relaxed, functioning only in the direction of insuring sleep.

This position of the censor in the dream state is responsible for all of the peculiarities which the dream manifests. Were the censor absent, or completely relaxed, all of the unconscious wish-material would rush forward in its undisguised horror. But this is an impossible, or at least an intolerable, condition. The censor merely allows these wishes to express themselves in disguised form, so that they may enjoy a temporary and pleasurable expression and yet not distress the dreamer. Consequently, the dream, as the dreamer remembers it, is confused and blurred, often unintelligible and absurd. This *manifest* dream is as confused and incoherent as the "censorable wishes" make it. "On the one hand, the worse the censorable wish, the greater the distortion; on the other hand, however, the stricter the censor himself is at any particular time, the greater the distortion will be also." [22]

The *latent* dream thoughts form the basic materials for dream construction and exist in the unconscious in the form of wishes; they appear in the *manifest* dream (the dream we remember vaguely in the morning) in a variety of distorted forms.

The manifest dream-content is the disguised surrogate for the unconscious dream thoughts, and this disguising is the work of the defensive forces of the ego, of the resistances. These

---

[20] *The Origin and Development of Psychoanalysis,* 46.

[21] *An Autobiographical Study,* 83.

[22] Which Freud admits is only a convenient term for a condition, and not a thing in itself. *A General Introduction to Psychoanalysis,* 114, 116.

prevent the repressed wishes from entering consciousness during the waking life, and even in the relaxation of sleep they are still strong enough to force them to hide themselves by a sort of masquerading.[23]

A dream is, therefore, the disguised fulfillment of an unconscious wish.[24] The fact that the censor is relaxed gives the dream a significance for clinical procedure; the fact that the censor still operates creates difficulties of interpretation and has given rise to innumerable studies of the vagaries of the " dream-consciousness." The dream has a language and grammar of its own, founded on the necessity for disguising the dream thoughts. It is this area of expression that has so impressed and interested the poet and novelist, has opened up new possibilities for the expression of unconscious states in fiction, and served as a basis for some theories of poetry and aesthetics generally. The fact that the dream is a compromise between conscious and unconscious states serves both the analyst and the modern novelist. In the case of the analyst, with whom we are concerned at present, the resistances the unconscious wish meets in the dream are a clue to the difficulties the patient offers the analyst in the latter's office.[25]

The interpretation of dreams proved an important step in the development of Freud's technique. It served as one of the most useful substitutes for the method of hypnosis which Freud had abandoned. It supplemented ably the actual clinical procedure

---

[23] *The Origin and Development of Psychoanalysis*, 48.

[24] Sigmund Freud, *The Interpretation of Dreams*, tr. A. A. Brill (New York, 1913), 136.

[25] *New Introductory Lectures on Psychoanalysis*, tr. W. J. Sprott (New York, 1933), tried to restate the *difficulties* of interpreting the dream and of using it for clinical purposes. " The resistance which we come across during the process of dream-interpretation must play some part in the formation of the dream as well." *Ibid.*, 25. He points out also that the dream is " a pathological product, the first member of the series which includes the hysterical symptom, the obsession and the delusion among its members; it is differentiated from the others by its transitoriness and by the fact that it occurs under conditions which are part of normal life." *Ibid.*, 27. Sigmund Freud, " The Employment of Dream-Interpretation in Psychoanalysis," in *The Collected Papers of Sigmund Freud*, II, 306-309, warns the analyst against considering dream interpretation as an end in itself. ". . . its use should be subject to those technical rules that govern the conduct of the analysis throughout." *Ibid.*, 309.

One of the most skillful and accurate of all applications of technical dream analysis to literature can be found in Arthur Koestler, *Arrival and Departure* (New York, 1943), 52, 62-65, 95, 102.

by furnishing a " document of the unconscious " which suggested a means of gaining access to the repressed wish. Finally, since all persons have dreams, and some very " good " people have very " bad " dreams, it served to convince Freud of the common basis for the interpretation of human behavior in general, not only of the behavior of neurotics. This last was most welcome to Freud, who believed that he had secured a means of studying human nature more penetrating than any psychology had hitherto offered.

He was prepared, therefore, to offer a general theory of the development of psychic life and to support his theory with much evidence from his clinical experience. One of the peculiarities of the patient's reaction to the treatment, Freud noticed, was his habit of returning (in the expression of symptoms or in reacting to the physician himself) to an early fixation—the phenomenon of regression. It was natural enough that Freud should have placed so much stress upon infantile sexuality in his effort to explain neuroses.

> The work of analysis which is necessary for the thorough explanation and complete cure of a case of sickness does not stop in any case with the experience of the time of onset of the disease, but in every case it goes back to the adolescence and the early childhood of the patient. Here only do we hit upon the impressions and circumstances which determine the later sickness.[26]

Correct interpretation and effective cure depended upon an examination of the patient's entire psychic development. Freud was struck by the fact that the repressed wishes he encountered in his clinical experience were almost always sexual.[27] Freud claims that his early teachers and collaborators, had each suspected the sexual basis of neurosis, but each had been repelled by the idea and had withdrawn from a consideration of it. But in spite of this ill omen he continued to insist upon the problem of sexuality. The combined facts—the fact of regression in the transference-

[26] *The Origin and Development of Psychoanalysis,* 55. See also, 50.
[27] This does not mean that all dreams are also sexual dreams. Dreams of childhood are almost always simple wish-fulfillments and derive their content from certain deprivations of the day before. See *The Interpretation of Dreams,* 107-12; *A General Introduction to Psychoanalysis,* Lecture 8, pp. 101-109.

neurosis, and the fact that neuroses seemed almost inevitably to have a sexual basis—induced him to make up a study of the sexual life from the very beginning. The publication of his *Three Contributions to a Theory of Sex* [28] aroused much bitter opposition, which Freud put aside as " conventional resistances "; [29] the book had much to do with the revision of child-education, under such leaders as Melanie Klein and Freud's own daughter Anna.

Freud first noticed that the word sex itself was often ambiguously applied and that there was little agreement as to its essential meaning. It might be used to determine sex differences; it might refer to the sexual act; or it might be used to refer to the indecent and the obscene. [30] In any case important phenomena of human behavior were excluded. These must be regarded as examples of degeneration, though simply calling them " degenerate " did not help to explain their presence or to ferret out their causes. [31]

The invert and the pervert needed more careful classification and explanation. They should be treated as examples either of " those whose sexual object has changed " or of " those whose sexual aim has changed." [32] The traditional reaction was of disgust and indignation. Freud thought it essential to understand sexual aberrations if we wish to know the truth about sexual normality. He came to the conclusion (a conclusion he had suspected long before 1905) that all sexual normalities *and* abnormalities spring from the very earliest, infantile sexual life. Such a contention, of course, threatened to disabuse us of one of our strongest sentiments—the " angel " theory of childhood. Everyone (except the children themselves) had believed that before puberty the child is asexual, has no interest in sexual activity, until such time as society finds it expedient for him to

[28] First published, Leipzig and Vienna, 1905; first translated into English by Dr. A. A. Brill, 1910.
[29] The term *resistance* has often been used by psychoanalysts as a means of disposing easily (and psychoanalytically) of all objections to psychoanalysis. See the satire on the use of this term in Mary McCarthy, *The Company She Keeps* (New York, 1942), and reaction to it in Mable Dodge Luhan, *Movers and Shakers* (New York, 1936). Cf. *The Origin and Development of Psychoanalysis*, 54–55.
[30] *A General Introduction to Psychoanalysis*, 262–63.
[31] Sigmund Freud, *Three Contributions to a Theory of Sex*, in *The Basic Writings of Sigmund Freud*, 554–55.
[32] *A General Introduction to Psychoanalysis*, 263–64.

be interested in sex. This attitude is at least partly responsible for " the peculiar amnesia which veils from most people (not from all) the first years of childhood, usually the first six or eight years." [33] This " amnesia " is easily observed in the treatment of neurotics, and it can be explained in terms of a very effective repression, in which both the individual and society cooperate.

Freud sees the sexual life of man as having three stages, which begin with the cradle and extend through the period of adolescence. Infantile sexuality arises from the limited sphere of sexual activities, ignorance of the act of copulation, and the dominance of the pleasure principle over the child's early life. The child seeks immediate gratification of its instinctual desires, and development leads to sexual inquisitiveness and to an indiscriminate search for forms of gratification.[34] Introduction to sexual activity is usually accidental, and it involves some of the most tender mother-child relationships. Sexual predispositions arise from a mixture of curiosity and desire for gratification. Education in sex-life begins early and plays its most severe role when the child is organically least inclined to regard sexual activity as important. The period from six or eight to twelve or fourteen years constitutes what is called the " latency period "; during this period the psychic forces of " loathing, shame, and moral and esthetic ideal demands " operate most effectively. (*Three Contributions,* 583) There are reasons why the child loses interest in sex at this time: " The sexual feelings of these infantile years would on the one hand be unusable, since the procreating functions are postponed—this is the chief character of the latency period; on the other hand, they would as such be perverse, as they would emanate from . . . impulses which in the individual's course of development could only evoke a feeling of displeasure." (*Three Contributions,* 584)

The new interest in sex puberty has for its aim what is socially desirable and necessary—propagation. The manner of sex-education in the other two periods, the extent to which the child

[33] *Three Contributions to a Theory of Sex,* 581.
[34] Freud calls this tendency in children the " polymorphous perverse " disposition; the indiscriminate nature of the child's interests arises from a lack of " discretion " in the selection of both sexual aim and object. If it is not controlled in the " latency period," it may lead to aberrations. *Ibid.,* 592.

has regulated his interests in conformity with " normality," is now responsible for the sexual character of the adolescent. Perversions and inversions can be traced to the sexual life of the earlier periods and to the failure to bring the sexual interest around to both the opposite sex and the socially approved aim which ordinarily governs sex interests. The balance between sublimation and repression is only subtly maintained, and slight deviations from the purpose of normal sex-education in the early periods may continue throughout life, damaging the person's hope for a normal sex life.

A word should be said about Freud's explanation of the dynamics of sex. Much confusion has resulted from the simple fact that Freud has expanded the conception of sexuality to include not only child sexuality but sexual aberrations. There is perhaps no term in the psychoanalytic glossary that is less accurately understood than the term *libido*. The *libido* is simply " sexual energy "; it is a form of " hunger energy," whose satisfaction is usually obtained by its investment in a sexual object. But this sexual energy may be withdrawn from its object and " taken back into the ego "—that is, it may be invested in the ego itself, and become *narcissistic libido*. Freud was distressed and even angered to find that this term was so grossly misunderstood. Much of this confusion was caused by Jung's reinterpretation of the term as meaning " psychic instinctive energy in general." In Freud's view, such a definition of *libido* renders it unfit for scientific use and forever blurs the application of it to the problem of sexual development. (*Three Contributions*, 611, 612)

ii

Freud's interest in the larger problems of human behavior awaited only the perfection of his clinical procedure and the incidence of a sufficient number of cases and experiments for adequate generalization and speculation. He was ready, after this groundwork had been laid, to consider " metapsychology," a term he described as the " final result of psychoanalytic research "—the extension beyond the realm of therapy into the field of descriptive psychology. " I propose that, when we succeed in describing a mental process in all its aspects, dynamic, topographic and economic, we shall call this a *metapsychological* presentation." [35] This is a logical outcome of the clinical procedure.

Another desirable inference came from the number and variety of cases with which Freud had to deal. The problem of explaining the source of many dream symbols, which seemed to have little or no connection with the intellectual or somatic disturbances of the previous day, led him to suspect a " layer of antiquity " which persists through the centuries as a basis for folk-thinking and dream-expression. On this point (among others) Freud and Jung fought bitterly, in the controversy which was to lead eventually to their separation. On the surface there seems to be little difference of opinion; Freud admits the existence of a " phylogenetic reference " in dream symbols. " The antiquity into which the dreamwork carries us back is of a double aspect, firstly, the individual antiquity, childhood; and secondly (in so far as every individual in his childhood lives over again in some more or less abbreviated manner the entire development of the human race), also this antiquity, the phylogenetic." [36]

But Jung and his followers maintained that " mental patients and neurotics reproduce in every detail the myths, cosmogonies, and primitive conceptions of the early ages of man." [37] Freud's chief objections to this conclusion were, first, that it was arbitrarily thorough, and second, that it was a means of excluding the important matter of sex-relationship and the function of the libido in the life of man.[38] Freud was convinced, however, that his studies in the analyst's office did confirm certain generalizations about human behavior which could be found demonstrated most clearly in folk and primitive psychology. Among these was the all-important " oedipus complex " which he first formulated in *The Interpretation of Dreams*,[39] explained in *Three Contributions to*

---

[35] Sigmund Freud, " The Unconscious," in *The Collected Papers of Sigmund Freud*, IV, 114.

[36] *A General Introduction to Psychoanalysis*, 167.

[37] Wittels, *Sigmund Freud*, 182.

[38] There was also, of course, Jung's insistence that the analyst should set himself up as a religious leader and guide, " prophet and saviour to his patient." *Ibid.*, 191.

[39] It has been the habit of psychoanalysts to use this concept as a means of analysing literature; cf. Otto Rank, *Das Inzest-Motiv in Dichtung und Sage* . . . (Leipzig, 1926); Ernest Jones, *Hamlet and Oedipus* (New York, 1949).

a Theory of Sex, and, finally in *Totem and Taboo* used as a means of clarifying many of the peculiarities of human behavior. One of the chief of these is the savage's dread of incest and the rigid social rules he formulates to protect himself against it; anthropologists have referred to these restrictions as exogamy.[40]

Taboo, a word of purposeful ambiguity, refers to an object that is both sacred and dangerous. The taboo symbolizes an ambiguous relationship between a group and the authority which governs it. Men in a primitive society therefore "assume an *ambivalent attitude* toward their taboo prohibitions; in their unconscious they would like nothing better than to transgress them but they are also afraid just because they would like to transgress, and the fear is stronger than the pleasure. But in every individual of the race the desire for it is unconscious, just as it is in the neurotic."

Hence the basis of taboo is "a forbidden action for which there exists a strong inclination in the unconscious." (*Totem and Taboo*, 55, 56) The taboo is constantly in danger of violation, precisely because it is subject to this unconscious wish; if it should be violated, such an act must be expiated through "renunciation." [41] By a comparison with the compulsion-neurosis, Freud hoped to throw light upon the taboo concept. The taboo ceremonial is the "correct counterpart to the compulsive action of the neurosis, in which the suppressed impulse and the impulse which suppresses it meet in mutual and simultaneous satisfaction." This ambivalence is best seen in the attitude toward the dead, in which the motives of hostility and tenderness reappear in strength. The question of guilt and responsibility for the death is directly related to the unconscious wish (present in some degree in normal persons) for the death of the loved one. The ambivalence is reproduced in the burial ceremony, in which fear of punishment is expressed through a ritual warding off of "demons."

This characteristic of primitive society seems to have persisted through the centuries and has been modified by culture. It has

[40] *Totem and Taboo*, tr. A. A. Brill (New York, 1927), 5. First published, Vienna, 1913. Among his sources, Freud used James George Frazer, *The Golden Bough* (Edinburgh, 1890).
[41] Later, Freud was to explain this ambivalence of desire and remorse, when he developed his idea of the *super-ego*. See *New Introductory Lctures*, 82–92.

remained a part of human tradition because it has always resided in the unconscious, which is not amenable to change. Treatment of it, in accordance with the varying cultural forms which the reality principle assumes, has varied and altered, but the unconscious wish remains, and is especially observable among neurotics. (*Totem and Taboo*, 90, 125) [42] On the basis of this similarity between primitive thought and modern neurosis, Freud gave a psychological description of the history of culture, dividing this history into the three most striking developments of the human psyche.

> . . . the animistic phase corresponds in time as well as in content with narcism, the religious phase corresponds to that stage of object finding which is characterized by dependence on the parents, while the scientific stage has its full counterpart in the individual's state of maturity where, having renounced the pleasure principle and having adapted himself to reality, he seeks his object in the outer world. (*Totem and Taboo*, 158)

The development of *conscience* as a substitutive control over the unconscious also has a place in this description. If conscience can be explained as an inner recognition of the undesirability of certain wish impulses, it may also be construed to suggest the means of checking the unconscious wish or of punishing the individual for having submitted to it.

From the total picture of totem and taboo Freud draws certain conclusions. In the first place, the development of man from his primitive origins is in many respects analogous to the child's psychic development. Secondly, the hatred-love feeling toward the parent, which Freud has termed the oedipus complex, also shares in the establishment of primitive totem-taboo formulas. The brothers band together against the father, whom they both love and envy. The result of this organization against parental au-

---

[42] Since this is merely an objective summary of Freud's position, it does not presume to criticize it. An excellent appraisal of Freud's work in anthropology may be found, however, in an article by A. L. Kroeber, "Totem and Taboo in Retrospect," in *American Journal of Sociology*, XLV (1939), 446–51. Kroeber's criticism rests mainly upon Freud's confusion of a "timeless psychological explanation" with "an historical one" and also "the curious indifference which Freud has always shown as to whether his conclusions do or do not integrate with the totality of science." *Ibid.*, 448–49.

thority may be the removal of its object; if so, renunciation and remorse follow, and " racial conscience " sets up laws against a recurrence of such action.[43] Freud is not unwilling to suggest that the basis for much (primitive as well as modern) social and moral action is the oedipus, or parent, complex. In this manner he has explained the function of the unconscious in preserving the remnants (that is, those remnants which are consistent with enduring psychic nature) of primitive " customs, ceremonies, and laws." (*Totem and Taboo*, 276)

In *Moses and Monotheism*,[44] Freud presented a specific illustration of his earlier views of primitive society. The murder of Moses, which he accepts tentatively from the researches of Ernst Sellin, is an act which is to be explained in terms of the ambivalence already discussed in *Totem and Taboo*. The reappearance of Moses in the form of the Messiah led again to the act of " murdering the father." The sense of guilt again resulted in the murder of the father, this time the Son of the Christian Trinity. This second murder forms the basis, according to Freud, of the doctrine of original sin; the Christian communion is a relic of the sacrificial feast of the totem cults. The Christians have, however, reconciled themselves to the fact of the father-murder, while the Jews persist in denying it, and for this they suffer persecution.[45]

In the year 1913, Freud was fairly well launched in his effort to apply psychoanalysis to diverse fields and to relate it to ethical and philosophical problems: he had suggested the analogy between individual and racial development; he had made some tentative remarks about conscience and had suggested it as a sort of liaison officer operating between individual and race; he had given the oedipus complex much prominence as a fitting characterization of family relationship and of its larger, racial implica-

---

[43] Thomas Mann has used this explanation in his Biblical novels, *Joseph and His Brothers* and *Young Joseph*. Indeed, he may be considered one of the few outstanding modern writers who have availed themselves of this phase of Freud's thought. Though there is much here which might contribute to a new theory of tragedy and a new concept of the historical novel, the influence of Freud's earlier works, on the dream and on sexuality, has thus far crowded out a mature consideration of this other. See below, Chapter VII.

[44] Tr. Katherine Jones (New York, 1939). Parts were published in the psychoanalytic journal, *Imago*, in 1937.

[45] Cf. S. W. Baron, " Review," in *American Journal of Sociology*, XLV, 471–77, for a criticism.

tions.[46] He was ready, therefore, to discuss problems of society and social relationships. This he did in a series of small monographs, digressive outpourings of his mind as he pondered over the larger implications of psychoanalysis. In 1921 he addressed himself to the problem of group psychology and its relation to the individual ego. Commenting on the phenomenon of group behavior, he noted that " when individuals come together in a group, all their individual inhibitions fall away, and all cruel, brutal, and destructive instincts, which lie dormant in individuals as relics of a primitive epoch, are stirred up to find free gratification." Groups demand illusions; they " constantly give what is unreal precedence over what is real. . . ." [47] The individual ego gives way in a group and all egos of a group concentrate upon a single, central object.

He carried this analysis further, and discussed in some detail one of the fairest of man's illusions in another of his small monographs, *The Future of an Illusion*. The masses have no natural inclination for instinctual renunciation; they must have both institutions and leaders. These instinctual drives have already been made clear by a study of their beginnings in the infantile stage of sexuality. Though for the most part, on the surface of society, one observes a regular obedience to these institutional inhibitions, there are many who conform to them only " under the pressure of external force." Man in the mass fears the licentiousness of nature and its psychic components. Culture, therefore, must " defend us against nature." In this defense, religion plays an important part. The gods have a task set before them: " They must exorcise the terrors of nature, they must reconcile one to the cruelty of fate . . . and they must make amends for the sufferings and privations which the communal life of culture has imposed on man."

The gods are a substitute for the father figure, the result of a mixed attitude of fear and helplessness. Hence religion is a well-organized, self-perpetuating illusion, founded upon man's unconscious wishes. An illusion is a special form of attitude toward

[46] The incest motive in Joyce's *Finnegans Wake*, for example, is coupled with mythological disguises which bring the individual and race together on the same plane of dream thoughts.

[47] *Group Psychology and the Analysis of the Ego*, tr. James Strachey (New York, n. d.) . First published, Vienna, 1921. Pages 17, 20.

the wish, however, for it has little or no relation with reality. Freud disapproves of the illusory character of religion precisely because (like the fantasy or the dream) it serves to satisfy a wish without submitting it to the sober influence of the principle of reality. If we were both strong and honest, he said, we would admit " honestly the purely human origin of all cultural laws and institutions." [48] Continuation of the illusion thwarts psychic growth; the " true believer " merely protects himself against an individual neurosis by participating in a universal neurosis.

The third of these speculations, *Civilization and Its Discontents*, discussed in greater detail the source of man's unhappiness. For the pains of life we have substitutive gratifications which serve to distract us from the unhappiness which would otherwise be our lot. The original aim of life is happiness—that is, pleasure. This is also the instinctive aim of unconscious wishes. This drive for pleasure, which Freud has termed the *pleasure principle*, comes into conflict with the entire external world. Therefore man is " wont to reduce its demands for happiness just as even the pleasure-principle itself changes into the more accommodating reality-principle under the influence of external environment. . . ." [49] The development of " the reality test " caused the establishment of many " counter illusions," such as religion and art. Art, though it cannot protect us against suffering, offers compensations for it.[50] Both the superior force of nature and the instinctual drive for pleasure forced man to establish severe safeguards against the instincts. Such a rigid institutional bulwark against the pleasure principle produced reactions—such as the " return to nature " theory which, forgetting the source of social prohibitions, regarded them as standing in the way of natural

[48] *The Future of an Illusion*, tr. W. Robson-Scott (New York, 1928). First published, Vienna, 1927. Pages 19, 30, 73. See below, Chapter VII, for further discussion of Freud and Kafka concerning this matter.

[49] Sigmund Freud, *Civilization and Its Discontents*, tr. Joan Riviere (New York, 1930), 28–29.

[50] " Unfortunately, psychoanalysis too [i. e., as well as aesthetics] has less to say about beauty than about most things. Its derivation from the realms of sexual sensation is all that seems certain; the love of beauty is a perfect example of a feeling with an inhibited aim. . . ." *Ibid.*, 39. Freud's remarks on aesthetics usually take this form. Though he has studied the motivating force of Leonardo's career and troubled himself over the neurotic components of an obscure German novel (Wilhelm Jensen, *Gradiva*), it is not in Freud's remarks on aesthetics that his importance for literary critics lies.

happiness. A community is in itself a safeguard against individual license. Society is therefore built up on the renunciation of instinctual gratifications. But it is, after all, an extension of the family relationship. Hence resignation, renunciation, and sublimation, all of them phases of the denial of the pleasure principle, are parts of social organization. Not only are perversions considered counter to the social use of sex; heterosexuality, though it may be normal so far as the selection of an object is concerned, is unsocial, for it involves complicated readjustment and legal problems and endangers the socially acceptable institution of monogamy.

The commandment to love one's neighbor as oneself is in essence a prohibition; for it tacitly recognizes that " men are not gentle, friendly creatures wishing for love . . . but that a powerful measure of desire for aggression has to be reckoned as part of their instinctual endowment." [51] The struggle between the ego and the libido has, in the majority of cases, resulted in a victory for the ego, and the ego has been able to rely upon society for help; this victory often has a disastrous price " of great suffering and renunciation." When the aggressive instinct is conquered by the ego, it turns back to (is introjected into) the ego, and there begins the disposition toward self-criticism and flagellation which is known as conscience. The aggressiveness becomes an inner torment, associated with feelings of guilt and remorse, whether for an anticipated or an accomplished " crime of the instincts." The ego therefore dreads not only authority itself, but also the conscience, or super-ego. " The first one compels us to renounce instinctual gratification; the other presses over and above this toward punishment, since the persistence of forbidden wishes cannot be concealed from the super-ego." [52]

Civilization, therefore, has a double problem: it has to aid the ego in regulating the drive toward instinctual gratification; it must rehabilitate the ego after the destruction caused to its moral sense by the introjection of aggressive instincts. Perhaps a reasonable relaxation of unnecessary modes of suppression will

[51] *Civilization and Its Discontents*, 75, 85. Hence, Freud explains, the communist assumption that aggressiveness is based upon the institution of private property is " founded on an untenable illusion." *Ibid.*, 88.
[52] *Ibid.*, 111.

accomplish both; perhaps the opportunities which psychoanalysis offers for an understanding of instinctual drives and the limitations of the pleasure principle will serve to diminish the pain of adjustment to social needs.[53]

iii

Freud had made much progress from the beginnings of his theories; his far-reaching applications of psychoanalysis to the fields of religion, sociology, and aesthetics made it unlikely that the original clinical terms would suffice. He was concerned in expanding his description of the " anatomy of the personality " to include factors that would explain the interaction of its elements. Metapsychology required an expansion of the Freudian glossary. The original division of the psychic life into conscious and unconscious arose from Freud's eagerness to show that " experimental psychology " had neglected a vast sphere of psychological life, a study of which is indispensable for an adequate understanding of human behavior. He found, after a short time, that the term " unconscious " could not describe a single element of the psychic construction, but was a characteristic of several elements, whose position in psychic geography was not neatly delimited or defined. In *The Ego and the Id* he attempted to redefine the psychic constitution and to establish the proper relationship between consciousness and unconsciousness. First of all, he noticed that there were " degrees of unconsciousness," or rather, two kinds of unconscious: " one which is transformed into conscious material easily and under conditions which frequently arise [the preconscious] and another in the case of which such a transformation is difficult, can only come about with a considerable expenditure of energy, or may never occur at all [the unconscious]." [54]

[53] This psychoanalysis of society has met with opposition from optimists and communists alike. Among the latter, Christopher Caudwell and Francis Bartlett have been most vocal. See *Science and Society*, III (1939) , 64–105. One communist has attempted to show that Marxian sociology and Freudian psychology supplement each other: Reuben Osborn, *Freud and Marx* (New York, n.d.) . For a thorough consideration of Freud's analysis of ego and society, see Herbert Marcuse, *Eros and Civilization* (Boston, 1955) .

[54] *New Introductory Lectures*, 101.

The ego is both conscious and unconscious: in that fact lies the explanation for the conflict between instinctual pleasure and reality which takes place within it. The *id* is the repository of all basic drives, the ego's enemy, " the obscure inaccessible part of our personality." It is entirely unconscious, hence remote from our understanding and difficult to manage. What we know about it has been gathered from our interpretation of dreams and of neurotic symptoms. The concepts of logic and order with which our conscious minds and our ego are so familiar are absolutely foreign to it—as are the other acts of orderly thinking, such as syntax and time-space relationships. It possesses only an " impulsion to obtain satisfaction for the instinctual needs, in accordance with the pleasure principle." [55]

This reinterpretation of the unconscious calls our attention to another element of the psychic life: the *preconscious system*, which faces upon the external world, from which it receives perceptions. From the preconscious the ego receives these perceptual stimuli, and it is prepared to protect the organism against them. The precarious state of the ego is now obvious. It must serve the principle of reality and at the same time pay heed to the impulsive demands of the id. It serves to order and organize the mental life of the individual and enlists in its aid such logical processes which are altogether foreign to the id. The ego has a third master to serve—the super-ego, conscience, which originated in parental authority and in the aggressive impulses of the ego which have been turned back upon themselves. In the face of these manifold duties, it is not surprising that, given society as it is and granting the complicated nature of our family and moral structures, the ego should often give way to forms of anxiety: " reality anxiety in face of the external world, normal anxiety in face of the super-ego, and neurotic anxiety in face of the strength of the passions in the id." [56]

Two other terms required redefinition, and upon their clarification depended much that was relevant to Freud's philosophical

---

[55] *Ibid.*, 103, 104. Of course, the id entertains no active hostility for the ego. There is no such thing as an actual *conflict* between the two. The ego, rather, is caught between the id and reality, and is forced to effect a compromise.

[56] *New Introductory Lectures*, 109–10. See below, Chapter VII, for more information concerning the problem of anxiety.

position. The first of these, the "sovereign tendency" of the instinctual processes, he termed the *pleasure principle*.[57] This is the principle which expresses the aim of all the unconscious wishes and brings them into conflict with the complicated structure of the external world. Since the instinctual drives were seldom fully satisfied, and since the world of fantasy and hallucination did not often offer a satisfactory substitute, "the mental apparatus had to decide to form a conception of the real circumstances in the outer world and to exert itself to alter them. . . . What was conceived of was no longer that which was pleasant, but that which was real, even if it should be unpleasant."[58] The only activity which did not have to submit to the "reality test" was the act of fantasy-making—in poetry and painting. The reality principle is not the opposite of the pleasure principle; it merely serves to safeguard it. It leads to unpleasantness only in those circumstances which bring the organism into too rude contact with the outside world.

This early statement (1911) of the two principles of mental functioning underwent some change in 1920, when Freud published his provocative essay, *Beyond the Pleasure Principle*. In the first place, the individual has ways of repeating what were originally unpleasant incidents, in such a manner as to gain mastery over them. Freud observed that this "compulsion toward repetition" in human beings was general and only more intense in neurotics. The expressions of a "repetition compulsion" seem to show an instinctive character; it is characteristic of an instinct to strive for "the reinstatement of an earlier condition, one which it had to abandon under the influence of external disturbing forces. . . ." Freud goes to biology for an explanation of this new "compulsion"; the tendency of the organic is to return to the' inorganic. The goal of all life is death; "the inanimate was there before the animate."

If this were altogether true, then death would long since have dispensed with all of animate matter. But not all organisms act

---

[57] *The Collected Papers of Sigmund Freud*, IV, 14. It is important to note that Freud began as early as 1911 to clarify the discussion of the pleasure principle.

[58] *Ibid.* Note that conflict with reality may lead to three specific varieties of disagreeable result: "unlust," pain, and anxiety. This last is frequently employed as a protective device, felt actually in anticipation of danger.

in this manner. The reproductive cells fight to secure the immortality of their own species. The sexual instincts are therefore the " life instincts." The pleasure principle, as redefined, and as qualified by the reality principle, strives to keep the psychic apparatus as a whole " free from any excitation, or to keep the amount of excitation constant, or as low as possible." [59] The pleasure principle, therefore, favors the " organic necessity " of returning to an inorganic state.

This is Freud's answer to questions about immortality. He allows no compensation for the feeling that the instinctual drive contributes to the destruction of the organism. But the sex instincts, he says, by a process of selection and coupling serve the end of keeping the organism alive. Love (Eros) is the champion of life, engaged in a relentless struggle against Death.[60]

iv

In this brief summary of the development of Freud's theories there are three important stages, each of which has had its influence upon thought and expression in fields other than psychology: the clinical, the " metapsychological," and the " practical." Since the clinical was by necessity the first to be developed, and the expressions of it were first published and translated, it was of first importance for the field of literary criticism. The further clarification and refinement of terms made necessary by Freud's adventures in what he calls " metapsychology " caused some interest and much confusion in lay reading circles, but the peculiar conservatism of the average educated person—that is, his willingness to let the *first* expression of a man's theories stand for the *whole*—made this phase of Freud's work less serviceable and less influential than the first. The " practical " applications of psychoanalysis—the manner in which it touched upon the fields of ethnology, philosophy, theology, and aesthetics—resulted in a wide variety of

[59] *Beyond the Pleasure Principle*, tr. C. J. Hubback (London, 1922), 44–45, 47, 81. First published, Vienna, 1920.
[60] This relationship of love with death is the subject of much of the talk associated with Dr. Krokowski in Thomas Mann, *The Magic Mountain* (New York, [1927]), 164-67, 462.

publications, many of them of doubtful critical importance. The real importance of Freud for the literature of his own lifetime came from the great popularity of his earlier works.[61] The problem of his influence involves, first of all, an attempt to determine what Freud meant precisely by certain terms which eventually found their way into popular usage; from that point, it will be possible to study the manner in which such terms were received and used. Both the original meaning of a term and its subsequent distortion are important for a study of influence.

Freud came upon the concept of the unconscious at a time when the orthodox psychology was for the most part limited to the study of consciousness and the limits of conscious knowledge. To be sure, the problem of the unconscious had been studied,[62] but at no time had a serious effort been made to explore the unconscious itself, and thus to isolate it from theological and epistemological preconceptions. Apparently the unconscious is the negation of conscious understanding; hence one may say that it is impossible to " know " it. If it is a sphere of mental, or psychic, activity, accessible to knowledge, it must be proved to be an active psychic entity, and not simply the " place where thoughts go when they disappear." Actually, Freud considered the unconscious as the " real psyche ": " its inner nature is just as unknown to us as the reality of the external world, and it is just as imperfectly reported to us through the data of consciousness as is the external world through the indications of our sensory organs."

It may be said that the approach to the unconscious was originally formed because of the inadequate picture of mental-affective life which consciousness afforded. The most complicated forms of mental life seemed to occur " without exciting the consciousness of the person." Since we " know " only through consciousness, these types of psychic activity must be communicated to us in some way or other. Yet there is no *direct translation* of the unconscious into consciousness; we must alter considerably our laws of conscious knowledge in order to understand the offerings of the unconscious. The analyst at any rate must recognize that

---

[61] Not including, of course, the monographs on anatomy, or even the earlier studies of hysteria. For the list of these, see Wittels, *Sigmund Freud*, 273–76.

[62] Eduard von Hartmann, *The Philosophy of the Unconscious*, tr. W. C. Coupland (New York, 1931). First published, Berlin, 1868.

" the effect on consciousness is only a remote psychic product of the unconscious process and that the latter has not become conscious as such; that it has been in existence and operative without betraying itself in any way to consciousness." [63] If such is the case, how can we ever hope to analyze the unconscious? As far as its physical character is concerned, we do not know it at all, but we can infer much from its " points of contact " with the conscious mental system. Freud has explored and analyzed these in great detail in three of his best known earlier books.[64] Through them we grow to understand, by studying their " peculiarities "—that is, their differences from conscious laws of presentation—and by noting the manner in which these peculiarities appear and reappear.

The unconscious is, therefore, a reservoir of that of which we are not conscious. Its mode of expression—that is, its points of contact with the conscious world—varies with both individual and occasion. In this variation we note that the unconscious has a life of its own, or at least an affective condition, certain apparently strong instinctual drives and a command over psychic energies which, in neurotics especially, seem to overpower the means of conscious control which men have at their disposal. When we examine the difficulty of understanding this psychic area, we note that there are *two kinds* of unconscious—the simple latent mental states, which are easily accessible, and the states which appear, through some obstruction or other, to be permanently hindered from becoming conscious. These two kinds, the Preconscious and the Unconscious, correspond to the degrees of *forgetting* to which we are susceptible. Ordinary forgetting does not exert any undue pressure upon the unconscious, but is merely a matter of relative interest, whereas dynamic forgetting involves an attitude toward and a fight against that part of the unconscious which is thus treated:

> . . . a mental act commonly goes through two phases, between which is interposed a kind of testing process (censorship) . In the first phase the mental act is unconscious and

---

[63] *The Interpretation of Dreams,* 485, 486.
[64] *The Interpretation of Dreams, Psychopathology of Everyday Life,* and *Wit and Its Relation to the Unconscious.*

belongs to the system Ucs; if, upon scrutiny of the censorship, it is rejected, it is not allowed to pass into the second phase; it is then said to be "repressed" and must remain unconscious. If, however, it passes this scrutiny, it enters upon the second phase and thenceforth belongs to the second system, which we will call the Cs. . . . It is not yet conscious, but it is certainly *capable of entering consciousness*, . . . that is, it can now, without any special resistance and given certain conditions, become the object of consciousness [The Preconscious].[65]

Freud was much preoccupied with the need to further clarify the nature of the unconscious and to delimit its sphere. But his position, once taken and here described, was not radically changed. The new designation, the *id* (made in 1923), simply pointed out that several spheres of mental activity were either totally or partially unconscious; but this did not alter Freud's earlier views about the peculiarities of the unconscious or about the means by which it is made accessible to consciousness.

For several reasons, students of psychology welcomed this discussion of the unconscious. Certain writers thought it a sharp attack upon rationalism; they believed that it finally disposed of the hampering limits imposed upon thinking by too rigid logical and syntactic systems. Since these systems were the only ones with which they were familiar, they resorted to metaphors and allegories as a means of admitting the unconscious to the world of thought and discussion. These metaphors for the most part depended upon the "world of darkness" for their objects of comparison. The unconscious was something "deep," "dark," "cellarlike"; it was the area from which came all that was brutally opposed to the "good life."

Another term given wide currency in the twenties was *repression*. It was the peg upon which discontented Americans hung all of their resentment with the moral world around them. As a term of disapproval it relaxed disciplines and smoothed the way to seduction. It was the easiest form of rationalization of familial impiety and extramarital indulgences. It made love "free" and

[65] "The Unconscious," *loc. cit.*, IV, 104-106.

helped to condemn fidelity as smug and conventional. What did Freud mean by this term?

Our brief analysis of the unconscious suggested that repression is the mechanism by which unconscious impulses or drives are forbidden access to conscious life. If we disapprove of or are afraid of an object in the external world, we can have recourse to flight. But we cannot (physically) flee something which is within us; "the ego cannot escape itself." In other words, "Repression is a preliminary phase of condemnation, something between flight and condemnation; it is a concept which could not have been formulated before the time of psychoanalytic research." Only those impulses whose satisfaction it is apparently possible to put off are repressed. It is impossible, for example, to put off indefinitely a hunger drive, without causing death to the organism. The direct path to instinctual expression and to subsequent satisfaction is, in cases of repression, blocked; and the repressed instinct, instead of going directly back to the unconscious, is diffused. "It ramifies like a fungus, so to speak, in the dark and takes on extreme forms of expression, which when translated and revealed to the neurotic are bound not merely to seem alien to him, but to terrify him by the way in which they reflect an extraordinary and dangerous strength of instinct." [66]

Thus the repressed instinct does not "give up" when it is denied entrance into consciousness. It expresses itself digressively, disguisedly, in "derivatives." This reaction to the resistance of consciousness gives rise to numerous peculiarities of behavior, some of them healthy, others unhealthy. There are devious methods of conforming to the external world, and in a sense each "fragment" of a repressed instinct becomes hypocritical—that is, it grants the authority of the repressing mechanism at the same time that it devises methods of eluding it.

Repression, like a social statute, requires a constant and energetic renewal and re-enforcement; ". . . if this were discontinued, the success of the repression would be jeopardized, so that a fresh act of repression would be necessary." [67] There is a constant struggle going on with the repressing force, and, during sleep, the repressed instinct finds ways of availing itself of an official satur-

[66] *Ibid.*, 84, 87.   [67] *Ibid.*, 89.

nalia, or relaxation of discipline. The repression, however, continues to operate, primarily because the repressed instinct, if allowed access to experience, would prove *painful*—that is, the energy at its command would serve to injure the ego if it were allowed complete expression. The analyst becomes aware of the nature of the patient's repression when he examines the latter's resistance to treatment. Repression, therefore, is at first a psychic matter; it represents the control of the instinctual drives in accordance with the principle of reality. Not to submit to the latter would mean disaster, for energies in themselves do not possess self-control; they are simply " energetic." Since the ego is the repressing agency, we are obliged to examine the relationship of the ego with the outer world. Established institutions, the ethical preconceptions which govern our lives, are merely auxiliary forms of the reality principle which add power to the " thou-shalt not's " of our emotional life. Perhaps this notion carries us far from our discussion of the actual mechanisms of repression, but it is the sense in which repression is popularly known. To remove the restrictions upon the instinctual life which society has raised would not in itself make for a healthier individual. Divorce, for example, releases a person so that he is (legally) able to make another selection of sexual object. It does not, however, free the ego from its original responsibility—which is to check the instinctual drive from excessive and painful gratification. Repression operates, therefore, quite independently of legal agencies for repression. It is a question of psychic energies purely; and a " cure " which makes the repressed material conscious to the patient does not allow him free use of it; it merely points to him a way of dealing with it intelligently within the world in which he has to live.

The sexual instincts are, for one reason or another, most often subject to repression. In a sense, adjustment to them is normal, since the problem of sexual adjustment is concerned primarily with the selection of a suitable object. But confusion concerning the meaning of *libido* has raised all of the ghosts which at one time were thought to be forever laid. Most people who read Freud in the twenties but did not study him carefully thought that he was an advocate of free love who argued that sexual freedom was the only pathway to happiness. On the level of intellectual discussion the *libido* was confused with the *unconscious,* as though the terms were interchangeable. Freud explained that he emphasized the sexual instincts because his clinical experience convinced him of their importance. In a great majority of cases the repressed materials *were* sexual, but that does not exclude the possibility of other instinctual drives. Freud wished to point out, however, that an explanation in terms of other instincts frequently missed the mark because it often assumed either that no sexual wish was involved or that the sexual wish was merely servant to another, more basic drive. Freud insisted that in most cases it was the other way round.

It is perhaps incorrect to talk about "*the* libido," as though it were a separate psychic entity which changed only superficially and had an existence independent of other elements of the psychic life. It is also a mistake to think of libido as subject to extinction, or temporary annulment. As a matter of fact, libido is scarcely accessible to ordinary measuring devices. It is psychic energy, distinguished from other types of psychic energy by its distinct chemical nature; it is "a force of variable quantity by which processes and transformations in the spheres of sexual excitement can be measured." Libido can be measured only in connection with its investment in an object. "We can then see it as it concentrates and fixes itself upon objects, or as it leaves those objects and passes over to others, from which position it directs the individual's sexual activity; . . ." [68] Libido is, therefore, flexible and maneuverable, is often invested in objects or receives stimulus from objects which have little or no connection with the socially approved end-product of sexual activity. There is little or no point in using the term to refer to instinctive life in general. Careful analysis of the phenomenon of narcissism, or "autoeroticism," [69] requires recognizing the ego and libido as separate—so that the ego may be the object of libido-investment, may become a love-object. Such is indeed the case in the earliest stages of infantile sexuality. [70]

[68] *Three Contributions to a Theory of Sex,* 611.
[69] A term derived from Havelock Ellis, though Ellis uses it in a slightly different sense. See *ibid.,* 586, n. 1.
[70] *A General Introduction to Psychoanalysis,* 359.

The three terms we have selected for special analysis—the unconscious, repression, and libido—are most frequently cited in discussions of Freud; their interdependence is noted only when one looks at Freud's theories as organic. For the most part, however, they were broken off from the parent theory and used independently as critical bludgeons or victims. This habit of accepting or understanding a doctrine only in separate fragments is not unusual. It is incorrect to say that a theory influences a community organically, unless the theorist is in a position to control its applications; translation of theory into practice is often hazardous.

Had psychoanalysis remained exclusively a therapeutic procedure, known only to a few who practiced it correctly and constantly under the supervision of "the master," an ideal control situation might have been possible. But a theory of human behavior is different from a theory of physics. The former deals with aspects of human behavior which have always been of great interest to human beings in general. A discovery in physics or astronomy, such as that by Copernicus, can affect the course of human behavior only when it is retranslated and becomes through its implications, rather than through its original or established truth, a matter of controversy in theology or ethics. The dynamics of translation, the transference of an idea from a sphere remote from to a sphere close to human interests, must be considered as essential to the study of influence. One does not say, "I think that the earth revolves around the sun; therefore I will lead a dissolute life." The syllogism must be complete, and each part of it must be subjected to the tests by which ideas are ultimately accepted or rejected by the average mind. These tests are only infrequently logical; ordinarily they are based upon previous acceptances or rejections, which in their turn are illogical and prejudicial.

But psychoanalysis needed little or no translation into the fluid language of human interests. It dealt with human materials; and, more than that, it started from an assumption that was *prior* to the prevailing bonds of social governance. There was little possibility that the psychoanalyst might flee into mere theory when severely criticized. The theory was itself based upon the most intimate preoccupations of daily life. Psychoanalysis could not remain confined to abstract theorizing. Nor did it wish to. The peculiarities of the doctor-patient relationship were soon aired and condemned. The analyst, it was said, ruined lives under the pretext of saving them. The patient fell in love with the analyst, and too frequently the analyst was unscrupulous in availing himself of such a reaction. Thus the popular view of the condition described by Freud as *transference*. Freud admitted that transference placed a grave moral responsibility upon the analyst, one that called forth all of the sterner qualities with which an analyst should be equipped before he thought of beginning practice.

When the patient comes to an analyst for treatment, only part of his " capacity for love " has been developed—that is, directed toward objects. It is highly probable, therefore, that the " unused " libido will be " turned also toward the person of the physician." This is especially true since the analyst is dealing with matters which concern the patient deeply. The peculiarity of transference, however, is not its occurrence but its intensity. This is a peculiarity which becomes clear only " when we consider that in this situation the transference is effected not merely by the conscious ideas and expectations of the patient, but also by those that are under suppression, or unconscious." [71]

In order to understand this state of affairs, it is necessary to bring to our discussion another clinical term, which has also been broken off from psychoanalysis proper by critics and used in one or another peculiar manner—the fact of *resistance*. The patient, though told that he must " reveal all," cannot do this because some of what he knows or subsequently learns about himself is on the periphery of repression, or is a disguised form of repressed materials. He therefore *resists* the desire of the analyst to get a faithful transcript of his mental life. Resistance is an agent of repression, designed to maintain the status quo and to impede any attempt to violate it.[72]

The attachment of the patient to the physician *favors* resistance. The transference is a means of deflecting the interest

---

[71] Sigmund Freud, " The Dynamics of the Transference," in *The Collected Papers of Sigmund Freud*, II, 313, 314.

[72] See *A General Introduction to Psychoanalysis*, Lecture 19, pp. 248 ff. " The resistance which the patient shows is highly varied, exceedingly subtle, often difficult to recognize, Protean-like in its manifold changes of form. It means that the doctor must become suspicious and be constantly on his guard against the patient." *Ibid.*, 248–49.

from the material the patient does not want to divulge to another means of disguise which the repressed material assumes. Eventually all of the problems for which the patient had once sought the analyst's aid have to be resolved in the field of transference. The transference may be either negative or positive; indeed, in the negative transference the resistance is most clearly to be seen. The astute analyst can make the transference serve his purpose by " lifting " the negative transference and by carefully manipulating the positive transference so that it will change from an erotic deviation from the main purpose of analysis to an active cooperation with the physician.[73] The negative transference, or hatred of the analyst, may, however, reach such a stage as to render treatment useless. Analysis is in a sense a battlefield on which the patient and the analyst struggle for supremacy: the patient, that he might simply " discharge his emotions "; the analyst, so that he can induce the patient to " fit these emotions into their place in the treatment and in his life-history, subject them to rational consideration, and appraise them at their true psychic value." [74]

Since the positive transference is in all cases erotic in character, Freud is deeply concerned over the problem of treating it wisely. First of all, the transference-love is not genuine love but a product of the analytic situation. If that is the case, should not the analyst adopt a moral attitude and preach to the patient? Should he urge the patient " to renounce and to sublimate the promptings of her instincts as soon as she has confessed her love-transference . . . ? " Such a procedure would deprive the analyst of using the transference as an agent of the cure. Even worse for the analysis would be " giving in to " the temptation which the transference offers; the patient would have achieved her object, but the physician not his. A cure would be utterly impossible, for the authority of the analyst would have disappeared under the

---

[73] " The Dynamics of the Transference," *loc. cit.*, 318.

[74] *Ibid.*, 322. Since in this respect, the analyst becomes a sort of " priest " in the community, the transference has been the subject of bitter controversy, and has served as the basis for several satirical treatments in fiction: Rose Macaulay, *Dangerous Ages* (New York, 1921); Waldo Frank, *The Bridegroom Cometh* (New York, 1939); McCarthy, *The Company She Keeps*. The transference love is also crucial to the relationship of the hero and heroine in F. Scott Fitzgerald's *Tender Is the Night* (New York, 1934). Much " post-Freudian analysis " has insisted on the analyst's significant role in redirecting the patient's life, with a view toward altering its future course.

pressure of the humiliation suffered. The only reasonable and safe procedure is to steer a middle course.

> [The physician] must guard against ignoring the transference-love, scaring it away or making the patient disgusted with it; and just as resolutely must he withhold any response to it. He must face the transference-love boldly but treat it as something unreal, as a condition which must be gone through during the treatment and traced back to its unconscious origins, so that it will assist in bringing to light all that is most hidden in the development of the patient's erotic life, and help her to learn to control it.[75]

v

In addition to the mismanagement of such details as the above, the reception and use of Freud as a critical or literary influence involved appropriation of major works, which were taken as a whole and which served, more than any others, to determine the direction of the influence.[76] Of these the two chief single influences were the " Dream-Work " in *The Interpretation of Dreams* and the *Three Contributions to a Theory of Sex*. Each of these deserves special attention at this point.

The importance of the " Dream-Work " for the thought of the twenties cannot be overestimated. Not only was it the central

[75] Sigmund Freud, "Further Recommendations in the Technique of Psycho-analysis: Observations on Transference-Love," in *The Collected Papers of Sigmund Freud*, II, 382, 385.

[76] This by no means exhausts the number of terms whose misuse dictated the manner in which psychoanalysis was received.

A *complex*, for example, was regarded as a term which might be applied to almost any attitude at all; in the popular mind it came to mean the same thing as a behavior pattern, especially one which was distasteful to the person using the term. Hence its use changed from a purely clincal to a pejorative sense.

Sublimation was accorded the favor of the populace as the only term by which psychoanalysis paid deference to conventional morality and religion. In Freud's definition, it meant simply the re-adaptation of the sexual energies to goals which existed outside the sphere of sexual activity.

Projection, a term less often used, but still susceptible to misinterpretation, signified in clinical terms the transference of an affect from one object to another, or in other words rationalizing an emotional state by referring to a substitutive cause.

section of the work on dreams,[77] but it also furnished the chief clues to a knowledge of the peculiar nature of the unconscious. Since the unconscious could not be "known" except in terms recognizable to consciousness, and since it is nevertheless known, or at least felt, in a variety of ways, it follows that its peculiarities rest upon the inability of a conscious system of communication to report it accurately. In other words, the conscious means of expression—language, syntax, logic—presuppose a world which is amenable to such restrictions. One of their functions is to create order from chaos. All conscious processes assume conformity. The dictionary is a catalogue of linguistic conformities; the systems of arithmetic and algebra argue a conformity in the treatment of numbers and signs; grammar (which is, after all, the logic of language) and logic demand conformity so that order may be maintained. Even allowing for the many exceptions in everyday life and in the evolution of speech- and thought-forms, the external world is orderly because the rational mind has seen it advisable to restrict digressions from conformable patterns. This is perhaps both necessary and good, but it restricts our ability to appreciate or grasp the significance of any forms of living which do not easily conform. The unconscious is entirely without a language. What we know of it is in terms of our own systems of communication; and, on first view, that is all but unintelligible. If we wish to know what the distorted and apparently unrecognizable expressions of the unconscious really mean, we shall have to dispense at least temporarily with our accustomed methods of research; we shall have to go to occurrences least understandable in terms of accepted systems of communication.

If we examine a dream, our report of it seems either senseless or disagreeable, or both. That is, the *manifest* dream, or that which we remember and report, rarely bears any relation—or, at any rate, any significant or acceptable relation—to our accustomed modes of thought. This is because the manifest dream is simply a translation of the *latent* dream content, or dream-thoughts, but the values we ordinarily apply in translating from one language

---

[77] Cf. *New Introductory Lectures*, 16–17. Freud was himself aware of the difficulties involved in the spread of his ideas. "A few formulae are generally known, and, among them, several which we have never put forward, such as the statement that all dreams are of a sexual nature. . . ." *Ibid.*, 17.

to another do not apply. It appears as though we are never sure at any time what any one element of the manifest dream may mean. Yet the dream has characteristics; the interpretation can proceed, not according to laws, but with certain warnings and with a preparatory sense of what the dream elements may ultimately mean. The larger divisions of dream-interpretation are: (1) the " latent dream-thoughts " which exist in the unconscious; [78] (2) the repressing and censoring agency, which, through its varying severity and laxity, enables the dream-thoughts to " come through " in disguised form; and (3) the manifest dream content, which represents the dream as we remember and report it. If we recognize the importance of the censor, we can interpret the manifest dream elements as having some relationship or other with the latent dream-thoughts. For one thing, the manifest dream is highly *condensed*—the dream as reported is " reserved, paltry, and laconic when compared with the range and copiousness of the dream thoughts." [79] There are no absolute ratios of condensation, but we may be sure that every element of the manifest dream " enjoys a manifold representation in the dream thoughts." The *condensing activity* of the manifest dream has some peculiar results: for example, the composite images of persons and portmanteau words. Since the latent thoughts are always visual, words are in general treated " as things " by the dream, " and thus undergo the same combinations, displacements, and substitutions, . . . as ideas of things." (*Interpretation*, 277) The play on words which results is similar to the linguistic habits of children.

We cannot be sure that an element in the manifest dream is important because it has a high degree of psychic intensity. The speaker who wishes to make an impression may emphasize a word by inflection of voice or by a gesture; but emphasis is not a sure indication of importance among the dream elements. This is true because of a " psychic force," which " deprives elements of high psychic value of their intensity and may give the impression of importance to an element of little significance." This is the mecha-

[78] They are thoughts only so far as they have been pushed out of consciousness by the repressing force; that is, they have an ideational quality, derived from the experience before repression. Other than that, they are not thoughts at all.

[79] *The Interpretation of Dreams*, 261. Future references to this book are in text, under short title *Interpretation*.

nism of *displacement,* which disfigures and distorts the manifest
dream so that the unconscious wish is not recognizable. It *must
not* be recognizable for the very reason that the censor must not
be informed of it.

We have already observed that the latent dream does not
enjoy the advantages of neat logical distinctions; nor can it employ
relational concepts as a means of indicating either its unity or its
disparity.[80] The interpretation of dreams has afforded ways of
determining the manner in which substitutes, if any, have been
found for these relational concepts:

> *and:* the dream indicates the and- relationship in the form of
> simultaneity.
>
> *because,* or *since:* the causal relationship is indicated by the
> juxtaposition of the " premise " dream with the " result "
> dream; (*Interpretation,* 292) or, the dream may manage
> it simply by changing one image for another, thus indi-
> cating crudely the source of the change.
>
> *either-or:* the disjunctive, or alternative, is managed in the
> dream by " taking both members of this alternative into
> one context, as though they were equally privileged."
> (*Interpretation,* 294) " Either-or," therefore, becomes
> " both-and."
>
> *no, none, not: no* does not appear to exist in the dream;
> antithesis is usually reduced to unity.
>
> *if:* the conditional relation is represented by simultaneity;
> that is, not " if he should do this," but " when he does
> this."

Similarity, correspondence and contiguity are represented in the
dream " by concentration into a unity." Thus, if A resembles B in
one or many particulars (of appearance or attitude), the dream
will represent both A and B in a composite form. To take one of
Freud's examples: " ' A is ill disposed towards me, and B is also ';
I make a composite person of A and B in the dream, or I conceive
A as doing an unaccustomed action which usually characterizes

---

[80] What appears to be an " intellectual component " is part of the dream
material, and " *not the representation of intellectual activity in the dream.*" *Ibid.,*
290.

B." Therefore, the common feature, the *hostility* of both A and B, is inserted. (*Interpretation*, 298)

Inversion is one of the most common means of dream-representation, and a very handy one indeed, for purposes of eluding the censor. The sequence of time is often inverted—for example, the conclusion of an argument may be at the beginning of a dream.[81] Or, the attitude of one person toward another may be inverted. For example, " His father upbraids him because he arrives so late," may mean, " He is angry at his father *and* his father is always too early."

The dream is concerned at all times with presenting the latent dream-thoughts in every permissible way. Since the dream-thoughts are incapable of accommodating abstractions, the latter are transformed into concrete terms, terms which are capable of visual expression. What the conscious mind abhors (ambiguity in word construction) the dream welcomes; for ambiguous verbal constructions are suitable " to the expression of more than one dream thought," and hence favor the mechanism of condensation. " A word being a point of junction for a number of conceptions, it possesses, so to speak, a predestined ambiguity, and neuroses . . . take advantage of the conveniences which words offer for the purposes of condensation . . . quite as readily as the dream." For the same purpose the dream may take words in their " original or etymological " meaning instead of their present, abstract form. If a proper name resists visual representation, it will be distorted considerably, or even replaced by " very far-fetched references." (*Interpretation*, 315, 325)

Another important means of representation is the *dream symbol*. The question of symbolism relates to the problem of folk metaphor and its persistence in the unconscious. Freud has noted in several places the tendency in the primitive mind to draw broad comparisons, with little regard for accuracy of resemblance.[82] The dream symbols are therefore looser in construction than the metaphors and similes of literary art; their comparisons appreciate, not the precise and complex details of resemblance of the metaphor, but the more universal and most obvious forms of relationship.

---

[81] Cf. the first " sentence " of *Finnegans Wake*.

[82] See *Interpretation*, 322; *A General Introduction to Psychoanalysis*, Lecture 10, pp. 122–40; Ernest Jones, *Papers on Psychoanalysis* (Baltimore, 1938), 129–86.

Yet they too are obscure in the sense that the things or acts compared are not immediately appreciated as alike; when the resemblance is pointed out, however, it appears so obvious as to be unmistakable. The peculiar fact about dream symbols is that they exist in the unconscious and hence may have little or no resemblance to any intellectual or somatic stimulus of the " dream day." [83] Though there has been much controversy over the place of symbols in dream-interpretation,[84] psychoanalysts seem agreed that some symbols are to be found " ready made in the Unconscious," and that they form a link with the history of culture.

One final characteristic of dream formation, which Freud calls *secondary elaboration*, is less important for the dream itself but helpful in explaining certain peculiarities of the manifest content. Secondary elaboration occurs when the censor, " which has never been quite asleep, feels that it has been surprised by the already admitted dream." (*Interpretation*, 390) Hence we have such expressions as " Well, it's only a dream after all," or we note expressions of satisfaction or dismay which seem inconsistent with the actual content of the dream.

The variety of suggestions that these characteristics of the dream offer has a direct relationship to the problems of language and style some twentieth-century writers encountered. If we regard consciousness and unconsciousness as one behavior-continuum, there remains the fact that the unconscious does not respond to the devices for ordering and control of conscious life; a complete picture of the mental life of any person places a responsibility upon both writer and reader; both are obliged to shift their centers of attention. This can be more demanding than the intellectual skill required to understand a literary conceit. The question of its appropriateness and of the dividing line

[83] Jones has discussed the psychic dynamism of the dream symbol more clearly than Freud: the symbol " always constitutes a regression to a simpler mode of apprehension. If the regression proceeds only a certain distance . . . , the result is metaphorical. . . . If, owing to the strength of the unconscious complex it proceeds further—to the level of the unconscious—the result is symbolism in the strict sense." Jones, *Psychoanalysis*, 186.

[84] Stekel has emphasized the symbol so much as to furnish catalogic short cuts to dream interpretation. Jung bases his interpretation of symbols upon a theory of the unconscious which includes all the relics of antiquity; hence symbols point to a variety of religious and ethical concepts inherited by the unconscious from the " race mind."

between the clinical and the literary may well be postponed for a consideration of some examples of this type of literature.

The *Three Contributions to a Theory of Sex* was also received with incredulity and amazement. It can be said to have influenced concepts of behavior and to have furnished a rationale for revolutions against accepted standards of familial behavior. If family standards were subjected to scientific scrutiny, they might not survive the analysis. Yet such terms as the oedipus complex and the electra complex became catch words for writers whose province had always been the field of domestic relationships. It is not that these problems would not have continued as legitimate subjects for treatment in fiction had Freud never made his "three contributions." But, for better or for worse, Freud's contributions made writers more conscious of these problems and gave them at least the illusion that they were legitimately transferring scientific terms and descriptions to the field of art. The novels of the twenties emphasized the themes; aided by the skeptical attitude toward older standards, the novelists gave their family portraits undeniably Freudian qualities.

chapter II

SPREAD OF
FREUD'S THEORY

i

Enough might be said about Freud's relationships with his followers to illuminate the journey of Freudianism from Vienna to the capitals of Europe and America. The family relationships of the Freudians have the value of showing the extent to which Freud became known in the early years of the twentieth century.

By 1907 Freud had completed four of the books that were directly responsible for his reputation. Since none of these was as yet translated into English,[1] the interest in them was confined to the medical and psychoanalytic fraternities. The stimulus for the development of psychoanalysis as a "school" came through the Zurich group, headed by Carl G. Jung and Oscar Pfister. Though the friendship between Jung and Freud was short-lived, it furnished the initial opportunity for decentralizing the psychoanalytic movement.[2]

In 1907 Freud learned of the great interest the Swiss psychia-

---

[1] The first of the four to be translated was *Three Contributions to a Theory of Sex*, 1910. For the story of Freud's slow progress to fame, see Ernest Jones, *The Life and Work of Sigmund Freud* (New York, 1953, 1955), volumes 1 and 2.

[2] This Freud has never hesitated to admit. Cf. *The History of the Psychoanalytic Movement*, 947–48. " I have repeatedly acknowledged with gratitude the great efforts of the Zurich School of Psychiatry in the spreading of psychoanalysis, especially those of Bleuler and Jung, and I do not hesitate to do the same today [1916], even under such changed circumstances." *Ibid.*, 947.

trists were taking in his contributions, and in the spring of 1908, the first Psychoanalytic Congress was held. From that time until 1913, the relations between Freud and Jung were cordial and their interests mutual. The break came at the 4th Psychoanalytic Congress, in 1913, when Jung's colleague, Maeder, read a paper on the dream. It was there that Freud saw clearly what he had long suspected—that Jung's interpretation of psychic phenomena was radically different from what Freud's long experience had permitted him to accept. To Jung the dream indicated that the unconscious harbored not only the "animal" but also the "divine" in man, and that such key terms as the oedipus complex were only symbols, to be traced back to a more fundamental source.[3] The character of Jung's first important contribution to "analytical psychology," *Wandlungen und Symbole der Libido,*[4] published in 1911–12, shows well the independence of Jung's thought. As Fritz Wittels suggests, a study of this work will explain to anyone the reason for Jung's break from Freud: "In the first part of the book, Jung is still being towed in Freud's wake. In the second part, however, the libido is created genetically and is desexualised. . . ."[5]

The break with Alfred Adler was likewise motivated by a difference in opinion about a central concept. For Adler the desire

[3] Cf. Wittels, *Sigmund Freud*, 178. In fact Jung was to develop a theory of the "collective unconscious" which actually tutored the personality by referring in dreams to mythical archetypes, *a priori* ideas residing in the unconscious, "this absolute inner order of the unconscious that forms our refuge and help in the accidents and commotions of life." See Jolan Jacobi, *The Psychology of Jung* (New Haven, 1943), 42–43.

[4] *The Psychology of the Unconscious*, tr. B. M. Hinkle (New York, 1916).

[5] Wittels, *Sigmund Freud*, 181. That is, Jung thought of libido as equivalent to all psychic energy, both the "human" and the "divine"; hence opportunity was afforded for religious and didactic additions to purely clinical and therapeutic procedures. This difference between Jung and Freud is essential; it is a difference in temperament as well as in philosophic approach. In the scores of books on psychoanalysis which appeared in the period from 1915 to 1930, the difference is mentioned and forms one of the bases for the innumerable controversies which characterized the history of psychoanalysis. Jung was not without his champions among the writers and artists of our century.

Among those who sponsored and wrote for the Paris-American magazine, *Transition* (1927–38), Jung was a favorite. His explanation of the creative artist's "exceptional" alliance "as it were a 'direct contact'—with the unconscious" (Jacobi, *The Psychology of Jung*, 27) attracted the *Transition* avant-gardists. Eugene Jolas told me in August of 1943 that Jung was an active sponsor of *Transition*. The surrealists, on the other hand, were almost unanimously (and usually unwelcome) supporters of Freud.

for power, and its consequent psychic complications, was the *modus operandi* of man's behavior. In the case of "weak men" this will-to-power manifests itself in what Adler calls the "masculine protest." He recommends that men have "the greatest possible freedom of action," so that they may fulfill their desire for power and be spared the feeling of inferiority which appears among the inhibited.[6] In *The History of the Psychoanalytic Movement*, Freud attempts to give his reasons for breaking with Adler:

> Adler's theory was, from the very beginning, a "system," which psychoanalysis was careful not to become. . . . Psychoanalysis has a greater interest in showing that all ego strivings are mixed with libidinal components. Adler's theory emphasizes the counterpart to it; namely, that all libidinal feeling contains an admixture of egotism. This would have been a palpable gain if Adler had not made use of this assertion to deny every time the libidinal feelings in favor of the impelling ego components. His theory thus does exactly what all patients do, and what our conscious thinking always does; it rationalizes, as Jones would say, in order to conceal the unconscious motives.[7]

It was necessary, therefore, to ask Adler to leave the movement; this Freud did in 1911,[8] and since then Adler has had a wide following of his own, especially in America; he calls his brand of psychoanalysis "Individual Psychology."

Of Freud's relations with his other followers, it is perhaps enough to say that there were many subsequent departures from the ancestral manor and that Freud felt keenly about them.[9] This

---

[6] Wittels, *Sigmund Freud*, 147.

[7] *The History of the Psychoanalytic Movement*, 966–67. Contrast Phyllis Bottome, *Alfred Adler: a Biography* (New York, 1939), 55–67.

[8] For a description of the manner in which this was done, see Wittels, *Sigmund Freud*, 150–51. "It should be noted that political influences played a part in these joint resignations. Adler and his nine friends were all Socialists." *Ibid.*, 151. In 1939 Wittels published a "recantation" of much that he had said in his biography, but Freud, in his letter to Wittels (published as a preface to the book), praised him for clearing up so well the matter of Adler's defection.

[9] The other important dissenters include Wilhelm Stekel and Otto Rank. His "loyal followers" include such men as Theodore Reik, Fritz Wittels (the "prodigal son"), Ernest Jones, Sandor Ferenczi (perhaps the oldest of them), and A. A. Brill.

side of Freud's nature is important only because, as a result of it, the psychoanalytic stream was muddied at its very source, and it required a careful study indeed to distinguish between terms which were originally " Freudian " and those which were subsequently used in different contexts by dissenting writers.

One of the most important links with the new world was the energetic and loyal work of Dr. A. A. Brill, who first encountered and studied Freudian clinical psychology at Jung's Clinic of Psychiatry, in Zurich, Switzerland. In 1908 he arranged with Freud for the translation of the latter's principal works.[10] Between that time and 1938, when he gathered together the " basic writings " and gave them a wide distribution through the agency of the Modern Library, Brill was to Freudianism in American what Ernest Jones is to the movement in England. He often met with artists, sociologists, and psychologists, and discussed with all of them the significance of the " new psychology." In his literal translations the works of Freud have been read by thousands.

He was ready and waiting, when in 1909, Freud crossed the Atlantic for his first and only visit to America; he had been invited to come to Worcester, Massachusetts, there to participate in the celebration of the twenty-fifth anniversary of Clark University.[11] With him came Ferenczi and Jung; present to receive him were Ernest Jones (then at Toronto) and Brill. While in the United States, he met William James and spoke briefly with him, and he converted James J. Putnam of Harvard University from an opponent to an enthusiastic advocate of psychoanalysis. Putnam's sponsorship was keenly appreciated by Freud, but it was received with mixed feelings. " Yielding too much to the great ethical and philosophic bent of his nature, Putnam later required of psychoanalysis what, to me, seems an impossible demand. He

[10] A. A. Brill, " The Introduction and Development of Freud's Work in the United States," in *American Journal of Sociology*, XLV (1939) , 323. See also Brill, " Reflections, Reminiscences of Sigmund Freud," in *Medical Leaves*, III (1940) , 19: " [from 1908] until 1918 I gave most of my leisure time to the translation of Freud's works. In addition to my work as translator I have taught, read and discussed his theories until this very day."

[11] These five lectures were first published in the *American Journal of Psychology*, XXI (1910) , 181–218. Known as *The Origin and Development of Psychoanalysis*, they constitute one of the best of Freud's earlier summaries of the movement. Since they were given in 1909, they are free also of the often irritating quibbling which he felt was necessary, once Jung and Adler had left him.

wished that it should be pressed into the service of a certain moral philosophical conception of the universe; . . ." [12]

The visit to America may well be said to have laid the groundwork for the subsequent popularity of psychoanalysis in the United States. Since Ernest Jones was later to become the leader of the movement in England, and to play an important role in one of Freud's most widely publicized adventures—that is, his flight from Vienna to London in 1939—the gathering in Worcester had further importance. Its immediate effect on the American public was not startling. The interest in psychoanalysis was still for the most part confined to medical and psychological journals. No translations into English of Freud's works were as yet available. Freudianism was still in a period of formulation, even in Vienna and Zurich. There was some effort at popularization, but no tidal wave of interest and controversy as swept the United States in the twenties.[13] Intellectuals and artists early saw the possibilities of the new psychology. Brill speaks of writers who "came to me from everywhere wanting to know about it," after he had published a paper on dreams sometime in 1910 and had received a two-page notice in the New York *Sunday Times*.[14]

ii

The first reference made in America to psychoanalysis appeared in an article by Boris Sidis in the *Journal of Abnormal Psychology*, in 1906. The issue of the *American Journal of Psychology* for April, 1910, besides printing in English Freud's lectures, published articles by Jung, Stern, Jones, and Ferenczi—the most complete and best statement of psychoanalysis then available in English.[15] The questions these articles and subsequent

---

[12] *The History of the Psychoanalytic Movement*, 951.

[13] There is no justification for such a sweeping statement as that by Harry Hartwick, *The Foreground of American Fiction* (New York, 1934), 128: "After 1910 the newspapers were packed with references to this new doctrine; and men in the street began quoting a jargon of strange phrases. . . ." Since he follows closely the information given in Mark Sullivan, *Our Times: the United States, 1900–1925* (New York, 1932), IV, 166–76, it may be instructive to consult p. 170 of this work. Sullivan is more conservative and cautious about his statements.

[14] A. A. Brill to Frederick J. Hoffman, November 18, 1942.

[15] Vol. XXI: Carl G. Jung, "The Association Method," 219–69; Wm. Stern,

contributions to "the press" debated were not of a sort which would interest the layman; nor was it likely that such journals enjoyed any great or effective circulation. Freudian theory was to be spared, for a few years at least, the rapid assimilation which was to be its fate in the twenties. To be sure, there were a few early notices in the popular magazines—among them, an article by H. Addington Bruce in the *American Magazine*, which included a photograph of the leading psychoanalysts at Clark University. Bruce treated the movement (along with other activities in the field of psychology) as an interesting curiosity, whose lasting contribution had yet to be tested and approved: "Thus far, it must be said, no other leading psychopathologist has accepted this sweeping, audacious theory. But it is being pressed vigorously by Freud and a rapidly increasing band of disciples. . . ." [16]

Popular reception of any idea which was in the beginning defined technically is possible only in certain circumstances: (1) The idea must be translated into the language in which discussion is possible. (2) These translations must receive due notice in the journals which are read regularly by the educated layman. (3) They must have—intrinsically—a value which will be appreciated by the lay mind; that is, the ideas must be either startling, novel, or basic to an intelligent consideration of human behavior.

The importance of translation cannot be overestimated. Brill's role, therefore, is significant. In 1913, he translated the third edition of *Die Traumdeutung*; [17] this and the *Drei Abhandlungen zur Sexual-Theorie* (the third edition of which he translated in 1918) contained most of what was to be tagged as "Freudianism" by the layman. Among other books which Brill was to give to the English-speaking public were the *Zur Psychopathologie*

"... Testimony and ... the Study of Individuality," 270–82; Ernest Jones, "Freud's Theory of Dreams," 283–308; Sandor Ferenczi, "The Psychological Analysis of Dreams," 309–28.

[16] "Masters of the Mind: Remarkable Cures Effected by Four Great Experts Without the Aid of Drugs or Surgeons' Tools," in *American Magazine*, LXXI (1910), 71–81.

[17] The third edition differs from the first two in being enlarged through the addition of dream interpretations and references to other works on the subject which Freud had consulted in the years after 1900. The translation is quite literal, almost clumsily so, but Brill does not hesitate to substitute case studies of his own when Freud's examples prove to be "untranslatable." See *The Interpretation of Dreams*, 277, 324. The changes are made in cases of dreams dealing mainly with the use of words in dreams.

38952

des Alltagslebens (translated 1914) and *Der Witz und seine Beziehung zum Unbewusztsein.* (1916) These last two works were accepted by the lay public as interesting additions to and applications of the central theories of Freud.[18] But early attention was fairly well confined to the work on dreams.

In that work such magazines as *Forum, McClure's, Century, Dial,* and *Nation* indicated a mild interest. Their aim was chiefly to give this " uncharted area " of the psychic life sufficient enlightenment so that the layman might test for himself the validity of Freud's conclusions. Edward M. Weyer suggested to his readers that, if one of them doubted the nature of Freud's conclusions,

> . . . he should submit a few of his own dreams to the test. He may verify for himself many of Freud's assertions, if he will keep a dream diary, and will adopt the habit of picking the skeletons of his own dreams immediately upon waking in the morning. The wealth of his own dream life will probably astonish him at first; then he will come to know himself as the proprietor of a busy theatre—owner, spectator, and critic in one.[19]

Among the pioneers in the work of presenting the dream work to the public was the Reverend Samuel McComb; unlike Weyer, however, McComb insisted that the dream showed the " orderly process of the mind " and refused to allow much for the claim that " all dreams are pre-eminently of a sexual origin." To his comments on Freud, he adds many references to dreams in which the supernatural plays a leading role. The article, on the whole, disapproves of the points which Freud considered most important to an understanding of the dream, and McComb brings his own preconceptions to bear upon the " new psychology ": " A dream is then an allegory, like the Pilgrim's Progress, which, indeed, with unconscious insight, its author sets forth under the guise of a dream." [20]

---

[18] Cf. the popularization given *Psychopathology of Everyday Life* by Bruce Barton, who reports an interview with Brill in the article, " You Can't Fool Your Other Self," in *American Magazine,* XCII (1921) , 11–13 ff. See also, Alfred Kuttner, " A Note on Forgetting," in *New Republic,* I (1914) , 15–17.

[19] Edward M. Weyer, " The New Art of Interpreting Dreams," in *Forum,* XLV (1911) , 593. A few of the articles appeared before the translation of *Die Traumdeutung.*

[20] Samuel McComb, " The New Interpretation of Dreams," in *Century,*

In their efforts to make Freudian psychology intelligible to the layman, the early commentators resorted to analogy and metaphor. We have such an explanation as that by Edwin Tenney Brewster, who pictures the psychic life as follows: " The conscious soul keeps house in a tidy little apartment . . . [underneath which lie] cellars and galleries and caverns, full of strange things. . . ." [21]

The publication of Brill's translation was the starting point of critical reaction. The *Nation* greeted *The Interpretation of Dreams* with some little misgiving. The general tendency in the new psychology, it suggested, was " to over-emphasize the potency of erotic influence in all of experience, and in the field here considered the results of this preconception are conspicuous, leading to improbable and revolting explanations." [22] Horace Kallen, less easily offended, and more interested in the clinical value of Freud's work, insisted that " the ultimate test of Freudism lies not in argument but in its clinical adequacy, and in the ease and simplicity with which it applies to other problems and illuminates other obscurities in the psychological jungle." [23]

In June and July of 1915 *Everybody's Magazine* published the first thorough popular account of the new psychology, in two articles by Max Eastman. All devices for making a difficult subject easy and entertaining were employed. Eastman begins by saying that these new theories may affect the lives of hundreds of thousands of men and women in America. Simple case studies are used to illustrate the " magic " of psychoanalysis. The author gives a brief summary of Freud's career and of the beginnings of dream-interpretation. Psychoanalysis, says Eastman to his popular audience, " is a technique for finding out what is in the unconscious mind. And the unconscious mind is the place where those desires and fancies go which we are not willing to acknowledge even to ourselves." Under the heading " The Menace of Submerged Desires," Eastman characterizes the mind as " like a . . . mysterious well of water, whose conscious surface is not large but which

LXXXIV (1912), 665. McComb objected especially to the conception of dream as wish-fulfillment. He seemed to think that if a dream were purely a wish-fulfillment, it allowed no scope for nobler motives in man's psychological makeup.

[21] Edwin Tenney Brewster, " Dreams and Forgetting: New Discoveries in Dream Psychology," in *McClure's Magazine*, XXXIX (1912), 715.

[22] Review of Freud's *Traumdeutung*, in *Nation*, XCVI (1913), 504.

[23] Horace Kallen, " The Mystery of Dreams," in *Dial*, LV (1913), 80.

spreads out to great distances and great depths below." The author cautions his readers, however, that psychoanalysis is not an easy excuse for all sorts of license and dissipation.[24]

In the second article the simplified explanations are illustrated in the accepted manner of the day, by George Brehm. One full-page drawing shows a young man making a passionate though formal request of his companion that she become his wife. She is sitting on the sofa, her face marked by obviously painful hesitation. The drawing is designed to illustrate the psychoanalytic explanation of old maidery: " She's a typical ' Old Maid,' " says the caption. " She really loves him but she can't make up her mind to take him. Why? In her ' unconscious' there is a vision of an ' ideal man,' and this vision is really just an infantile image of her father or her brother." The second article in the series concentrates mainly upon popular applications of Freud's *Psychopathology of Everyday Life*, as its title certainly suggests.[25]

These two articles did for the general public what reviewers and special writers for the *Nation* and *New Republic* were doing for the educated layman, what the men and women of Greenwich Village and of Mabel Dodge Sterne's " circle " were doing for the intellectuals and artists. Despite the great over-simplification of Freudianism and the use of inaccurate metaphors in his explanation, the articles aroused a very active curiosity about the new psychology, a curiosity which was to be more than satisfied in coming years.

iii

By 1915 psychoanalysis was also fairly well launched in the magazines from which the intellectual of that day drew his information. The work on dreams had been the bridge to an understanding of Freud's basic assumptions. The movement was still new; it had aroused the interest of psychiatrists and, to a lesser extent, of clergymen, and it was beginning to be appreciated by

[24] Max Eastman, " Exploring the Soul and Healing the Body," in *Everybody's Magazine*, XXXII (1915) , 741-50.

[25] Max Eastman, " Mr. Er-er-er—Oh! What's His Name? " in *Everybody's Magazine*, XXXIII (1915) , 95-103.

the layman as well. In the field of ethics, Edwin B. Holt, taking his cue from Putnam's suggestion that psychoanalysis had much to say for a reinterpretation of philosophic notions, published his work on *The Freudian Wish and Its Place in Ethics.* (New York, 1915) This book placed an altogether un-Freudian construction upon the motivity of the wish. The wish was to be the emotional successor to the " sensation," as previous psychologists had characterized the psychic life. The wish, intelligently perceived or felt, was the guide to a course of action: it was given " pragmatic sanction." In fact, " the whole drama of life hinges on the development and reciprocal modification of motor settings, that is, of purposes and wishes incorporated in the body." (p. 61) That the wish, as Freud examined it, seemed often to lead, not to " purposive action " but to defensive action and hence to neurosis, did not seem to bother Holt, who conceived of the wish as dynamically geared to the good, the expedient, and the socially permissible.[26]

All of the problems of the twenties seemed to have been anticipated by the early pioneers. " False analyses " and other quackery, they hastened to suggest, were not to be blamed on Freud.[27] It was Walter Lippmann, recently from Harvard, who anticipated the difficult course of psychoanalysis once it became the prey of popularizers and after-dinner symposiums. It was Lippmann who invited Brill to speak at one of Mabel Dodge Sterne's " evenings," and it was also he who warned against the misunderstanding which must inevitably come from drawing-room discussions and " psyching." His criticism was directed chiefly against " people [who] will criticize Freud on the basis of a dinner-table conversation or perhaps on the reading of his book about ' The Interpretation of Dreams.' . . ." Freud's psychology is of such interest to the layman because he touches at the very heart of human interest. For that reason, however, people resent and reject what does not appeal to them in his psychology, and thus distort it. If we allow him to speak without interruption, he will

<hr>

[26] In a sense Holt was aware of the clinical sources of the Freudian wish. He saw a world in which wish and reality needed only the principle of " discrimination " to be joined in effective harmony. See pp. 134–35.

[27] Cf. Alfred B. Kuttner, " The Freudian Theory," in *New Republic,* II (1915), 183, and his review of Holt's book, in *New Republic,* II (1915), 9–10.

probably " emerge triumphant." " When I compare his work with the psychology that I studied in college or with most of the material that is used to controvert him, I cannot help feeling that for his illumination, for this steadiness and brilliancy of mind, he may rank among the greatest who have contributed to thought." [28]

In a letter of November 18, 1942, Lippmann explained his early acquaintance with the theories of Freud. [In the spring and summer of 1912]

> I had been a pupil at Harvard of William James and of Graham Wallas and was preparing to write a book on politics, which was published under the title, *A Preface to Politics.* I had a close friend who shared a cabin in the Maine woods with me while I was writing that book. He had been a patient of Dr. Brill and was engaged in translating the *Interpretation of Dreams* into English. His name was Alfred Booth Kuttner. I read the translation as he worked on it and discussed it with him and began to see how much Freud had to contribute to the psychology which I had learned at college. If you care to examine *A Preface to Politics*, you will see the effects. It may interest you to know that the book was reviewed by Freud in his journal, " Imago."

A Preface to Politics appeared in 1914. The book is studded with references to the major intellectual interests of the time— among them, the theories of Nietzsche, Bergson, and Freud. Lippmann's discussion may well be regarded as a preliminary summary of the moral, social, and political controversies of the immediate future. It is a call for a new, more appropriate " order of thinking." Society has too long simply answered evil by prohibition or taboo. Lippmann asks that we follow out the suggestion of William James, to find a " moral equivalent " of all evil. The idea of so channelizing the energy of original desires that they may be most happily used by society follows the Freudian discussion of sublimation. The burden of Lippmann's advice is that we stop applying artificial restrictions to our desires, but begin by understanding our inner natures. On the basis of intelligent introspection we may be able to develop a political morality more

[28] Walter Lippmann, " Freud and the Layman," in *New Republic*, II (1915), 9–10.

consistent with the actual nature of man and at least not detrimental and oppressive, as are some of our present legal institutions and practices.

Through the stimulus afforded by Mabel Dodge Sterne's group and the pre-twenties version of Greenwich Village, Freudianism became a rival to the war as a subject of interest. On the one hand it was denounced as a " psychological humbug " which accepts for publication " the very quintessence of inanity "; [29] on the other hand it was hailed as a corrective of the errors of the confessional and the rallying cry of the feminist movement. Florence Kiper Frank suggested that " The Freudian searching into motives is the accredited material of the novelist; the use of dream symbols the very stuff of the poet." [30] Note in this connection the controversy which went on over Warner Fite's review of Jung's *Psychology of the Unconscious* in the pages of the *Nation*. This respectable professor described all utterances of the psychoanalysts as " of the same order; not merely sexual, but abnormal and obscene." He resented the fact that the respectable, normal, conscious self is made out by psychoanalysts to be a fool. " The Freudian's contribution consists in converting the suggestions rejected or suppressed, the leavings of the conscious self, into a second fully organized personality, a demoniacal Alter Ego, crafty and mysterious, lustful and malevolent." He granted that Freud shows " evidences here and there of fine feeling," but insisted that they are " scattered among the fruits of an ingeniously obscene imagination." [31]

Among the answers to this review was that of Samuel Tannenbaum, a practising analyst, who objected to Fite's confusion of the Freudian with the Jungian school and insisted that a truth may not be palatable but is none the less true.[32] Samuel Eliot protested that this " undesirable emphasis upon sex " was merely

[29] J. Victor Huberman, as reported in *Current Opinion*, LX (1916), 35.

[30] Florence Kiper Frank, " Psycho-analysis: Some Random Thoughts Thereon," in *Little Review*, III (1916), 15–17. She believes, however, that Freud will eventually prove more important for the physician, Jung for the layman. She predicts, quite accurately, that " It will take perhaps another five years for the discussion of psychoanalysis to penetrate the popular consciousness." *Ibid.*, 17.

[31] Warner Fite, " Psycho-analysis and Sex Psychology," in *Nation*, CIII (1916), 127–29. It is more an indictment of Freudian psychology than a review of Jung's book.

[32] Samuel Tannenbaum, Letter, in *Nation*, CIII, 218.

hindering the development of a valuable treatment of neuroses.[33] C. Ladd Franklin, on the other hand, applauded Fite's courage in dealing openly with " the absurdities of the Freudian doctrine. . . . The whole trend of thought is no less a prostitution of logic—of scientific acumen and method—than it is of a decent morality." Using the prevailing war hysteria to advantage, Franklin condemned this new psychology as a product of the " German mind," which was " to a certain extent undeveloped when contrasted with the logical and moral sanity of the non-German civilized nations. . . ." [34]

There is much in these letters that helps to illuminate the study of Freud's influence. For one reason or another, the writers bring to their subject (whether with sympathy or hostility) their preconceptions of what a psychology may be permitted to say about the life of man. In many respects, referring to a thing as having been said seemed the equivalent of advising that it ought not to have been said. Judgment proceeded along such lines as these: " This is bad because it is expressed by a man from a nation with which our friends are at war "; or, " This is bad because it overreaches the bounds of polite morality "; or, " This cannot be true because I have not experienced it." A legitimate criticism might have been directed against those who admired psychoanalysis as a " cure-all " or who employed it to excuse personal excesses. But the forces of misunderstanding operated as fully in one direction as in another; and sane, sober discussions were limited to but a few pages of the contemporary magazines. People brought either their predispositions or their ignorance to the door of psychoanalysis—and expected the one to be obeyed or the other to be excused. One thing was sure to happen—a doctrine so avidly praised and so avidly condemned was bound to interest the thoughtful people of the time.

That Mabel Dodge Sterne should have gathered together so many of these " thoughtful souls," men and women of such diverse views as John Reed, Walter Lippmann, Margaret Sanger, Maurice Sterne, and Hutchins Hapgood, is a mystery which only the combined psychologies of Mrs. Sterne herself and of the American intellectual in general can resolve. She all but established the

[33] Samuel Eliot, Letter, in *Nation*, CIII, 219.
[34] C. Ladd Franklin, Letter, in *Nation*, CIII, 373.

pattern of the " free-lance intellectual " of the early twentieth century. Since her psychiatrist-doctor, Bernard Sachs, had advised her to live apart from her husband, she went again to psychoanalysis when she felt bored or in need of a confirmation of her own prejudices. She thus illustrated well what Waldo Frank was later to point out as one of the weaknesses of psychoanalysis, and what Freud himself recognized and deplored—the expensiveness of treatment.[35] She moved from one analyst to another, and was at the same time interested in other kinds of " healing." Under treatment from Dr. Smith Ely Jelliffe, she came to the conclusion that " Psychoanalysis was apparently a kind of tattletaling. I was able to tell not only everything about myself but all about Maurice [Sterne]." After a time she shifted from the " Jungian " analysis of Dr. Jelliffe to the " Freudian " analysis of Dr. Brill.[36] With Brill she was later to conduct a correspondence on the " problem " of her relations with D. H. Lawrence.[37]

We have already noted that the curiosity of the young intellectual had been aroused. Brill mentions Theodore Dreiser, who, he says, gave him credit for influencing his " views on life." The great advocate of psychoanalysis in Greenwich Village, Floyd Dell, speaks of his introduction to the new psychology in Greenwich Village, in 1914:

There must have been at that date a half dozen or more people in the Liberal Club who knew a good deal about psychoanalysis, and a score or so more who were familiar enough with the terms to use them in badinage. I began reading books about psychoanalysis and was at first incredulous

---

[35] Waldo Frank, " Sigmund Freud," in *Virginia Quarterly Review*, X (1934), 536. " The time required by an analysis, and the expense, make the method (under our present system) available chiefly to the type of idle woman and parasitic man who are not worth saving at the price of the lengthy effort which the analyst must devote to readjusting them into a morbid world." In " Turnings in the Ways of Psychoanalytic Therapy," *loc. cit.*, 392–402, Freud suggests psychoanalytic clinics for the poor, and admits that the procedure of analysis might have to be modified in adjustment to such an expansion.

[36] Luhan, *Movers and Shakers*, 439, 498. By 1923, Mrs. Sterne had remarried once again, this time to Tony Luhan. All of her books, therefore, give her later name; references to Mrs. Sterne and Mrs. Luhan are, of course, to the same person.

[37] Mabel Dodge Luhan, *Lorenzo in Taos* (New York, 1935), 270. " In a final panic I hastened to New York to consult Dr. Brill, good old Brill, sitting in his office like a kindly ghoul, laughing at mysteries, with a quick name for any subtle dilemma."

about dream interpretation, until I tried association [a method of interpretation which Jung had developed] on one of my dreams with convincing results. . . . I think it was late in 1916 that I began being analyzed, not for any particular neurotic difficulty, but because I thought it might be helpful to me in my love life and literary work, as it proved to be. Everyone at that time who knew about psychoanalysis was a sort of missionary on the subject, and nobody could be around Greenwich Village without hearing a lot about it.[38]

For the old *Masses,* which Dell helped Max Eastman to edit, the interest in psychoanalysis was happily associated with the fast approaching dawn of an intelligent day. The discussions centered upon woman's suffrage, liberalization of the divorce laws, and other problems which an enthusiastic interest in Freud might associate with his theories. Thus argued the Village intellectuals: Freud's writings have pointed out the importance of sex in human life and have suggested an intelligent reappraisal of social and moral restrictions. We must therefore count him as one of us. This was before the impact of the Marxist revolution had been felt, and one's personal sex relations were still as important as social well being; indeed, the two were interdependent.

But all of these references are in reality preliminaries to the postwar twenties, which were to witness the real penetration of Freudianism into the thought of England and America. There was no lack of discussion of Freudianism before and during the war. But the ordinarily slow process of transferring an interest from scientific journals to the popular consciousness was made even slower by the preoccupation with questions of war and peace. Freud himself confined his writing to papers on clinical procedure; between 1913 and 1918 no major work by him was released to the public. His "Thoughts for the Times on War and Death," [39] written early in 1915, reflected his mood at the time. Meanwhile, Jung, situated securely in the haven of Zurich, Switzerland, carried on as usual, and found an opportunity to carry psychoanalysis to the intellectuals exiled there during the war—among them, James Joyce.

[38] Floyd Dell to Frederick J. Hoffman, September 17, 1942.
[39] First published in *Imago,* IV (1915), 1-21. See also *The Collected Papers of Sigmund Freud,* IV, 288-317.

chapter III

FREUDIANISM—
AMERICAN AND ENGLISH

---

i

Despite its attractiveness to the general public Freudianism was primarily a contribution to psychology, and especially to psychiatry, or " medical psychology." It had more than an ordinary interest for the cultured layman because it dealt fearlessly with those aspects of human behavior which are his common concern but had not up to that time been the subject of dining-room or parlor conversation. There must have been a special reason why in the years following the war its popularity increased at a tremendous rate—why it became, in a sense, a plaything of the intellectual and of the wealthy, the subject of unending discussions in the cafes, the speakeasies, and the salons. The type of opposition it met indicated that it was not acceptable in those circles which upheld the values of the past; the fact that it was enthusiastically received by many of the younger intellectuals might indicate that it furnished them with a critical weapon against the standards they had but recently repudiated. Both the negative and positive advantages of psychoanalysis appealed to the postwar generation: it gave them an apparently justifiable means of " scoffing scientifically and wisely " at the old standards, and it furnished an opportunity to search for new bases of human conduct. Freud's work served as a revolutionary document; it pointed away from the past.

Few thought seriously enough to search in it for an alternative social or moral program. Freudianism merely suggested to the individualists a way of defending themselves against the apparent collapse of the older culture. The postwar world first sought adjustment through the new psychology, then—when it had wearied of it or found it inadequate—sought for release in economic protest. The figures of Freud and Marx dominated the twenties and the thirties.[1] The young men and women first repudiated the psychological and ethical sources of their civilization; later many of them concentrated upon the economic framework of their world. Assuming an interest in the common man whom they had only recently discovered, they organized against the economic evils of the world. It was with the "*moral* protest" that the widespread influence of Freud was associated.[2]

The "transvaluation of values" seemed grounded upon extreme opposition to everything taken for granted before and during the war. In the words of one of them, the young intellectuals of the twenties were "Humanists turned upside down. For each of the Humanist virtues they had an antithesis. . . . Yet the Esthete and the Humanist both were products of the same milieu, one in which the productive forces . . . were regarded as something alien to poetry and learning."[3] Since Greenwich Village had before served as a haven for refugees from American culture, it was bound to become a sort of show place of American bohemianism and the center of discussions in the *Saturday Evening Post* and the New York dailies. What the Villagers thought and talked about was, if not front-page copy, at least good editorial material.[4] So far as this colorful but disorganized group of intellectuals had any coherent set of guiding principles, Malcolm Cowley has formulated them. The principal object of attack was

---

[1] Cf. Floyd Dell, *Homecoming: an Autobiography* (New York, 1933) , 293–94.

[2] Though psychoanalysis was usually associated by the conventional man with radicalism in behavior, there were times when it offered a new way of discussing the "drive for money and power." It could be linked, however ungraciously, with the psychology of salesmanship and of personnel work. It is not surprising, therefore, to see adaptations of the *Psychopathology of Everyday Life* and of *The Interpretation of Dreams* in popular, success magazines. See *American Magazine*, XCII (1921), 11–13; XCIX (1925) , 29.

[3] Malcolm Cowley, *Exile's Return: a Narrative of Ideas* (New York, 1934) , 38.

[4] Cf. George Britt, "Montmartre in Manhattan," a series, in New York *World Telegram*, May 16–21, 1932.

the " standardization of society "; their principal aim was to re-assert the free life of the pagan, as they saw it; their principal method was to get rid of the psychic sources of maladjustment by confessing their sins to a psychoanalyst.[5]

In the pages of Bobby Edwards' provocative magazine, *Quill*, the question of Greenwich Village morals was argued back and forth. Edwards' principal task was twofold: to claim for the Village the position of pioneer in the arts and in morals and at the same time to defend its reputation against those who wished to slander it. The two tasks were not altogether incompatible. " Greenwich Village has gone through radicalism, license, Freud-ism, free love, and synthetic gin—and has finished with all that," he said in August, 1923. " Here is one of the rare places in America where there are ideals, moderately decent deportment and comparative seriousness in artistic expression." His references to psychoanalysis are frequent and usually half-serious, half-flip-pant. " Now the principal motivation of sex is the dreadful ructions of the subconscious mind which apparently dwells on nothing else. It is the vile animal mind we have inherited. . . . And if you don't let your subconscious do as it wishes you get complexes which do everything from spoiling your digestion to making you a faddist." [6]

In the issue of February, 1923, Edwards expresses himself as tired of " This Anti-Puritan twaddle " which formed the substance of much intellectual discussion in the Village. The entrance of Freud into the Village precincts, says Edwards in July of 1923, was made through the Washington Square Book Shop; and, in December of the same year, the editorial spleen is especially strong:

> Now there remains the embarrassing subject of the great pollution of Village and American literature by that Freudian insidiousness, Psychoanalysis.
>
> Of course there are terrible people who will speak frankly about dubious matters and unfortunately the reading public is not immune to curiosity about subjects that have no place in the curriculum of a Methodist seminary. . . . Freuding

---

[5] Cowley, *Exile's Return*, 69–71.
[6] Bobby Edwards, Editorial, in *Quill*, VIII (1921) , 25.

parties are frowned upon by the better Villagers as severely as petting parties. . . .

As far as one can see who has not studied medicine, . . . Freud means nothing at all. But as interpreted by many whose knowledge of German is hazy, the worst possible is read into the jumbled psycho-romantic ramblings of the unfortunate Austrian savant.

For the Villagers the conditions they scorned and had fled needed labels, and the new psychology conveniently supplied them. The term Puritan was separated from its historical context and extended to include almost all of the guardians of the nations' morality and business. The sinful virtues of the founding fathers had been visited upon their sons, who were tainted with an original sin that no baptism could remove. In a word, the nation had fallen victim to a serious moral illness—repression. The Puritan had "repressed" all normal reactions to sensible living, and as a result his descendants were sex-starved and pitiful. Materialism had pushed aside normal life as inexpedient and had substituted Success for sex. All of this was not merely a subject of conversation; it was the theme of a number of postwar books on American culture.[7] One of the most astute observers of "young America," Leo Stein, suggested that American lack of experience and naïveté would be compensated for by a study of science and psychology, which would reveal depths in the human psyche not yet known in superficial America:

What our experience did not teach us, for that experience was quite blunted against the armor of our optimistic complacency, we are about to learn from science. The newer individual psychology, especially identified with the name of Freud, is telling us a number of things which in part we should have known, and it is probable that one of the reasons

---

[7] Waldo Frank, *Our America* (New York, 1919), *In the American Jungle* (New York, 1937), *Salvos: an Informal Book About Books and Plays* (New York, 1924); Ludwig Lewisohn, *Upstream* (New York, 1922), *Midchannel: an American Chronicle* (New York, 1929), and others. Harvey O'Higgins, *The American Mind in Action* (New York, 1924), attacked prominent Americans of the past from this point of view. See Randolph Bourne, "Portrait of Sophronisba," in *History of a Literary Radical, and Other Essays* (New York, 1920); "The Puritan's Will to Power," in *Seven Arts*, I (1917), 631–37.

why it is being accepted so much more easily here than in the centers of a wiser and more reflective civilization, is that on the whole, we feel rather less attainted by it.[8]

Many of the Villagers suggested that the secret of maladjustment lay in the institution of marriage. The American businessman was universally held up as illustrating the effect of repression upon personal happiness. There was no direct solution to this problem—but there was constant discussion and much experimenting. It was natural that Freud should be quoted as an authority on sexual experiment, as it had been natural for him to have furnished the label for the " great American illness." But Freud did not bring about this revolution in sex morality. The revolution simply drew upon him—as it did upon Havelock Ellis and Krafft-Ebing, and a host of others as a means of justifying its opinions and its acts. The cry was " unconventionality," and " attitudes ranged from tolerance of experimentation to approval rather than from condemnation to tolerance." [9] The motives for this attitude were not all artificial. To many sex freedom meant a safer way to married happiness; the choice of a partner required some thought, and marriage should not be undertaken as a business arrangement or as a means of securing wealth and power.[10] For many of the experimenters, however, love was an enigma not easily solved by talk; the modern freedom of sexual selection did not guarantee happiness. Indeed, " modernism " was often so confusing that it stood in the way of marital compatibility.[11] The desire to be " modern " ran counter to the basic instincts of man and woman, so that it did not help to remedy an admittedly bad situation. Man is led away from happiness,

---

[8] Leo Stein, " American Optimism," in *Seven Arts*, II (1917), 90.

[9] Caroline F. Ware, *Greenwich Village, 1920–1930* (Boston, 1935), 236; cf. 240, 255–56.

[10] Dell, *Homecoming*, 288–89; cf. his *Love in the Machine Age* (New York, 1930), a detailed study of sex behavior in the modern age. See also his " Marriage and Freedom," *Liberator*, IV (1921), 16–21.

[11] Thus we have Felix Fay and Joyce Tennant, failing to " make a go " of it because of Felix's " modern ideas," *Moon Calf* (New York, 1920), 344 ff. In the sequel, *Briary Bush* (New York, 1921), 128, Felix, converted from his " modernism," resents the discussion of modern marriage: ". . . did they really think that his and Rose-Ann's marriage was to be, as it were, a sociological performance for the benefit of onlookers? " Cf. the lengthy discussion of the marriage relations of Paul and Janet Glover, in Ludwig Lewisohn, *Stephen Escott* (New York, 1930), 193 ff.

through sublimation, in order that he may serve civilization. " '. . . on the defeat of nature . . . depends the continuance of human culture.' " As a result, the modernists rebel against all sentimental notions of sex, against all masculine possessiveness: " The modern woman—some modern women—are rebelling against their overvaluation as love-objects." [12] The modernist as well as the conservative denies the ideal function of sex: " possession of beauty, for such a being as man in such a universe as this, *means* sexual possession— " and " [Man scarcely understands] the great mystery of Eros which both your radicals and your conservatives seek to cheapen, the former as sin, the latter as a matter of no importance." [13]

Though many sincere persons did not seek to exploit freedom or to look upon free love as the privilege of the " back stairs," those who viewed Greenwich Village as a place of sin were willing to believe that all " modernists " had surrendered themselves to a pagan orgy. There was apparently no mean between the extremes of the inhibited and the uninhibited. This explains, perhaps, why the eyes of the average man turned toward the Village in horror, amusement, and envy. America as a whole, and especially that part of America eager to participate in minor social revolutions, was in the mood to accept someone as its guide in matters of personal conduct. They had, early in their lives, " learned the practicality and cynicism that is safe only in unregenerate old age." [14] Freud's discussions of sex had long since been translated; and the practice and mispractice of psychoanalysis had been the means of spreading the language of the new psychology so that it was fairly widely misunderstood by 1920. Psychoanalysis had the lure of the new idea, the fad; as such it impressed the readers of the " slicks " and of the metropolitan dailies. Discussion of sex answered a need, for the young people of the

[12] Lewisohn, *Stephen Escott*, 211.

[13] *Ibid.*, 216.

[14] John F. Carter, " ' These Wild Young People,' by One of Them," in *Atlantic Monthly*, CXXVI (1920), 302.

Perhaps an extreme indication of young America's anxious search for moral and aesthetic guide is the announcement in the first issue of a Greenwich Village little magazine, *Playboy*, I (1923), 6: " D. H. Lawrence, Arthur Schopenhauer, Walt Whitman, Friedrich Nietzsche, Jesus Christ, Robert Hillyer, Elie Faure, William Blake, John Peale Bishop and Edmund Wilson Jr., Lord Dunsany, Clive Bell, King Solomon and Carl Sandburg, Playboys all; let them speak for us! "

twenties at least *thought* it had been unduly restricted. Psychoanalysis was, among other things, intimately associated with the desire for greater freedom among the postwar generation. Rabbi Stephen Wise, in a sermon reported in the New York *Times*, appealed for greater moderation in matters of " promiscuous discussion " of vital problems; " let psychoanalysis remain in the workshop of the scientist and the laboratory of the physician." [15] Sex has its place, but it should be kept there. It is absurd to explain everything in terms of sex desire. Man does not live by sex alone: " He had violent, unfulfilled desires for Brahms concertos and free verse and Hollywood and constitutional amendments." [16] Freud was neither the originator nor the guiding spirit of this movement. He had written some books and had initiated a new clinical procedure, and they were at the disposal of the young men and women of the twenties.

The public interest in psychoanalysis was vastly stimulated by scores of popularizers, who attached Freud, Jung, Adler, and others to their own beliefs.[17] The chief of these were André Tridon,[18] A. A. Brill, Frederick Pierce, and George Green.[19] Tridon's books are designed to allay any and all fears of difficulty; they chat with the reader, as their author chatted with women's clubs at " psychic teas." Though many psychoanalysts succeeded only in confusing their readers further, Tridon brought a " comfortably diluted version of Freud within the capacity of anyone.[20] This " diluted version " was further made available by countless references in the daily papers and magazines of the English-speaking world. What, in summary, was the popular notion of psychoanalysis?

[15] New York *Times*, November 21, 1921, 6:3.
[16] Viola Paradise, " The Sex Simplex," in *Forum*, LXXIV (1925), 111.
[17] Mark Sullivan, *Our Times*, IV, 171, estimates that, by the 1920's, " there were more than two hundred books dealing with Freudianism." He does not attempt to list them.
[18] *Easy Lessons in Psychoanalysis* (New York, 1922); *Psychoanalysis: Its History, Theory, and Practice* (New York, 1919), and others. " Like Herbert Spencer, who played a similar part with regard to Darwinism," said Pierre Loving, in *Quill*, VII (1920), " Tridon is the talented magician whose wand converts the tangled jargon of the various schools into simplicity."
[19] Brill, *Fundamental Conceptions of Psychoanalysis* (New York, 1922); Frederick Pierce, *Our Unconscious and How to Use It* (New York, 1922); George Henry Green, *Psychoanalysis in the Class Room* (New York, 1922). Cf. Ruth Hale, " Explaining Freud," in *Bookman*, LV (1922), 302–304.
[20] Bernard DeVoto, " The Well-Informed, 1920–1930," in *Forays and Rebuttals* (Boston, 1936), 224.

For one thing it was " talk about dreams." Most people knew that dreams had a new significance as an index of character, and dream analysis became a parlor game. Men and women were advised to make collections of their dreams, and with the aid of a little reading, to search for " hidden complexes " and thus to form estimates of their friends' character. Such amateur analysis of dreams was a subject for ready satire or for serious consideration in the fiction of the time.

Psychoanalysis was also thought of by the popular mind as a rationalization of sex-looseness; indeed the average man was forced to remark this fact, for it was pointed out to him from both the editorial and the clerical pulpit. Protests mounted against the age of licentiousness which Freud had ushered in. It was regarded as a " justification of immorality by science." [21] This misconstruction of Freud's theories was fought against by those who had studied Freud; but those who were ignorant of Freud scarcely ever heard these protests against his misuse. " Popular Freudianism " admitted, therefore, all of the enormities against which Freud had long since warned.

Psychoanalysis was, as well, a subject for drawing-room conversation. It was the key by which access could be had to the " best circles." Sandor Ferenczi, Hungarian analyst, suggested that in America the interest " is somewhat superficial and that the deeper side is somewhat neglected." [22] Psychoanalysis was a delightful excuse for " talking about oneself." In this way, the terms of psychoanalysis became " household words "—repression, fixation, sublimation, complex (*all* behavior patterns or attitudes were " complexes ") , defense mechanism—were badly misused labels attached at almost any time to a sentence, or included in a summary analysis of character.

To some, all psychoanalysts were quacks; others realized the values of the new practice, but pointed unhappily to its abuses. Since it was but newly developed, and since no working set of regulations had thus far been widely accepted, psychoanalysis

[21] London *Times*, December 4, 1920, 10e. The *Times* article goes on to refute this claim and to explain the true meaning of psychoanalysis. This is also the burden of a New York *Times* editorial, March 29, 1921, 14:5, which criticizes G. K. Chesterton for his superficial remarks about Freudianism.

[22] New York *Times*, June 5, 1927, II, 4:3.

appeared to be an easy prey for charlatans. In London alone, runs one complaint, " there are scores of so-called ' analysts,' male and female, who without possessing any qualifications or having undergone any real training either in medicine or in psychology, manage to secure high fees by imposing on the credulity of nervous or hysterical women." [23] This condition, it was hoped, would produce " its own antidote "—a wholehearted campaign against such quackery. The danger was obvious—to anyone who had studied the clinical difficulties of the " transference," and who understood the intimate nature of the doctor-patient relationship, it was obvious that in unskilled hands psychoanalysis was " worse than worthless." [24]

The reception of Freud had been adulterated by misinterpretation and superficial enthusiasm. It was not surprising that Freud and his theories should stimulate two reactions he had anticipated—indignation and horror—and one he had sincerely feared—delight. Indignation was expressed by such men as G. K. Chesterton, who denied that psychoanalysis could be a science, for no true science could have become so fashionable: " It is a characteristic of sincere scientific speculation that it *cannot* at any given moment be applied generally to public affairs except with the utmost caution and the most copious dilutions of common sense." [25] The " crime of the Freudians " was that they discussed " subjects which polite people do not discuss in mixed companies, or at all if they are particularly sensitive." [26] Opponents suspected that psychoanalysis had simply furnished an excuse for talk which, in terms of decency and good taste, might well be dismissed from polite discussion.

Further, if the discoveries of Freud were to be applied universally, there was no longer any dividing line between the normal and the abnormal, and every person might turn to brooding introspection over illnesses he has never had.[27] How can one possess

[23] Letter, in *New Statesman*, XX (1923), 654.

[24] Editorial, in New York *Times*, September 12, 1921, 12:5.

[25] Gilbert K. Chesterton, " The Game of Psychoanalysis," in *Century*, CVI (1923), 35. Cf. London *Times*, July 26, 1921, 12b.

[26] Editorial, in New York *Times*, September 25, 1922, 14:5, cf. *ibid.*, November 12, 1922, II, 6:2; " Frightened Analyst," in *Nation*, CXII (1921), 908; " Analyzing the Psychoanalysts," in *Review of Reviews*, LXXVI (1927), 322–23.

[27] New York *Times*, January 4, 1922, 7:1, March 24, 1922, 24:2; London *Times*, April 23, 1921, 7d, December 29, 1925, 7d.

sufficient discrimination, or fortitude, to realize that self-control was as adequate a bulwark against "abnormality" as ever? Psychoanalysis was said to encourage a pessimistic view of life, to have destroyed all or most of man's illusions. It was easy, therefore, to blame suicides upon the new psychology: Mercy Rogers, for example, who, after reading 102 books on psychoanalysis and allied subjects, despaired of her life and turned on the gas.[28]

Despite this gloomier view, Americans at any rate enjoyed the "fad" as a welcome diversion. The journalist's reaction was to take a train to Vienna and to report on the appearance and habits of "the great man."[29] Hollywood hoped to induce Freud to collaborate with script writers, and to advise them on the deeper psychological problems of love.[30] The secrets of the psychoanalytic confessional were gladly divulged at the usual space-rates for magazine stories.[31] Psychoanalysts who made America their home, or who visited America, were also "good copy," and the public was liberally supplied with reports of interviews with them.[32] Advice to the working girl was given the spice and flavor of the "New Psychology."[33]

Obviously the terminology was either too difficult or too drab for popular treatment. Though the intellectual might appropriate terms from his own acquaintance with the theory, and

[28] New York *Times*, January 4, 1922, 7:1; cf. *ibid.*, March 24, 1922, 24:2; London *Times*, April 23, 1921, 7d, December 29, 1925, 7d.

[29] Cornelia Stratton Parker, "The Capital of Psychology," in *Survey*, LIV (1925), 551–55; Raymond Recouly, "A Visit to Freud," in *Outlook*, CXXXV (1923), 27–29; Odette Pannetier, "Appointment in Vienna," in *Living Age*, CCCLI (1936), 138–44.

[30] New York *Times*, December 21, 1924, VII, 3:8; cf. also, London *Times*, August 4, 1925, 8b, for report of a film "dealing with psychoanalysis" to be made in Vienna "supervised by Professor Freud and explaining his system." The New York *Times*, July 31, 1938, IX, 3:7, reported that Freud might be asked to come to America to help with the picture, *Dark Victory*.

[31] Cf. Lucian Cary, "How It Feels to Be Psychoanalyzed," in *American Magazine*, XCIX (1925), 29 ff.; Virginia Terhune Van de Water, "I Am Psychoanalyzed," in *Century*, CXIII (1926), 224–29.

[32] Brill: New York *Times*, July 31, 1921, III, 7:1; *American Magazine*, XCII (1921), 11–13. Adler: New York *Times*, April 10, 1927, II, 5:3. Wittels: New York *Times*, October 21, 1928, X, 7:1. Ferenczi: New York *Times*, June 5, 1927, II, 4:3.

[33] Luhan, *Movers and Shakers*, 510. In the list of "excitements" for the popular mind may be included the presence of ten "eminent psychiatrists" at the trial of Leopold and Loeb (1924), and the newspaper coverage of this trial. See Grace Adams, "The Rise and Fall of Psychology," in *Atlantic Monthly*, CLIII (1934), 86.

might even understand them, a widespread discussion of such terms called forth the best efforts of the public press to give them vividness and color. Perhaps all scientific terms are metaphors, in that they determine the nature of an abstraction by comparing it with its nearest concrete parallel. But the term " unconscious " was as colorless a label as had ever been given to an area of psychic activity. If the unconscious was "not conscious," then what was it? That is, how may we describe it so that it may make an impression in the public mind? How can we denounce the unconscious as such, or explain it to those who are unwilling to work with abstractions? There is a wide selection of clichés from which to draw, once one has decided upon what moral coloring to give the term. The unconscious is " brutal "—that is, it corresponds to our animal nature, as the conscious life attests to our rational nature.

The unconscious would appear to be a region resembling the zoological gardens, with all the keepers on strike. A host of unnoticed and unsuspected desires and passions are constantly roaring and raging in their cages. And the only hope for peace for the unfortunate patient is for the Psychoanalyst to open the cages and set their inhabitants free.[34]

The unconscious, being evil, is capable of intrigue and conspiracy against the " law and order " of the conscious mind. In view of that it is not inconsistent to label it the " Machiavelli " of the psychic life. " Apparently once the machinations of the subconscious [35] are brought to light, we can generally deal with them

[34] Arthur E. J. Legge, " Mental Healing," in *Quarterly Review*, CCXXXVIII (1922), 260. Notice how the analyst, consistent with the metaphor, is the " suspicious character " who sneaks in and releases the animals while the keeper (the censor) is absent.

[35] The layman scarcely ever bothered to differentiate the *subconscious* from the *unconscious*; for him the two terms were interchangeable. There are two separate terms, signifying different psychic areas:—*Unterbewusst*, for the subconscious;—*Unbewusst*, for the unconscious.—This latter he emphasized more and more fully as his conception of psychic topography was further clarified. Ernest Jones, in *The Life and Work of Sigmund Freud*, supplies this highly important note: " Freud took care never to use the term *unterbewusst* (subconscious), which he regarded as misleading; it suggests merely something that is slightly less conscious. On one early occasion, however, he used *subconscient* in French." (vol. 1, p. 403)

The same problem occurred in the matter of the two terms *repression* and *suppression*. The latter is liberally and often mistakenly used in translations of Freud's earlier works and in popular commentaries on Freud in the early twenties.

ourselves. It is only when the plots of that Machiavelli are concealed from us that he can harm us." [36]

Apparently the unconscious is also a primeval or mythical den; one critic refers to the libido as the loathsome " dragon that wallows in the unconscious." [37] To Aldous Huxley, the unconscious, " we are told, is a sort of den or inferno to which all the bad thoughts and desires which clash with our social duties in the world are sent." [38] For G. K. Chesterton, talk about the unconscious was " some ridiculous mythology about every man having inside him a sort of aged and microcephalous monkey. Wistful and melancholy poems are written about how trying it is to have a monkey inside him, and ethical essays earnestly debate whether the man should own the monkey or the monkey the man." [39] All but the last two of these examples were designed seriously to inform the reader or to influence him either for or against the doctrine of Freudianism. The censor (a term which is sufficiently metaphorical in itself) was variously termed as a " policeman," " a watch-dog," or a " Guard." [40]

All of these references should give the impression that Freud was well known, hastily received, and badly misinterpreted. Advocates and opponents joined in clouding the atmosphere and in making it difficult for the average layman to grasp the real significance of Freudianism. But it is hardly likely that any thinking, literate person who in any way associated himself with the world of letters failed to encounter the new psychology. It is more than likely that he was unable to escape getting too much of it. If he had not read any books on the subject, he was bound to come across it in almost any discussion; if he did not go out, he

Freud's original terms were: *Unterdrückung* for suppression; *Verdrängung* for repression.

[36] E. W., " The ABC. of Psychoanalysis," in *Living Age*, CCCIX (1921), 101.

[37] George M. Cullen, " Psychoanalysis Attacked," in *Living Age*, CCCX (1921), 107.

[38] Aldous Huxley, " Our Contemporary Hocus-Pocus," in *Forum*, LXXIII (1925), 317–18.

[39] Chesterton, " The Game of Psychoanalysis," *loc. cit.*, 41–42.

[40] Cf. London *Times*, January 25, 1929, 14c; report of a lecture by Sir Robert Armstrong-Jones, who used substantially the same " extended metaphor " which Freud employed in one of his earliest popular lectures: *A General Introduction to Psychoanalysis*, 256. Indeed, Freud has often been accused of simply inventing a mythology or a " word-reality " corresponding to no existing things. Cf. Huxley, " Our Contemporary Hocus-Pocus," *loc. cit.*, 317; Samuel Tannenbaum, as reported in the New York *Times, March* 19, 1922, VIII, 4:6.

was just as likely to discover it in newspaper or magazine, or to notice its application in the works of his fellowwriters whom he ordinarily examined; if he did not read or speak to people, then he was safe from it.

ii

The reaction of the intellectual differed from the popular reaction in both degree and kind. It was a more serious reception; the pardonable motive of curiosity is insufficient to explain his interest. The intellectuals would rather " psych " each other than eat. They were so fascinated by "this lingo about the libido" that Susan Glaspell was to exclaim in despair, "'You could not buy . . . a bun without hearing of someone's complex.'"[41] Margaret Anderson and Jane Heap spent their evenings searching for "the Achilles heel in everybody's psychic set up. . . ."[42] Hutchins Hapgood noted the degenerative treatment of Freudian psychology: "every Tom, Dick, and Harry in those days was misinterpreting and misapplying the general ideas underlying analysis. It was a typical case of the natural exaggeration of a new set of thoughts, making them often ridiculous."[43] Since Mabel Dodge Sterne had first been psychoanalyzed in 1916, many of her friends had tried it. They did so for various reasons—out of curiosity, boredom or genuine need; for purposes of testing the validity of the theory, or in order that they might improve their writing.[44]

Floyd Dell, recognized by many as an authority or at least an interesting discussion-leader in matters of interest to the intellectual of his time, gives a fairly complete picture of his experience with psychoanalysis. He had become interested in the

[41] Albert Parry, *Garrets and Pretenders: a History of Bohemianism in America* (New York, 1933), 278.

[42] Margaret Anderson, *My Thirty Years' War: an Autobiography* (New York, 1930), 186.

[43] Hutchins Hapgood, *A Victorian in the Modern World* (New York, 1939), 382–83. Hapgood overcame one of his strongest objections to psychoanalysis—its expense—by analyzing himself. He gathered together all of his old letters and read them: ". . . those objective documents took me back to the origin of my psychoses, and thereby cleansed and purified a suffering being."

[44] John Farrar, "Sex Psychology in Modern Fiction," in *Independent*, CXVII (1926), 669.

new theory through a reading of Burton's *Anatomy of Melancholy*, but had long before this become used to the "jargon of psychoanalysis" which he had heard since he first came to "the Village," in 1914. In the midst of his first novel, he suffered from a "creative amnesia" and was forced to stop writing. Accepting the advice of his "dearest friend and former sweetheart," he consulted Dr. Tannenbaum, who agreed to treat him at a negligible expense. The arrangement was ideal, the kind of analytic situation which every analyst might well "dream of." Dell lost no time in resistances: "Memories, dreams and associations poured out of my mind in a never-ending torrent." He agreed not to disturb his emotional life by falling in love during the time of treatment. Excellent cooperation saved the analyst much inconvenience: "My psychoanalyst gave me no interpretation of my dreams, but let me interpret them myself; nor did he tell me I had a terrific mother-complex and was narcissistic, had a great deal of unconscious homosexuality and a variety of other frightful-sounding traits; I found all that out myself, and told him." [45] Dell was more than pleased with the results. He hailed the new psychology as "an idea of the same importance as the Copernican idea, the Darwinian idea, the Marxian idea . . ."; soon his friends were being psychoanalyzed and were using psychological small talk in their conversations.

Psychoanalysis suited the young intellectual of the twenties for several reasons. He had not too long before rejected (for the most part cynically) the traditional moral and social *structure—* in part, his residence in Greenwich Village was testimony to that— and he was not yet ready to accept another system so fully developed as, for example, the Marxist. What he wanted in the twenties was a *method*, a psychological approach to and justification for his own soul-searching; he welcomed psychoanalysis because it did not legislate against his desires or restrict them within the mores of his (for the present) hateful society. Psychoanalysis was made to order for his personal revolt against tradition. That the young men and women of the Village were not always absolutely self-confident about their revolt is a point Joseph Freeman

[45] *Homecoming*, 293, 295. Cf. Dell, "A Literary Self-Analysis," in *Modern Quarterly*, IV (1927), 149.

is careful to make: " Sons and daughters of the puritans, the artists and writers and utopians who flocked to Greenwich Village to find a frank and free life for the emotions and senses, felt at their backs the icy breath of the monster they were escaping. Because they could not abandon themselves to pleasure without a sense of guilt, they exaggerated the importance of pleasure, idealized it and even sanctified it." [46]

The revolt of the postwar twenties was in its essentials a " romantic protest " against moral and social inconveniences. It is true, of course, that Emma Goldman's *Mother Earth,* and Max Eastman's *Masses* and *Liberator* had been interested even at an earlier time in the dissemination of socialist theory; Karl Marx was not forgotten. But many, if not all, of the intellectuals of the twenties thought of the revolt as one for the present at least dominated by a personal soul-searching and a mind so free and so open that it could quite freely entertain contradictory theories without being upset in the slightest. Psychoanalysis suited most of them because it was new, unorthodox, shockingly frank, and because it implied—though it certainly did not advise—a more liberal view of sex matters.

This was the " mania psychologica " of the twenties, the " insatiable passion for intricate mental analysis." [47] That it should have affected the quality and nature of twentieth-century fiction is not surprising. While Freud was being debated on all levels of comprehension, writers modeled their studies of character on the therapeutic situation. The hero of this type of fiction was only infrequently a genuine subject for clinical treatment; but he was frequently pale, shy, sensitive, given to much introspective brooding over the world, which struck him as being harsh and importunate. His experiences with the other sex were less affairs than adventures in understanding. No single motive explained any single act; rather, any one act presupposed a variety of motives, intricately bound with the " hidden life " of the character.[48] Critics complained of the crude obviousness with which psycho-

[46] Joseph Freeman, *An American Testament: A Narrative of Rebels and Romantics* (New York, 1936), 117.

[47] Houston Peterson, *The Melody of Chaos* (New York, 1931), 8.

[48] John Crowe Ransom, " Freud and Literature," in *Saturday Review of Literature,* I (1924), 161. Cf. Adams, " The Rise and Fall of Psychology," *loc. cit.,* 85.

analysis was introduced into their reading matter. It is the chatter of the drawing room which is being " spread, all too plentifully, on the printed page." [49]

The truth was that writers were eager for an approach to characterization that avoided the gentility of Jane Austen, the sentimental heaviness of Dickens, and the socially diverting realism of Howells. They felt that sex was *their* problem; that they had but recently discovered it under layers of social restriction; and that psychoanalysis furnished a ready set of descriptive terms for their purpose. Thus they substituted the complex for the simple, the abnormal for the normal, the novel for the conventional. They often managed these materials badly. They often used Freud, and psychoanalysis generally, as an excuse for exploiting the interest in sex. The novels which reveal this kind of exploitation rarely outlived the fashionable interests in the situation of which they took advantage; probably none of them was intended for more than an immediate popularity. Not all writers, however, were clumsy manipulators of their tools. Some of them at least gained access to hitherto ill-defined ways of explaining human situations.

The fiction of the twenties reflected—and, quite naturally— the intellectual's preoccupation with psychoanalysis. The several classifications Maxwell Bodenheim gave this fiction are perhaps harsh and arbitrary, but they repay examination:

> the sensual melodrama, written in an awkwardly forced style and unsuccessfully wavering between Whitman and Baudelaire, such as Waldo Frank's *Rahab*; the novel in which sensuality adopts a heavy, clumsy, and naïvely serious mien, such as the stories and novels by Sherwood Anderson, in which young men lie upon their backs in cornfields and feel depressed by their bodies, etc.; the novel in which sensuality becomes half flippant and half sentimental, and plays the youthful ape to sophistication, such as the creations of F. Scott Fitzgerald; the novel in which sensuality, sordid and undressed, fights with longing for business success, a proceeding that occurs in the ponderous fiction of Theodore

---

[49] Raoul Reed, " Psychoanalysis in Literature," in *Freeman*, V (1922), 490.

Dreiser; the novel in which sensuality sneers at itself and wonders whether the gain is worth the effort involved, a quality recently exhibited in Ben Hecht's *Erik Dorn*; and the endless novels in which sensuality runs after romance, nobility, and domestic bliss.[50]

Some of these categories are only incidentally related to the "psychoanalytic novel." Psychoanalysis may have suggested to many novelists that the broad disclosure of sensuality is a valid approach to the art of characterization, but that is highly improbable. Bodenheim's critical rejection and its motivation are in a sense symptoms of the "Freudian illness." They show the extent to which the mind of the critic had been turned aside from the actual study of Freudian influence.

If psychoanalysis contributed anything worth preserving or even studying in the literature of this period, it is not to be found in extravagant demonstrations of sensuality or adolescent attacks upon the mores, but rather in its sponsorship of, or at least its concessions to, introspection. The novel of the future, says one critic near the end of the decade, will require a strong, " dynamic mind to synthesize these tortuous despairs—now inescapably an element of the European mind—with the lust for earth that must be the basis of any attempt to create an image of it. . . . No simple form will be sufficient for the analysis he will have to make of life complicated by the release of ancient terrors by Freud's and Einstein's contributions to his consciousness." [51] The most challenging thinkers, those who most appealed to the intellectuals of the day—Schopenhauer, Nietzsche, Bergson, and Freud—were men not interested so much in erecting systems of thought as in giving philosophical justifications for a point of view and a position taken with respect to an unsatisfactory environment.

There were novels which revealed their authors as serious students of psychoanalysis and it is necessary to consider them regardless of their intrinsic value, if we are to get a clear picture. Among the novels of Ludwig Lewisohn, for example, *Stephen*

[50] Maxwell Bodenheim, "Psychoanalysis and American Fiction," in *Nation*, CXIV (1922), 684.

[51] Brian Penton, "Note on the Form of the Novel," in London *Aphrodite*, VI (1929), 443.

Escott and *The Island Within* [52] employ psychoanalysis, not always subtly, but frequently with effectiveness. The first deals with the problem of marital unhappiness and its psychological implications. Fundamentally, it is a defense of genuine marital harmony and an attack upon " modernism " in sex experiment. In *The Island Within*, Arthur Levy joins the ranks of the psychoanalysts, and from this vantage point views the modern world. These are not great novels, but they are certainly not gross displays of sensuality. They represent an artist of some talent turning his knowledge of psychoanalysis to some creative purpose, and are a testimony of the value of psychoanalysis for a writer who will use it intelligently. [53]

The reception of Freudianism in the twenties was not always soberly sincere or indiscriminately enthusiastic. The excesses which were noted with either sadness or alarm were also satirized. The picture of old ladies, led by their own " contrariness " to the analyst's office, is grotesque enough and a fit enought subject for the novelist. Much of the emphasis in Rose Macaulay's *Dangerous Ages* is devoted to Mrs. Hilary's search for a companion to whom she can talk about herself. For Mrs. Hilary, psychoanalysis was the answer to a lonely woman's prayer; it was " far better than the confessional—for priests, besides requiring only those portions and parcels of the dreadful past upon which you had least desire to dwell, had almost certainly no interest at all in hearing even these, but only did it because they had to, and you would be boring them." [54] The intrusion of psychoanalytic chatter into a hitherto peaceful domestic scene is the subject of one of the plays first produced by the Provincetown players, Susan Glaspell's *Suppressed Desires*. [55] The devices by which Stephen and Henrietta Brewster are parted and then re-united are only ordinary theatre, but Mabel, the naïve sister of Henrietta has some lines which

[52] New York, 1928.

[53] The novels of Conrad Aiken, Waldo Frank, and Sherwood Anderson might with some justification also be discussed here.

[54] P. 86; see also pp. 35–36, 65, 84.

[55] Published in *Plays* (New York, 1930), 231–71. First produced at Provincetown, Mass., 1917. Bobby Edwards, Editorial, in *Quill*, XIII (1923), 14, says that *Suppressed Desires* introduced Freud to many who had to read him to understand the play. "It is the only blot on the record of the little theater movement that this most foul and insidious of German propaganda should have been innocently distributed by them."

merrily discuss the faddish nature of popular interest in Freudianism. Throughout the satirical literature of this period, much attention was paid the misguided efforts to make psychoanalysis a familiar discipline and the tendency to overestimate its treatment of infantile sexuality. Among the subjects satirized were the amateur psychoanalyst; [56] the question of the sexual instincts, " The error of the Viennese "; [57] the tendency to apply psychoanalysis to biography and history; [58] and the invasion by psychoanalysis of literary criticism.[59]

Though many of the writers of the twenties turned later to studies of economic oppression, and though for many of them psychoanalysis was merely the object of ridicule, it was ultimately to have an important influence over modes of thought and methods of writing. Terms in themselves have little value. A technique transferred from one field to another loses some of its native quality and importance, and there is also the chance that it will not be adjusted readily to the needs of its new environment. Freudianism was destined to persist in the thirties, though in modified form, and with far less of the chicanery and " stuntism " which both marked and marred its appearance in the twenties.

iii

Was Freud a fad? Was psychoanalysis doomed to disappear, once the leisure for studying it and talking about it had ceased to exist? In the thirties there was little decrease in the number of attacks on Freud as a danger to our moral and social world, but the debate about his genuine value needed to be settled. The medical profession still quarreled over the legitimacy of psycho-

[56] See Aldous Huxley, " The Farcical History of Richard Greenow," in *Limbo* (London, 1920), 65–68.

[57] See Aldous Huxley, *Antic Hay* (London, 1923), 149.

[58] Simeon Strunsky, " The Scandal of Euclid: A Freudian Analysis," in *Atlantic Monthly*, CXXIV (1919), 332–37, a " review " of the hypothetical book, *Sex Elements in the First Five Books of Euclid*.

Euclid's attachment to the " eternal triangle " is said to be traced to " a profound attachment developed by the geometer at the age of two for his grandmother on the father's side. . . ." *Ibid.*, 333.

[59] Harvey Wickham, " Did Shakespeare Murder His Father? " in *Catholic World*, CXXXIV (1932), 538–46, a burlesque of the Freud-Rank theory of the motivation for *Hamlet*.

analytic therapy, and there was no relaxation of the disciplining of quacks and charlatans.[60] The dominating question concerned Freud's position as a scientist. He had always maintained that psychoanalysis was a science and that its entire procedure was based on scientific assumptions.[61] The topography of the psychic life was a " closed system," a " rigorous determiinsm," secure against any " psychic leakage " and able to explain all acts of the psyche because of the addition of the unconscious to its world.[62] Scientific caution, however, did not allow many workers in the field to agree with him. They debated Freud's theories as though they were members of a club, passing on his eligibility for membership. The questions they raised were not designed to reassure the Freudians; the answers scientists gave were even less assuring:

(I) There is no genuine basis for accepting the unconscious as a legitimate field of scientific investigation. One can only guess at the meaning and nature of the unconscious; this guesswork must be limited, if it is to receive scientific sanction. To continue, " the unconscious, admittedly, was not directly known. If it were, it would not be unconscious, but conscious. Its existence, therefore, could only be inferred from events happening in consciousness . . . the unconscious became a rag bag for pet theories and a fruitful breeding ground of myths, myths which only too readily crystallized into dogmas." [63]

(2) Since Freud attaches too much importance to the unconscious, he has to rely upon metaphors for a description of mental life, and his work is therefore only a sort of " poetized science," proceeding chiefly by analogy with sober scientific investigation.[64]

---

[60] Cf. Terence Greenidge, " The Growth of Psychoanalysis," in *Spectator*, CLXII (1939), 490. The British Medical Association throughout the twenties and early thirties parried the question of the " dangers of psychoanalysis," as reported in the London *Times*, September 23, 1922, 9c–d; July 18, 1925, 14b; July 19, 1926, 9b; July 22, 1929, 8e; January 14, 1931, 10c.

[61] See *New Introductory Lectures*, Lecture 35, p. 248.

[62] See Jones, *Psychoanalysis*, 11–14; cf. Theodore Schroeder, " Deterministic Presupposition of Psychoanalysis," in *Open Court*, XLI (1927), 90–102. ". . . the psychoanalyst's hypothesis must be deterministic, and not moralistic, if his research is to have meaning or value for him." *Ibid.*, 97.

[63] C. E. M. Joad, " Psychology in Retreat," in *New Statesman and Nation*, IX (1935), 956.

[64] David B. Klein, " Psychology and Freud: an Historico-Critical Appraisal," in *Psychological Review*, XL (1933), 447–48. Klein defends Freud's use of analogy

(3) The concepts based on the instinctual life may be valid so far as they operate within a narrow clinical framework, but the shift from therapy to speculation involves a reinterpretation of values, which Freud has not adequately made.[65]

Parallel with this discussion ran the debate concerning Freud's relationship with Marx. Since the latter was, in a sense, to succeed Freud in the popular mind, the legitimacy of Freud's presuppositions about society were considered important. Some Marxists thought of Freudian therapy as a good means of discovering the ills in a bourgeois society.[66] For the most part, however, Marxists were convinced that psychoanalysis was adjusted to bourgeois society and denied the value of therapy if its aim was to send the patient back into society with no desire to change it or to fight its evils.[67] For this reason, and also because the "myth of the unconscious" involves one in questions of superstition and suggestion, these critics insisted that Freud can never be of any service to the materialism of Karl Marx.[68]

These debates proved two things: that the popular, capricious interest in Freud was giving way, at least in part, to a serious con-

as a cogent means of scientific description. Cf. W. Béran Wolfe, "The Twilight of Psychoanalysis," in *American Mercury*, XXXV (1935), 390–91.

[65] Carney Landis, "Psychoanalysis and the Scientific Method," in *Science*, n.s., XCIII (1941), 486. Cf. Knight Dunlap's severe attack, as reported in New York *Times*, September 10, 1938, 19:1; Waldemaar Kaempffert, in New York *Times*, October 1, 1939, II, 8:1: "It is the speculator in Freud which irritates any one who is familiar with the rigorous methods of physical science."

[66] Osborn, *Freud and Marx*, 245–56; Harry Slochower, "Freud and Marx in Contemporary Literature," in *Sewanee Review*, XLIX (1941), 315–24. Slochower goes so far as to maintain that Freud and Marx "employ a similar strategy and follow related pursuits, that, at any rate, each offers a contribution which the other can employ and thereby complete their respective patterns." *Ibid.*, 320. Slochower's studies of such modern writers as Franz Kafka and Thomas Mann employ Freudian and Marxist ideas alternately or in combination.

[67] Francis H. Bartlett, "The Limitations of Freud," in *Science and Society*, III (1939), 69 ff.; Caudwell, *Illusion and Reality*, 185; Waldo Frank, "Sigmund Freud," *loc. cit.*, 536; W. H. Auden, "Psychology and Art To-day," in *Arts To-day* (London, 1935), 19.

[68] Sidney Hook, "Marx and Freud, Oil and Water," in *Open Court*, XLII (1928), 20. The Marxists were not the only men who criticized Freudianism for dealing inadequately with the social determinants of neurosis. A group of psychiatrists and psychoanalysts has recently criticized Freud for his "biological orientation of values" and has suggested that cultural determinants (not necessarily economic) should be more completely noted in analysis. Among the most active of this group are Karen Horney and Abraham Kardiner. See Eliseo Vivas, "The Legacy of Sigmund Freud: Philosophical," in *Kenyon Review*, II (1940), 173–85. For a recent criticism of the "neo-Freudians," see Herbert Marcuse, *Eros and Civilization* (Boston, 1955), 238–74.

sideration of Freud's position in modern thought; and, that the
psychological individualism of the twenties was now passing.

The old quarrels with pulpit and press continued through the
thirties. Freudianism was still regarded as a convenient scapegoat,
and even furnished material for political manipulation.[69] The
sensibilities of the clergy were further violated by Freud's publication of *The Future of an Illusion*.[70] The clergy believed, not
only that Freud had released hordes of new demons, but that he
had appropriated the confessional, an honorable and traditional
means of laying moral ghosts. The " Freudian confessional " was
inferior because its lay priests could not bring to it a moral system
but were satisfied with merely informing their sinners of their
infamies. They are " without power to convey the priceless grace
of absolution." [71] Good and evil must be clearly determined, and
this determination had always been the duty and the prerogative
of religion.[72] A horrified public was also displeased by the notion
that Freud's neurotic patients should bear any resemblance to
normal human beings.[73] This time critics expressed disappointment that the " Freudian crusade " had failed in its purpose—to
rid us of our puritan inhibitions, or to substitute a healthier sex
attitude for the one it asked us to repudiate.[74] Freud's preoccupation with the " irrational sources of behavior " was, in one in-

[69] The " case of Starr Faithfull," reported in the New York *Times*, June 21,
1931, I, 2:3. The New York State legislature was asked by State Senator William
Lathrop to prepare a bill, providing for an investigation of psychoanalysts.
[70] Cf. review of the book by Atkinson Lee, " The Freudian Illusion," in
London Quarterly Review, CLIX (1934) , 507–13.
[71] Claude C. H. Williamson, " The Dangers of Psychoanalysis," in *Catholic
World*, CXXXVI (1932), 296; cf. Reginald J. Dingle, " Psychology and Original
Sin," in *Dublin Review*, CC (1937) , 134–44.
[72] Herbert S. Schwartz, " Psychoanalysis and the Devil," in *Commonweal*,
XXV (1937) , 659–61. ". . . ' instinct ' . . . is none other than the devil masquerading
in scientific dress." *Ibid.*, 661. See Denis de Rougemont, *Le Parte du Diable* (New
York, 1943) , reviewed by C. G. Wallis, in *Kenyon Review*, VI (1944) , 150–56.
" Psychoanalysis can be defined as an attempt to reduce ' sin ' and ' Evil ' to
subjective mechanisms, which medicine can learn to control. . . . In the eyes of the
Freudian there is no Devil, but merely a belief in the Devil, springing from the
' projection ' of a guilt-complex. Heal this complex, and there won't be belief in
the Devil any more, nor consequently any Devil." Rougemont quoted by Wallis, 154.
[73] E. S. Waterhouse, " Psychoanalysis: a Success or Failure? " in *London
Quarterly Review*, CLV (1931) , 29–30.
[74] ". . . the psychoanalysts have consistently failed to follow through and
either rid us of our puritan sexual complexes, or give us a brave new morality to
replace the hush-hush ethics of an ascetic Christianity." Wolfe, " The Twilight of
Psychoanalysis," *loc. cit.*, 387.

stance, compared with the " romantic notions " which hastened the rise of Hitler.[75]

Most of these reactions were continuations of the attitudes of the twenties; discernible in them was an effort to understand Freud and a greater determination to give him his place. Practising psychologists tried sincerely to clear up the " verbal muddle " which the indiscriminate use of terms had long since caused.[76] For the most part, however, the popular mind had accepted psychoanalysis—though it may never have heard of Freud—as a part of its daily life. It was already becoming interested in the new " craze "—Watson's Behaviorism.[77] Failure of psychoanalysis to prevent, account for, or effectively cure the depression of 1929 was at least partly responsible for this shift. Economic changes in the United States and elsewhere almost from the beginning of the thirties emphasized the urgent need of a unified social program and standard. It is perhaps as simple as that: men were no longer permitted the luxury of personal soul-searching when the political and social ills of the nation were widespread. To the group with which Joseph Freeman associated, the doctrines of Marx and Freud seemed equally true; yet it was apparently impossible to reconcile the one with the other. The average psychoanalyst, says Freeman, looked upon " the radical's hatred of capitalist society as a mental derangement," and psychoanalysis might often afford the radical a backdoor escape into bourgeois society. But for the loyal and enthusiastic radical, psychoanalysis ceased to furnish completely satisfactory answers to the questions of the thirties: " Experience convinced us that Freud had discovered important truths about sex and it could not be denied that sex was a decisive human activity. . . . But as a system of sociology [Freudianism] was worthless. . . . What counted now in the world of reality was not so much the origin of the search as its object." [78]

[75] J. Gaudefroy-Demombynes, " Freud, Source Mystique du Romantisme Hitlérien," in *Mercure de France*, CCLXXXV (1938) , 478–83. That is, Freud and Hitler are alike in their use of and enthusiasm for the irrational.

[76] Karl Menninger, " Pseudoanalysis: Perils of Freudian Verbalisms," in *Outlook*, CLV (1930) , 363–65, a careful attempt to explain to the lay mind the precise meaning of such terms as fixation, repression, etc.

[77] Adams, " The Rise and Fall of Psychology," *loc. cit.*, 88.

[78] Freeman, *An American Testament*, 301. Freeman later regained much of his old interest in psychoanalysis; the novel, *Never Call Retreat* (New York, 1943) uses the psychoanalytic report as a structural medium.

iv

The *Interpretation of Dreams* was some twenty-seven years old
when a group of expatriates established the magazine *Transition* in Paris, in 1927. In the intervening years, much had
occurred to the new approach to dream-interpretation, and critics
had toyed with the idea that the dream furnishes a clue to the
creative mind.[79] *Transition*, an experimental journal, principally
for American writers, began early to deplore the corrupt state
of twentieth-century language. With Eugene Jolas as editor, in
the early thirties it organized its protests into a " credo " which
denounced rational communication as superficial and insisted that
the " language of the night life " must at least supplement it.
While the *Little Review* in America simply published Joyce's
Ulysses as an " adventure in new writing," *Transition* looked upon
Work in Progress as a document of protest against " the word."
Transition stood as the embattled bastion of " the new language "
and fought stalwartly for it against such foes as *The Modern
Quarterly*, *This Quarter*, and Wyndham Lewis' *Enemy*.[80] Though
Transition says nothing about the *mechanisms* of the dream by
which the " language of the unconscious " may be deduced and
imitated, it is well aware of the importance of the dream itself
as the clue to the " new understanding ": " The study of the
dream . . . is a poetic-esthetic liberation. It solidifies our artistic
perceptions and gives the poetic creation a universal significance
that leads to the metaphysical and the mythological in all its
fabulous possibilities." [81]

This liberation from language is, according to Jolas, a symptom of a greater struggle for cultural rebirth—not a Marxist struggle, for the Marxists are deeply concerned over words, but a
struggle of creative individualism. " In a world which is in a

[79] Among them, Prescott, *The Poetic Mind*.
[80] *Modern Quarterly*, devoted to Marxian criticism and edited by V. F.
Calverton, contributed an entire issue to the controversy. *This Quarter*, in several
of its editorials, announced itself as opposed to " chaos in language," III (1930),
129–41. Wyndham Lewis late in the twenties refuted the notion in his *Enemy*, I
(1927), a periodical which published almost nothing but Lewis.
[81] Eugene Jolas, " The Dream," in *Transition*, XIX-XX (1930), 47.

state of flux the assumption that language for purposes of creative expression has been fixed once and for all is no longer tenable." [82]

Though Freud originally formulated the method of dream-interpretation, it was Jung who, in Jolas' estimation, gave dream symbols their importance for the artist. The artist must go to psychoanalysis to observe the process of dream-interpretation, but the neurotic and the poet cannot be classified as one and the same person. Jung, making his debut in the pages of *Transition*, underscores this rejection of Freudian therapy, and emphasizes the fact that the poetic vision is part of the deep reservoir of all art. The poet is greater by far than the neurotic: " He is the collective *man*, the carrier and former of the unconsciously active soul of mankind." [83]

The artist is no mere " channel " through which impressions flow. He must reorganize consciously what he has experienced unconsciously. The artist, therefore, aware of the source of all great truth, is capable of transforming his dream-life into the philosophies of all ages. " What the faculties of a conscious being —sense and reason—know under the name of objective reality is not the Real. The ultimate reality which confounds itself with life, can only be attained in the interior of ourselves, in the Unconscious." [84]

In the twenty-seventh issue of *Transition*, Jolas printed the answers to a questionnaire he had mailed to the creative artists and critics of his acquaintance. These men were asked if they had " ever felt the need for a new language to express the experiences of [their] night mind?" They were further requested to report " any ancestral myths or symbols in [their] collective unconscious." [85] The answers constituted a modern symposium on the influence of psychoanalysis on the creative mind. All but one of them either repudiated or were ignorant of Jung's notion of a " collective unconscious." That the dream was of importance to creation, however, many of them were willing to assert, and a few agreed that language would have to be altered to accommodate

[82] Jolas, " The King's English Is Dying; Long Live the Great American Language," in *Transition*, XIX-XX, 141.

[83] Carl G. Jung, " Psychology and Poetry," in *Transition*, XIX-XX, 41.

[84] Albert Béguin, " The Night-side of Life," in *Transition*, XXVII (1938) , 201.

[85] Eugene Jolas, " Inquiry into the Spirit and Language of Night," in *Transition*, XXVII, 233.

itself to the dream. This point of difference between Jung and Freud, which was based primarily upon a disagreement about *emphasis*, was not settled by the questionnaire, but Jung's theory did not seem to meet much practical corroboration.[86]

That the dream itself is one of the significant sources of creation was affirmed, however. In two respects Freud's work on the dream influenced the manner of writing and plot construction in the literature of the thirties: (1) The devices which dream-interpretation revealed were significant contributions to experimental writing, and a knowledge of them helps one to understand such writing. (2) The dream itself took a definite place in the construction of plot or the explanation of motivation. It was one of the devices by which an action could be anticipated by the reader, and it afforded a view of the character's inner life. The twentieth-century artist wished to believe that he possessed more than an arbitrary device for enclosing a story within a framework. The dream was for him a way of pointing to the complexity of a character's motives and his diverse range of possibilities for action. For example, Conrad Aiken—who in 1915 had read Freud's *Interpretation of Dreams* in the English translation, considers the dream an essential means of explaining the sources of action. In the *Great Circle* (1933) Andrew Cathers' spiritual crisis is explained in a long dream, which takes us back to his childhood and gives all of the essential clues. This use of the dream (often very skillfully introduced) is to be found also in the novels of Waldo Frank, Ludwig Lewisohn, Thomas Mann, and Arthur Koestler.

Freudian applications to literature and criticism were challenged anew in the thirties, and Jung's theory of the " collective unconscious " furnished an alternative which pleased many writers. Jolas felt that Freud, " By reducing everything to the dogma of a neurosis, . . . eliminates layers of poetic genius that are essential for esthetic understanding." [87] Herbert Read, however, valued that side of psychoanalytic theory because it enables the critic to determine the role which neurosis plays in the act of creation.

---

[86] *Transition* began by printing a number of surrealists, but Jolas' theory of language and creation differs from surrealism in his insistence upon the mystical and religious resources of the unconscious and the consequent importance of the Dream for reality. See his *I Have Seen Monsters and Angels* (Paris, 1938), 9–18.

[87] Eugene Jolas, " Literature and the New Man," in *Transition*, XIX-XX, 15.

" There is much in literature that is on the border-line of reality; it would be useful for the critic to be able to determine by some scientific process the exact course of this borderline." [88]

The quality of this discussion of psychoanalysis indicates a serious concern with essential aesthetic problems. Two essays by Thomas Mann [89] helped to give Freud a place among the great thinkers of his time. But the protest against the novel " disguised as clinical report " justifiably continued. " Is there a legitimate distinction between a well-written case-report and a thoroughgoing psychological novel? " queried Leo A. Spiegel,[90] puzzled over the enormities which abuse of a theory might cause. Even here, however, the criticism is tempered by a realization that it is the abuse and not the theory that is at fault.

Certain important peculiarities may be noted in the reaction to Freud in the thirties. For one thing, while the twenties had given only sporadic essays in Freudian aesthetics, men of the thirties explored the linguistic and aesthetic possibilities in the newly discovered unconscious. Much of the energy and attention of young writers was directed toward problems of sociological criticism and Marxist tutored creation. Freudianism, though less popular, was given a more serious evaluation than it had received in the twenties; its ultimate place in the intellectual life of the twentieth century was tested, and its immediate value compared with that of the economic theories of Marx. The role of psycho-. analysis in the protest novel of the thirties was relatively slight. This is understandable since the reality with which this kind of novel dealt was tangible and harsh—the world of policemen, and bread lines, and union meeting halls. The discovery of the " subliminal " sources of human behavior aroused an intense and apparently lasting interest in both literary artist and critic.

In the years since 1940, two developments of interest to literary criticism have taken place. One of these is the rapid

[88] Quoted in A. W. Ramsay, " Psychology and Literary Criticism," in *Criterion*, XV (1936) , 631.

[89] " Freud's Position in the History of Modern Thought," in *Criterion*, XII, (1933) , 549–70, and " Freud and the Future," a speech given in honor of Freud's eightieth birthday and printed in condensed form in *Saturday Review of Literature*, XIV (1936) , 3–4 ff.

[90] " The New Jargon: Psychology in Literature," in *Sewanee Review*, XL (1932) , 476.

progress made by Jung in influencing the critical uses of psychoanalysis. This was made possible because of the growth of interest
in myth and because of Jung's willingness to expand the theory
of archetypes beyond the narrow familial basis insisted upon in
Freud's discussions of the phylogenesis of the human life. Though
there is much criticism of Jung's lack of exactness and his tendency
to over-emphasize the role of psychiatrist in the patient's life (see
Edward Glover, *Freud or Jung*, New York, 1950), his type of
analysis has had an especial appeal to those interested in interpreting literature in terms of mythical and archetypal origins. In the
second development, there was a careful extension of many of the
Freudian techniques to literary criticism and to a study of language. The most successful of these investigations was Ernst Kris's
Psychoanalytic Explorations in Art (New York, 1952). This
significant book brought much of the Freudian usefulness to
criticism up-to-date and applied to it several of the disciplines
contributed by modern criticism. Chapter ten of this book,
" Aesthetic Ambiguity " (written in collaboration with Abraham
Kaplan), is one of the most incisive applications of Freudian psychology to criticism ever to be made. These two principal developments are quite opposed in their stress, scope, and effect.
While archetypal criticism (as in the work of Maud Bodkin) is at
present more popular, there is no reason for assuming that the
more sober and cautious work of men like Kris will not endure
beyond it.

chapter IV

THE PROBLEM
OF INFLUENCE

i

Freud's theories have had such an elaborate career that it may seem impossible to distinguish genuine influences from merely apparent or obviously false ones. Though our survey thus far should make the reasons for this difficulty fairly clear, we may try to bring them within the sharp focus of a summary.

(1) Psychoanalysis was not immediately welcomed or accepted, whether by the medical fraternity, the schools of psychology, or the general public. It was at least ten years before the new psychology was cautiously accepted, and twenty before it enjoyed, or suffered, the attention of the general public.

(2) Freud and his earliest co-workers experimented for some time with names and terms, under the impression that they had discovered a new approach to age-old problems; they wished to differentiate it from the old, either by an original use of old terms, or by inventing new terms. While *Freudianism was being discussed* on all levels of understanding, Freud was himself modifying and extending his terminology, in an effort to make it more precise or more comprehensive. A conspicuous example is Freud's attempts to determine accurately or conveniently the geography of the psyche. From 1912 to 1924 he was steadily improving and defining the terminology related to the functional reaction to unconscious life.

(3) The dissenting psychoanalysts confused the issue still further by taking the Freudian terminology and shaping it to their own needs. Thus, we must distinguish between Freud's definition of *libido* and Jung's use of the term; between Freud's suggestions about symbolism in the dream, and Stekel's use; and so forth.

(4) The attitude toward an idea, or toward a body of theory, very often becomes fixed and determined in the lay mind long before the theory itself is ready for a final estimation.

(5) Besides these considerations, there are other difficulties which stand in the way of a correct and intelligent grasp: the problem of a technical study, and of its transference to the world of " ready and easy discussion "; the multiplication of difficulties involved in popularizing—the " false entrances and exits " which popular eclecticism uses.

(6) Finally, we may suggest that the professional and ethical guardians of society are sensitive to change. There results, a mass of well-intentioned but obviously biased hostility; and hostility is an extremely important means of spreading any notion, concept, or idea, because it is helped by a functioning prejudice. Our notions of the devil are, for the most part, derived from sources which are hostile to the devil. Though abstract considerations of evil may satisfy the philosopher or theologian, the poetic or mass mind is seldom satisfied until it " *sees* " the abstraction. This can be abundantly proved by reference to the manner in which abstractions were paraded—in full costume—before the eyes of Elizabethan spectators. It is the basis of popular allegory.

It is not at all surprising that the writers, of the twenties at least, should have been a bit confused about the exact meaning of Freudianism. The writer brought to the confusion his own preconceptions and prejudices. Many of the young intellectuals of the twenties confused the issue further by accepting Freudian terms immediately upon hearing them, or by attaching at the most a summary sketch of their meaning. Thus *repression* as Freud defined it lost much of its original meaning in a discussion; but it gained new cultural ingredients from the particular area in which it found an audience. The single term repression, therefore, suffered a variety of changes, which may be formulated as follows: Freud's definition of the term: *Repression, minus* what has been lost through hasty generalization or inadequate knowledge of its source-meaning, *plus* cultural ingredients which have been attached to the already altered concept, *equals* repression as American convention imposed upon free sex expression, or *neo-Puritanism*.

The factor of metaphor must also be considered. Hence the *mechanism* of repression was often replaced by the picture of a *repressed person*, or a repressed people. In the matter of an amateur or aésthetic usage of a term, the example is more important than the term it is designed to illustrate; and the term acquires the qualities of its illustration, and loses its original accuracy or " abstract purity."

All excessive or extremist reactions, which act as the barriers to clear understanding—such as indignation, horror, enthusiasm—affected the nature of Freud's debut in the society of the intellectual. Consider for a moment the " levels of comprehension," on any one of which a writer may, according to his tastes and learning, have encountered a fragment of Freudian theory:

(1) The level of accurate understanding: such understanding may be had only from reading intelligently the material in the original language. Such men as Waldo Frank, Ludwig Lewisohn, and Thomas Mann were equipped to do this.[1]

Freud ←———→ writer

(2) The level of translation: here one must add a third figure, so that at least three persons participate in " the learning process "—for example, Freud, Brill, and Conrad Aiken, or Freud, Brill, and Eugene O'Neill.

Freud ←———→ translator ←———→ writer

(3) The level of summary or survey: here originator, translator, and lecturer all intervene before the writer discovers the doctrine.

---

[1] This, of course, does not mean that the theory will remain accurate and unchanged after the writer has used it for his own purpose, or that it need be. He may, after all, find certain parts of it obdurate and difficult, unsuited to an aesthetic purpose. Thus he may alter it and adjust it to his own needs. Though a theory loses part or all of its " laboratory or lecture-room effectiveness " in the course of such a metamorphosis, the artist may have performed a genuine service in breaking down the barriers between one discipline and another.

Freud ⟵———⟶ translator ⟵———⟶ lecturer ⟵———⟶ writer

or

Freud ⟵———⟶ lecturer-translator ⟵———⟶ writer

(4) The level of fragmentary presentation; such as a " Mabel Dodge Sterne evening " or a tea at the Woolfs. A variety of barriers are here set up, any one or all of which might have been present in a given instance: the manner in which the subject is introduced, the discussion which took place before it was introduced, the predispositions of the person or persons who " led the discussion " or with whom the theory seemed most to be associated, and finally, the intervention of other theories—such as those of Havelock Ellis, Westermarck, or Karl Marx—by which the topic of discussion was colored. Of such was the nature of Sherwood Anderson's " education " in Freudianism, as in many other matters.[2]

Freud ⟵———⟶ translator ⟵———⟶ lecturer or
popularizer ⟵———⟶ speaker ⟵———⟶ listener

In all of these situations, the nature of the writer bore heavily upon his relationship with Freudian theory, and in many respects was the deciding factor—though, in a few, it was *altered by* the experience. Thus, a writer might have said: " This is what I have known all along—what I have written about "; or, " This is interesting, and it may help me to see more clearly; I can use it "; or " This is sheer nonsense; it will interfere with my genuine appreciation of human affairs, if I allow it to." As a result of one or another of these expressed attitudes, the writer may dismiss Freudianism summarily, satirize it gleefully, or embrace it religiously; or he may soberly consider Freudianism itself and lampoon the idle gossip of literate but stupid enthusiasts.[3] The occasions

[2] Margaret Anderson, *My Thirty Years' War*, 38; Sherwood Anderson, *Memoirs* (New York, 1942), 243.

[3] Cf. Phyllis McGinley, " Tragedies of the Psychopathic: the Painful Case of Mr. Pring," in *Forum*, XCIV (1935), 32–33:

> Go find frustrations of your own
> Lest, like poor Pring, you sit alone
> No more a host, no longer guest,
> Unwept, unhonored, unrepressed!

See James Thurber and E. B. White, *Is Sex Necessary?* (New York, 1920); Thurber, *Let Your Mind Alone* (New York, 1937).

described in level 4 were numerous; they were among the most effective agencies for spreading any theory in the twenties. They were also a means of distortion. This artificial situation has done much to affect the manner in which theories are entertained in our century.[4] In one of his novels, Waldo Frank describes several of the avenues of approach to Freud which were open to the young intellectual. On one drunken occasion, Freud slips into the conversation incidentally; here he is a sort of social scapegoat: " the unmarried men and the married women ought to give Freud a million dollars, yes and the married men ought to sue him for a million, yes and the professional painted ladies ought to hang him, he's caused a hell of a lot of unemployment. . . ."

During a more temperate evening Freud gets a bad second in a struggle with Marx. Present are a psychoanalyst, a communist, several others who make only occasional remarks. The Marxist has the floor for most of the evening; the Freudian has written a monograph on *Hamlet*, and is peeved because he has too little opportunity for airing his views. " They ate and drank: Cariss, touched in his vanity because he had not said *his* word— Barbarian! the psychoanalytic Truth doesn't exist for these Marxists. . . ." Later, however, Cariss has ample opportunity both to discuss his theories and to demonstrate his practice of them.[5]

The creative artist works, it appears, within a complex environment, and his originally naïve view of human behavior is subject constantly to qualification and modification by circumstances in that environment. Ideas, concepts, and theories are seldom if ever received in a state of purity. The act of creation is thus obstructed as often as it is helped by suggestions and distractions originating in that environment. This obstruction is aided and abetted in a great number of instances by the willful independence of the artist himself. Writers who have a sufficiently healthy and independent view of their world and who also possess a confident mastery of their craft may produce great or satisfactory works with apparently little aid or hindrance from their immediate surroundings. Indeed, it is the task of the creative artist

---

[4] See, for example, Carl Van Vechten's description of an evening at Edith Dale's (Mabel Dodge Sterne's) , in *Peter Whiffle: His Life and Works* (New York, 1922) , 136 ff.

[5] Frank, *The Bridegroom Cometh*, 352, 399.

to work independently of them, or at the most to assume the role of judge or analyst of them.

Allowance must be made for the peculiar nature of the aesthetic point of view. What actually happens to a writer when, after a long period of preliminary discussion and thought, he submits to the necessities of his art? He does not usually begin by lining up representative texts on his table, and piecing together fragments from them. The creative artist is first of all aware of the *idea* to which he hopes to give aesthetic form of one sort or another. His use of suggestions from the world from which he has momentarily absented himself will depend upon his recognition of their relevance to his mastery and view of the idea. Theory is thus inferior to aesthetic practice at the moment of such practice.

The clue to influence may be seen in the word *relevance*. This is not, however, the relevance which critics discover after a poem, play, or novel has been published. It is a relevance momentarily comprehended, a service theory performs for the writer. This independence of theory gives the writer a great advantage over his intellectual guides. They are his servants, not his masters or tutors. Recognition of them is usually qualified and altered in accordance with an aesthetic and not a scientific or philosophic point of view. Hence a writer selects freely from them; his selection is not always accurate, or fair to them. They do not dictate specifically or explicitly to the artist *during* the moment of creation.

If this is true, what if anything can be said about influence? The aesthetic experience is in an important sense a moment of creation, an aesthetic *present*, bounded in time by a sociological and ethical past and future. In other words, the writer's intellectual environment affects and alters his attitudes and views *before* he yields to the necessity for aesthetic decision. Equally important is the fact that, once a work of art has been published, or put on exhibition, it is again subjected to the judgment and criticism of its environment.

The intellectual and sociological preliminaries to the creative act are, of course, the sum total of theory with which the artist is in some way familiar, plus the circumstances under which he becomes familiar with them. Their effect upon him depends for the most part upon their attractiveness, their appropriateness to his interests. Suggestions from the discipline of psychology may seem much more appropriate to him than suggestions from the fields of physics or chemistry; this is especially true if he is interested in understanding motivations of human behavior, or in testing his own experience by comparing it with social experience. This interaction between subjective and social experience bears an important relationship to the ultimate nature of an artist's point of view. The artist normally has a sense of insecurity in his relationship with the outside world, an insecurity which derives from the *difference* between him and the social norm. This insecurity is alternately great or trivial as his environment appears certain or confused. The instability of our age reacts upon the artist by intensifying his own feeling of uncertainty. Its peculiar contribution to modern aesthetics is to increase the artist's desire for aesthetic solutions to political, social, and philosophic problems. He is eager for new knowledge, and he distrusts or scorns traditional knowledge. He is thus influenced by the thought of his time because he is not altogether confident of his own powers of integration. It is in this way that the act of creation is prepared for, in the world outside the sphere of subjective interests and convictions. The artist differs from other men primarily in the *intensity* of his need for security. He differs from the philosopher and scientist, perhaps in the emotional and prejudicial point of view he brings to the world of theory, which he examines halfseriously, or altogether too seriously, and often indiscriminately.

Psychoanalysis enjoyed a great advantage over other bodies of theory because of its greater attraction for the artist. It was, after all, a new and bold interpretation of human behavior. For one thing, it flattered the subjective importance of the artist himself, for it suggested deep and significant sources of independent behavior. Again, it gave him new clues for the study of himself and his world, clues which were all the more attractive because in their superficial nature they opposed the established notions of institutional behavior. It is quite possible that Freud has influenced the writing of our time more radically than other theorists because the subject matter with which he dealt was more intimately related to aesthetic interests. But he did not, except for a few minor examples, *control* the act of creation. The independence of aesthetic attitudes asserted itself powerfully, as it does in most examples of creative activity. Freud's influence has in the main been implicit rather than explicit. The power of aesthetic independence is such that it invariably changes original doctrine from its original systematic and explicit character to a condition of contradictory and unsystematic influence. Original doctrine loses the dogmatic or didactic character which it originally possesses— and *must* possess if it is to be accepted without qualification. In the course of an artist's career, there is a strong and a critically important tension between doctrinal certainty and subjective skepticism. It is probably incorrect to judge influence simply by measuring the external facts of any cultural history. It is even more incorrect to assume that an influence has taken place because a work of art merely *corresponds* to a body of theory—that is, that the conclusions or characteristics of a work of art are similar to those suggested by a certain brand of psychological investigation or by a philosophical system.

The measurement of influence must consider several matters: the degree to which a body of theory is current; the degree *and* nature of discussion which that body of theory undergoes within the time and in the place in which the artist lives; and the attitude of the artist toward theorizing in general and toward a specific body of theory. We need to determine the nature and quality of the artist's variation from exact theory. This course may be difficult, but it is also very rewarding, for it does more than prove a point. It pays strict attention to the peculiarities of the aesthetic point of view; it ultimately results in an honest and exact appraisal of our cultural history; and it gives to the artist a deserved and merited personal integrity.

In the course of literary history the position of the artist is strongly affected by the professional criticism of his contemporaries. There have, of course, been many critics who were also artists, and many artists who occasionally took to criticism, for one reason or another. For the most part, however, criticism has been a field apart from creation. The critic's relationship to his time is intellectual and often axiomatic. His attitude toward the ideas and theories of his time is usually more objective than the artist's, since he is obliged not to grasp the world intuitively but to appraise it intellectually. He is therefore in a better position to understand ideology but less able to sympathize with the difficulties of creation or to comprehend the ambiguous nature of its results. The critic is thus closer to the intellectual world, and it is his ideal task to demonstrate the value of aesthetic contributions to it. The controversies of his time are in an especial sense his own, and he is one of the arbiters of taste and belief. The effect of a critic's disposition and temperament often lies in his preference for one body of thought as opposed to another. Far from interpreting the artist to his world, he often arbitrarily selects a body of theory, or a synthesis of several, and views all works of art from this vantage point.

The role of the critic is to examine quite objectively the ideologies of his time, with a view toward noting their applicability to or difference from aesthetics. He must also recognize quite candidly and intelligently the important modal differences between intellectual or scientific and emotional or aesthetic points of view. Thus, the purpose of a psychoanalyst is not to represent the tragedy in human life but to remove it. A critic who insists that a novel is exactly like a series of psychoanalytic case-histories fails to grasp the essential difference between a patient and a fictional character. More than that, he makes the greatest mistake of all in failing to see that the analyst views his patient scientifically and objectively and that the author often views his characters subjectively. The analyst's function is both descriptive and prescriptive; the writer does not advise his characters or his readers in the same way at all. Nor does he examine his characters with scientific caution. No writer is, therefore, literally a " Freudian "; one may only say that he might have been interested in the aesthetic possibilities of Freudianism and have exploited them in one imperfect way or another.

ii

It is another thing, however, for a critic to judge psychoanalysis itself, with a view toward estimating its good or bad effects upon literature and evaluating its suggestions for a new interpretation of the personality of the artist. This occupation is a legitimate one; it belongs not to the examination of single works but to the field of aesthetics, more specifically to the psychology of aesthetics. And since such work is important for an artist's final estimate of himself, we might well look for a moment at the contribution of psychoanalysis to aesthetics.

The writer was well able to find psychoanalysis in a number of places. That its companion-subject, sex freedom, was often closely linked with it, either in causal sequence or as an associate matter, both speeded the influence of popular Freudianism and barred the way to an understanding of the actual theory. Freud's contribution to literature, then, may be regarded as twofold: association of his name and theories with analyses of character and society, and adaptation of portions of his theories to theories of writing and style. For Freud, psychoanalysis had little enough to say *about* the artist; but his statements about art are not so important as his contributions to the subject matter and style of art.

As to the former, his remarks are infrequent and scattered, though he was bolder in such fields as philosophy and ethnology, and his psychoanalyst followers did not possess his timidity in matters of aesthetics and literary criticism.[6] The artist is for Freud a " neurotic " who seeks and finds in art a " substitutive gratification " for his " thwarted desires."

> The artist is originally a man who turns from reality because he cannot come to terms with the demand for the renunciation of instinctual satisfaction as it is first made, and who then in phantasy-life allows full play to his erotic and ambitious wishes. But he finds a way of return from this world of phantasy back to reality; with his special gifts he moulds

---

[6] Cf. Otto Rank's *Das Inzest-motiv in Dichtung und Sage . . . ; Art and Artist* (New York, 1932).

Freud's own statements about the artist are contained in *The Collected Papers of Sigmund Freud*, IV: " The Relation of the Poet to Day-Dreaming," 173–83, " Contributions to the Psychology of Love: . . . ," 192–202, " Formulations Regarding the Two Principles in Mental Functioning," 13–21; *Leonardo da Vinci: a Psychosexual Study of Infantile Reminiscence* (New York, 1910); *A General Introduction to Psychoanalysis*, Lecture 23, pp. 326–27; *Civilization and Its Discontents*, 38–39. See Louis Fraiberg, " Freud's Writings on Art," *Literature and Psychology*, VI (1956), 116–30.

his phantasies into a new kind of reality, and men concede them a justification as valuable reflections of actual life. Thus by a certain path he actually becomes the hero, king, creator, favourite he desired to be, without pursuing the circuitous path of creating real alterations in the outer world. But this he can only attain because other men feel the same dissatisfaction as he with the renunciation demanded by reality and because this dissatisfaction, resulting from the displacement of the pleasure-principle by the reality-principle, is itself a part of reality.[7]

Thus the artist helps the world to soften the impact with the "reality-principle," because he is more skillful in the matter of averting the clash between desire and the harsh, external world; ". . . he makes it possible for others, in their turn, to obtain solace and consolation from their own unconscious sources of gratification which had become inaccessible."[8]

This extension of therapy to aesthetics comes very close to regarding the artist as a successful neurotic; whereas the patient is obliged to give up his neurosis, or to redirect it by means of effective sublimation, the artist is applauded and honored for his. This assumes a close association between the instinctive life and the life of the imagination, and it further tends to disparage the creative act of a subjective means of avoiding rather than an objective plan for shaping reality. It is one of the points from which the literary critic transfers the therapeutic situation to the field of biography and the "clinical interpretation" of literature. Many artists and art critics scoffed at the notion, and held that it was just another evidence of illegal poaching on the preserves of formal aesthetics.[9] It is easy to see how this approach to the imaginative life might lead to abuses. Albert Mordell, for example, one of the extremists, accepted the Freudian hypothesis

[7] "Formulations Regarding the Two Principles in Mental Functioning," *loc. cit.*, 19.

[8] *A General Introduction to Psychoanalysis*, 327.

[9] Clive Bell, "Doctor Freud on Art," in *Nation and Athenaeum*, XXXV (1924), 690–91. Roger Fry, "The Artist and Psychoanalysis," in *The New Criticism: an Anthology of Modern Aesthetics and Literary Criticism* (New York, 1930), 193–215. Cf. Review by W. C. Blum, "Impossible Purity," in *Dial*, LXXVIII (1925), 318–23. See also Lionel Trilling's honest and intelligent discussion of this point, "The Legacy of Sigmund Freud," in *Kenyon Review* (1940) II, 162–68.

literally: " A literary work stands in the same relation to the author as the dream to the patient." The source of much re-explanation of creative genius will be found " in the infantile love life of the authors." " When we say that a genius is a man who discovers a new truth or depicts beauty, we really mean that he is a man who, having experienced a repression, has been led to make certain conclusions from that event which society has not wished to admit. . . ." [10]

The advantage to literature of that sort of criticism is indeed negligible. Yet we must admit that Freud is himself responsible for this direct translation of therapy into aesthetics. It cannot be simply dismissed, for it is part of the picture. This is not to say, however, that the use of clinical evidence in the discussion of literature is necessarily bad or distorting. A study of poets need not distort the understanding of their poetry. The greatest defect of this kind of biographical analysis lies essentially in its ignoring the work or merely using it as accessory evidence for the analysis of the writer.

Those critics who went, not to Freud's statements about artistic genesis, but to the results of psychoanalytic research for clues about the imaginative life, made a happier selection and were more successful in avoiding extremist conclusions. This much, they believed, was true: that the dream was a rich source of clues for a new interpretation of the imaginative life. Since the manifest dream, properly interpreted, revealed facts of significance about the unconscious, they were led to believe in a close correspondence between the dream-life and artistic creation. Since in the dream-state the hold of the practical world is temporarily suspended, the imagination has relatively free play, and " creates a world completely fanciful—or fantastic—in which it ranges at will." This according to Frederick C. Prescott, can be the source of a clearer understanding of the poetic imagination. In the " free play of the dream consciousness," thought loses its analytic and abstract character and becomes " purely imaginative and concrete." The poet has the same difficulty that the patient encounters in the analytic situation, though for the former it is more easily encompassed and the results are generally more

[10] Albert Mordell, *The Erotic Motive in Literature* (New York, 1919), 6, 11, 114.

pleasing—the task of turning the visual, concrete thing into words. The poet is less disturbed than the " man of affairs " by bounds set ordinarily to free expression; in this respect, his mind compares favorably with the child's. The primitive and childish mind is more poetic than the advanced mind, which has been " forced " into purposive thought. " The *undirected,* purposeless ever-interested mind of the child, who loves and greedily desires, later develops, through suppressions and laws of one sort or another, a set of mores, a code, by which he is subsequently to live."

The poet considers these bounds lightly, and is more easily able to get back to the blessed anarchy of childhood.[11] His task is, therefore, somehow to communicate his dream-life as beautifully and with as little intervention from the rational, abstracting activity of his world as possible. It is to " make the unconscious conscious " but not to destroy its beauty in so doing. Prescott, of course, excludes all poetry whose aim is to persuade or dissuade, didactic or philosophic poetry, the materials for which are drawn from the rational, waking mind. For him, the " imagination of the unconscious " comprehends " not our immediate and selfish desires, but the deeper feelings and aspirations which we share with members of our race." [12] This approach to poetic creation involves two separate considerations: first, a proof that the source of much poetic inspiration lies in the unconscious, especially as revealed in the dream; and, second, a study of the mechanism of the dream-life and its association with the mechanics of poetic expression. Prescott is concerned with both problems; we know that Freud has described the processes by which the latent dream becomes manifest, the " dream-work ": " If we call

[11] Prescott, *The Poetic Mind,* 17, 43, 69. Dr. Brill said that he and Prescott had conferred frequently about the latter's book, checking it with Freudian theory, and that Prescott had in turn helped Brill with his translations. Interview of December, 1942.

[12] *Ibid.,* 116. At this point, Prescott shies away from the Freudian conception of the unconscious and accepts instead the Jungian notion of a universal or " collective unconscious," in which strivings which the external world considers " good "—the mystic's distillation of primal forces—operate to ennoble the poet's imagination. " I think careful consideration might show that the responsibility of the individual to society or to morality in conscious thought and action is one thing, and the responsibility in visionary unconscious thought quite another; and that, though the dreamer is freed from social obligation in a narrow sense, he is brought into relation with the mind of the race in a larger way and thus subjected to a more profound control." *Ibid.,* 116–17.

the corresponding action of the mind in forming of poetic images the Poetic work (or *Dichterarbeit*), the question is how far the principles of the one are applicable to the other."

For each of the devices of the dream-work the poet has analogous methods. The poetic image is often a composite; the metaphor has sufficient amgibuity in it to suggest a variety of concrete images—it is a mode of condensation; ". . . whereas in true prose, words should have one meaning, . . . in true poetry they should have as many meanings as possible." [13] Similarly, the composition of figures in fiction may be compared with the processes of composition and identification in dreams, especially in the case of autogenic characters in which the author divides himself to form characters.[14]

Critical exploitation of psychoanalysis has been marked often by abuse and misunderstanding. Not only have critics often sinned against good critical sense by forcing the writers of the time into pigeonholes of theory; they have frequently mistreated Freud's original remarks about the psychological nature of the artist. Three at least of modern critics may, however, be said to have shown great intelligence in their appropriation of Freudian materials; Herbert Read, Edmund Wilson, and Kenneth Burke have made important contributions to a sane estimate of Freud's meaning for modern aesthetics.

Read is quite impartial in his use of psychoanalytic theory; he selects from the theories of Freud, Jung, and Adler, as he judges each to be appropriate to his purpose. The important effect of modern psychology upon aesthetics, Read believes, lies in its calling the attention of critics to the " organic " sources of poetic form, " form imposed on poetry by the laws of its own origination, without consideration for the given forms of traditional poetry."

---

[13] Prescott, *The Poetic Mind*, 169, 173. The terms "true prose" and "true poetry" refer to a distinction which he has made earlier; he would prefer to consider poetry not the product of formal training, but the product of a certain type of "poetic" inspiration. "The same creative faculty which produces poetic verse produces also prose fiction, in narrative and drama. . . ." *Ibid.*, 8.

[14] The ever-present autobiographical figure in fiction is similar to the ever-present ego in the dream. Freud: "Dreams are absolutely egotistic," and "If I do not know behind which of the persons which occur in the dream I am to look for my ego, I observe the following rule: that person in the dream who is subject to an emotion which I experience while asleep, is the one that conceals my ego." *The Interpretation of Dreams*, 299, 300n.

This return to a study of the psychological sources of creation demands some revision of our notions of the personality of the artist. Read makes an interesting distinction between the personality and the character of the artist. Character, he says, " can be explained as a disposition in the individual due to the repression of certain impulses which would otherwise be present in the personality; . . . an enduring disposition to inhibit instinctive impulses *in accordance with a regulative principle.*" The personality of the artist is thus in frequent conflict with his character, which seeks to prohibit his full use of the unconscious sources of aesthetic expression. The character of modern expression may thus be explained in terms of the modern analysis of psychic behavior. The physical power of the instincts is regulated and modified by the strenuous efforts of the ego to keep it within bounds. " What is suppressed in consciousness may be found active in the imagination, which might be identified with the preconscious of Freud's phraseology." Read's use of this phraseology is demonstrated in his discussion of Marcel Proust:

> It is the phenomena of the mind in its conscious, unconscious and even preconscious phases of repression and censorship, that Proust is describing in words not far removed from the scientific vocabulary of psychoanalysis. But I doubt very much that Proust had any exact knowledge of psychoanalysis; at many points we must regard his work as a confirmation, or an anticipation, of the observations of Freud. Proust speaks of the heart, and Freud of the mind; but these are interchangeable concepts.[15]

Read's principal contribution to criticism is his careful delineation of the areas of aesthetic activity. Criticism of literature and analysis of the psychology of the artist are two different activities, though they may be mutually helpful. Further, the critic must affirm his identity and mark the limits between himself and the analyst. " The psychologist," says Read, " is indifferent to literary values, . . . and may even definitely deplore them, especially when they represent the trimming of subjective phantasies under the influence of some objective standard or tradition." No work of

[15] Herbert Read, *Form in Modern Poetry* (New York, 1933) , 5, 13, 17, 20, 28.

art can come simply from an *understanding* of any field, no matter how intimately related it may be to the preoccupations of the artist. However, a study of psychoanalysis may help the critic to realize, "more quickly and more reasonably than the normal man would realize from *his own* experience, such facts as the subjectivity of love and the general law of determinism in which all our emotions and ideals are bound." [16]

Psychoanalysis helps us to understand the problem of creation by offering a reasonable explanation of the aesthetic disposition. Further, the Freudian analysis of psychic geography—the discussion of id, ego, and superego, that is—is convenient, for it is as accurate a picture of man's unconscious life as can be had within the limits of psychological metaphor. Freud may not have been totally correct in his analysis of the artist as a neurotic. "The essential point to notice," however, says Read, "is that psychoanalysis seems to show that the artist is initially by tendency a neurotic, but that in becoming an artist he as it were escapes the ultimate fate of his tendency and through art finds his way back to reality." [17]

For Edmund Wilson the body of psychoanalytic theory also aids the critic in his attempt to judge the merits of his contemporaries. Wilson is concerned with two matters: the ideological framework within which aesthetic activity takes place, and the assistance which psychological biography affords in the final evaluation of a writer. But Wilson does not accept a wholesale psychoanalysis of writers. The critic, he says, is not a scientist who can mix his elements and predict the results of their combination. The Freudians have contributed a certain exactness and suggestiveness to an important tendency which "had already got well started before ": "the interpretation of works of literature in the light of the personalities behind them." Wilson notes Freud's study of Leonardo da Vinci, but regards it as case history rather than criticism. The dangers of this method are implicit in its deceptive simplicity: "The method has led to bad results where the critic has built a Freudian mechanism out of very slender evidence, and then given us merely a romance based on the sup-

---

[16] Read, "The Nature of Criticism," in *Collected Essays in Literary Criticism* (London, 1938), 126, 127.
[17] *Ibid.*, 140.

posed working of this mechanism instead of a genuine study of the writer's life and work."

In this warning Wilson does more than serve notice to those who think that bad psychoanalysis makes good criticism. Psychoanalysis, like Marxism, is another of the ideological extensions of a critic's own perception. He must still be able to tell good from bad literature, to estimate a work on the basis of its formal excellence or its poverty of talent. "No matter how thorough and complete our explanations of works of literature may be from the historical and biographical points of view, we must be ready to try to estimate the relative degrees of success attained by the products of the various periods and the various personalities in some such way as Eliot and Saintsbury do." [18]

Thus the theories of Freud and of Marx, so far as they have been pertinent to the critic's task, have increased his understanding and enriched his perception, so that he may be able to do justice to the literature of his time. Wilson's position enables him to oppose both the purely ideological interpretation and the purely textual criticism of literature. A novel is supplementary to a body of psychological theory; and we may know more about each by studying the other. This is above all a reasonable point of view. And, as it develops in his own criticism, it leads to eminently satisfactory and humane appraisals of ancient and modern literature. The virtue of moderation in the matter of literary taste lies in its honest and sensible use of the "equipment" of the critic and its skillful avoidance of violent dogmatism of one extreme or the other. Such moderation is necessary and especially helpful in an occupation in which one's use of "special disciplines" is always suspect.[19]

Kenneth Burke employs Freudian terminology and theory as he does all else that interests him. Of all modern critics he is most aware of the diversity of influences which have gone to make up our intellectual and critical pattern. For him, the greatest critical

[18] Edmund Wilson, "The Historical Interpretation of Literature," in *The Intent of the Critic*, ed. Donald A. Stauffer (Princeton, 1941), 55, 57.

[19] Among Wilson's essays which apply suggestions from psychoanalysis to literature are these: "Dickens: the Two Scrooges," "Justice to Edith Wharton," and "Philoctetes: The Wound and the Bow," in *The Wound and the Bow* (New York, 1937); and "The Ambiguity of Henry James," in *The Triple Thinkers* (New York, 1948).

need is to extend the range of conceptual usage, so that it may meet the complex intellectual needs of the modern mind. One encounters, therefore, a bewildering varity of allusions to the theorists of our time; and there is also a constant shifting of meanings and terms within the ample boundaries of Burke's critical attitude. Burke believes that no simple or systematic explanation of modern thought is possible, for modern society is complex. The proper approach will therefore be as complex as is its subject; he advises what he calls a " perspective by incongruity," by means of which one may see all attitudes and theories with a kind of comic allowance for their contradictions and for the confusion which their mutually exclusive presence creates: " The progress of humane enlightenment can go no further than in picturing people not as *vicious,* but as *mistaken.* When you add that people are *necessarily* mistaken, that *all* people are exposed to situations in which they must act as fools, that *every* insight contains its own special kinds of blindness, you complete the comic circle, returning again to the lesson of humility that underlies great tragedy." [20]

All of the contributions to modern thought have served paradoxically both to explain and to observe man's views of the universe. Burke's aim is to provide a vocabulary which if used not literally but flexibly and from the point of view of what he calls " comic self-consciousness," will enable man to comprehend the entire universe and all of the self-contradictory acts of mind and body within it. This is putting obscurity to work; it requires a patient and ever-increasing renunciation of the desire for easy clarification.

It is with this point of view in mind that we must approach his use of Freudian terminology. Like other theorists, Freud has furnished the modern mind with a set of terms or concepts, behind each of which there is a very active nucleus of theory. What Burke does, in essence, is to separate these concepts from each other, consider each as a suggestive unit, and then test their relevance to other concepts, drawn from a variety of sources; to do the same with these other concepts, until all ideas supplement each other suggestively but illogically.

What I should like most to do would be simply to take

---

[20] Kenneth Burke, *Attitudes Toward History* (New York, 1937) , I, 51–52.

representative excerpts from [Freud's] work, copy them out, and write glosses upon them. Very often these glosses would be straight extensions of his own thinking. At other times they would be attempts to characterize his strategy of presentation with reference to interpretative method in general. And finally, the Freudian perspective was developed primarily to chart a psychiatric field rather than an aesthetic one; but since we are here considering the analogous features of these two fields rather than their important differences, there would be glosses attempting to suggest how far the literary critic should go along with Freud and what extra-Freudian material he would have to add.[21]

So far as the neurotic and the poet both act symbolically, psychoanalysis reaches into aesthetics. But literary criticism must note the essential differences between neurotic symbolism and poetic symbolism. Likewise, insofar as the poet is a subject of psychoanalytic investigation—that is, his mood of concentration is similar to that of the neurotic—ideas, obsessions and terms may be considered complementary, but only if we account again for the *original* difference of purpose between psychoanalysis and aesthetics. With such caution as is necessary to preserve literature from losing its identity in the scientific laboratory, Burke considers such suggestions from psychoanalysis as dream symbolism, sex motivation, and the method of free association. Whatever remains after the purely clinical emphasis has been accounted for may be grouped under the term " poem as dream." Above all, the peculiarities of the dream work, known as condensation and displacement, are of value, as the " creative violation " of orthodox syntax and the logic of perceptual reality. In the end, one has to admit that Freudianism must be qualified by aesthetic theory, to the extent of readjusting the emphasis which the analyst's office places upon certain things and including other ideas which psychoanalysis either omits or under-emphasizes.[22]

[21] Kenneth Burke, " Freud—and the Analysis of Poetry," in *American Journal of Sociology*, **XLV** (1939) , 391.
[22] An important application of Freud's analysis of dream language and ambiguity appears in the work of William Empson. See especially, *Seven Types of Ambiguity* (London, 1930) , *passim*; and " Alice in Wonderland," in *Some Versions of Pastoral* (London, 1935) .

iii

Such criticism as this has justified some attention because of its intelligence and because of the suggestions it offers for a final aesthetic appraisal of Freudian influence. We may note that critics have been concerned with two kinds of inquiry: the psychological nature of the artist, and the suggestions which psychoanalysis has made regarding modern efforts to revise and alter the formal and stylistic character of literature. This latter problem is central to the study of modern aesthetics.

The experimental writing of the twentieth century saw in the unconscious a linguistic problem which required a revision in the matter of imagery and symbolism. Many writers were willing to go beyond the mere " stream of consciousness " manner of arranging phrases in a fluid pattern, and of suspending the control of space-time over mind. For them the " stream " must resemble the " flow " of the unconscious psychic life. Hence the eccentricity, and the unintelligibility of much modern experimental writing. An ideal approximation to the unconscious cannot be looked for in literature; even when words are most plastic—that is, when they suggest a variety of meanings and lend themselves readily to visual diffusion—they are still words, and as such only indirectly represent the affective and concrete " life of the unconscious." Yet words are the writer's tools. He cannot employ paints or electric wires; nor can he leave the page blank, as one irate critic suggests.[23] If the unconscious is so difficult to represent, why bother? Why renounce our habitual communication to find what even Freud admits is accessible to the conscious mind only by careful and painstaking inference? Isn't a metaphorical description more satisfactory than a " faithful transcript "? The experimenters reply that, for various reasons, it is within the range of artistic possibility—though, perhaps, not within the range of the reader's comprehension [24]—to reproduce the unconscious.

[23] Joseph Prescott, " James Joyce: A Study in Words," in *PMLA*, LIV (1939), 314. " Joyce will call his next work *tabula rasa* and will regale the reader with hundreds of pages of closely bound paper, every one of which will be innocent of printer's ink. . . ."

[24] We have *Transition* proclaiming among other things, " the Plain Reader be damned! " " Proclamation," in *Transition*, XVII (1929).

They believed that this "new writing" should follow, not the laws of ordinary communication, but the dictates of the unconscious itself. Since this is a repudiation of the laws governing communication, it may be considered an instance of the hyperindividualism that characterized much of the revolt of the twenties. Surrealism is its foster-child. The surrealist would go directly to the unconscious itself and leave out the intermediate avenues by which it approaches consciousness. Freud "discovered" the unconscious by devious methods, and he found that we can have access to it by measuring the peculiarities and disguises which distinguish its attempts to break through to reality. The surrealists wish to integrate dream with reality (by which they mean, of course, "make reality subservient to dream"). Surrealism is an extreme example of what has come from Freud's exploration of the unconscious mind of man. But Freud explored the unconscious, not by "remaining within it" but by measuring by means of it the complex and deep resources of the human psyche. As Herbert Muller has put it: " He [Freud] conceived the unconscious as primary only because more rudimentary, and sought always to control it. They [the surrealists] conceive it as the source of beauty and truth, and seek to exploit it." [25]

The coincidence of Freud's with surrealist thinking—André Breton had once planned to become a psychiatrist—called attention to the possibilities of the dream-life. It was the surrealists' intention not only to exploit these possibilities for themselves but also to sponsor the irrational or unconscious life as the property of all men. They tried to ally themselves with the Communist

[25] Herbert Muller, "Surrealism: a Dissenting Opinion," in *New Directions in Prose and Poetry, 1940*, ed. James Laughlin (Norfolk, Conn., 1940), 553. Cf. Kenneth Burke, "Surrealism," *ibid.*, 563–79. Muller's essay on surrealism, though intelligent and just, is another indication of his growing distrust of the irrational in literature. He sees in almost every literary use of irrational themes a suspicious alliance with the forces of evil in modern society—more specifically, with Hitler. In his *Science and Criticism* (New Haven, 1943), a book otherwise temperate and wise, he refers to this change of heart: ". . . in my book on the modern novel, written some years ago, I noted the obvious limitations and excesses of D. H. Lawrence's work but ended by stressing its values. I felt, rightly or wrongly, that in a science-governed age both literature and philosophy needed his impassioned rendering of the 'unknown modes of being' and his exaltation of old ways of feeling. Today I should stick by almost any given sentence in the chapter. Yet I should also shift my emphasis and dwell more on the dangers of Lawrence's attitude. In Hitler's world there are men enough to glorify the Unconscious, rally behind the instinctive and irrational." *Ibid.*, 15 n.

International, claiming kinship on the grounds of their common hatred of bourgeois morals and restrictions.

It is with their influence upon aesthetic theory and practice that we are most concerned, however. It is their purpose, says David Gascoyne (who since 1938 has no longer been one of them), "to extend indefinitely the limits of 'literature' and 'art' by continually tending to do away with the barrier that separates . . . the printed page or the picture-frame from the world of real life and action." [26] More specifically they are interested in exploiting the aesthetic possibilities of unconscious metaphor, hoping to find within the unconscious a riot of imagery and unsyntactic profusion, "a perpetual flow of irrational thought *in the form of images*."

Surrealism began with the destructive nonsequiturs of Parisian dadaism. Dadaism was launched noisily in Zurich, Switzerland, in 1916, and continued in Paris until about 1922. Perhaps it was the desire to subject revolt to some form of aesthetic discipline which caused the establishment of surrealism. In the words of its first manifesto, surrealism wished to destroy the restrictions of rationalism because "'the methods of logic are applied nowadays only to the resolution of problems of secondary interest. . . . Under colour of civilisation, under pretext of progress, all that rightly or wrongly may be regarded as fantasy or superstition has been banished from the mind.'" [27]

The attachment to Freud is more than accidental. The surrealist practice was first to reject all of the limitations of the ego, sublimation as well as repression; secondly, to use the unconscious as source of both aesthetic and moral departures from the norm; and finally, to break loose altogether from the analyst's control and tutoring of the unconscious, to which the analyst of course attached primary importance. Subsequent additions to surrealist theory have accepted the unconscious desire or wish as the end of activity, poetic or otherwise.

The three principles of surrealistic aesthetics and morality are called the Objective Hazard, Estrangement of Sensation, and Black Bile. The first is perhaps the most strictly original contribution. It begins by assuming that the unconscious desire is the

[26] David Gascoyne, *A Short Survey of Surrealism* (London, 1935), x.
[27] Quoted, *ibid.*, 59–60.

single arbiter of action. Freud's cautious and almost lifelong preoccupation with the Pleasure Principle and the Reality Principle is thus eliminated at one stroke. The Objective Hazard disregards this example of psychoanalytic caution. Freud had insisted that, although the unconscious drive is for immediate satisfaction of instinctual desires, this drive is halted and its energies retarded by the rude shock with reality and the consequent efforts of the ego to protect the psyche from any repetition of its painful experience. Surrealists regard such precautionary efforts on the part of the ego and its social assistants as mere interference. The unconscious, instinctual desire must leap out of its prison and find brutal and violent satisfaction.

> We live in Society, we have desires, and we find obstacles to their realization; we are fighting for the realization of our desires. We are fighting against all obstacles to their realization. Our morality leads us to an ethic of desire because the artist in following what Freud called Pleasure as opposed to Reality expressed desires more clearly than other men do, and takes the lead in the field of hope.[28]

The second of the three principles, Estrangement of Sensation, is of course linked with the linguistic and illogical habits of the unconscious as they are exposed in the manifest dreams and in other situations developed by the psychoanalyst. The literature of surrealism regards the eccentricity of language and the illogical suspension of intelligible comparison as central to its expression of reality. "Everything that produces estrangement, from a broken motorcar to the Pyramid of Cheops, from deep sea life to the dance at the Savoy in Harlem, can produce this estrangement and therefore be poetic."[29] There is no such thing as formal beauty in surrealist aesthetics. The surrealist relies upon the shocking—comically shocking—persistence of disorder to convey its poetic or pictorial impression of unconscious reality. The image ought to "bring about the fusion of two mutually distant realities." Thus the image of Lautréamont (nineteenth-century predecessor of surrealism), the "'chance meeting, on a

[28] Nicolas Calas, "The Meaning of Surrealism," in *New Directions in Prose and Poetry, 1940* (Norfolk, Conn.), 389.
[29] *Ibid.*

dissecting table, of a sewing machine and an umbrella ' " succeeds in bringing "about the union of two mutually distant realities upon a plane equally unrelated to either of them." [30] The surrealist will go to the dream report as often as it furnishes examples of such coincidences. But later statements by surrealists lead one to believe that they have not been altogether satisfied with what the dream report has to offer. "I think we have exaggerated," says Calas, "the poetic value, not of the unconscious image, but of the free-association method which is the *modus operandi* of psycho-analytical confession. . . . There is in [the poet's] care no psycho-analyst to command the rhythm of the poem like a God, a father or a lover; unless the poet discovers the rhythm himself his images will remain inert." The limitations of the analyst's procedures—which the surrealist never really considered anyway—have struck him as endangering the freshness and originality of surrealist expression; for the symbols and images of the dream do recur with monotonous regularity and similarity. The great difference between the surrealist poet and the analytic patient must again be stressed: "Freud's patients are merely victims; the poet, by the sole fact that he creates, is a *hero*, a hero who suffers assuredly, who feels inferiorities which are often terrible, but one who has discovered a world he can explore and conquer, a world, moreover, of high social significance, and cannot be degraded to the rank of patient." [31]

The third of these principles, Black Bile, Breton's *l'humour noir*, is a kind of introjected irony, an irrational laughter which the poet expresses when he is aware of the violent incongruities of unconscious reality. Freud had shown in his *Wit and Its Relationship to the Unconscious* that the intention behind laughter can be quite cruel.

> Surrealism, thanks to the discoveries of Freud, has managed to go very deeply into the process of affective reaction and has discovered that when irony becomes really revolutionary (from the point of view of the poet) it becomes something much more cruel than what is understood when we use the

---

[30] Gascoyne, *A Short Survey of Surrealism*, 66.
[31] Nicolas Calas, "The Light of Words," in *Arson*, I (1942), 16.

term irony. . . . It is laughter of the most disagreeable kind and with the most disturbing effects.[32]

This laughter does not exclude the scatological, though it does not necessarily exalt it. It is a humor associated with the shock of dislocation from conscious signposts of good and evil.

These and other indications of the totally irrational must be associated with the history of Freud's influence on modern literature; the influence is undeniable. The surrealists, however, have themselves marked the limits of their debt to Freud. They reject all but his description of the unconscious, and they accept that, not for the reasons for which Freud himself introduced it, but for their own reasons. Their contributions to modern literature are perhaps more symptomatic than constructive. Some value must be admitted in their unceasing attacks upon credulity, for the imagery of surrealistic poetry is often accidentally striking and effective, and the plastic representation of incongruity is a ceaseless hindrance to stuffy platitudes about the " spiritual significance of the arts."

iv

Freud's interpretation of the dream has remained an important influence. As a result of it the writer has revised his view of himself as an artist, and of his responsibility to his readers. Experimental writers expect their readers to participate in the creative act in an ingenious way. The elements of commonalty which any reader of nineteenth-century fiction may enjoy are not so easily accessible. If a writer is not merely capricious—that is, if his images are not so remote that only he knows what they mean— then the reader may discover the meanings for himself. The traditional dramatic critics speak of a suspension of judgment necessary for an acceptance of theatrical conventions. The modern reader is forced to a " suspension of censor " in order that he may explore, with his author, the devious ways of dream-consciousness.

[32] Calas, " The Meaning of Surrealism," *loc. cit.*, 390. For a brief but concise study of the sources of surrealism in nineteenth-century French literature, see Wallace Fowlie, *Age of Surrealism* (New York, 1950) .

Freud speaks of "secondary elaboration" as a means by which the censor operates with respect to a dream already completed. The reader, when he says, "This is grotesque; this is absurd," reacts in essentially the same way as the dream-self, when it remarks, "Well, after all, it's only a dream."

At this point the analogy between patient and reader breaks off. So far as adopting the analyst's point of view will help make the path to understanding simpler, the reader may do so; but he is no more interested in "curing the hero" than a reader of conventional fiction is interested in having the villain put to death or the heroine enjoy a full-dress wedding. There is a point at which the aesthetic and the scientific points of view part company. Psychoanalysis may have rich suggestions for the artist, but curing the hero is not one of them.[33]

Freud's therapy dealt with neurotic patients almost entirely, but the intellectual of our time accepted his conclusions concerning character as universally applicable, for two reasons: (1) Freud had shown in the *Psychopathology of Everyday Life* and *Wit and Its Relationship to the Unconscious* that the distinction between normal and abnormal was primarily one of degree and not of kind, and that every person was at least potentially neurotic. (2) Observation of the life around him and of the world within him led the young intellectual to much the same conclusion.

The influence of abnormal psychology upon character analysis was readily admitted. Whether the hero of our twentieth-century novel is an analyst (as in the case of Lewisohn's *The Island Within*) or a patient (as in Arthur Koestler's *Arrival and Departure*), certain conclusions about his character derive their psychological quality from the analytic environment. What we speak of as the "struggle of wills" in traditional fiction, becomes, for the "clinical novelist," a struggle against the forces of repression. What might have been considered an honorable submission to fate, or the beautiful expression of filial piety is explained as an infantile fixation or a "parental complex."[34] As a result of the introduction of psychoanalytic theory, there was a renewed interest

---

[33] Cf. Chapter VIII, for discussion of Sherwood Anderson and psychoanalysis.
[34] Thus, in May Sinclair, *The Life and Death of Harriet Frean* (New York, 1922), 97, Priscilla had fallen ill only as a means of holding her husband: It was "pure hysteria. Robin wasn't in love with her and she knew it."

in neurotics; they were regarded as a mirror of the world. The danger is that this preoccupation with the "abnormal or eccentric" does not prove anything except that people are often neurotic or abnormal. Shakespeare's fools are honorable persons, conveying important truth in the guise of nonsense, which they often found necessary because the world had closed the door on "common sense." Dostoevski's Prince Myshkin is, after all, a wise man in his way, whose sympathy and naïveté reaches depths not appreciated by those ambitious and sensible people around him. But the twentieth-century writer, instead of assuming that the normal and abnormal were not isolated types—as Freud had suggested—often took the abnormal for the normal. This pessimistic view of life was part of the tradition of revolt; perspective was frequently lost. The pessimism of the naturalist assumed that external forces left no room for individual free will; man was a plaything of these forces. The pessimism of the psychological novelist is an extension of this same naturalism. Freud explained that no fact of the mental life was without its cause. The psychological novelist would like to regard his pessimism as of a deeper dye. To some writers of his type, the search for life was more accurately a "search for death." One might explain all this by remarking that modern man held to no fixed illusions; but the larger world-negation came to adjust desire to reality. When the opportunity for social protest offered itself, many of these novelists gladly turned to it, for it at least offered an object of attack outside the self.[35]

Despite the devious course which Freudianism took after it left the clinical environment of its origins, we may sketch the main Freudian contributions to literature. (1) *The Interpretation of Dreams*, and especially the chapter on the "Dream-work," affected writers variously. It suggested the existence of an unconscious life in which patterns of conduct were not superficial, but complex. It offered the dream as a convenient summary of character-motivation, and even as a part of the plot-structure itself.

[35] In this aspect of twentieth-century fiction the popular notions of both Adler and Jung also played a role—though these were usually referred (if they were referred to anything at all) to their sources in Freudian psychology. The "inferiority complex" and the extrovert-introvert division of types were both often lumped together as "Freudian terms."

It called the attention of writers to the need for a new language—
a language based upon the devices of condensation, displacement,
multiple determination, and secondary elaboration. In so doing,
it suggested to experimentalists the idea of employing " absurdities " in their writing—that is, a repudiation of what is logical
and syntactic, for what is illogical and ungrammatic.

(2) *The Three Contributions to a Theory of Sex*, together
with other books of the time, and Freud's earlier book of *Introductory Lectures* furnished a set of psychological terms which were
often applied with more facility than judgment. Among the traditional situations which novelists have exploited for ages, the
psychological novelist made some alterations in treatment. The
parent-child relationship, if it was allowed to extend beyond the
period of adolescence and caused a subsequent disparagement of
" masculine qualities," was treated as a form of oedipus complex—
though individual writers gave this idea their own modifications.
The " eternal triangle " remained triangular, but it was often
treated as a problem of modern sex-ethics. Forms of maladjustment were often regarded as signs of ego-fixation, or narcissism.

(3) Freud's monographs on social and theological matters
had only a limited and an indirect influence. The pessimistic conclusion that social institutions, and the arts as well, were mere
illusions occasionally stimulated writers to underline their study
of modern pessimism. Waldo Frank, for example, regarded the
altering of an institution as insufficient for social change, since
institutions were, for the most part, " hampering illusions of
power and order." Freud's doctrine of the recurrence of certain
phylogenetic patterns, which he developed in *Totem and Taboo*,
influenced Thomas Mann's treatment of the Joseph story. Mann
also hopefully emphasized Freud's brief reference to the future
of analysis as a task of building and strengthening the ego by
means of making its union with culture and society more and
more attractive and its task of regulating the id correspondingly
easier.

(4) The clinical situation was itself responsible for many
incidental sub-plots and especially for satire. The idea of resistance claimed much interest both in discussions and in satires of
such discussions in literature. The transference situation was ideal

material for satire, and was generally treated satirically. The psychoanalyst was himself a new fictional type—though it is extremely doubtful that he will ever reach the status in fiction which the kindly or courageous physician has long enjoyed.

Of the many diverse influences which affected twentieth-century writing, Freud was an important one. He was, however, only a single member of a large fraternity of thinkers who had some bearing upon the thought and the fiction of the twenties. It is now our problem to estimate the diversity and the strength of Freud's influence, by examining in detail the works of a number of novelists—among them, James Joyce, D. H. Lawrence, Sherwood Anderson, Waldo Frank, Franz Kafka, and Thomas Mann.

chapter V

INFROYCE

i

The four books with which the name of Joyce has been associated give freely of their autobiographical information.[1] The ideas with which Joyce grew up, and which never left him, though he repudiated most of them, are given careful attention in *A Portrait of the Artist as a Young Man*;[2] the Dublin materials, with which he never ceased working, were first suggested in the book of short stories, *Dubliners*[3] and given detailed treatment in *Ulysses*,[4] and in *Finnegans Wake*.[5]

[1] Excluding his books of poems, slender volumes which have almost no significance for an understanding of his prose. Louis Golding, *James Joyce* (London, 1933), 9–21, and Rebecca West, *The Strange Necessity* (Garden City, New York, 1928), 1–215, have attempted to fit the poems into the Joycean "canon" and to find some relationship between them and the prose works. For Joyce's poems, see William Y. Tindall, ed., *Chamber Music* (New York, 1954).

[2] Written by 1914; published, February, 1914, through September, 1915, by Ezra Pound in *London Egoist*; published, New York, 1916, London, 1917.

[3] Written by 1907; published, London, 1914, New York, 1916.

[4] The complicated history of the publication of this book is given in Herbert Gorman, *James Joyce* (New York, 1939), 291–324. See also R. F. Roberts, "Bibliographical Notes on James Joyce's *Ulysses*," in *Colophon*, n.s., I (1936), 565–79. Perhaps the most thorough consideration of Joyce's reputation and summary of Joyce criticism is *Joyce: The Man, the work, the Reputation*, by Marvin Margalaner and Richard M. Kain (New York, 1956).

[5] Published serially to end of Part III in *Transition* I, II, VI, VII, XI, XIII,

The three major influences which these books reveal are the Catholic scholarship and Jesuit training which Joyce encountered though probably not systematically in his college life, the tradition of Irish myth and politics which was a part of the background of every thinking Irishman of his time, and a love of music, which he seems to have inherited from his father. All three of these occupied his attention throughout his life; and he never forgot or failed to use the Dublin that had given them to him. Among the minor themes which figured in the Joycean counterpoint were the death of his mother, his disillusion over his father's greatness, his self-imposed exile from Dublin, which in a sense dictated his attitude toward the life he describes in his stories, and the literary life of Dublin. The peculiar characteristic of Joyce's mind was that, though he managed to reject outwardly most of the ideas or theories which made demands on his loyalty or credulity, he never really put aside any of them; his defiant *non serviam* was always tempered by a reluctance to give up any heritage that had sufficiently impressed him. He loved the things he hated.

We can understand, therefore, the importance of the exile theme in Joyce's works. His life after 1902 was a succession of advances toward and retreats from his native city. Paris, Dublin, Zurich, Trieste, Rome, Dublin, Trieste, Zurich, Trieste, Paris: his itinerary from 1902 to 1939 reflects the restlessness of his exile. From 1904 until 1914 he alternated between Trieste and Rome, turning over in his mind the idea of *Ulysses*, quarreling with his publishers over the publication of his earlier books, and teaching languages at the Berlitz schools and at the Commercial Academy in Trieste. In 1914 Ezra Pound helped to launch Joyce's career as a published writer. Early in 1915 he moved his family to Zurich; there they were to spend over three years, until the end of the war, this time exiles in a literal sense.

These wanderings are not without importance for our study. Joyce's move to the Continent resulted in a considerable enlargement of the range of his intellectual interests. The continental flavor of Trieste intellectual life impressed him at a time when he was least inclined to respect the tradition of his native city.

XV, XVIII (1927–1929); additional sections published in nos. XXII, XXIII, XXVI, XXVII (1933–38); published, New York, 1939.

Neither the form nor the content of *Dubliners* reveals anything startling to the reader. The stories are written in the best tradition of the short story, skillfully and shrewdly describing the lives of Irish citizenry. We may, therefore, share with Paul Elmer More his amazement—though we are not obliged to share his critical obtuseness—when he first comes upon *Ulysses* and *Work in Progress.*[6] How, he asks, can a man, " capable of writing the last scene of ' The Dead ' . . . wallow in the moral slough of *Ulysses* and . . . posture through the linguistic impertinences of *Work in Progress* . . .? " [7]

There is a great difference between *Dubliners* and *Ulysses*; it is not in subject matter, for both deal with the same materials. Does the great difference lie in the " moral approach," as More would have us believe? It is partly that, and the reasons are obvious enough. Joyce is a transitional figure; his training in Irish schools, his preoccupation with Aquinian problems in ethics and aesthetics, which he gives us so vividly in *A Portrait of the Artist as a Young Man*—these form merely a part of his life. More important for an ultimate evaluation of his work was the continental influence to which he was subjected while he lived in Trieste, Rome, and Zurich. For that reason, one must see in clear outline his career in Trieste and Zurich: (1) His interest in continental matters was evidenced as early as 1901, when he reviewed favorably one of Ibsen's plays. (2) The rather slight poetry, published as *Chamber Music,*[8] reflects his earliest attempts to find an audience. (3) *Dubliners* was completed in 1907; by the time it was published, seven years later, Joyce had turned away from its form, but not from its content.

By 1907 Joyce had finished paying tribute to the spirit of his past and was busy with the work which explains his rejection of this past.[9] *A Portrait of the Artist as a Young Man* ends with

[6] Provisional title for *Finnegans Wake*, as it was published serially in *Transition*.

[7] Paul Elmer More, " James Joyce," in *American Review*, V (1935) , 130. More answers the question in his own way: *Ulysses* is the " pursuit of art as an abstraction, divorced from the responsibilities of life. . . ." Hence Joyce's career after *Dubliners* reflects the modernist's desire to scoff at moral demands on conscience and his " love of disintegration " in preference to the humanist tradition. *Ibid.*, 140–55.

[8] Published, London, 1907, New York, 1918; another slim volume, *Pomes Penyeach*, was published in Paris by Sylvia Beach in 1927.

[9] For information about the progress of this book, see Theodore Spencer's

the defiant note which was to carry Joyce through all of his subsequent intellectual experiences. "I will not serve," Stephen
says, and he means by that, that the old gods are dead for him,
that he will serve only himself. As Joyce leaves for the Continent,
he dedicates himself to a program which is clearly anticipated in
the *Portrait*: (1) to preserve himself intact; (2) to satisfy his
intellectual interests; (3) to seek the universal in art. It is not
merely the tradition which Joyce describes so painstakingly in this
book, but the attitude Stephen-Joyce adopts toward it.[10] In
Trieste, where he finished the *Portrait*, he was already engaged in
preliminary plans for *Ulysses*. The progress toward its completion
was slow and halting, and was affected by a revision of his attitude
toward form and style.

One of the many new influences to which Joyce was susceptible at the beginning of his work on *Ulysses* was psychoanalysis.
The seven years before Joyce began writing *Ulysses* were the most
fruitful early years for psychoanalysis; and both Trieste and Zurich
were important centers of the new psychology. Joyce could have
read Freud in Trieste, as he eagerly read other men who offered
him new perspectives. In the isolation of Zurich, where he lived
for more than three years, Joyce continued his writing, hostile to
too-frequent demands on his time, yet aware of the other intellectuals in his group.[11] Zurich was also the center of Jung's school
of psychoanalysis. It would be incorrect to say that Joyce was
spellbound by psychoanalysis, or preoccupied with it during his
stay in Zurich; but he must surely have known much about it.
He had at least one important connection with it. Mrs. Harold

"'Stephen Hero': the Unpublished Manuscript of James Joyce's 'A Portrait of
the Artist as a Young Man,'" in *Southern Review*, VII (1941), 174–86. *Stephen
Hero*, an earlier and much longer draft of the *Portrait*, was published in 1944; a
new edition, with additional pages, appeared in 1955. The difference from the
Portrait lies in the more extensive and complete portraits of the members of the
Dedalus family. Its principal value is the opportunity it affords for a study of the
Dublin life and background which Joyce gave up when he left for the continent.
". . . the most interesting portion of the manuscript—a very considerable portion—is
concerned with Stephen's views on art and its relation to life." *Ibid.*, 179.

[10] Emotional attributes of this attitude are treated with some penetration and
more dullness in Joyce's only published play, *Exiles*, written in Trieste, 1914–15,
performed in Zurich, 1917, published, 1918, London and New York. Cf. Bernard
Bandler II, "Joyce's Exiles," in *Hound and Horn*, VI (1933), 266–85.

[11] See Frank Budgen, *James Joyce and the Making of Ulysses* (New York,
1934). On p. 26 Budgen mentions Jung as part of the "intellectual atmosphere."
The birth of dadaism took place in Zurich in 1916.

McCormick, the only daughter of the late John D. Rockefeller, Sr., in Zurich at this time, contributed a thousand Swiss franks to Joyce's support, then later withdrew her gift because he refused to be psychoanalyzed.[12] Joyce's connection with the Zurich group, though at the most only peripheral, is nevertheless interesting because it demonstrates that he was aware of psychoanalysis, must have learned much about it, and might have been attracted by its literary possibilities.

Upon such slim evidence as this, critics have hailed Joyce's *Ulysses* and *Finnegans Wake* as literary products of the interest in psychoanalysis. Mary Colum, for example, takes the influence as a settled matter:

> . . . [the method used by Freud] is really the process followed by Joyce in the celebrated monologue of Marion Bloom with which *Ulysses* ends. . . . Joyce's new puzzling book, *Work in Progress*, is an attempt to carry the revelation of the unconscious life many stages further than in *Ulysses* . . . [he] tries to depict the whole night-life of the mind. . . . Joyce's mastery of the interior monologue is the second point in his technique in which he is likely to remain unsurpassed, and for this mastery he *undoubtedly* owes a great deal to Freud.[13]

Like Mrs. Colum, Lionel Trilling bases his remarks upon a study of internal evidence: " James Joyce, with his exploration of the numerous states of receding consciousness, with his use of words as things, a concept basic to the Freudian interpretation of dreams, with his pervading sense of the interrelation and interpenetration of all things, and, not least important, his familial themes, has *perhaps* most thoroughly and most consciously exploited Freud's ideas." [14]

Two other comments need to be considered here. Both of them are based upon the coincidence of Jung's and Joyce's residence in Zurich. Harry Levin suggests that Joyce " *could scarcely* have resisted " the influence of the Zurich school. He regards the

---

[12] Gorman, *James Joyce*, 237, 264. Gorman says that Joyce refused " flatly and angrily " to be psychoanalyzed by Doctor Jung.

[13] Mary Colum, *From These Roots* (New York, 1937) , 346–49. Italics mine.

[14] Lionel Trilling, " The Legacy of Sigmund Freud; II: Literary and Aesthetic," in *Kenyon Review*, II, 157. Italics mine.

dream work as " Joyce's license for a free association of ideas and a systematic distortion of language." [15]   The other critic is Eugene Jolas, editor of *Transition* and advocate of a new " language of the night." He was closely associated with Joyce, was the most active of the group which sponsored Joyce's experiments in writing; he was himself very much interested in psychoanalysis, and especially in the psychology of dream-interpretation. Jolas at times seems to be formulating an aesthetic mainly in order to explain and to justify Joyce's contributions to his magazine.[16] It is not at all surprising that we come across the following remark in James Laughlin's critical appendix to Dujardin's *Les Lauriers sont Coupés:* " Eugene Jolas pointed out to me not long ago that Zurich, where Joyce was living when he was planning Ulysses, was an active center of the psychoanalytic movement. Joyce *could not have failed* to be exposed to Freud or to be influenced by his studies of the unconscious. . . ." [17]

Jolas told me in August of 1943 that Joyce had known Jung quite well in Zurich and later in Paris, that Joyce knew psychoanalytic literature and that he used the suggestions of Freud's *Interpretation of Dreams* in *Finnegans Wake.* Jolas remarks elsewhere that " Joyce had a passion for the irrational manifestations of life," but that he had nothing in common with the surrealists

[15] Harry Levin, *James Joyce: a Critical Introduction* (Norfolk, Conn., 1941), 89, 185–87. Italics mine. Later Levin points to the influence of the Freudian mechanisms of dream-work and wit which seem to be developed in *Finnegans Wake:* " His neologism is the joint product of the three types of verbal wit that Freud has discriminated—condensation, displacement, allusion. . . . Through ' portmanteau words' Joyce is able to instil a Freudian undertone in his small-talk."

[16] *Transition* is noted chiefly for the serializing of *Work in Progress* in its issues, from 1927 to 1930. The magazine had begun by publishing a number of the surrealists, and for a time featured Gertrude Stein as well as Joyce. Ultimately Jolas broke off altogether from the surrealists; at no time can his philosophy of language and aesthetics be compared with surrealism. The latter numbers of *Transition* develop Jolas' own philosophy, which he calls *Vertigralism.* See his essay, " Surrealism: Ave atque Vale," in *Fantasy*, VII (1941), 23–30.

[17] Eduard Dujardin, *We'll to the Woods No More* (Norfolk, Conn., 1938), 149–50. Italics mine.

Other critics who have linked Joyce with Freud: James Douglas, review of *Ulysses*, Sunday London *Express*, May 28, 1922. The usual ranting reaction, referring to psychoanalysis as the " dirty and degraded cult . . . ," quoted by Gorman, *James Joyce*, 296. J. Middleton Murry, *New Witness*, August 4, 1922. Bernard DeVoto, " Freud's Influence on Literature," in *Saturday Review of Literature*, XX (1939), 10.

Neither Proust nor Joyce, DeVoto says, " would have written as he did without the instruments that Freud fitted to their hands. . . ." Helen V. McLean, " Freud and Literature," in *Saturday Review of Literature*, XVIII (1938), 18.

and psychoanalysts. He was very much interested in talking over and describing his dreams. The evidence Jolas offers supports the reasonable conclusion that Joyce was interested in all theories, both traditional and modern, and that he saw literary possibilities in many of them.[18]

All of these critical references would appear at the most confirmatory, at the least unnecessary, if Joyce had mentioned this influence directly in his own books.[19] No reference to any of the psychoanalysts appears before *Ulysses*; in the library scene of that novel, Stephen Dedalus refers to " Saint Thomas . . . whose gorbellied works I enjoy reading in the original, writing of incest from a stand-point different from that of the new Viennese school. . . ." (*Ulysses*, 203) This single reference [20] to psychoanalysis can scarcely be said to have settled the issue, but it does serve to include the new psychology among the matters Joyce considered. The last work, *Finnegans Wake*, contains numerous references to Freud and Jung by name and to psychoanalytic terms and theories. In Part I, he combines the names of the two men and discusses the theories to which Freud first gave printed form in 1905:

> . . . we grisly old Sykos who have done our unsmiling bit on 'alices, when they were yung and easily freudened, in the penumbra of the procuring room and what oracular comepression we have had apply to them! could . . . tell . . . that *father* in such virgated contexts is not always that undemonstrative relative (often held up to our contumacy) who

---

[18] Eugene Jolas, " My Friend James Joyce," in *Partisan Review*, VIII (1941) - 82–93.

[19] We have at present almost no letters by Joyce which concern matters of aesthetics or influence. Most of the letters printed in Gorman, *James Joyce*, are about the tedious details of publication. As David Daiches puts it, letter to Frederick J. Hoffman, November 12, 1942, " His critics friends and biographers seem to have combined in an unmentioned conspiracy to conceal Joyce's sources." The Gilbert Stuart collection of the *Letters* (New York, 1957) contains very few mentions of psychoanalysis, and those are of little consequence except for marginal insights. See, for example, the letter of June, 1921, in which he describes Jung as " the Swiss Tweedledum who is not to be confused with the Viennese Tweedledee, Dr. Freud," and complains that he " amuses himself at the expense (in every sense of the word) of ladies and gentlemen who are troubled with bees in their bonnets." (p. 166)

[20] So far as can be determined from a use of Miles L. Hanley's *Word Index to James Joyce's Ulysses* (Madison, Wis., 1937). Joyce does not mention the names of any of the " Viennese school."

settles our hashbill for us and what an innocent all-abroad's adverb such as Michaelly looks like can be suggestive of under the pudendascope and, finally, what a neurasthene nympholept, endocrine-pineal typus, of inverted parentage with a prepossessing drauma present in her past and a priapic urge for congress with agnates before cognates fundamentally is feeling for under her lubricitous meiosis when she refers with liking to some feeler she fancie's face.[21]

Joyce's references to psychoanalytic terms and concepts are numerous: he talks about " that limbopool which was his subnesciousness " (*Finnegans Wake*, 224) ; he suggests Freud's remarks about the birth trauma in the phrase, " prepping up his prepueratory " (274) ; he includes one of Adler's terms in the sentence, " Charles de Simples had an infirmierity complexe before he died a natural death " (291, n. 8) ; he describes Freud as " the lewdningbluebolteredallucktruckalltraumconductor!" (378) When Shaun defends himself against charges of incest, he says: " Somebody may perhaps hint at an aughter impression of I was wrong. No such a thing! You never make a more freudful mistake, excuse yourself! " (411) [22]

In the trial scene, in which Earwicker is accused of incest, Jaun (the same " person " as Shaun) says to the " judges ": " Would ye ken a young stepschuler of psychical chirography, the

[21] James Joyce, *Finnegans Wake* (New York, 1939) , Part I, 115. A paraphrase of the passage:

> We psychoanalysts who have soberly studied the early sexual life of children have been able to discover some surprising things about them. We can, for example, say that the father is not just the man around the house who pays the bills; we can assure you that any remark passed innocently enough in an analysis might, upon close examination, be a very important clue; finally, we can tell what a neurotic patient, a nymphomaniac of a certain type (reference to Jung's *Psychological Types*) , with an " Electra complex," is *really* thinking about when she refers to some person for whom she has a fancy.

" priapic urge for congress with agnates before cognates " suggests that the patient has some tendency toward narcissism; " present in her past " has reference to Freud's emphasis upon the persistence of infantile sexuality in adult behavior (a fact also suggested by the adjective *prepossessing*) ; " drauma " is, of course, a portmanteau word, suggesting *trauma* plus *drama*. All but two (" yung " and " of a certain typus ") of these references go back to Freud's *Three Contributions to a Theory of Sex*.

[22] The word *aughter* may be puzzling until it is noticed that Shaun is Earwicker himself, disguised in his dream (he is also Earwicker's son Kevin); *aughter*, of course, means *other* plus *daughter*.

name of Keven . . . ?" (482) Though Jerry (Shem) and not Kevin is most closely associated with Joyce in *Finnegans Wake*, it is tempting to think that Joyce is here referring to himself as a student of "psychical chirography." [23] Near the end of the trial, the dream of Earwicker comments on the effect of psychoanalysis on twentieth-century thought: "God has jest. The old order changeth and lasts like the first. Every third man has a chink in his conscience and every other woman has a jape in her mind." (486) [24]

Finally, in a dialogue which follows the "trial," Joyce refers again to psychoanalysis, in such a manner as perhaps to indicate his own relationship to it:

> You have homosexual catheis of empathy between narcissism of the expert and steatopygic invertedness. Get yourself psychoanolised!
>
> —O, begor, I want no expert nursis symaphy from yours broons quadroons and I can psoakoonaloose myself any time I want (the fog follow you all!) without your interferences or any other pigeonstealer. (522)

If it is not taking too much for granted to read into this passage Joyce's attitude toward psychoanalysis, it can be defined as follows: Joyce wishes to be "let alone"; he knows pretty well how to analyze his own character; and, wherever psychoanalysis goes, the intellectual atmosphere is befogged by terms and half-understood concepts. This goes for any other theorist who wishes to penetrate to the secret of his life.

These references in *Finnegans Wake* [25] may seem to suggest

---

[23] The word *stepschuler* may suggest that Joyce considers psychoanalysis as a "second intellectual father," acquired through his experiences in Trieste and Zurich.

[24] These words are spoken by one of the "judges," who then proceeds to cross-question Shaun-Earwicker in a manner that suggests a burlesque of the doctor-patient relationship. The "judge" finds himself pleased with the questioning: "Again I am deliciated by the picaresqueness of your irmages." The word *irmages* is probably a combination of *Irma* and *images*; Freud's *Interpretation of Dreams* refers constantly to a dream which he himself experienced, the dream of "Irma's injection." See *Interpretation of Dreams*, Chapter II, pp. 80–102. In a combination of legal and psychoanalytic phraseology the "judge" advises his patient-defendant: "Put from your mind that and take on trust this. The next word depends on your answer." *Finnegans Wake*, 487.

[25] The list is by no means exhausted. See also Part I, 119, 123, 173, 178, 187; II, 271, 290, 295, 299, 337, 363; III, 417, 422, 439, 460, 470, 474, 476, 480, 481, 515,

that Joyce was following psychoanalysis as the only legitimate influence of his literary career. This is not at all true. Joyce had many interests, and each of them played some role in determining the unusual character of his two last books. But the mention of psychoanalysis is not merely *incidental* to the structure of *Finnegans Wake*. Among the several theories that helped to determine the form of that work were psychoanalysis and Vico's cyclical theory of history.

What is the actual place of psychoanalysis in Joyce's literary career? (1) We are fairly certain that Joyce had or admitted no knowledge of Freud or psychoanalysis before he left Dublin on his tour of continental cities. (2) We have some biographical data to assure us that he encountered psychoanalysis, first casually in Trieste, then more thoroughly in Zurich. (3) From internal evidence, we can assert that some time during the writing of *Ulysses* he learned about psychoanalysis, and that by 1922 he had read almost all of the works of Freud and some of the works of Jung. It is also clear that his was not a superficial knowledge, for his references to psychoanalysis in *Finnegans Wake* presuppose a familiarity with terms and concepts unusual for the layman. There is a very striking correspondence between Joyce's shift to literary experiment and his spiritual renunciation of his earlier tradition. In other words, Joyce's search for " new gods " convinced him that a new approach in literature was also necessary.

ii

This new approach was no invention of Joyce's. In 1887 Eduard Dujardin had written the first " stream-of-consciousness " novel, *Les Lauriers sont Coupés*.[26] Forty-four years after the fact, Du-

---

524, 525, 526, 527; IV, 623. A passage on p. 515 is especially interesting for critics: " Happily you were not quite so successful in the process verbal whereby you would sublimate your blepharospasmockical suppressions, it seems? " I take this to mean: Perhaps (and fortunately too—*haply* plus *happily*) the author has not been too successful in disguising by his verbal tricks Earwicker's repressed psychic life. If Joyce had been entirely successful, no critic would have managed to explain the book.

[26] Since Joyce's interest in the book was announced it has appeared in an English translation by Stuart Gilbert under the title *We'll to the Woods No More*. Joyce read Dujardin's novel for the first time in 1917.

jardin explained what he had done. The "interior monologue," as he designated it,

> . . . is the speech of a character in a scene, having for its object the direct introduction of the reader into the interior life of the character, without any interventions in the way of explanations or commentary on the part of the author; like other monologues, it has *theoretically* no hearers and is not spoken. But it differs from the traditional monologue in these respects: in the matter of content, it is the expression of the most intimate thoughts, those which lie nearest the unconscious; in its nature it is a speech which precedes logical organization, reproducing the intimate thoughts just as they are born and just as they come; as for form, it employs direct sentences reduced to the syntactical minimum; thus in general it fulfills the same requirements which we make today for poetry . . .[27]

This is a clear enough statement of the author's intention. But several things in it should be pointed out: (1) the close analogy with the "traditional monologue"; (2) the characterization of the monologue as the "*speech* of a character in a scene"—as though the only necessary difference were that a character talk to himself, instead of to others; (3) Dujardin's insistence that the thoughts are "those which lie nearest the unconscious," an assertion which is not borne out in his practice. Most of the thoughts in his novel lie remarkably close to the conscious, so close indeed that when the hero turns to talk to his friend Charvainne, the transition from monologue to dialogue is slight and offers little if any distinction between the two levels.

As a matter of fact, writers and critics are both confused by the idea of "interior monologue" and the "stream of consciousness." One fundamental distinction it does make, and this Dujardin has already made clear: the distinction between the external speech of average, sane persons and the thought which underlies this speech, or which exists quite independent of any speech at all. But the stream of consciousness is not a sharp enough cate-

---

[27] *Ibid.,* 153–54. Quoted by Laughlin in his critical appendix. The original is in Eduard Dujardin, *Le Monologue intérieur: son apparition, ses origines, sa place dans l'oeuvre de James Joyce* (Paris, 1931).

gory to include all the diverse forms of writing which it ordinarily labels. Further classification should be made, so that one can see on first examination what a particular example of the "school" purports to do. First of all, the interior monologue is a natural stylistic companion of the psychological novel. It is, at any rate, based on the assumption that personality is not static and that motivation may be explored in the psychic life of a character as well as, or instead of, expressed in a presentation of his overt acts or speech. "The realization, which this technique implies, of the fact that personality is in constant state of unstable equilibrium, that a mood is never anything static but a fluid pattern, 'mixing memory with desire,' marks an important new development in the tradition of psychological fiction. . . ." [28]

Writers who were aware of modern psychology frequently altered their conception of personal dynamics. For them, any given action cannot be defined or represented simply; the niceties of social conduct such as those described in the traditional novel appeared to them superficial. They needed some instrument that would enable them to penetrate beneath the consciousness of their characters. They felt that traditional fiction, no matter how complex it tried to be, managed only to classify its characters—and, in their estimation, "to classify was to condemn."

The techniques employed in the stream-of-consciousness novel are designed to capture for us the sources of human behavior it is the task of the mind to keep from consciousness. For the coherence of our controlled waking lives, it wishes to substitute the incoherence of our psychic lives.

Its defining feature is exploitation of the element of incoherence in our conscious process. This incoherence characterizes both our normal and our abnormal states of mind. The natural association of ideas is extremely freakish. Our psyche is such an imperfectly integrated bundle of memories, sensa-

---

[28] David Daiches, *The Novel and the Modern World* (Chicago, 1939), 26. In recent studies of the stream-of-consciousness novel, the following useful distinction is made: stream-of-consciousness refers to the *type* of novel in which several techniques are used to explore various levels of consciousness; the most important of these is the interior monologue. See Melvin J. Friedman, *Stream of Consciousness* (New Haven, Conn., 1955), and Robert Humphrey, *Stream of Consciousness in the Modern Novel* (Berkeley, Calif., 1954).

tions, and impulses, that unless sternly controlled by some dominating motive it is likely to be at the mercy of every stray wind of suggestion.[29]

When we reflect that the two essential governors of all social life, space and time, are an important part of conscious control, we can see that the stream-of-consciousness novel all but upsets two of the three pillars of fictional representation.[30] No conscious action is conceivable except within the boundaries of space and time. As a matter of fact, when we cease being aware of them, we are *unconscious.* Stream-of-consciousness fiction does not do away with space-time; for even a stream flows either rapidly or slowly, and exists in space. A psychic stream must likewise exist in both space and time. But both of these fundamental categories are now subsidiary to the study of complex human behavior; and space-time schemes are substituted for the accepted and recognized pattern of ordinary waking life.

It seems that the stream-of-consciousness novel has been described too narrowly, with too little attention to its variants. The expression used does not account satisfactorily for the varying degrees of depth to which the new techniques commit us. The designation " stream of consciousness " does not really clarify the wide variety of uses to which it is allegedly put. There are actually at least four levels of writing, and each has its own system of referenfes to space and time: [31]

(1) The *traditional,* which applies readily all of the accepted conscious controls and uses the recognizable systems of communication it is our custom to study and serve. Within the bounds of this manner of writing all, or almost all, types of behavior can be described, but they must be labeled, or at least inferred within the range of ordinary comprehension. Thus, when Samuel Butler speaks of Ernest Pontifex's report to his parents of his life at school, he describes a situation which on another level might be

[29] Joseph Warren Beach, *The Twentieth Century Novel* (New York, 1932) , 517.

[30] The third, *character,* is the point of departure for the psychological novelist; he is willing, therefore, to suspend the other two, or to revaluate them, because he feels that the traditional novelist has failed in adequately reproducing the third.

[31] There are other techniques, competently discussed by Melvin Friedman in *Stream of Consciousness,* internal analysis and sensory impression among them. See Friedman, chapter 1.

presented in an altogether different manner: " Here Ernest's unconscious self took the matter up and made a resistance to which his conscious self was unequal, by tumbling him off his chair in a fit of fainting."[32] This type of novel is, of course, capable of much complexity of analysis, especially if it employs variations of the Jamesian " central intelligence." But it is still not a stream-of-consciousness novel; the internal analysis of characters' minds remains within the range of objective narrative. Perhaps the technique of internal analysis comes closest in the fiction of Virginia Woolf to the margin of conscious attention.

(2) The level of the " preconscious "[33]—or, of " conscious revery "; the chief difference from logical discourse is its greater fluidity and its less obvious attachment to the rules of sentence structure and word-meanings. This is the " interior monologue " of Eduard Dujardin's novel: " The *carriage moving along the streets*. . . . A single one in the unnumbered host of lives, thus I go my way, one by distinction among the rest; and so the Now, and Here *this hour striking*, this world of life, all these come to being within me. . . ."[34] It is the " day-dream," and its frame of reference is always the working world. All but a few of the modern novels employ it, at one time or another, to indicate a release from the unconscious, or to bring the reader back, for a moment, to a recognizable world.[35] On this level the time-space reference is obscure, but the character frequently refers both to the time of day and to objects in space, borrowing the traditional notions of both time and space for the purpose of identification.

(3) The level of the " subconscious "—in which the conscious mind releases much of its control over the will. Sometimes this control seems all but suspended, but it is nevertheless present and determines much of the content, if not precisely the direction, of the flow of thought.[36] and image. The psychoanalytic parallel may

---

[32] Quoted from *The Way of All Flesh*, by Beach, *The Twentieth Century Novel* (New York, 1932), 33.

[33] See above, pp. 28–29, for Freud's explanation of the " Preconscious." Cf. Freud's " The Relation of the Poet to Day-Dreaming," *loc. cit.*, 173–83.

[34] Dujardin, *We'll to the Woods No More*, 109. Italics mine.

[35] See, for example, Conrad Aiken, *Blue Voyage* (New York, 1927), 10–13: Demarest's encounter with the American businessman on shipboard.

[36] The use of the term subconscious is purely arbitrary here, and does not argue a distinction between subconscious and unconscious in psychoanalysis.

be found in the analyst's "benevolent despotism" over the patient's reminiscences. Here the dream is often effectively employed, as it is in therapy, but the flow of the psychic life is not governed by the mechanisms of the dream-work. Since consciousness is relatively remote, some substitute must be furnished for the rational space-time continuum. This substitute is usually of the author's own suggestion, and a wide variety of ingenious devices —some effective, some merely artificial—are employed to give the reader clues about the surroundings. Perhaps the best examples of writing on this level are William Faulkner's *As I Lay Dying* and *The Sound and the Fury*.

(4) The level of the "unconscious"—in which the literary style and content both attempt to break completely from rational control and to approximate the behavior of the psychical unconscious. In this last case, rational controls are present, though they appear in the form of a censor, and their function is primarily to distort rather than to impede the flow of unconscious expression. On this level, the mechanisms of the dream-work are particularly effective, and any reference to actual time or space comes in the form of what Freud has called "secondary elaboration." The best example of this form is, of course, Joyce's *Finnegans Wake*, though Conrad Aiken's *Great Circle* [37] sometimes employs the language of the dream for its effects.

Though the stream-of-consciousness novel existed long before Freud's work on the dream or his subsequent statements about the unconscious, it is his "depth psychology" which has been responsible for the variations upon an original and somewhat limited form. It is possible to measure the *position* of any given fictional "stream," with reference to both consciousness and unconsciousness.

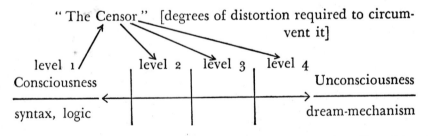

"The Censor" [degrees of distortion required to circumvent it]

level 1   level 2   level 3   level 4
Consciousness   Unconsciousness
syntax, logic   dream-mechanism

----

[37] 86–181. It may be said that the great proportion of surrealist writing (especially surrealist poetry) is produced on this level.

It is also possible to determine the accuracy of a literary representation of the psychic life; this does not imply that an accurate
transcription of the psyche is necessarily great, or even good, art.
The study of the stream of consciousness raises a question
.which is of some aesthetic importance. It concerns the position
of the analyst in relation to the legitimate role of the artist. If
there were no distinctions between the fields of psychology and
art, the accurate transcript of the therapeutic situation—a psychoanalytic " case history "—would also be great art. That this cannot
be true Freud has himself seen clearly: " In considering dreams
reported by a poet one may often assume that he has excluded
from the report those details which he perceived as disturbing and
which he considered unessential." [38] This is a caution for all good
analysts who may be fooled into accepting the dream reports of
capricious artists. In it lies the key to the aesthetic problem with
which we are concerned. A " completely accurate " dream report
may not be as dull as a market report, but it certainly does not
qualify as good writing. We may answer the question in summary:

> The psychoanalyst and the artist may both use the dream—or
> other approaches to the unconscious—as legitimate materials.
> But the purpose of one is essentially different from that of
> the other. The psychoanalyst is interested in sober fact; the
> artist, in imaginative elaboration. Whereas the one may re-
> gard transference-love as a danger or a barrier to " the cure,"
> the other may look upon it as material for satire or tragedy.
> But the fact still remains that the artist has borrowed his
> tools from the scientist; and wild, indiscriminate fury, even
> though it may be called divine, does not produce great art.

One final, related question is appropriate. To what extent
may obscurity serve to embellish art, and at what point does it
cease to be the expression of obscurity and become mere obscurity
of expression? Shall we dismiss a work simply because it is unintelligible? When an artist employs a device which according to
him is a means of revealing the unconscious, his work is usually
accompanied by commentary and explication—just as the patient's
dream requires considerable explanation and interpretation be-

[38] *Interpretation of Dreams*, 379.

fore it becomes, not conscious (for the manifest dream is conscious, though absurd to the waking mind) , but intelligible. It
may be that interpretation and comment are indispensable accom-
panists of experimental writing, at least until the means of such
interpretation becomes a part of the reader's own mental equipment. This may explain, in some part, why so many experimental
writers append notes to their works, or why the appearance of
Work in Progress in the pages of *Transition* provoked a collection
of explanatory essays, some eight years before Joyce's work appeared in completed form.[39] Such explanation may be both legitimate and valid; the essential aesthetic judgments remain to be
administered once the work is finally brought into conscious
awareness. The two questions pertinent to all works of art are
then applicable here as well: (1) Has the artist understood his
materials, and has he used them wisely and well? (2) Did the
method employed have an aesthetic significance which justified its
being used? In short, could not the artist have employed other
materials to better advantage? In the case of Joyce, we can at
least attempt to answer the first of these questions.

iii

Ulysses is not a document of the unconscious. It is a highly individualized, objective statement, with narrative continuity and
rigid plot structure. In it are to be found all the levels of writing,
from the traditional to the unconscious. But the salient aesthetic
fact is its great emphasis upon the interior world as the external
world impinges upon it. Having once decided to forsake the
ordinary regulations for a fixed narrative, Joyce is obliged to turn
to his own inventiveness for substitutes. There are traces of Dujardin's influence, as in the first episode, where we find Stephen,
Buck Mulligan, and Haines at breakfast, and later on the beach.
Here is an explicit statement of theme: Telemachus at home, un-
happy, plagued by guilt of conscience, ready to embark on a search
for he knows not what.

The details of the day (June 16, 1904) are neither moving

[39] Samuel Beckett *et al.*, *Our Exagmination Round His Factification for
Incamination of Work in Progress* (Paris, 1929) .

nor tragic. To all appearances, it is an ordinary day, beginning at eight in the morning in the Martello tower where Stephen is lodging, and ending between three and four in the morning of the next day in the house of Leopold Bloom, canvasser of ads, and cuckold to a concert singer. What has happened? [40] Stephen collects his pay from his master at the school, wanders into the newspaper office to deliver a letter, is next seen in the library, explaining his theory of Shakespeare's *Hamlet*, wanders through the book shops, where he spies his sister Dilly, reappears in the maternity hospital where for the first time he speaks with his " spiritual father," Bloom, then leaves for a riotous round of the pubs, has an adventure in a bawdyhouse, and is taken in tow by Bloom, who offers to put him up for the night. Bloom begins the day by feeding his wife, his cat and himself, goes to the funeral of Paddy Dignam, from there to the newspaper office on official business, has lunch, hunts for a book for his wife, wanders into the Ormond bar to write a letter to Martha Clifford, his sad compensation for cuckoldry, runs against Irish patriotism and braggadocio in Barney Kiernan's tavern, flirts with Gerty McDowell at the beach, goes to the maternity hospital, trails Stephen from there to the brothel, takes him under his care and escorts him to the house of Bloom where they have a cup of cocoa and discourse on various subjects without much common interest; and finally, having failed to induce Stephen to stay the night, crawls into bed beside Molly Bloom, not the first who has shared that bed in those hours.

The drama, however, is one of inner conflict: the two men are portrayed against a complex spiritual and physical background. It is a narrative of inner states objectively treated. Throughout the day the minds of Stephen and Bloom wander—that is, their states of consciousness vacillate from full possession to revery to unconscious fantasy and hallucination.

Since *Ulysses* explores the states of mind below consciousness, plot structure needs to be indicated in devious ways; that is, it

[40] There are many summaries of *Ulysses*, to which the reader may be referred: Stuart Gilbert, *James Joyce's Ulysses; a Study* (New York, 1934) ; Richard Kain, *Fabulous Voyager* (Chicago, 1947) ; see also Richard Ellmann, " The Backgrounds of *Ulysses*," *Kenyon Review*, XVI (Summer, 1954) , 337–86, and Hugh Kenner, *Dublin's Joyce* (Bloomington, Ind., 1956) ; Philip Toynbee's " A Study of James Joyce's *Ulysses*," in Seon Givens, ed., *James Joyce: Two Decades of Criticism* (New York, 1948) , 243–84, is especially valuable.

must not intrude too obviously upon the consciousness of the reader. One perceives the continuity of the narrative by catching the repetition of motifs as they reappear in later episodes. The comic theme of the cake of soap, which Bloom shifts from pocket to pocket during the day, and finally, in the " Ithaca " episode, takes out and uses, is intended as a sort of minor odyssey, and its connection with Bloom's emotional life is important for Joyce's study of his character. Similarly, the pamphlet announcing the arrival of J. Alexander Dowie, American evangelist, and the news of the sinking of the *General Slocum*, recur infrequently and inconspicuously in subsequent episodes. The former is also a clue to the time sequence, for it has been crumpled up and thrown into the river, and it finds its way, by the end of the narrative, to the bay and out into the sea. Joyce also employs word motifs which, as they are recombined in the subconscious mind, reappear in altered form in later episodes. Such, for example, is the confusion in Bloom's mind between *Beaufoy* (Philip Beaufoy, whose prize story he has read earlier in the day) with *Purefoy* (Mrs. Mina Purefoy, who lies in the hospital, awaiting her nth child). Thus the odyssey of Bloom rests upon tenuous and accidental combinations of words; each time a word recurs, it is added to the psychical context of the moment and a mutual influence takes place which redirects Bloom's intention and subsequently his action.[41]

The demands of such intensity of narration (768 pages, covering some fifteen or sixteen hours) are so great that space and time are subjected to the pressure of the psychic world. Space values are often completely suspended, and simultaneity takes the place of conjunction. Time subserves interest, expands and contracts in accordance with the demands of the moment—until it is completely suspended in the hallucination of the nighttown scene.

In *Ulysses* Joyce is concerned chiefly with the full development of character; he insists upon being impartial and objective, and refuses to insert the ordinary clues to development, since he believes it is the reader's obligation to find common interests in the mind processes of Bloom and Stephen. Such characterization relies upon depth of consciousness and consistency of inner states

[41] Joyce, *Ulysses*, 156, 366. Cf. Hanley, *Word Index to James Joyce's Ulysses*, 391–92.

rather than upon equilibrium between external action and intention. The level of both conscious and unconscious thought determines the literary style of any single episode. Thus, in the opening episode, character is presented in the traditional manner, the adjectives and adverbs supplied by the author, the dialogue offered in the ordinary fashion as the fictional *modus operandi:* " Stately, plump Buck Mulligan came from the stairhead, bearing a bowl of lather on which a mirror and a razor lay crossed. A yellow dressing gown, ungirdled, was sustained gently behind him by the mild morning air." *(Ulysses,* 5)

In the " Proteus " episode Stephen, alone, allows his mind to wander over notions which are part of his own psychic life. Things are no longer objectively determined by the author's control but suggest mental associations belonging to the subliminal world of the character. " The cords of all link back, strandentwining cable of all flesh. That is why mystic monks. Will you be as gods? Gaze in your omphalos. Hello. Kinch here. Put me on to Edenville. Alpha, alpha: nought, nought one." For the moment, Stephen's eyes are closed, and space and time have been annihilated. Psychic values overpower objective things. Words are treated as things. " Where is poor dear Arius to try conclusions? Warring his life long on the contransmagnificandjewbangtantiality. Illstarred heresiarch." (39)

In the " Calypso " episode we encounter the mind (this time, of Bloom) on the level of the preconscious. External objects are close to consciousness and suggest a train of thought just below the conscious awareness of everyday life. Since Bloom is an ordinary man and since he is occupied with the quite usual business of getting breakfast, the emphasis is not deep or tragic; the speculation is trivial: " They call him stupid. They understand what we say better than we understand them. She understands all she wants to. Vindictive too. Wonder what I look to her. Height of a tower? No, she can jump me." (55)

This monologue about the nature of " catness " is notable for its immediate intelligibility and for its looseness of thought sequence: the shift of pronoun antecedents is Bloom's own—*they* (meaning people generally, the popular estimate) to *they* (referring to cats and their relations with humans) . For the most part

Bloom's monologue is of this character. In the " Hades " episode, he is riding in the funeral carriage with Stephen's father and others, when he suddenly spies his rival, Blazes Boylan, and is confused and embarrassed. He tries to cover up his confusion by looking down at his nails and recalling Molly's body:

> Mr. Bloom reviewed the nails of his left hand, then those of his right hand. The nails, yes. Is there anything more in him that they she sees? Fascination. Worst man in Dublin. That keeps him alive. They sometimes feel what a person is. In-stinct. But a type like that. My nails. I am just looking at them: well pared. And after: thinking alone. Body getting a bit softy. I would notice that from remembering. What causes that I suppose the skin can't contract quickly enough when the flesh falls off. But the shape is there. The shape is there still. Shoulders. Hips. Plump. Night of the dance dressing. Shift stuck between the cheeks behind. (91)

Here Bloom's preoccupation with his own thoughts is more in-tense and his motives are mixed. Hence the shifts of idea are more rapid, as though Bloom were shying away from something he does not want to admit. Throughout the passage one notices the projection of his own inadequacy to the looseness of the female, the search for an adequate rationalization of his own position. His attention seeks an object remote from the disturbance which the sight of Boylan has caused. But Boylan is always there; never mentioned directly, he nevertheless dictates the nature of Bloom's remarks about his own appearance. The monologue is a reflection of Bloom's disturbed mind and an effort to evade the task of facing directly the cause of the disturbance. Face the facts? That is impossible when the facts are facing you. The primary object is to avoid a direct clash with the facts; to think them over calmly when one is far away from them—better not to think of them at all, or to disguise them in trivial speculations about one's dress and figure.

These are instances of " conscious revery "; but Bloom also has his moments when circumstances require a deeper mono-logue. Such is the case in the " Sirens " episode, in which he, in search of Martin Cunningham, stops at a pub to write a letter to Martha Clifford. He sits down, looking at the white letterpaper:

Blank face [the paper]. Virgin, should say [paper confused with Martha Clifford]: or fingered only. Write something on it: page. If not what becomes of them [shift to thoughts about frustrated women]? Decline, despair. Keeps them young [Sex]. Even admire themselves [Loose women]. See. Play on her. Lip blow. Body of white woman, a flute alive [Musical image for sex]. Blow gentle. Loud. Three holes, all women. Goddess I didn't see. They want it: not too much polite [The image abandoned]. That's why he [Boylan] gets them. Gold in your pocket, brass in your face. With look to look: songs without words. Molly that hurdygurdy boy. She knew he meant the monkey was sick. Or because so like the Spanish. Understand animals too that way. Solomon did. Gift of nature.

Ventriloquise. My lips closed. Think in my stom. What?

Will? You? I. Want. You. To. (281)

The rationalization of the " Hades " passage continues here, but there is a more fluid expression, a freer flow of images, less awareness of external objects. The punctuation of the last line is necessary to indicate pauses, a desire to contemplate fully the idea indicated by the context. There is less attention to trivial distractions, a greater willingness to submit them to the preoccupations of his inner self. (He is here picturing Molly, eager to submit to Boylan's will.)

It is in the " Circe " episode that Joyce most closely approximates the frame of psychological reference known as the unconscious. Mr. Middleton Murry refers to this episode as the " Walpurgisnacht " of *Ulysses*, and Gilbert analyzes the theme as black magic and hallucination.[42] Stephen has broken away from the maternity hospital, and, acting upon a suggestion from his friends, determines to spend the night in the pubs and brothels. Bloom, his paternal instinct aroused through unconscious association of Stephen with his dead son Rudy, follows him and finally locates him in the house of Bella Cohen. The state of hallucination is induced in Bloom by exhaustion, in Stephen by alcohol. Under these influences, both Bloom and Stephen have visions, in which

[42] Gilbert, *James Joyce's Ulysses*, 299.

the past merges with present and future, and the unconscious wishes and anxieties of each are given form in disguising images. All incidents of the day combine in disguise with several of the past; the repressed guilt feeling of both Stephen and Bloom is now expressed in traumatic drama. Stephen appears as Cardinal Primate, Bloom as Lord Mayor of Dublin. The soap appears in the charade, as does the druggist who gave it to Bloom. All of the social theories which Bloom timidly suggested in the " Cyclops " scene are now dramatized in Bloom's unconscious. In the course of this fantastic scene, Joyce summarizes all previous episodes in a litany chant, which the " Daughters of Erin " recite. (488) Alexander Dowie, who has appeared previously only in a pamphlet and a billboard notice, now takes form in the Bloom-Stephen unconscious as a hallucinatory Elijah: " No yapping, if you please, in this booth . . . Florry Christ, Stephen Christ, Zoe Christ, Bloom Christ, Kitty Christ, Lynch Christ, it's up to you to sense that cosmic force. Have we cold feet about the cosmos? No. Be on the side of the angels. Be a prism. . . ." (496–97)

Bloom's father appears, the symbol of shame in Bloom's unconscious, and Stephen's mother, whose fancied grudge against Stephen forms one of the minor guilt-motifs throughout the day, renews her complaint, acting as Stephen's conscience. Inversion of sex roles takes places between Bella Cohen, the whore-mistress (who becomes " Bello ") and masochistic Bloom. (517 ff.)

In all of this several important points are clear: (1) the hallucinations are inevitably composed of distortions of the day's incidents, some of them apparently trivial, others of some importance to both Stephen Dedalus and Leopold Bloom; [43] (2) complexes and fears, inadequacies of personality, are all dramatized in terms of their effects upon the unconscious; (3) despite the dramatic form, the language is adjusted to the intensity of the unconscious situation. Though Joyce did not need any study of psychoanalysis in order to represent this nighttown scene, he has obviously availed himself here of several psychoanalytical facts. The scene

---

[43] The "transvaluation of psychic values" of which Freud speaks, *Interpretation of Dreams*, 285–88, is here well developed. Thus such trivial matters as the cake of soap and the evangelist are endowed with an absurdly high importance, out of proportion to their trivial place in the events of the day. In fact, the soap, the evangelist, and other ostensibly insignificant details enjoy an accidental importance throughout the book.

is not simply "black magic"; its use of filial-sexual themes, of burdens of conscience, of masochism in the Bello-Bloom incident, all point to an understanding of the unconscious, and a literary representation of repressed materials which subsist within it.

Molly Bloom's forty-four page revery, on the other hand, does not approximate the language of the unconscious. Indeed, she is very much awake and very much alive. However, it should be noted that for her the dividing line between wish and its conscious satisfaction is slight and ineffective. She may be regarded as a literary demonstration of naïve desire, whose ease of satisfaction argues a freedom from restraint uncommon in society but secretly longed for by many. The absence of punctuation points to a release from the slight hold which the social amenities ordinarily have upon her. In contrast to Bloom's pizzicato musings Molly's mind flows through present and past without pause. It is readily fed by the sights and sounds of the night, and only when she has finally settled down for a night's sleep does it relax from the holds of her bodily interests. Hence, though the device of one continuous, loose sentence is admirably suited to the moment, there is nothing particularly unusual about the style; nor is it difficult to follow the trend of her thought, since the one theme, the "universal Yes," dominates it at all times.

iv

The dream of Humphrey Chimpden Earwicker is, however, a complete panorama of unconscious life. Here are employed all of the devices which Freud explained in chapter seven of *The Interpretation of Dreams*. But *Finnegans Wake* is no mere transcript of a dream. In fact, it is a whole series of dreams, varying in their psychic intensity, changing their object repeatedly and encompassing the entire life of man. The materials of H. C. E.'s "dream day" are only a small part of the whole. Joyce's store of learning and his preoccupation with the exile themes of his entire life allow one to believe that Joyce himself shares the dream state with Earwicker: actually, Joyce is Jerry, the "penman" twin of Kevin. The inclusion of so much material which could not have been the part of even such an exceptional tavernkeeper as Earwicker is explained on two accounts: (1) The dream bears reference to certain primitive symbolic survivals in the unconscious, archaic symbols which persist through the centuries and are the common heritage of all peoples. This is a convenient peg on which to hang (2) the cyclical theory of history, which is the contribution of Vico, among others, to Earwicker's dream.

In other words, Earwicker is the common representative of all men, " Here Comes Everybody " (32), whose unconscious dream life proceeds " In the name of the former and of the latter and of their holocaust. Allmen " (419). The " Vico road " which this dream takes—here the reference is to an actual road near the site of Earwicker's place of business—corresponds to a historical pattern of three cycles, in which man passes from primitive to complex life to dissolution and thence back to his primitive beginnings:

> In the beginning was the thunder: the thunder set free Religion, in its most objective and unphilosophical form—idolatrous animism: Religion produced Society, and the first social men were the cave-dwellers, taking refuge from a passionate Nature: this primitive family life receives its first impulse towards development from the arrival of terrified vagabonds: admitted, they are the first slaves: growing stronger, they exact agrarian concessions, and a despotism has evolved into a primitive feudalism: the cave becomes a city, and the feudal system a democracy: then an anarchy: this is corrected by a return to monarchy: the last stage is a tendency towards interdestruction: the nations are dispersed, and the Phoenix of Society arises out of their ashes.[44]

The author has justifiably taken liberties with the dream only as he has imposed an alien theory upon the mind of an average man—only to prove that this average man is, when least disturbed by the incidents of his average day, a prototype of all men. For the psychological basis of this blending of myth with dream content, Joyce has gone to Jung's concept of the " collective unconscious "; for the mechanisms of the dream mind he relies entirely upon Freud. As in the case of *Ulysses*, Joyce has scattered clues which

[44] Beckett *et al., Our Exagmination,* 5.

enable the reader to mark his course. One such is Earwicker's stammering; another, the incessant play on the word *Guinness*; a third, a series of refrains which though constantly distorted in the course of the dream work, retain their original connection with the whole.

This, then, is the stream of unconsciousness method in its most thorough literary application. We have already observed that the latent dream content (the unconscious source of dream thoughts and wishes) goes through a wide variety of changes and disguises as it seeks expression in the manifest dream. The devices of condensation, displacement, and dramatization are all present here, but the real emphasis is upon the *power of words* to evoke dream images and to stand in the place of the visual content, so strong and so necessary in the actual dream. In the " Circe " episode of *Ulysses*, the repressed wishes and fears of Stephen and Bloom are dramatized; stage directions furnish the latent content with adequate visual emphasis. Here *words* are treated as *things*, and sounds take the place of visual images in all cases in which the latter are not sufficiently served by the dream situation itself. Here also Joyce's immense learning in foreign languages comes to his aid. It affords him an opportunity to subscribe to one of the dream's language habits—the tendency to substitute the etymological meaning of a word for its present meaning, if the latter is too abstract for adequate representation. The following, cited by Margaret Schlauch, is an illustration of this device in operation: the " gracehoper " has a " ' pair of findlestilts to supplant him ' [in this case] the writer reminds us of the root-meaning of ' subplant ' as ' to plant under,' rather than the modern ' supplant.' " [45]

The effectiveness of " the word " as a means of combining the dream-life of Earwicker with the racial history of man is nowhere better demonstrated than in the " Anna Livia Plurabelle " chapter. (196–216). Here we are given the impression of the flow of a river (the Liffey) from its source to its juncture with the sea through the gossip of two women who wash clothes on its banks; the story of a young girl growing old; the concentration—through semantic shift—of all the river names of the world; and the symbol

[45] Margaret Schlauch, " The Language of James Joyce," in *Science and Society*, III (1939), 486.

of the elm and the stone, which persist thereafter in the text to signify life and death.

The purpose of *Finnegans Wake* is clearly to render dream-life into words. Miss Schlauch considers the purpose successfully accomplished:

> For this unique task it seems to me that the linguistic medium chosen is eminently appropriate. It is a symbolic medium. The language of polysemantic verbalism achieves an effect *comparable* to the multiple imagery of a dream, although it uses speech as dreams cannot do.[46] Just so an innocent narrator of a dream, no doubt unwittingly, reveals a whole world of connotations to a trained psychoanalyst listening to him.[47]

The linguistic habits of the dream-life, united under the terms *condensation* and *displacement,* are all abundantly revealed in Joyce's work. The ambiguity of a word serves the purposes of condensation, and the manifest dream is therefore likely to contain many examples of what Miss Schlauch has called " polysemantic verbalism." Puns and portmanteau words are no strangers to the dream, as Freud has abundantly shown; they constitute one of Joyce's chief devices: " And of course all chimed *din width* the *eatmost* boviality." and " *Eins* within a *space* and a *wearywide* space it *wast ere wohned* a Mookse " (58). In the latter passage, the combined use of modern English, middle English, and German can be noted. The dream, incapable of accommodating abstractions, converts *in medias res* into " in midias reeds " (158); in another instance it uses the same devices to convert a religious line (the first line of the *Confiteor*) into a disguised sexual reference:

---

[46] This is not entirely the case. Dialogue does take place in the dream, and speeches can be reproduced, though they do not represent any actual intellectual activity in the dream.

[47] Schlauch, " The Language of James Joyce," *loc. cit.,* 487–88; cf. Prescott, *The Poetic Mind,* 304–15; Michael Stuart, " Mr. Joyce's Word-Creatures," in *Symposium,* II (1931), 459–67. Carola Giedion-Welcher, " Work in Progress: a Linguistic Experiment by James Joyce," in *Transition,* XIX-XX, 174–83; Archibald A. Hill, " A Philologist Looks at *Finnegans Wake,*" in *Virginia Quarterly Review,* XV (1939), 650–56. Cf. the complaint of Sean O'Faolain, in " Almost Music," in *Hound and Horn,* II (1929), 178–80 (a review of " Anna Livia Plurabelle "), and the objections of Professor Stoll, *From Shakespeare to Joyce.*

> mea culpa   mea culpa
> May he colp, may he colp her,
>   mea maxima   culpa
> may he mixandmass colp her! (238)

The Irish term for whiskey (the word which awakens Finnegan) is used in a double sense in the line, " usquebauched the ersewild aleconner " (319), which may be interpreted to mean " the wild [or erstwhile, or homosexual] Irishman O'Connor debauched with whiskey [Usqueadbaugh]." When Jaun arrives at the convent to deliver his " mock sermon " the girls make " a tremendous girls-fuss over him pellmale " (430). Throughout, lines from Shakespeare are distorted in the dream-work: " Where it is nobler in the main to supper than the boys and errors of outrager's virtue." (434).[48] At times the play on syllables is such as to hint readily at the disguised wish: " I'll be strictly forbidden always and *true* in my own way and private where I will long long to *betrue* you along with one who will so betrue you that not once while I *betreu* him not once well he *betray* himself." (459) Here the complicated, disguised incestuous relationship of Earwicker and son Jaun (Kevin) and daughter Isobel is ultimately revealed by the triumph of the " ay " sound over the " ue," allowing the incest idea to slip through the censor's controls.

The manifest dream also shows considerable ingenuity in circumventing the difficulty of proper names and adjusting their sounds to the sense of the moment. Joyce's use of this device has a double significance, for it aids in the translations of myth into dream-life. Frequently it is the means by which a junction is formed of mythical and local matter.

> Nobucketnozzler and the Guinnghis Khan (24).
> (Nebuchadnezzar)   (Genghis Khan)
> a cleopatrician in her own right . . . (166)

A variety of distortions of Shakespeare's name occurs: " Shaggspick, Shakhisbeard, Scheekspair, Great Shapesphere." (177, 191, 295). The distortion may imply an attitude toward the original —as in the case of " Delude of Isreal " (331); or it may offer the

---

[48] Cf. Parody of Polonius, III, 579.

key to an interpretation of a fable; the " gracehoper," for example, " contrited with melanctholy,"—this phrase refers to the compromise effected at the Council of Augsburg (416).

One further service the dream performs—that of disguising the ego by distorting his name or his personal appearance. Since the letters H. C. E. stand for both the local pub owner and the mythical everyman, this disguise is especially appropriate to Joyce's purpose. It is used in two different ways: (1) by distorting the name itself; (2) by playing upon the sounds of Earwicker, the last name.

There are many instances of the first: Haroun Childeric Eggeberth; Howke Cotchme Eye; Hocus Crocus, Esquiloacus ("his thousand-first name "); Hotchkiss Culthur Everready; Hery Crass Evohodie; Haveth Childers Everywhere. The second form derives from the source-meaning of Earwicker—*earwig*, a pesky little gnat-like insect, which buzzes in the ear of the dreamer; the French, *perce oreille* is used as the basis for another series of disguised names: the ballad of Persse O'Reilley; Purseyriley; Perseoroyal; pearce orations, etc.

We become aware of the shifts in dream intensity by occasional " lucid comments " by the dreamer; this is especially clear when dawn appears and the light disturbs the sleepers, or when the sound of the clock penetrates the sleeper's consciousness. At the beginning of the dream, Earwicker, not yet thoroughly asleep, is afraid of disturbing Ann: " Aisy now, you decent man, with your knees and lie quiet and repose your honour's lordship! " (27) Later, his dream self hears the sound of the clock striking, but soon readjusts itself: " Tolv two elf kater ten (it can't be) sax." (403) The last section, devoted to the dream life of Ann, shows the transition from dream to consciousness. The objects in the room, the children in their beds, abandon their misshapen dream contexts and appear as real things in a real world. And with this realization, there appears in actual words what the incest theme of the entire dream has implied: " you're changing, acooshla, you're changing from me, I can feel. Or is it me is? I'm getting mixed " (626). That is, the love life of Earwicker and his wife has passed, and they must now turn their attention to their children's lives. But the love energies of Ann (Anna Livia

Plurabelle) will persist in the love lives of all her children: " I can see meself among them, allaniuvia pulchrabelled " (627).

These experiments with words and sounds subserve the historical and the psychological themes. Since the unconscious is not aware of either space or time,[49] Joyce is able to employ simultaneity as a substitute for the usual orderly sequence of events. Hence the composite figures which find their way into the dream lives of Earwicker and his wife are historical or mythical personages superimposed upon the present. " The reader must be prepared at times to visualize several related images simultaneously, realizing that these images are not necessarily bound together by surface-obvious associational chains but that their range may include any desired point in political or religious history, legend, fable, mythology, science, mathematics, current events, etc." [50]

Joyce's labor of some fifteen years has resulted in a complex representation of racial and personal unconscious. He is himself aware of the difficulty which the critics will meet in trying to untangle this " steady monologuy of the interiors " (119). His explanation of method is to be found in the text:

> (. . . with increasing lack of interest in his semantics, allowed various subconscious smickers to drivel slowly across their fichers), unconsciously explaining, for inkstands, with a meticulosity bordering on the insane, the various meanings of all the different foreign parts of speech he misused and cuttlefishing every lie unshrinkable about all the other people in the story, leaving out, of course, foreconsciously, the simple worf and plague and poison they had cornered him about until there was not a snoozer among them but was utterly undeceived in the heel of the reel by the recital of the rigmarole. (173–74)

In other words, he has allowed his interest in the subliminal world to upset his regard for precise semantics and, with an almost overbearing care for details, to jumble syntax, to bring in foreign words and meanings—deliberately excluding the simple narrative

---

[49] Cf. Freud, *New Introductory Lectures*, Lecture 31, p. 104: more strictly, the *id* which is wholly unconscious.
[50] Beckett *et al.*, *Our Exagmination*, 156.

style which might have appeased his critics. As a result, he has been able to introduce an assortment of linguistic oddities, historical tags and ends, ". . . once current puns, squashed quotatoes, messes of mottage, unquestionable issue papers. . . ." (183) and if one wishes to, and expends the effort to disentangle these " inversions of all this chambermade music," he may identify " the whirling dervish . . . self exiled in upon his ego . . . writing the mystery of himsel in furniture " (184).[51] Hence this parade of words, this " shemming amid everyone's repressed laughter " (190) has a meaning, and a study of the Freudian dream-mechanism helps to reveal it—but not that alone. " The lowquacity of him " (424)[52] requires also a patient attention to the music of word-sounds: ". . . if an ear aye sieze what no eye ere grieved for " (482). The sentient power of the word is the bridge of understanding; its ambiguous structure affords diverse clues to interpretation and is, according to Joyce, the proper vehicle for an elaborate but compressed history of humanity. Such is the challenge thrown to the critic: he is a fool who contents himself with literal meanings, without grasping the rich variety of connotations which every word and phrase possesses. Those who devote all their lives " to make a ghimel pass through the eye of an iota " (120) will find no pleasure here.

v

The particular *clinical* attitude towards problems of sex adjustment in the twentieth century was not mere coincidence. We have already seen how sadly critics referred to the " good old days " when sex had its proper and discreet place in the scheme of things. Freud had come to the conclusion that neuroses were predominantly of sexual origin because his clinical experience had presented overwhelming evidence that this was the case. One of the central stages in education for civilization, he maintained, occurs when both nature and society cooperate in turning the child's interest away from sexual matters and toward education

---

[51] This is Earwicker, of course, dreaming about his son Jerry (" Shem the Penman ").

[52] Here Kevin (" Jaunty Jaun ") is discussing his brother Jerry.

in adjustment. If this education is too severe, sublimation might easily give way to repression, and normal outlets for sexual expression be shut off.

Joyce's handling of sex themes is a direct consequence of his interest in the unconscious. Repressed instinctual drives have no place to go but the unconscious; and this applies also to terms which are not part of the ethical-social treatment of sex matters. As Freud explains: " Owing to the repression brought about by civilization many primary pleasures are now disapproved by the censorship and lost. But the human psyche finds renunciation very difficult; hence we discover that tendency-wit furnishes us with a means to make the renunciation retrogressive and thus to regain what has been lost." [53] Both distress and amusement over obscenity are the result of a carefully trained repression of the nature as well as the labels for certain common functions. When these repressed materials are released from the unconscious, we are ashamed, shocked, and amused. The obscenities in *Ulysses* and *Finnegans Wake*—though in the latter case they are more effectively disguised, because the psychic censor is often more effective than the legal censor—are there because they are part of the life of the unconscious.

Joyce's portrait of love in Dublin lacks both the romantic gloss Hollywood ordinarily gives it and the shame with which the pulpit often characterizes it. The cuckoldry in *Ulysses* seems to have at least the plausibility an objective description confers upon it. Joyce obviously goes beyond the realistic description of prostitution and extra-marital indiscretions. His conception of character motivation recognizes all of the bases for human relationship which psychoanalysis has identified. In the " Circe " episode of *Ulysses* these repressed or only partially revealed tendencies are all given dramatic representation.[54] And in Molly Bloom's monologue the earthy importance of these matters is climaxed by the " eternal affirmative ": " I suppose that's what a woman is supposed to be there for or He wouldn't have made us the way He did so attractive to men. . . ." (765)

Lionel Trilling has remarked that familial themes are one

---

[53] *Wit and Its Relation to the Unconscious*, 697.
[54] Cf. Edwin B. Burgum, " *Ulysses* and the Impasse of Individualism," in *Virginia Quarterly Review*, XVII (1941) , 564.

of Joyce's most conspicuous uses of Freud. Stephen's ambiguous attitude towards his parents is most clearly seen in his confusion of defiance with fear of his dead mother. He has refused to kneel and pray for her at her deathbed. The feeling of guilt which that refusal stimulates haunts him throughout the day, and is climaxed in the " Circe " episode:

> (Stephen's mother, emaciated, rises stark through the floor in leper grey with a wreath of faded orange blossoms and a torn bridal veil . . .)
> Stephen: (choking with fright, remorse, and horror) They said I killed you, mother. He offended your memory. Cancer did it, not I. Destiny. (564–65)

The search which ultimately leads to Bloom's meeting with Stephen is motivated in two ways: Stephen's disgust with his own father and Bloom's remorse at the death of his son Rudy, whose loss Bloom considers responsible for encouraging and justifying Molly's sexual adventures.

In *Finnegans Wake* the family of Earwicker is the focal point of Joyce's universal portrait of man. Earwicker, a man of some fifty or sixty years, keeps a pub in Dublin; his wife Ann has long since lost her hold upon him. They have three children: Isobel, a daughter of some twenty or so years, and the younger twins, Kevin and Jerry. Earwicker is preoccupied with his children. The affection he once felt for his wife is now easily transferred to his daughter. And his fondness for one of the sons, Kevin (Shaun, Jaunty Jaun) has in it suspicions of homosexuality. The incest theme appears first when Earwicker is disguised as Tristram, wooing Iseult (Part I), whose name assumes various other disguises during the night. The climax of both themes, the incest taboo and the homosexuality taboo, appears in Part III, in which Kevin and Isobel both figure. Kevin and Earwicker are both important to the subsequent "trial scene," in which Earwicker is accused of incest by his son.

The incest theme is disguised in a variety of ways. The dream points out that it is " so analytical plausible! " (299) —that is, that psychoanalysis has revealed it to be a natural consequence of familial associations. Further disguised argument for it is found in the reference to "those hintering influences from an angel-sexonism." (363) The "Judgment" handed down to Earwicker convicts him of incestuous relations with two of his children: "Whereas by reverendum they found him guilty of their and those imputations of fornicolopulation with two of his albow-crural correlations. . . ." (557) [55]

The monologue of Molly Bloom in *Ulysses* and the dialogue of "Anna Livia Plurabelle" represent Joyce's tribute to the sexual importance of womanhood. Anna Livia Plurabelle is both the River Liffey, nourishing the soil, and fruitful womankind. As Earwicker is "Everybody," Duke Umphrey as well as "Haveth Childers Everywhere," Anna Livia symbolizes the eternal feminine: "Anna was, Livia is, Plurabelle's to be" (215). Both Molly and Anna Livia are lustful, "shameful" creatures—two portraits to be added to the gallery of famous loose women. Though the latter portrait may be considered a parody on the sentimentalists —as was the "Nausicaa" episode in *Ulysses*—Joyce is perhaps least satirical here, and most interested in the beauty of sounds and images: "She was just a young thin pale soft shy slim slip of a thing then, sauntering, by silvamoonlake. . . ." (202)

Joyce's interest in psychoanalysis, as we have seen, while certainly not central, has played an important role in determining the style and content of his last two novels: (1) He regarded the dream work, and especially the suggestive ambiguity of words as a factor of much importance in the development of experimental writing. (2) More than any other writer of his time, he was aware of the several stages by which the individual recedes from consciousness, and of the aesthetic problem involved in each case. (3) He thought that much of character motivation could be more adequately developed by recourse to the psychoanalytic explanation of familial relationships than by any other method.

Joyce is not enchained or imprisoned by the power of his unconscious life. He is a very careful, painstaking, "conscious" artist, aware of modern psychology and interested in it, yet after

---

[55] Other references to homosexuality, incest, and other sexual perversions include: II, 215, 238, 279, n. 1, 297; III, 318, 342, 349, 352, 364, 411, 414, 419 (reference to Oscar Wilde), 422, 431, 433, 435 ("onanymous letters"), 449, 454, 461, 465, 480, 499 ("adipose rex"—a reference both to Earwicker's physical appearance and to the oedipus complex).

all independent of it as well. We would be doing violence to the integrity of the aesthetic consciousness, either to criticize Joyce for employing psychoanalysis inaccurately or to condemn him for using it at all. The true measure of his art is not the judgment of any scientist but the analysis of his use of what materials he considered aesthetically attractive and suitable. In such an analysis a knowledge of psychoanalysis is helpful both to the reader and the critic.

chapter VI

LAWRENCE'S QUARREL
WITH FREUD

i

In May, 1913, when *Sons and Lovers* was published by Duckworth of London, Lawrence was pointed out as a novelist with exceptional insight into such psychoanalytic problems as incest-horror and the oedipus complex. Yet that novel was written before Lawrence had any real acquaintance with Freud, and before he mentions Freud in any of his letters. Such Freudian criticisms of *Sons and Lovers* were at best exaggerated. *Sons and Lovers* demonstrates that Lawrence needed no theory except his own to aid him in his analysis of character. Most important, *all* of Lawrence's work bears ultimate reference to his own experience, no matter how many suggestions of " alien theory " it may contain.

When we examine Lawrence's habits of reading, we find him either enthusiastic or bitter over the literary offerings of his contemporaries; we discover that his reading interests are based upon what books he has available at any given moment of his life and upon what his particular mood happens to be. He was opposed to intellectual analysis at all times, though especially so in his early life, the life described in *Sons and Lovers* and " E. T's " *A*

Personal Record. The intellectual experience of the early years, as described by " E. T." moves from one position to another—from T. H. Huxley and Haeckel, to Kant, Schopenhauer, and Nietzsche: " In all his reading he seemed to be groping for something that he could lay hold of as a guiding principle in his own life. There was never the least touch of the academic or the scholastic in his approach." (112–13)

Lawrence's reading was sporadic, by reason both of his habit of traveling to the ends of the earth, and therefore having to rely on anything he could get, and of his habit of measuring all influences by his emotions rather than by his intellect. To say that Lawrence was superficial is to neglect certain important personal determinants of his thought. His *distrust* of the intellect, of its cynicism and " whimpering futility," gave him his sole basis for an attack upon the " academic chairs of virtue." But in this repudiation not only the strictly skeptical, or the rigidly logical minds suffered; those who seemed to have something to say to him, or who spoke along the same lines, were also rejected. Bergson, for example, bored him: " He feels a bit thin." [1]

He would seem, therefore, the most thoroughgoing anti-intellectual of his time. But one must speak in paradoxes about this paradoxical figure. With the statement, " Lawrence rejected everything," must be linked the judgment, " Lawrence rejected nothing." He *never gave anything up*. He assumed a critical ambivalence of acceptance-rejection in all his reactions to the intellectual world around him. It was through no ordinary fickleness of mind that he responded to any influence in this way. It is a mistake, therefore, to say that Lawrence was influenced by Freud, or Bergson, or Nietzsche; one can only say that " Lawrence was influenced by Lawrence." Another point ought to be made, in order to clarify the problem of influence: he often used reading as a test of his emotional state; likewise, he frequently resorted to writing to " clear his mind." Horace Gregory points out that Lawrence's two essays on psychoanalysis were motivated in this manner: " the writing of such essays offered him the means of checking-back results of his convictions, and . . . by this process

---

[1] Letter to A. D. McLeod, April 26, 1913, in *The Letters of D. H. Lawrence* (New York, 1932), 121.

he was enabled to unroll himself like a map and thus review (in the only way he knew how) the existing worth of his beliefs."[2]

Lawrence's reading was never impersonal. He measured books as he did persons; for him there was little if any distinction between them. Hence, his evaluation of John Middleton Murry, for example, was not in terms of Murry's mind, nor in terms of his literary or critical talents, but almost entirely in terms of Murry's ability to "get along" with him—that is, to enter sympathetically into Lawrence's emotional life. The difference between their minds is important. The sensitivity of Lawrence was dynamic: the difference was one between an angry mood and a sulking introversion. Murry held tenaciously to critical categories which had been tested and found satisfactory to his taste; Lawrence had from the beginning insisted upon a dynamically personal and subjective tribunal at which ideas—*any* ideas—were to be tried. Hence Murry from the beginning admits that he cannot understand Lawrence: "Lawrence's ideas are rather difficult for me to get hold of, because he uses all kinds of words in a curious symbolic sense to which I have no clue."[3]

So far as we can determine, Lawrence's interest in Freud came at the same time as his whirlwind courtship of Frieda. Frieda has explained her own interest in Freud, which began just before she met Lawrence: "I had just met a remarkable disciple of Freud and was full of undigested theories. This friend did a lot for me. I was living like a somnambulist in a conventional set life and he awakened the consciousness of my own proper self."[4] Lawrence caught Frieda's enthusiasm for "things German" almost immediately; and, in his trip to Germany, soon afterward (1912), he found time to explore both the language and the literature of her native land. How much of Frieda's own personality went into the revision of *Sons and Lovers*, one can only guess; but it is sufficient to say that the "Miriam" of that novel lost her hold upon Lawrence; and that the novel was altered in detail and in point of view as a result.[5] Before the final draft was

---

[2] Horace Gregory, *Pilgrim of the Apocalypse*, 58.

[3] John Middleton Murry, "Reminiscences of D. H. Lawrence," *New Adelphi*, 3 (1930), 270.

[4] Frieda Lawrence, *Not I but the Wind* (New York, 1934), 3.

[5] *Ibid.*, 56. The final draft was written in Gargnano, Italy, with "Frieda helping."

ready for the publishers, perhaps during the time of revision, Lawrence was listening to Frieda's explanations of Freud and arguing with her about Freud's contribution to modern thought. " Yes, Lawrence knew about Freud before he wrote the final draft of ' *Sons and Lovers,*' " Frieda tells me in a letter of November 21, 1942. " I don't remember whether he had read Freud or heard of him before we met in 1912. But I was a great Freud admirer; we had long arguments and Lawrence's conclusion was more or less that Freud looked on sex too much from the doctor's point of view, that Freud's ' sex ' and ' libido ' were too limited and mechanical and that the root was deeper."

These arguments and discussions may have affected the final structure of *Sons and Lovers* in one way at least: Lawrence may have increased the emphasis in the novel upon the mother-son relationship, to the neglect of other matters, and given it the striking clarity which it enjoys in the published book. But the relationship was there long before Lawrence's final revision; and he did not allow any clinical or psychological commentary to interfere with the literary excellence of the novel as a whole. It is doubtful that the revision of *Sons and Lovers* was more than superficially affected by Lawrence's introduction to psychoanalysis; Freudianism belongs to a later period in Lawrence's development. The influence of Lawrence on the psychoanalysts was another matter altogether. They hailed *Sons and Lovers* as the most penetrating study of the oedipus complex yet to be found in English literature. Lawrence was at first pleased and amused, then became interested in psychoanalysis—as though he had anticipated it and therefore expected it to clarify his own mind. Dr. David Eder began to attend the " Lawrence evenings " and to undertake a serious discussion of Freudian theory, especially as it influenced the reading of *Sons and Lovers.* Lawrence studied psychoanalysis with his usual intense interest, but was soon disappointed with its " odor of the laboratory." He objected to its habits of analysis, which never " let one's feelings alone "; he complained that the psychoanalysts " can only help you more completely *to make your own feelings.* They can never let you *have* any real feelings."

ii

The excitement caused by *Sons and Lovers* in psychoanalytic circles did not, therefore, lead to any wholehearted acceptance by Lawrence of Freud, but it did give him some cause for reflection. He was anxious at first to point to the experience described in *Sons and Lovers* as " normal," but he gave the psychoanalysts careful attention—perhaps waiting for some way of proving them false. This opportunity seems to have come at the same time that he was himself formulating his " theory of being " in two essays, *Psychoanalysis and the Unconscious* (1921), and *Fantasia of the Unconscious* (1922). Here he has apparently subdued psychoanalysis and given it the disparaging label *scientific*, but he does not let psychoanalysis rest; his letters and book reviews refer to the new psychology almost until the time of his death. After the writing of *Fantasia*, he justifies his rejection of psychoanalysis on two grounds: (a) that it is just a " fad," unworthy of serious consideration, and (b) that it does not account for the problems of group-association, but fastens the physician's ego to the patient's in an unequal struggle for dominance.

As a support for his first objection, his letters to Mabel Dodge Luhan are most illuminating. He writes the much-analyzed Mrs. Luhan: " I rather hate therapy altogether—doctors, healers, and all the rest. I believe that a real neurotic is a half devil, but a cured neurotic is a perfect devil. . . . I would prefer that neurotics died." [6] When Lawrence hears of her interest in Jung, he is resentful; she reports his indignation in the following manner: " More attempts to know and to understand! More systems and more consciousness! All he wanted was the *flow* and not the knowing about it! " [7] He is sufficiently astute to recognize the real reason for Mrs. Luhan's interest in psychoanalysis—her restless search for " new " experience: " It all seems to me a false working-up, and an inducement to hysteria and insanity. I know what lies back of it all: the same indecent desire to have everything in the *will* and the *head*. Life itself comes from elsewhere." [8]

[6] Letter, December 4, 1921, in Luhan's *Lorenzo in Taos* (New York, 1932), 13–14.
  [7] *Ibid.*, 138.   [8] *Ibid.*, 151.

Lawrence did seem interested in one version of psychoanalysis —the un-Freudian analysis of Trigant Burrow, a New York psychologist. Burrow's theory of " group images " he reads with great interest and considers the only one of any value. Lawrence believes he shares with Burrow a distaste for science and the scientific method: " your criticism of psychoanalysis as practised is to the quick. . . . But do you know, I think you are really more a philosopher, or artist, than a scientist—and that you have a deep natural resistance to this scientific jargonizing." [9] The book to which Lawrence refers is Burrow's *The Social Basis of Consciousness.* In a review of it, he applauds Burrow again for his criticism of practising psychoanalysts. Therapy is simply an artificial conflict between the analyst and the patient; Burrow has discovered the artificiality of his position as an analyst; he " found, in his clinical experiences, that he was always applying a *theory.* . . . The mind could not be open, because the patient's neurosis, all the patient's experience, *had* to be fitted to the Freudian theory of the inevitable incest-motive." The analyst's intentions are good; he wants to set the patient free; but he merely substitutes one image for another, " the fixed motive of the incest-complex. . . . While the Freudian theory of the unconscious and of the incest-motive is valuable as a *description* of our psychological condition, the moment you begin to *apply* it, and make it master of the living situation, you have begun to substitute one mechanistic or unconscious illusion for another." [10]

These remarks to and about Trigant Burrow have the value of showing us Lawrence's attitude toward psychoanalysis near the end of his creative career. He is still interested in the psychology, but has long since convicted it on the counts of its scientific nature and its inadequacy as a psychological guide for living. The inert, dead mass of clinical material did not interest Lawrence in the slightest; but he always credited psychoanalysis with value as a descriptive science. Similarly, he distrusted the analytic situation; it placed too much emphasis upon complete submission on the part of the patient. Lawrence was unwilling to have any one

[9] *Letters*, 695; cf. 643, 693.
[10] D. H. Lawrence, " A New Theory of Neuroses," *Bookman*, 66 (1927), 314; reprinted in *Phoenix: The Posthumous Papers of D. H. Lawrence*, ed. Edward D. McDonald (New York, 1936), 377, 378.

person submit entirely to another; such a condition would destroy the organic individuality which gives life to so many of Lawrence's fictional heroes. The spark which kept alive a person's original self was in itself kept alive by clashes of personality, and not by submission.

Lawrence did agree with Freud in at least one particular—that the normal sex life of man had been disastrously repressed and neglected. Even here the differences between the two men are marked. Whereas Freud suggested that the source of most mental illness was repression of normal sex development, Lawrence argued that full expression of the personalities of both man and woman involved a genuine sex relationship, which went far beyond the mere " understanding " that modernists offered as the clue to sex happiness. These are not at all the same attitudes: Freud's is, in a sense, a negative approach; it is to *remove illness* that he is forced to emphasize sex. Lawrence, however, considers the sex experience (and all of its implications for family life) as basic to initial health and happiness. Sex experience is a part of Lawrence's " religion "—an important expression of the self in its search for vital mysteries. Hence, many of his characters find their most vital happiness or their most bitter disillusionments during and after such experience.

Lawrence believed that sex is the ultimate expression of a person's individuality. The " mass mind," as Lawrence saw it in operation during the First World War, or as he viewed it in the industrial centers of England and America, had sacrificed much to the principle of collective action. Under such conditions, sexual experience degenerates to insect lust (*Letters*, 231). Modern man had debased sex by looking at it in one of two ways: (a) as an interesting thing, which can be " known " and " experimented with " (or, thought about) ; (b) as lust, which shows no consideration for either self or object. Lawrence was in many respects a Puritan; he abhorred mere lust, which, he felt, lacked the emotional concomitants of joy and was merely the perversion of the life instinct: " There is a brief time for sex, and a long time when sex is out of place. But when it is out of place as an activity there still should be the large and quiet space in the consciousness where it lives quiescent " (*Letters*, 781). For this reason he is horrified by Aldous Huxley's *Point Counter Point*, though he has to admit that Huxley has "shown the truth, perhaps the last truth," about his generation, and "with really fine courage " (*Letters*, 765). He is opposed to sex censorship as much as he is to sex looseness; they are two sides of the same coin. The "censor- moron " hates nothing so much as truly vital and essential living. His prudery threatens "our developing and extending conscious- ness " (*Letters*, 769). But the modernist of the twenties repels him as thoroughly; the American woman especially, who "intel- lectualizes " sex: " The one woman who *never* gives herself is our free woman, who is always giving herself. America affects me like that " (*Letters*, 559).

Lady Chatterley's Lover contains Lawrence's most complete statement about sex. The novel argues for complete freedom, not from restraint, but from false prudery. Lady Chatterley is placed in an impossible situation—tied by bonds of sympathy and memory to a gentleman who has been paralyzed by a war injury but who insists upon holding her. "*Il n'a pas de quoi.*" In her first attempt to escape from her marriage, she meets with a representa- tive modernist, one who regards sex as an interesting and pleasant pastime, and flattering to his ego, but who has never really ex- perienced it in the manner of which Lawrence approves: " it is in the passional secret places of life, above all, that the tide of sensi- tive awareness needs to ebb and flow, cleansing and freshening." [11] Lady Chatterley was destined to find these passional secret sources of life; in submitting to them, she threw aside all of her posses- sions—not only the husband she despised but all of his wealth. This theme of repudiation is necessary to Lawrence's life-view; for it involves condemnation of industrial society as one of the principal causes of life failure.[12] Mellors, the complete Lawren- cean man, furnishes the key to her final understanding of sex as a living thing; for he has kept aloof both from the repressive forces

---

[11] D. H. Lawrence, *Lady Chatterley's Lover* (Florence, Italy, 1928), 118.

[12] Clifford's wealth has been inherited, and it depends on the work of the mines. While Lady Chatterley has her secret affair with Mellors, Clifford is busy improving the collieries in a way which is to plunge the workers into deeper auto- matism. Cf. Gerald Crich's similar plans, *Women in Love* (New York, n. d.; first published, 1920), 240–65. Lawrence believed that the only true equality lay in the uninterrupted spiritual development of man; the machine imposed another type of equality upon this, and the result was chaos.

of modern industrialism and from the petty intellectualism of Clifford's tribe.

In the controversy over *Lady Chatterley's Lover* Lawrence engaged willingly and with enthusiasm. He tried to define the terms *pornography* and *obscenity*. The first term does not refer merely to a representation of sex: it is " the attempt to insult sex, to do dirt on it."

> In the degraded human being the deep instincts have gone dead. . . . It happen when the psyche deteriorates, and the profound controlling instincts collapse. Then sex is dirt and dirt is sex, and sexual excitement becomes a playing with dirt, and any sign of sex in a woman becomes a show of her dirt. This is the condition of the common, vulgar human being whose name is legion, and who lifts his voice and it is the *Vox populi, vox Dei.* And this is the source of all pornography.[13]

During the First World War, Lawrence had thought deeply of these matters, and he came to the conclusion that Christianity had misunderstood love throughout its history. Near the end of his life (1927), he published the short novel, *The Man Who Died*; if the life of Christ had come to an end as Lawrence describes it, instead of in the manner of the gospels, the problem of Christianity and sex might have been solved. The body of Jesus has been taken down and laid into the tomb; but he has not really died— or, rather, the life of the gospel accounts has been killed within him and he is free to find the true source of human vitality and happiness. Death has saved him from his own salvation. He has neglected his own body in pursuance of a spiritual mission. In a temple of Isis he meets the fulfillment for which he has been seeking, and he understands why he has been put to death: " I asked them all to serve me with the corpse of their love. And in the end I offered them only the corpse of my love. . . . If I had kissed Judas with live love, perhaps he would never have kissed me with death." [14]

The proper sex relationship is best demonstrated in an ideal marriage. As ever, Lawrence draws chiefly from his own experi-

[13] Lawrence, " Pornography and Obscenity," in *Phoenix*, 176.
[14] *The Man Who Died* (London, 1931), 137–38.

ence for his statement of marital harmony. Contrary to the impression given in most contemporary accounts, Lawrence was supremely happy only with Frieda. The violent quarrels were an important part of their relationship. His friends saw often that the tie with Frieda was indissoluble. Frieda herself never lost her conviction that the marriage was suitable: " I think the greatest pleasure and satisfaction for a woman is to live with a creative man, when he goes ahead and fights—I found it so. . . . Often before he conceived a new idea he was irritable and disagreeable, but when it had come, the new vision, he could go ahead, and was eager and absorbed." [15]

Lawrence's happiest years, when he was enjoying the first full realization of Frieda's love, inspired him to make a number of statements about the importance of man's love for woman: " I think the only resourcing of art, revivifying it, is to make it more the joint work of man and woman. I think the *one* thing to do, is for men to have courage to draw nearer to women, expose themselves to them, and be altered by them; and for women to accept and admit men " (*Letters*, 198) . He believed in marriage because he was happily married. But marriage was not complete unless it involved a violent clashing of supplementary natures. Man must surmount an initial objection to woman in order to realize her fundamental nature. Being kind, or benevolent, or liberal merely serves to overemphasize this objection. Lawrence sees the failure of all liberalism—the " twentieth-century enlightenment," founded upon philanthropy and improved sewage disposal—as the tendency to break away from essential physical values, which have always seemed a little disagreeable to civilized man. In modern literature the repulsiveness of man was finally being investigated—especially in the novels of Joyce, Huxley, and Gide. " For a long time, the *social* belief and benevolence of man towards man keeps pace with the secret physical repulsion of man away from man. But ultimately, inevitably, the one outstrips the other. The benevolence exhausts itself, the repulsion only deepens. The benevolence is external and extra-individual. But the revulsion is inward and personal." [16]

[15] Frieda Lawrence, *Not I but the Wind*, 194.
[16] Introduction to Dahlberg's *Bottom Dogs*, in *Phoenix*, 270. Cf. Freud, *Civilization and Its Discontents*, 66–67, n. 1.

Lawrence's criticism of modern sex attitudes is addressed to their failure to recognize the deep sources of vital experience, their tendency to prevent a complete and satisfactory sex experience. In this respect, both the " censor-moron " and the modern " free woman " err alike: the one in considering sex itself unwholesome; the other, in fearing its consequences. Neither is entirely honest; neither wishes life to be fully charged with elements of danger and beauty. In this indictment Lawrence includes all of modern science; scientists do not instinctively or intuitively grasp what they outwardly assert. They count, tabulate, announce results in bewildering figures, or in hesitant semi-conclusions. This is true, as well, of Freudianism, which substitutes the " intellectual-psychological " for the " intuitive-psychological."

iii

This hesitancy in matters of vital importance, which Lawrence believes to be a source of modern disintegration, is especially noticeable in the new psychology. Certainly the psychoanalysts were dealing with the most intimate and the most important matters affecting man's fate. Why did Lawrence not agree with them? His critical, philosophical works all refer at one time or another to psychoanalytic terms—the unconscious, the oedipus complex, repression, sublimation, etc. But his chief reason for reading psychoanalysis was to refute it; or, rather, to find his own explanations for the terms which psychoanalysis had offered him. His examination of Freudianism and his own suggestions, though they have many errors of interpretation, provide an excellent beginning for Lawrence's own vitalistic position.

He begins by claiming the Freud and his followers are " out, under a therapeutic disguise, to do away entirely with the moral faculty in man." Since Freud was searching for the basic elements of our being, he could not help revealing enormities and horrors, but only in the hope of ridding us of them:

> This is the moral dilemma of psychoanalysis. The analyst set out to cure neurotic humanity by removing the cause of the neurosis. He finds that the cause of the neurosis lies

in some unadmitted sex desire. After all he has said about inhibition of normal sex, he is brought at last to realize that at the root of almost every neurosis lies some incest-craving, and that this incest-craving is *not the result of inhibition of normal sex-craving*. Now see the dilemma—it is a fearful one. If the incest-craving is not the outcome of any inhibition of normal desire, if it actually exists and refuses to give way before any criticism, what then? What remains but to accept it as part of the normal sex-manifestations? [17]

The source of this erroneous conception of Freud is, of course, the controversy over *Sons and Lovers*. The last chapter of that novel shows Paul struggling against the pull of his mother toward death, or against the full realization of Paul's self. Freud had wished to call this strong influence the incest-striving which is subsequently subtilized or rejected, in accordance with the mother's hold over the child. The hold of Mrs. Morel over Paul is such that he cannot enter freely into any sort of companionship with Miriam, and is driven, in despair and exasperation, into the arms of Clara Dawes—a temporary affair, which too is stopped by the mother's will. Lawrence was troubled by this novel. How true was it? And, if it was true—if the hold of the mother was so powerful that it might ruin the life of the son—were the psychoanalysts right in giving it widespread, conscious attention? They were wrong, chiefly because they insisted that incest-striving was a normal thing: " Any inhibition must be wrong, since inevitably in the end it causes neurosis and insanity. Therefore the inhibition of incest-craving is wrong and this wrong is the cause of practically all modern neurosis and insanity." [18]

Freud did not, of course, attach moral judgments to his clinical findings; nor did he advocate the fulfillment of the incest-craving as a means of cure. The object of analysis is neither to

---

[17] *Psychoanalysis and the Unconscious* (London, 1923), 12, 20–21. Lawrence errs, of course, in assuming that " incest-craving " is characteristic of the unconscious, which Freudians have insisted should be called " natural." Actually Freud, in his *Three Contributions to a Theory of Sex*, has shown that the libido of the infant, does not distinguish from its objects, that it is not consciously recognized at all, and that the education of the child is in part a matter of directing the libido to some external object.

[18] *Psychoanalysis and the Unconscious*, 22.

find incest in the patient's infantile sex life nor to pronounce one or another sort of moral judgment upon it. It is chiefly to point out the *impracticability* of incest as a regulating factor in the patient's life. Implicit in Lawrence's criticism is the error of the lay critic, who believes that Freud opposes inhibitions; he does not countenance incest as a means of releasing man from the inhibition of his incest-craving, but suggests sublimation, re-direction, and re-formation of one's conscious controls over the early sex life. But Lawrence will not forgive Freud for "making sex conscious." So long as the "great affective-passional functions and emotions" remain unconscious and are enjoyed unconsciously, the question of sin never bothers man. "Adam and Eve fell, not because they had sex, or even because they committed the sexual act, but because they *became aware* of their sex and of the possibility of the act."

Lawrence replaced Freud's sober definition of the unconscious with a poetic, mystic affirmation. For Freud, he says, the unconscious is "the cellar in which the mind keeps its own bastard spawn. The true unconscious is the well-head, the fountain of real motivity." He would have us believe that the Freudian unconscious is made up solely of "the whole body of our repressions," as though it were this and nothing more. If this were true, then it would indeed suffer from comparison with the unconscious as Lawrence declares it. For the novelist, the unconscious begins where life begins. "We are trying to trace the unconscious to its source. And we find that this source, in all the higher organisms, is the first ovule cell from which an individual organism arises." [19] This is a mixture of psychological terminology and vitalistic biology—bold in its outlines, but not very accurate. Its essential difference from Freud's version lies in its insistence upon equating individual organic life with a "non-cerebral consciousness." For Freud the unconscious is not dependent upon any life outside itself, though the sexual instincts guarantee the immortality of any organic species.

This brings us to what is, perhaps, at the center of Lawrence's criticism. Freud has insisted that the unconscious exists without our knowing it; but he does admit that there is evident advantage in knowing it; and, if we are to have a cure, we must become aware of its peculiarities, subject them to the minds of both the patient and the analyst. This " cerebral " attack upon the unconscious is just another of the mistakes of modern science. " What we are suffering from now is the restriction of the unconscious within certain ideal limits." He refuses to grant two points: (1) that the unconscious is in any way dangerous, except for the timid and the impotent; (2) that becoming aware of the unconscious has any value, except for descriptive purposes. He insists that the longer we submit to an intellectualizing of unconscious processes, the less are we able to " live unconsciously "—unencumbered by the timid restrictions of the mind. Thus, he hopes to replace the sober, scientific version of the unconscious by his own: " It is that active spontaneity which rouses in each individual organism at the moment of fusion of the parent nuclei, and which, in polarized connection with the external universe, gradually evolves or elaborates its own individual psyche and corpus, bringing both mind and body forth from itself."

In view of the disagreement about the sources of human behavior, we can expect that Lawrence will also suggest a different picture of infantile and child psychology. While the discussion of sex etiology in Freud's *Three Contributions to a Theory of Sex* is a rather grim effort to destroy the notion of the asexual infant, Lawrence wishes to portray the child as a pagan, vigorous, and actively happy being. Indeed, the life of the child begins with the foetus, which is " radically, individually conscious." All of the newly born child's acts are instinctive, blind, " mindless ": " From the great first-mind of the abdomen it moves direct, with an anterior knowledge almost like magnetic propulsion, as if the little mouth were drawn or propelled to the maternal breast by vital magnetism, whose center of directive control lies in the solar plexus." [20]

Since the scientist has always referred to man's acts from an intellectual point of view, he has always considered bodily acts not a little objectionable. Even though Freud insisted upon the naturalness of certain bodily predispositions, he too looked upon these acts, these primal, healthy expressions of bodily sanity and

[20] *Ibid.*, 45, 108, 51, 55–56.

the drive of the id which compels them, as "reclamation projects for the ego." For the poet and the novelist, this procedure serves to kill the spontaneity of the child's early life. Several characters of Lawrence's novels are victims of this early psychological malformation. They either dwell in dreary vicarages or on estates, or are prey to the confining and crushing power of modern industrialism. For reasons of external pressure or domestic stupidity, the child is often forced into polite clumsiness when his natural habits of graceful impoliteness should be encouraged.

In *Fantasia of the Unconscious*, Lawrence carried his disagreement with Freud further. Though it is biologically true that "the rudimentary formation of both sexes is found in every individual," actually this is of little importance, compared with the fundamental and essential separateness of male from female. Both man and woman have their separate worlds; they supplement each other, but they are not interchangeable. The man has a mission, a destiny, to serve in this world; but he must return to "relax and give himself up to his woman and her world." [21]

The task of educating the child before puberty is accomplished largely by stimulating and reinforcing the vital zones of bodily activity. Physical stimulation, occasional rough handling, healthful spankings, are all recommended. Since Lawrence places so much emphasis upon the mature act of coition, infantile sexuality is of little importance for him. "True, children have a sort of sex consciousness. Little boys and girls may even commit indencies together. . . . [But] It is a sort of shadow activity, a sort of dream-activity. It has no very profound effect."

It is upon the relationship of man as man with woman as woman that much of life actually depends. This is important, but it is not solely important—and psychoanalysis, Lawrence believes, is responsible for misdirecting us. He insists that the sexual act is merely a renewal of life, and, as such, a path to other, significant group activity. This activity is not at all sexual, though each individual requires the renewal which coition grants. "The ultimate, greatest desire in men is this desire for great *purposive* activity. When man loses his deep sense of purposive, creative activity, he feels lost, and is lost. When he makes the sexual consummation

. . . even in his *secret* soul, he falls into the beginnings of despair." [22] Sexual union is, therefore, a reaffirmation of organic
unity and of the dignity of the individual soul—the "unconscious," Lawrence prefers to say, for the word "soul" has been
profaned.

In his chapter on "Sleep and Dreams," Lawrence's ambivalent acceptance-rejection attitude toward Freud is even more
noticeable. He believes that most dreams have as their source
physical disturbances of the day before—"pancakes for supper";
many of the peculiarities of dreams "are direct transcripts from
the physical phenomena of circulation and digestion." Yet he
does not deny the importance of repression, and he admits the
presence of mother-fixations in the dream: "The activity at the
lower center, however, is denied in the daytime. There is a
repression. Then the friction of the night-flow liberates the repressed psychic activity explosively. And then the image of the
mother figures in passionate, disturbing, soul-rending dreams." [23]

But man awakens with a hatred of his dream; the incest
images therefore have no importance. Lawrence finds in dreams
the seat of automatism, the enemy of spontaneity; activities denied
existence by the waking life are granted an automatic life in the
dream: "Any *significant* dream-image is usually an image or a
symbol of some arrest or scotch in the living spontaneous psyche."
But symbols in the dream represent no *release*; rather, they are
human wishes and drives, the "falling out of human integrity
into the purely mechanical mode." [24] It is obvious, therefore, that
for Lawrence the center of dream-activity is not the unconscious
at all, but the reverse of the unconscious—the expression of that
cerebral automaton which deadens spontaneous life.

The principal terms of Lawrence's quarrel with Freud may be
summarized as follows:

(1) Lawrence disapproved of him because he thought he had
brought into consciousness what had best remain unconscious.
The basis for true, vital life was the spontaneous functioning of
the non-cerebral self. Understanding anything is not a cognitive
act; it is the undeliberate functioning of ourselves as organic and
individual beings.

[22] *Ibid.*, 140, 151–52.   [23] *Ibid.*, 243, 245–46.   [24] *Ibid.*, 250, 253.

(2) The unconscious is not a source of evil; evil results from the weakening of unconscious processes, by making them spiritual and ineffectual.

(3) The mother-child relationship is vital so long as it remains on the plane of unconsciousness; it is the source of joy and life in the child and should not be interfered with by the intellect.

(4) Child-training should therefore be devoted entirely to the development of the bodily centers. This is made possible by the fact that there is no such thing as infantile sexuality, and fears about the perverted development of sex interests are unwarranted.

(5) Lawrence differentiates the sex aim of puberty and youth from the purely physical activity of the child, and denies Freud's application of the term *sex* to these earlier activities. He says further that man and woman are separate, isolated types, and that bisexuality is a " scientific myth."

(6) The importance of the act of coition is therefore central for Lawrence. It is the point of sexual relationship which enables man and woman to go to the deepest sources of their natures, and thus to understand themselves and to know clearly their separate and complementary roles.

(7) But man should go beyond the crucial union of egos which is the act of coition. For him it is the source of renewal, which should serve to drive him forward into creative group life. Woman offers the nucleus of further renewal, and supplements her husband's life by turning him back from time to time to the fountain source of his strength.

In all of this Freud seems a lonely outsider. Nevertheless, we should note this as one of many instances—indeed, one of the most interesting examples—of the union of psychologist with creative artist. For the metaphor of the unconscious, which Lawrence substituted for the notion of soul, he was grateful to the psychologist. The incest-motive and its associate, the oedipus complex, puzzled Lawrence, and forced him to re-explain, in terms of a highly original version of biology. The great barrier to an acceptance of Freud—a barrier which Lawrence magnified unjustly —was the determinism of Freud's system. This he joined to the mass of scientific theory, of much of which Freud himself disapproved. The surrealists *use* the unconscious as a source of literary novelty; Joyce found in it a few keys to linguistic change; Lawrence wished to *live* within the unconscious: "If only we would shut our eyes; if only we were all struck blind, and things vanished from our sight, we should marvel that we had fought and lived for shallow, visionary, peripheral nothingness. We should find reality in the darkness" (*Letters*, 282).

iv

Lawrence pleads for a denial of the intellect, a reassertion of "the blood" as a source of religious experience: "My great religion is a belief in the blood, the flesh, as being wiser than the intellect. We can go wrong in our minds. But what our blood feels and believes and says, is always true" (*Letters*, 96). He believed that one can achieve union with the primal sources of his being only through personal experience—experience into which he entered wholly and "mindlessly"; one avenue to such experience was the body of woman. In a sense, all experience between man and woman was a return to the mother; in this respect Lawrence held to the idea of incest, though he gave it an altogether un-Freudian, unscientific meaning:

> Beware of it—this mother-incest idea can become an obsession. But it seems to me there is this much truth in it: that at certain periods the man has a desire and a tendency to return unto the woman, make her his goal and end, finds his justification in her. In this way he casts himself as it were into her womb, and she, the Magna Mater, receives him with gratification. This is a kind of incest. . . . It is awfully hard, once the sex relation has gone this way, to recover. If we don't recover, we die. (*Letters*, 462)

Lawrence's "religion of the blood" assumes an equation of consciousness with affective states; consciousness, therefore, has little to do with cognition. That part of consciousness which is *mental* should never dominate bodily consciousness. He proceeded from this discovery of "cellular" consciousness to a religion which was a combination of pantheism and vitalism. He suggests also that there is a racial differentiation in consciousness —one historically conditioned, however, not inherent. " White consciousness " has become predominantly mental and nervous, remote from the sources of vital being. The Indians, on the other hand, more naïve, less civilized, are perhaps " giving themselves again to the pulsing, incalculable fall of the blood, which forever seeks to fall to the centre of the earth, while the heart, like a planet pulsating in an orbit, keeps up the strange, lonely circulating of the separate human existence." [25]

Lawrence's censure of Christianity and his championship of a vitalistic paganism are given expression in two of his later works, *The Apocalypse*, and the novel, *The Plumed Serpent*. In the first, he regrets that we have lost much of the splendor and meaning of Revelation; we are no longer united in one unconscious rhythm, but have disintegrated into selfish, destructive individuals. But the book of *Revelation* had recaptured much of the pagan spirit, which was later to be crushed by Catholicism and the Reformation. Modern man has occasional accesses to violent outbursts of desire—the state of consciousness which has been so effectively repressed and so superficially labeled by modern philosophers as the libido or *l'élan vital*.

The Plumed Serpent is Lawrence's answer to the cry for the resurrection of old gods. Since they have long since died out in the white consciousness, their revival should be left to the darker-skinned races—the Mexican Indian, for example. In the rhythm of ancient Indian dances, the heroine is led to abandon all of her white reserve. " She felt her sex and her womanhood caught up and identified in the slowly revolving ocean of nascent life, the dark sky of the men lowering and wheeling above." And she senses that this is something different from the collective white consciousness which she has watched during the World War. That was mere lust; this new consciousness of strength which lay " in the vivid blood-relation between man and woman " was the source of great power and happiness.[26]

Lawrence would replace (through what means he knew not, though he suggested several tentatively) the humanism of West-

---

[25] D. H. Lawrence, *Mornings in Mexico* (New York, 1934), 110.
[26] D. H. Lawrence, *The Plumed Serpent* (New York, 1933), 128, 398.

ern civilization with the new faith, the outlines of which he had already given in *Fantasia of the Unconscious*. Its basis was a pantheism which saw a sort of blood unity in the energy of all nature. The external, emotional substitute for prayer was love—the sort of love in which Rudolph Birkin believed. This is not the ordinary relationship of one person to another, but a clear recognition of the " isolated strangeness " of all men:

> There is, [Birkin told Ursula] . . . a final me which is stark and impersonal and beyond responsibility. So there is a final you. And it is there I would want to meet you—not in the emotional, loving plane—but there beyond, where there is no speech and no terms of agreement. . . . One can only follow the impulse, taking that which lies in front, . . . asked for nothing, giving nothing, only each taking according to the primal desire.[27]

In order to set aside the modern mental consciousness, we need to reinsure the polarity of bodily-spheres in the unconscious. One must never reject the body for the mind; the chief task is the preservation of the body's vital health. He is concerned, therefore, in his two essays on psychoanalysis, with an elaborate description of these bodily centers. The diaphragm divides the unconscious into two levels—the lower, dark and dynamic, the upper, objective and mental, though also dynamic. Stability of these centers is best maintained through avoiding excessive emphasis upon the mental spheres, and through a constant stimulation and exercise of the lower sphere; spanking for the child, coitus for the adult. From the time of his two essays on the unconscious (1921–1922), he read widely in several fields, looking for the social group that most fully lived his kind of life.

He attended throughout his life to a restatement of his religion; he was always finding something new to add to it in his reading and, most of all, in his personal experience. His rather disorganized statements on religion proceeded originally from a dislike of current religious practices. A new experience—such as meeting Tony Luhan or watching the Hopi Indian dance at Hoteville, New Mexico—might well suggest a fresh and original view,

[27] Lawrence, *Women in Love*, 165–66.

which led him finally to an avid search through books for some confirmation of his feelings. This was the method by which he had first encountered psychoanalysis, then defended himself against it.

In the Lawrencean unconscious there were certain centers of activity, among which was maintained an active vibrational relationship, or " polarity." The chief function of education should be to keep alive the lower, bodily-conscious centers; but Western society had overemphasized the centers of mental activity and had disturbed the balance of the human being by cutting short pure blood activity or by subjecting it to a sparse, mean, and petty intellectualism. He searched, therefore, for forms of society in which the basic and healthy polarity had been maintained. Though he had once said that he was bored by Bergson, it is clear that Lawrence's personal religion, so far as it was derived from reading at all, can be traced to Greek hylozoism and Bergson's *l'élan vital;* and the psychoanalysts furnished the concept of the unconscious, which Lawrence used as a substitute for soul, *l'élan vital,* and all other interpretations of vital energy.

v

Lawrence's novels are in one sense evidence of his spiritual development. As in his critical work, his novels reflect the controversialist and prophet, preaching a gospel which indirectly affected his manner of utterance. While Lawrence was not an experimentalist, in the sense that Joyce was, his novels are marked by original attitudes and methods. From the beginning of his career as novelist and critic he was disturbed over the concern with style and structure that seemed to often to mark modern literature. He resented also what he called the moderns' resignation, or their gloomy retreat before both nature and man; of Conrad he says: " why this giving in before you start, that pervades all Conrad and such folks—the Writers among the Ruins. I can't forgive Conrad for being so sad and for giving in." (*Letters,* 68) The odor of decay seems to prevail in modern fiction —a sense of the death which dwells in society itself. " I hate Bennett's resignation. Tragedy ought really to be a great kick at

misery. But *Anna of the Five Towns* seems like an acceptance—
so does all the modern stuff since Flaubert. I hate it. I want to
wash again quickly, wash off England, the oldness and grubbiness
and despair." (*Letters*, 66–67)

Lawrence thought the human individual worth preserving;
and he spent his life perfecting a plan whereby such preservation
might be possible. In his extremely lively, frequently disorganized
critical pieces, Lawrence demonstrated his own position by rejecting the ethical standards of his fellow authors. Hawthorne's
The Scarlet Letter, for example, is " unwholesome " because the
" sin " is exalted and symbolized, *ad nauseam*: " the sin in Hester
and Arthur Dimmesdale's case was a sin because they did what
they *thought* it *wrong* to do. If they had really *wanted* to be
lovers, and if they had had the honest courage of their own passion, there would have been no sin: even had the desire been
only momentary." [28]

The novel for Lawrence—any novel that deserved the name—
gave a creative view of life; it had a philosophy. Lawrence
brought to his reading of the works of others the same predispositions which we find in his own writing. No novel of any stature
was without its meaning for his own point of view. Melville's
Moby Dick, for example, which he regarded as a " great novel,"
was so because it carried with it a " didactic punch ":

> The essential function of art is moral. . . . But a passionate,
> implicit morality, not didactic. A morality which changes the
> blood, rather than the mind. . . .[29]

There is a danger that the novel will deaden the senses, will
merely present dead matter persisting in a dead world. But if it
is handled as a live portrait, it is at once the artist's best medium
and his best opportunity to convey the actual meaning of life,
" the changing rainbow of our living relationships." How can
creative art actually accomplish this? Life is so fluid that one
can only hope to capture the living moment, to capture it alive
and fresh: not the ordinary moment of an ordinary day, but the
critical moment of human relationships. This moment may ap-

[28] *Studies in Classic American Literature* (New York, 1923), 148.
[29] *Ibid.*, 254.

pear subtilized on the printed page, because human relationships are in themselves complex, and there is a wide divergence between external appearance and internal cause. How to capture this affective movement within the prison of cold print, without destroying that movement? " If you try to nail anything down, in the novel, either it kills the novel, or the novel gets up and walks away with the nail." [30]

This moment of vital human experience, in which the emotional life demands the most from man and woman, is the focal center of Lawrence's novels. Lawrence fastens upon it and pours into it the intensity of his entire spirit. Such a waiting for the instant, for what Whitehead calls an " event " in space and time, forces us to abandon ordinary standards of judgment. Form for Lawrence was relatively unimportant—though he was capable of writing carefully made short tales and novelle, his longer novels are held together by a succession of moments of crucial experience; its continuity is fitful, the *modus vivendi* a series of revitalized crises of human relationship. Since, as we have seen, the act of coition is one of the few acts in which the sources of energy are drawn upon profoundly, Lawrence often provides a vivid representation of such experiences.

Character always seems in a condition of unstable equilibrium with the external world. We are aware of affective states rather than of the names of the characters—though we may note, in passing, the color and sound which pervade the " circumambient air." " You mustn't look in my novel," he tells Edward Garnett, " for the old stable ego of the character. There is another ego, according to whose action the individual is unrecognisable, and passes through, as it were, allotropic states which it needs a deeper sense than we've been used to exercise, to discover are states of the same single radically-unchanged element." (*Letters*, 200)

For Lawrence a tragedy need not lead to a violent resolution in order to be powerful or tragic. For him tragedy consists in " the inner war which is raged between people who love each other." (*Letters*, 46) His characters, then, are the narrative investment of intensely charged affective states. One of the impor-

[30] " Morality and the Novel," in *Phoenix*, 532, 528.

tant qualities is the subtle complexity of an emotional state that a character assumes in a moment of crisis. Most obvious of these complex emotions is the hate-love ambivalence which qualifies any personal relationship, however happy it may appear. The understanding of Anna Brangwen with her new husband, for example, is ambiguous; it is at its height when she appears most to hate him. " His blood beat up in waves of desire. He wanted to come to her, to meet her. She was there if he could reach her. The reality of her who was just beyond him absorbed him. Blind and destroyed, he pressed forward, nearer, to receive the consummation of himself . . . he knew her, he knew her meaning, without understanding."

The investment of unconscious energies in three people, close to each other, and held together by the very thing which repels them, is a common enough situation in Lawrence's fiction. Mrs. Lydia Brangwen, Tom, and the daughter Anna are such a trio. Most often, however, the difficult, often violent, adjustments of one person to another mark the creative moment. When the young Anna marries her cousin Will, a battle of unconscious wills begins, vivified by their supplementary personalities: " They fought an unknown battle, unconsciously. Still they were in love with each other, the passion was there. But the passion was consumed in a battle. And the deep, fierce, unnamed battle went on. Everything glowed intensely about them, the world had put off its clothes and was awful, with new, primal nakedness." [31]

Horace Gregory has pointed to two symbols which in his opinion are central to Lawrence's thought, as it is revealed in the novels: the symbol of the cathedral arch, in *The Rainbow*, and the African statue of *Women in Love*. These and other symbols [32] inform Lawrence's novels with a significant and strangely appropriate continuity. The symbol for Lawrence is merely the means by which the affective state it kept alive—or the point at which

[31] D. H. Lawrence, *The Rainbow* (New York, n. d.), 86–87, 157. First published, London, 1915.
[32] Frequently, and especially in his later novels, a bird or animal symbolizes the dynamic caught in a moment of arrested motion: the horse in *St. Mawr* (New York, 1925), the bird in *Mornings in Mexico*, and *The Plumed Serpent*. Cf. also *The Ladybird and The Fox* in one volume (London, 1923). Only once does a musical instrument act as a significant symbol: the flute in *Aaron's Rod* (New York, 1922).

it stores its latent energy, awaiting new opportunities for discharge. Of *Lady Chatterley's Lover*, he says:

> Yes, the paralysis of Sir Clifford is symbolic—all art is *au fond*
> symbolic, conscious or unconscious. When I began *Lady
> Chatterley*, of course, I did not know what I was doing—I did
> not deliberately work symbolically. But by the time the book
> was finished, I realized what the unconscious symbolism was.
> . . . The wood is of course unconscious symbolism—perhaps
> even the mines—even Mrs. Bolton. (*Letters*, 832)

These are the two principal characteristics of Lawrence the novelist: the focalizing of an affective state, which frequently has to suffice for orthodox characterization; and the symbol, for the most part undeliberate—though the cathedral seems to be an exception—which acts as a fountain-source for all affective releases. The former dominates the earlier novels—*The Rainbow, Women in Love, Aaron's Rod*, and such shorter stories as " The Prussian Officer "; the latter governs, and often disturbs, the plot structure of the later novels—*The Plumed Serpent, The Virgin and the Gypsy, St. Mawr, The Man Who Died*. Only occasionally is the symbolic continuity of plot previsioned or recapitulated in a dream or vision; and the sparse use of dreams in Lawrence's novels is not surprising when one realizes his statements about dreams in *Fantasia of the Unconscious*.[33]

The story of Lawrence's development as a novelist runs parallel with that of his emergence as a thinker. The novel is Lawrence's best document; he frequently admits failure to treat satisfactorily in poetry what he often successfully manages in the novel. In the earlier novels the illustration is passionately revealed in moments of high drama; in the later novels the preaching intrudes, and *The Plumed Serpent* especially lacks the fine, subtle blending of text with context. The first are his most effec-

---

[33] See March's dream of the fox—in which she sees it as a symbol not only of its own cunning but also of Henry's persistent nature. *The Fox*, 124. Cf. also the vision of trampling horses which Ursula Brangwen experiences, *The Rainbow*, 459–63. The dreams of James Houghton are referred to only humorously, and have no significance for the plot of *The Lost Girl* (New York, 1921), 13: " Sad indeed that he died before the days of Freud. He enjoyed the most wonderful and fairy-like dreams, which he could describe perfectly, in charming, delicate language." They are child-like dreams of simple wish-fulfillment.

tive works of art; the last, the most vigorous announcements of his principles and attitudes.

Much as Lawrence was exposed to Freudianism, he retained his individuality, his independence of influence, to the end. In an important sense, Lawrence's novels are not in the least psycho-analytic. They do not employ, either crudely or satirically, the terms or concepts which appear in the novels of Ludwig Lewisohn or May Sinclair. Conrad Aiken's reference to " a muddy psycho-analytic mysticism " contains a half-truth, however. Lawrence was forever concerned with the failure of cognitive or mental con-sciousness. The artist, therefore, saw the same fault with the past as the psychologist had already observed: our intuition of human consciousness was incomplete. But the two men go their own ways, and it is perhaps unwise to measure the one by the standards of the other, for their development of the idea of consciousness becomes widely separate. Lawrence's investigation led him to place his faith in a form of religion as a synthesis of bodily and emotional expression. For Freud, religion was in itself an illusion, which, like art, furnished the ego with a " substitutive gratifica-tion." This difference of opinion is part of the natural and proper difference between artist and scientist. Lawrence's portrait of the unconscious allowed for little or no interference by the ego. Whereas Freud regarded the ego as the guardian (a badly con-fused guardian, it must be admitted) of the total self against its violation by the dark unconscious self, to Lawrence such a disci-pline caused interference with fundamental sources of emotional expression. In Lawrence's development as artist and prophet, Freud acted in the role of an irritant; Lawrence recognized that his antagonist had made profound discoveries about that world in which the artist was most interested. Both Lawrence and Freud explored the area from which we have since learned much about the role of the irrational in human affairs. Lawrence was ever aware of the fact that Freud was patrolling the same grounds.

chapter VII

KAFKA
AND MANN

i

"My writing was about you, in it I only poured out the grief I could not sigh at your breast. It was a purposely drawnout parting from you, except that you had forced it on me, while I determined its direction." [1] In this way Franz Kafka underscores the significance for him of his life-long struggle with his father. A struggle for recognition it was, fraught with misunderstanding, anxiety, scorn, and pain. The temptation is strong to give it the sole credit for all of the peculiarities of Kafka's writings. The formula is ready at hand. Nowhere in twentieth-century letters is there a better case for the Freudian. Yet Kafka's biography, when examined closely, does not permit of such easy interpretations. His spirit conceals an almost terrifying complexity of cross-purposes beneath an apparently simple exterior.

The Kafka environment is not at all unusual. His father was a successful wholesale merchant in Prague. Franz, born in 1883, was the only one of three sons who had survived birth. There were six years between him and the youngest of his three sisters.

[1] Max Brod, "Extracts from Franz Kafka's 'Letter to My Father,'" in Harry Slochower *et al.*, *A Franz Kafka Miscellany* (New York, 1940), 43.

He was a lonely child, his interests fairly well controlled from the start by the dominating interests and convictions of his father. Almost from the beginning, Franz's will and purpose failed to suit the pattern his father had naturally assumed all persons under his direct control would follow. Kafka's responsibility seemed therefore to involve the surrender of his uniqueness of personality to the will and wish of his father. Kafka recognizes that such submission makes simple the task of bringing up the child:

> In my experience, both school and home strove to obliterate individuality. This simplified the work of bringing up the child, while also simplifying life for the child, though of course he first had to taste the anguish caused by repression. . . . [My parents] did not acknowledge my individuality, but since I felt it—being very sensitive about it, and always on guard—I necessarily recognized in this attitude their disapproval of me. But if they condemned an avowed idiosyncrasy, how much worse were to be considered those idiosyncrasies which I kept hidden, because I myself found some wrong in them? [2]

Kafka's father was an excellent representative of the successful middle class. Because his life had proved its worth in material rewards and because he was not inclined in any way to recognize any other type of life, he regarded it as the only kind of experience a sane man would wish to have. Such an example might well have converted a son less inclined to question all models of behavior; for Kafka it was an obvious proof of his own inability. Once having decided upon the fundamental estrangement of the two personalities, Kafka imagined a strict division of the two points of view. The world of his father was both inaccessible and frightening. In whatever experience he had or wished to have, he was aware of the domination of that world over his individuality. At one time, says Max Brod, he had thought of collecting all his writings under the title *The Attempt to Escape from Father*.[3] Kafka saw in his father the model of an authority that

[2] Franz Kafka, "Autobiographical Sketch," in Slochower *et al.*, *A Franz Kafka Miscellany*, 51–52.

[3] Brod, "Extracts from Franz Kafka's 'Letter to My Father,'" in Slochower *et al.*, *A Franz Kafka Miscellany*, 43.

should not be questioned—that *can* not be questioned, without serious damage to the questioner. It is not a matter of reasonable action; all independent decision, whether made with good reason or not, will be implicitly or explicitly punished. Authority often overrules the question of human dignity; at no time does it permit the subject to escape without some scar, in memory of the unequal conflict.

In his biography, Max Brod often refers to this implicit resignation to the will of the father, this constant reference to the example of parental tyranny. Kafka, says Brod, overestimated his father's power over him, and this error of judgment prevented him from claiming any independent validity for his own talents. Any independent action, which he must inevitably take—since he was both by temperament and talent widely separated from his father's life—involved in consequence a sense of guilt. Kafka's life is an ever-shifting law-court scene, in which the son is always the defendant, the father both the prosecutor and the judge. In the course of this lifelong trial, the weight of argument brought forth by the defendant is intelligible and intelligent, a rational persuasion, grounded upon the principle of sufficient and good reason. The judgment and accusation, on the other hand, are often mysterious and vague. One is not always sure, either, that this accusation comes from the prosecutor; it appears at times to come from the defendant—a psychological trick that is essentially a form of self-accusation. Two important points stand out from the mass of court proceedings: the deeply certain and authoritative pronouncement of the judge, which must be accepted, though it is not entirely understood; and the vacillating querulousness of the defendant, as though he did not entirely trust the reasonableness of his own argument.

In " The Letter to My Father " [4] Kafka allows his father a " rebuttal." After some one hundred or so pages of careful explanation and penetrating criticism of the prosecutor-judge, the defendant breaks down, and allows him to cancel out, in a single, brief statement, the apparent dignity and reasonableness of the defense:

---

[4] It was preserved by his mother, who in her family wisdom did not allow her husband to see it.

While I openly blame you for everything, meaning just what I say, you are outdoing yourself in " cleverness " and " filial affection " by explaining why I am not to blame either. Of course here you succeed only apparently (that is all you want anyway) and between the lines it turns out that, in spite of all the talk about personality and essential nature and contradiction and helplessness, I was really the aggressor, while you acted only in self-defence. The results of your insincerity so far ought to be enough for you, as you have proved three things: first, that you are innocent; secondly, that I am to blame; and thirdly, that you are ready, out of pure magnanimity, not only to forgive me, but, what is more as well as less, to prove and to believe that I am innocent too, although this is contrary to fact. . . . I admit that we are fighting each other, but there are two kinds of fight. There is the knightly battle, where equal opponents are pitted against each other, each for himself, each loses for himself or wins for himself. And there is the struggle of vermin, which not only stings, but at the same time preserves itself by sucking the other's blood. Such is the professional soldier, and such are you. You are not fit for life, but in order to live in comfort, without worry or self-reproach, you prove that I have taken away your fitness for life and put it all into my pocket.[5]

In the short story, " The Sentence," this ambiguity and guilt-relationship are again explained. George Bendemann, a young businessman, has all but taken over his father's business and made a great success of it. He has also decided upon marriage, and he finds it difficult to break the news of his plans. The father, now weakened by age, has reluctantly depended upon George for the management of his business. From his bed, George's father upbraids him for taking manifest advantage of him. " ' I am still much the stronger,' " he cries. " ' How long you hesitated before becoming mature. . . . Now you know what was going on outside yourself. Before you only knew about yourself. You really were an innocent child, but in reality, diabolical!—Listen: I now condemn you to death by drowning.' " Dazed by the fearful sentence, George rushes out of his father's room, into the street, and leaps

[5] *Ibid.*, 49–50.

from the bridge, crying, " ' Dear parents! Yes, I have always loved you.' " [6]

There is something pitifully helpless in the powerful hold which Kafka's reference to his father has over the conclusion of his tales. So strong is his sense of debasement and of self-criticism that occasional glimpses of success on his own part almost inevitably bring about a sudden collapse of self-assurance. Aware that his father's world held almost all the keys to material security and success, he forswore the temptation to take up a writer's career and became a Doctor of Laws in 1906. He was engaged, apparently with some success, in a semi-state office in Prague. In 1912 he met a young woman from Berlin, " Fräulein B "; he became engaged to her in April of 1914, broke off the engagement in July of that year, was again engaged to her in 1916, and finally ended their relationship in 1917, pleading illness as an excuse. To some critics, this illness appears to have been brought about deliberately. In August, 1916, in a letter to Max Brod, Kafka sums up the advantages and disadvantages of married life. Alone, he will be free to concentrate upon his work, without any trivial cares or distractions. His powers will be available for his own uses. Married, he will be forced to dissipate his strength, all of it expended in the support of the " Blutkreislauf des menschlichen Lebens." [7] What he has accomplished, says Kafka, has always followed from his " having been alone," independent of conventional responsibilities. Kafka himself had suggested to Brod that his illness was psychically caused, a release from the obligation of marriage.[8] In the important " Letter to My Father " he shows the relationship—real or imagined, it apparently does not matter—between the " Verlobungskrise " and his father's hold upon him. The need of his father's approval has qualified his every decision.

The most important obstacle to marriage is the already ineradicable conviction that, in order to preserve and especially to guide a family, all the qualities I see in you are necessary—

[6] Franz Kafka, " The Sentence," in *Transition Stories*, eds. Eugene Jolas and Robert Sage (New York, 1929), 208, 210–11.

[7] Max Brod, *Franz Kafka: Eine Biographie* (Prague, 1937), 186. A translation of this book by G. Humphreys Roberts was published in New York, 1947.

[8] " ' Er stellt sie als psychisch dar, gleichsam Rettung vor der Heirat.' " *Ibid.*, 199.

and I mean all of them, the good and the bad, just the way they are organically united in you: strength, coupled with a tendency to ridicule the other fellow, health and a certain recklessness, speaking ability combined with aloofness, self-confidence and dissatisfaction with everyone else, sophistication and tyranny, knowledge of people and a distrust of most of them. . . . Of all these qualities I had comparatively few, almost none, in fact. And yet what right had I to risk marriage, seeing, as I did, that you yourself had a hard struggle during your married life, that you even failed toward your children. . . .

However, I did not ask this question; I only lived it, from childhood on. The problem of marriage was not the starting point of my self-probings anyway; I had always questioned myself over every trifle; in every trifle you convinced me, by your example and by the way you brought me up, as I have tried to describe it, of my incapability. And what was true, and justified you in all trifling matters, would of course be insurmountably true for the Highest, that is, marriage.[9]

One genuine source of unity there was between Kafka and his parents—their Judaism. Yet even here the relationship was not steadfast or assuring. His father, it seemed to him, accepted the religion in terms of his adjustment to "a certain Jewish social class." Hence the performance and fulfillment of his religious obligations, though punctual within their limits, was casual and perfunctory. Franz was bored with the whole thing. When, later in his life, he became intensely interested in Jewish thought and religion, it was to the excellent learning and impressive sobriety of his mother's family that he felt indebted. The memory of his father simply hindered Kafka's complete acceptance; "'. . . my new interest bore your curse.'" Though Kafka was in a sense reviving the Judaism of his family in his own study and devotion, this effort did not bring them closer together. His father apparently turned away from Jewish theology; this could only mean that "'you realized subconsciously the weakness of your own Judaism and of my Jewish upbringing, that you wanted in no wise

---

[9] Brod, "Extracts from Franz Kafka's 'Letter to My Father,'" in Slochower *et al., A Franz Kafka Miscellany,* 44.

to be reminded of it, and received all reminders with open hatred.' " [10]

It is impossible to determine accurately the extent to which this ambiguous relationship affected Kafka's wrting. It is far too easy to offer a simple psychological explanation—all the easier because such an explanation accounts for everything in his life and in his writings. "Any psychoanalyst," warns Klaus Mann, " could define Kafka's religious pathos—his humble and yet mistrustful fear of God—as the productive ' sublimation ' of an obvious ' father complex.' " [11] So far as an artist's aesthetic conscience and consciousness are affected by his personal experiences, the father-son relationship, it must be admitted, is responsible for much of the peculiarity of style and point of view which is Kafka's contribution to the world of letters. Indeed, this relationship takes many forms in Kafka's writings. In all cases where the masculine and feminine wills are in conflict over a moral issue, the masculine will overrules the feminine, and the circumstance of the hero does not permit him to question or effectively to contravene that will. The feminine will and being play an important role in the progress of Kafka's heroes—but this role stops far short of the doorway to understanding, sympathy, or ultimate salvation. Kafka will not accept the easy way of feminine sympathy—because this way is endlessly qualified by the power of the paternal-masculine. The role of women is secondary—and the female can only alleviate pain or torture, not remove it. Many of the painful situations in Kafka's stories arise from a misunderstanding and a lack of good will. The hero-victim *knows* the reasons for his innocence, has evidence of it (usually, however, no witnesses) ; but the guilt is supported by an overwhelming and desperate weight of circumstantial evidence. The hero, therefore, though innocent (or just, or right), may be implicitly guilty of being innocent! Against this paradox, feminine sympathy avails little; it can offer only petty subterfuge, for essentially its presence is trivial and unimportant.

Kafka found it all but impossible to understand his father

[10] *Ibid.*, 49.
[11] Klaus Mann, Preface to Franz Kafka's *Amerika* (Norfolk, Conn., n. d.) , xi.

partly because his sense of guilt prevented such understanding. To him, the authority invested in the father image was beyond understanding; his perplexity and disillusionment were both incredible and poignant. His father did not act reasonably; and yet his unreasonableness did not make it possible for Kafka to renounce him altogether, or to accept him unequivocally. Authority is always incomprehensible, says Kafka; one cannot reduce it to reasonable terms, compromise with it, or dismiss it with easy ridicule. There is no reasonable way of justifying one's father's way to his son. " It's impossible to defend oneself where there is no good will,' " Karl Rossmann tells himself after his interview with the Head Waiter of the Hotel Occidental has reached an impasse, and his circumstantial guilt is so rigidly fixed that he appears actually guilty.[12] This sense of a total collapse of reason in the face of irrational or mysterious circumstance sometimes assumes horrible forms. In the story " Metamorphosis," Gregor Samsa, a successful salesman who has been supporting his family, one day awakes and finds himself changed into an enormous bug. " Lying on his plate-like, solid back and raising his head a bit, he saw his arched, brown belly divided by bowed corrugations, on top of which the blanket was about to slip down, since it could not hold by itself. His many legs—lamentably thin as compared with his usual size—were dangling helplessly before his eyes." [13]

It is not a hideous dream. He has emerged from sleep into a world horrified and made furious by the change. The simple arrangement of his former world has collapsed. He has become an object of loathing. This shame and debasement which Gregor feels has in a sense been willed by him—this sudden collapse of the order of his everyday surroundings. For Gregor's father the metamorphosis is a demonstration of his son's malice. On one occasion the father, infuriated by the turn of events, throws apples at him, and one of these apples is imbedded in Gregor's back, causing a wound he suffers for more than a month. It " seemed to recall, even to his father, that Gregor was a member of the family, despite his present sad and loathsome shape, whom they could not treat as an enemy. Family duty demanded that they

[12] Kafka, *Amerika*, 188.
[13] Franz Kafka, " Metamorphosis," in *Transition*, XXV (1936), 27.

swallow their repulsion and tolerate him—tolerate him, and nothing more." [14]

Just as Gregor had somehow willed the metamorphosis—it is *his* crime and responsibility—so he must will to die, to remove the shame it has caused his family. He must, in other words, remove himself from the consciousness of his family, in atonement for having thought and willed independently of it. Gregor refuses, therefore, to take any food, and as a consequence the family is released from the responsibility of his loathsome presence. The metamorphosis is thus a symbol of man's willful denial of authority. That this authority is absurd, or unreasonable, does not alter the circumstances or reduce the guilt.

Kafka's failure to manage the father-son relationship has important implications for his eventual decision regarding the God-man relationship: incomprehensible demands for duty and obedience in the face of absurdity which is all too obvious to a person accustomed to the "reasonableness" of things. Only once did he suggest a plan or order which might accommodate incongruous moral and psychological ideas. *Amerika*, his first attempt at a sustained work of art, closes with the description of an immense spectacle—the "Nature Theatre of Oklahoma." Karl first learns of this project when he reads a placard announcing a recruiting for service in it. "If you think of your future you are one of us! Everyone is welcome! If you want to be an artist, join our company! Our Theatre can find employment for everyone, a place for everyone!'" Karl is amazed and incredulous: "Everyone, that meant Karl too. . . . He was entitled to apply for a job of which he need not be ashamed, which, on the contrary, was a matter of public advertisement." [15] Karl finds that everything promised is true. He is taken on as a student engineer, not because he is at all qualified for that profession, but because he had at one time *wanted* to become an engineer! The fact that he has no identification papers on his person does not seem to matter. His willingness and his desire are passport enough. This gigantic social project is the product of wish-fulfillment and a lively

[14] *Ibid.*, XXVII (1938), 83. Cf. Harry Slochower's suggestive comment: "We have here the reversal of Abraham's sacrifice of Isaac." "Franz Kafka—Pre-Fascist Exile," in Slochower *et al.*, *A Franz Kafka Miscellany*, 9.
[15] Kafka, *Amerika*, 272–73. Written in 1913.

imagination—Kafka had never visited America—through which he
saw the new world happily providing what his own world had
denied him. He would flee from his father and from the per-
plexing ambiguities of his personal world to the refuge of a world
fantastically designed for the unified and happy praise of God.[16]
This is an exception to Kafka's usual conception of man's struggle
for religious and ethical security. Its very superficiality points to
the fact that it is a single moment of release from the weight of
his ordinary cares and the uncertainty of his search.

His writing shaped itself in accordance with the difficulty in
and dread of the father-son relationship. Briefly, the circumstance
is as follows. Kafka felt an essential difference between his father
and himself—a difference in temperament and in talents. But he
did not throw aside his family because of this difference. His
father's strength and the strength of authority which was related
to it prevented him from adopting any simple expedient, such
as revolt or departure from the family circle. He allowed the
authority of his father to act as a judge of everything with which
he was subsequently concerned. When his decisions were arrived
at in some independence of judgment, they were qualified and
circumscribed by a feeling of guilt, which made them half-hearted
and ambiguous. A sense of utter helplessness, mingled with rage
and hatred, came over him. It seemed that he should accept what
to him seemed unreasonable, almost unintelligible. His struggle
for peace is characterized by an ambivalence of protest and submission—a protest against the unreasonableness, often absurdity,
of authority, a submission to its inevitability and its power. Here
we have qualities which when appraised logically cancel each other
out—absurdity, unreasonableness, attractiveness, love and hatred,
fear and suspicion. The effects are gruesomely comic, as in " Metamorphosis "; or wearisomely hopeless, as in *The Trial*; or exas-
perating, as in *The Castle*. Inevitably, however, the art of Kafka
is employed in describing the tortuous pilgrimage of a soul beset
with doubt and skepticism to some spiritual refuge, which is never
reached. The search always ends in an irrational confusion, in

[16] See " Die Welt als ein Schauspiel zum Preise Gottes! " Herbert Tauber,
Franz Kafka: Eine Deutung Seiner Werke (Zurich and New York, 1941) , 57. A
translation of this book by G. Humphreys Roberts and Roger Senhouse was published in London, 1948.

which all rational laws are suspended; it often ends in the death
of the hero.[17]

ii

Concerning this important and enduring fact of Kafka's life—his
ambiguous relationship with his father, and the sense of guilt
which it brought with it—Max Brod has had this to say:

> . . . it seems impossible to deny the applicability to Kafka's
> case of Freud's theories of the subconscious. And yet this
> interpretation seems too facile. For one thing Franz Kafka
> himself was thoroughly familiar with these theories and
> never regarded them as anything more than a very approxi-
> mate, rough picture of things. He found that they did not
> do justice to details or, what is more, to the essence of the
> conflict.[18]

Brod admits the opportunity for psychoanalysis, but insists that
it can never search deeply enough for essential causes, which in
his estimation are much more important than any psychological
interpretation can make them. That Kafka should have read Freud
is quite probable, for their homes were but a short distance from
each other, and for a time at least they were almost neighbors.
Slochower suggests that both the economic and the moral conditions of twentieth-century Austria were ready soil for " psychoanalysis and mystic doctrines." [19] There is scarcely any question of Kafka's knowledge of psychoanalysis, or its peculiar per-
tinence to his case. Were this a psychoanalytic study of biography,
it might be a simple matter for one to argue the case conclusively,
drawing for evidence upon Kafka's own admissions—in his notebooks, his letters, and elsewhere.[20] But such an easy treatment of

[17] His own death Kafka called a return to the father, a day of great for-
giveness. " ' Mein Leben ist das Zögern vor der Geburt.' " Quoted by Tauber,
Franz Kafka, 218–19.
[18] Max Brod, " Kafka: Father and Son," in *Partisan Review*, IV (1938), 21–22.
Cf. Brod, *Franz Kafka*, 31.
[19] Slochower, " Franz Kafka—Pre-Fascist Exile," in Slochower *et al., A Franz
Kafka Miscellany*, 9.
[20] Cf. Brod, " Kafka: Father and Son," *loc. cit.*, 22: ". . . it must be admitted
that Kafka himself, in stating that he had, not explicitly, or ' in ordinary thinking,'

a complex life and of its literary product might well cause serious omissions of interpretation; it would certainly not fully agree with more than one half of Kafka's own thinking about the matter, and would deny the relevance or importance of Kafka's own statements about psychoanalysis.[21]

What might Freud have said about Kafka's life? Hostility toward the father comes from a boy's love of his mother, his intense desire to " return to her," a desire which is constantly interfered with by the father, who bars the way and himself enjoys the love which the child thinks belongs to him. The hatred for the father is repressed, for several reasons, one of which is of course the father's strength and authority, another the fact that this hatred is not unmixed with a sense of duty, even at times a certain tenderness toward the father. The father is, therefore, the first important barrier to the child's free path to instinctual gratification.[22]

In 1909 Freud published " The Analysis of a Phobia in a Five-Year-Old Boy."[23] In this essay, and in a subsequent study of anxiety, he demonstrates the ambivalence of a child's attitude toward his father: " He finds himself in the jealous and hostile oedipus attitude to his father, whom, however, in so far as his mother does not enter the picture as the cause of dissension, he loves devotedly. Thus we have a conflict springing from ambivalence—a firmly founded love and a not less justified hatred, both directed to the same person."[24] The effect of this withdrawal of the mother's attention is twofold: first, the union with

formulated his attitude toward his father's superiority, but had ' experienced it from childhood on,' seems to confirm the psychoanalytic point of view. So do his remarks on his father's ' methods of training '—amplified in numerous diary entries dealing with his ' miscarried education '; and his letters on pedagogy, based on Swift's thesis that ' children should be brought up outside of the family, not by their parents.' " See also " Aus Zwei Briefen Kafkas über Kinderenziehung," in Brod, *Franz Kafka*, 261–68.

[21] For an exhaustive psychoanalytic interpretation of Kafka, see Charles Neider, *Kafka: His Mind and His Art* (New York, 1949). Paul Goodman's *Kafka's Prayer* (New York, 1947) employs psychoanalysis as one of several critical strategies.

[22] The mother herself sets up barriers too—such as are necessary for the education of the infant, to make him gradually independent of her. But the father's presence and his deliberate pre-emption of what the child blindly regards as his prerogative, is the most powerful of all barriers, and the most likely to lead to hatred and ultimately to anxiety.

[23] *Collected Papers of Sigmund Freud*, III, 149–289|

[24] *The Problem of Anxiety*, tr. Henry A. Bunker (New York, 1936), 38.

the mother, originally the only source of the child's sense of identity, is rudely shattered for long periods of time; secondly, the child's sense of importance (for importance is purely biological in infancy) is given a severe shock. His instinctive reaction is to strike blindly at the source of this discomfiture; when that move does not succeed, the child is forced into a none too strategic retreat. The " enemy " has aroused a number of as yet unformed emotions: respect, hatred, anger, disappointment—which, when combined with the child's natural love for his father (as a convenient " sex object "), cause a serious enough disruption of his simple life, and are his earliest introduction to the painful complexity of experience awaiting him in future life.

The measure of this disappointment, as well as of its effect upon the child's nature, is the strength of control with which the father orders and regulates his son's new-found relationship with his mother. Since the father's severity and " family zeal " can only be interpreted as a strong barrier to the child's gratification of his desires, the latter may very well, as he grows older and finds this barrier interfering in other ways as well, adopt a relatively strong and sometimes enduring resentment toward its source. In some cases, perhaps especially those in which the doctrine of obedience and the effect of painful and senseless discipline apparently dominate the child's growing awareness of his outside world, the mother also becomes a prisoner of the father's will. This is not to say that the mother actually *is* suffering from the father's rule (she may very well submit to it gladly, out of respect or love) ; rather, the child *assumes* or believes that his mother shares his imprisonment, since of course she is as anxious as he is to satisfy his wishes. Hence, the father becomes a tyrant; his authority is unquestioned; occasional relaxations of it are eagerly awaited and gratefully received. Protests against it on grounds of reason or justice only aggravate the wound; for reasonable protest does not avail against the tyranny.

Further, the child, after he has matured and recognizes independently a superficial difference between justifiable and unjustifiable commands of his father's will, may consider some of them absurd. If the will of the father resembles that of a tyrant, the absurdity of his command and the child's recognition of that

absurdity have very little chance of altering the effect of authority. Solutions to this intolerable situation are many: complete
severance of the family ties, suicide, murder. But each of these
presumes a strong will on the part of the son, a determination that
" this wrong will be shattered." If the will is weak—if it has been
all but drawn within the orbit of the father's will—the solution
is so unsatisfactory that it can scarcely be *called* a solution. The
child may very well spend his life in an endless search for independent decision; each such effort is liable to failure. He cannot
renounce his father, he cannot accept him. Each attempt to renounce him will be hindered by the desire (for the sake of peace)
to accept him. Every resolve to accept him will (because of the
implicit absurdity or unreasonableness of the tyranny) reawaken
in him the desire to renounce him.

The extension of this early father-son relationship—the " oedipus reaction "—affects the quality and intensity of the child's
acceptance of moral and social restrictions. Actually, Freud says,
the development of a conscience, the superego, replaces the oedipus relationship: " During the course of its growth, the super-ego
also takes over the influence of those persons who have been concerned in the child's upbringing, and whom it has regarded as
ideal models. Normally the super-ego is constantly becoming
more and more remote from the original parents, becoming, as
it were, more impersonal." [25] Thus the superego develops out of
the parental situation, using such objects or images as are readily
available in the child's heritage or surroundings—the school, the
church, the community—and, of course, acting as an inner deter-
rent both upon the id and the ego.

Psychoanalysis might thus have explained Kafka's affairs, and
should certainly have had little difficulty adjusting each of his
writings to that explanation. Kafka's ambivalent attitude toward
his father, and the power which his father apparently had over
him, affected the development of conscience, or superego, in his
personality. Kafka's God, therefore, bore a strange but a clear
enough resemblance to his father. His was a personal God, but
one with whom any intimacy or understanding was extremely difficult of attainment, almost impossible. The tyranny of this God

[25] *New Introductory Lectures on Psychoanalysis*, 92.

made his every step hesitant, recalled to him the egregious pre-
sumption of any moment of self-confidence, and made unthinkable the prospect of a mutual trust or obligation. The strange
conclusion of that morbid tale, "In the Penal Colony," suggests
ominously that the ingenious torture machine is after all just, and
that any reformist notions which might have made salvation easy
or sins readily forgiven, will eventually be overruled. Most of
Kafka's shorter stories deal symbolically with the strange figure
of the father and his family position. *The Trial, The Castle,*
and "In the Penal Colony" treat of the father-position transformed into the image of an inaccessible and incomprehensible
God, the whimsical God of the Book of Job, or the stern and
demanding God of Kierkegaard's *Fear and Trembling.*

The biographical sources of Kafka's art lend themselves
readily to a psychoanalytic exposition. This he himself admitted,
though he condemned the explanation as "too facile." The ultimate progress of his art goes beyond the limits of psychoanalysis.
It is an aesthetic statement of an irrational ethic—an ethic and a
religion that are beyond reason, or that demand a suspension of
reason to be comprehended. Such a position cannot employ a
single scheme; it is not bound or limited by the requisites of any
school of psychology or philosophy. Kafka shares with many
others, European and American, a distrust of simple rationalism.
Avoiding the confidence and optimism of late nineteenth-century
scientists, these men denied that science and its eighteenth-century
partner, rational religion, had satisfactorily answered the questions and resolved the paradoxes of the God-man relationship.

It is possible that Freud would have had more to say to Kafka
had the latter lived long enough to see his discussion of Judaism in
Moses and Monotheism. As it was, Kafka rejected psychoanalysis
at the threshold of the analyst's laboratory. The confidence of
psychoanalysis in its therapeutic procedures did not impress him.
The tendency to locate all spiritual and emotional depression
within the area of mental and nervous diseases suggested to him
that psychoanalysis was evading its essential responsibility. Simply
to bring the *source* of a neurosis to the surface, to subject the
irrational to conscious scrutiny does not, he said in effect, alter the
situation or improve it.

Try to understand it by calling it a disease. It is one of the many symptoms of disease which psychoanalysis claims to have uncovered. I do not call it disease, and I consider the therapeutic part of psychoanalysis a helpless error. All these so-called diseases, pitiful as they look, are beliefs, the attempts of a human being in distress to cast his anchor in some mother-soil; thus what psychoanalysis finds to be the primary source of religions is none other than the source of individual " disease." Today, to be sure, there is no religious unity, the sects are numberless and mostly confined to individuals, or perhaps that is only how it seems to any eye entangled in the present. But such anchorings which find real soil . . . are performed in his being, and afterwards continue to form his being (his body too) further in that direction. Who can hope for cure here? [26]

Psychoanalysis has had some important things to say about religion and the religious impulse. But, in Kafka's estimation, it is nonsense to regard a religious belief as merely a submission to the " impersonal father image " or a successfully religious person as using religion merely as an escape from a personal neurosis. Freud's interpretation of religion as an illusion on a grand scale might have received an answer from Kafka similar to the following: It is true that a religious belief can be called an illusion, if by illusion you mean a belief that receives no immediate—or even ultimate—justification in fact, no miracle which in some startling way adjusts the supernatural to a man-made causality. More than that, Kafka objects to the psychoanalytic treatment of beliefs as diseases, as though a laboratory or official pronouncement—this is contrary to reason, it is not reasonable or polite or in the best taste to subscribe to it—were to exorcise the paradoxes of faith in God. Freud described religion as one aspect of culture, as a large-scale sublimation, to which man contributes his fears and troubles, a kind of reservoir of unnatural shock. The gods, therefore, man-made as they are, are used as a means of comforting man against the terrors of nature, and as a spiritual (or illusory) refuge from the sufferings which an exacting communal culture

[26] Franz Kafka, " Meditations," in Slochower *et al.*, *A Franz Kafka Miscellany*, 70.

has made possible. Freud wishes us to get rid of these illusions, since they are wish-fulfillments, barring the way to an honest appraisal of man's weaknesses. The task of psychoanalysis is to shift the control from God to human society, to admit " honestly the purely human origin of all cultural laws and institutions." The result, he says, will be a healthy and courageous view of the world as it is, a moderate control of pleasure, a discreet governing of pain. The shock of reality should not lead to illusion or to large-scale theological schemata, but to an intelligent mastery of the situation, through knowledge or conscious awareness. For, at bottom, Freud believes firmly in the dictum that " Knowledge is Power," that a conscious awareness of biological and psychological mechanisms will lead to a sensible appraisal of them and adjustment to them. Such a readjustment will eliminate the unfortunate, neurotic detours which the human mind has had to take in the realm of the spirit. " The true believer," says Freud, " is in a high degree protected against the danger of certain neurotic afflictions; by accepting the universal neurosis he is spared the task of forming a personal neurosis." [27]

iii

Kafka's reaction to Freud's view of religion should be fairly clear. What Freud regarded as an aberration, a misconstruction or distortion of the process of sublimation, Kafka insisted upon calling a reality. There are three ways in which God may be imagined or called into the human consciousness. There is the reasonable God, who by a happy chance bore himself with the deportment of an enlightened gentleman, who gave a metaphysical guarantee to all who would purchase his clock-universe. In the face of catastrophes not listed in the rule-books, this God might be absolved from the responsibility, but each such absolution weakened in his polite constituency the respect accorded him. [28]

[27] *The Future of an Illusion*, 76, 77. This book was written in 1927, and Kafka could not therefore have read it. However, it is closely related with the general intention and purpose of psychoanalytic therapy, and Kafka had long before his death in 1924 inferred its conclusions from others of Freud's writings.

[28] The only opposition to such a God which might have in any way pleased the gentlemen of the Enlightenment is satire, such as we find in Voltaire's *Candide*. Kafka regarded satire—especially as directed against ethics or metaphysics

The second God-construction is a mythical figure, in whom the qualities of tenderness, mercy, kindness, and commiseration are essential as a means of protection against the harsh realities of human existence. This is in part what Freud calls the illusion whose future disappearance he hopefully predicts. Such a God may not be a reasonable being, but his lack of reasonableness is a prerequisite to his service to the community of men. Prayer to him and worship of him are both signs of the illusion as an operating principle in theology. He bears the burden of human sin and of physical and geological disturbance. Both Freud and Kafka would like to see such a vision óf God dissipated and destroyed: Freud because it interferes with the immense reconstruction project which science has undertaken for some two centuries or so; Kafka, because it is a deliberate and puerile denial of the reality of an actual God, whose ways are neither temperate nor comprehensible.

Thus, the third God-construction, the God of Kierkegaard and Kafka. Far from denying responsibility for evil in the world, for accidents in an otherwise perfect world, this God is indifferent to complaints against them. Far from acting as a tribune of easy justice or as a means of comforting refuge, he remains starkly cruel, cruelly whimsical, inaccessible to the yardstick of sufficient reason. His manner fluctuates incomprehensibly from good to evil to good, not because he is aware of any ethical dichotomy but because he is beyond all systems of ethical appraisal. Man's worship of the first God is a pastime, of the second a flight from reality, of the third an unreasonable and unreasoning acceptance. In the words of Pascal, whom Kafka studied with interest, man's finiteness of body and intellect limits his chances of either measuring or controlling the infinite:

> We sail within a vast sphere, ever drifting in uncertainty, driven from end to end. When we think to attach ourselves to any point and to fasten to it, it wavers and leaves us; and if we follow it, it eludes our grasp, slips past us, and vanishes forever. Nothing stays for us. This is our natural condition,

---

—as a low form of humor. Kierkegaard, of course, used it as a weapon against his contemporaries. But to satirize the ways of God was unthinkable, in the opinion of both Kierkegaard and Kafka.

and yet most contrary to our inclination; we burn with desire to find solid ground and an ultimate sure foundation whereon to build a tower reaching to the Infinite. But our whole groundwork cracks, and the earth opens to abysses.[29]

The majority of Kafka's writings describe man's relationship to such a God, personalized, an anthropomorphic judge to whom rational appeals are of no consequence, because he is not aware of, or is indifferent to, man's rational schemes for achieving salvation. This is why the Book of Job, the story of Abraham and Isaac, and the legend of Prometheus interested him profoundly. More specifically, he became attracted to the story of Abraham as a key to his philosophy, through reading Kierkegaard's *Fear and Trembling*.[30] To avoid certain pitfalls of easy interpretation, we ought to keep this in mind if we are to appraise correctly Kafka's literary work.

Kafka's style is above all realistic. The details are starkly clear. Kafka presents situations clearly and within easy range of the immediate understanding. " If the expressionists converted natural events into magic," says Slochower, " Kafka attempted to show the magic within the simple course of events." [31] Kafka regarded Flaubert as an arbiter of style; he too sought a clear approximation to the reality of the event he was describing. But this clarity, though painstakingly achieved, is illusory. Within the range of the reader's attention the facts are unmistakable, concretely realized, and plausible. Beyond the reach of this attention —at the point where the reader is called upon to fit a succession of events within a time, space, or thought sequence—obscurity sets in and the reader is forced to readjust his position, or to regard the book as a whole as absurd. It is only then that one realizes that it is not intended as representation, but as allegory and symbol.[32]

[29] Blaise Pascal, *Pensées* (New York, 1941), 25. Kafka rejected the notion of a Christian intermediary, the persuasive conclusion of Pascal's argument. Cf. Kafka, *The Trial* (New York, 1937), 198–99; Tauber, *Franz Kafka*, 216–17.

[30] Princeton, 1941. Written in 1843.

[31] Slochower, " Franz Kafka—Pre-Fascist Exile," in Slochower *et al.*, *A Franz Kafka Miscellany*, 27.

[32] More strictly as *symbol*. For, as Brod points out, allegory suggests a careful correspondence between abstract and concrete truth, whereas symbol allows for an endless process of interpretation and provides for shifts in meaning consistent with the nature of Kafka's quest: ". . . Sache der Spannkraft, die den Einzelfall ins Grenzenlose ausstrahlen läszt. . . ." Brod, *Franz Kafka*, 236–37.

Thus, the realism of details is designed to demonstrate that man's actions, considered singly, are comprehensible and plausible. The larger obscurity of plot and development is designed to show that man's actions in the aggregate, especially if man is engaged in a spiritual quest, are incomprehensible and strike one immediately as absurd.

Far more suitable to the nature of Kafka's thinking is the use of irony, or ironic comedy. In the eyes of Kafka's God, the strivings of man are pitiful and grotesque. More than that, he is indifferent to them, and they acquire their grotesqueness from man's own despairing observation of them. Man's earnest striving for a successful rapport with God leaves him breathless, and his efforts, considered from the perspective of the immediate future, are stupid. They are laughable; but laughter directed against oneself is likely soon after to lead to a meditative silence. It is as though an earnest endeavor or striving were suddenly to appear grotesque, as though the floor beneath the worshiper were suddenly to disappear. The measure of such irony is not the slapstick nature of any given situation, but the seriousness with which one has initially regarded the purport of events leading up to it. Max Brod describes one of many readings with which Kafka entertained his friends. "All of us laughed loudly [at one of Kafka's comical passages]. But we were soon silent. This was no laughter to which men were accustomed. Only angels would dare laugh thus. . . ." This was a new kind of laughter which Kafka's humor provoked, a laughter near to the sober insight into final truths, a "metaphysical laughter." [33] The crudity of many of Kafka's comical situations, reminding one as they do of circus clowning or vaudeville slapstick, is designed to point to the despairing conscientiousness of a man as he pursues his paltry way toward success, or God, or the evening dinner. "For though his humor persistently reminds us of the knockabout comedian and the circus," says Edwin Muir, "it is founded on the most grave and exact reasoning. Its originality lies in its union with the deepest seriousness. K's predicaments [of *The Castle*] are absurd, but they are also desperate." [34]

[33] *Ibid.*, 163.
[34] Edwin Muir, "Franz Kafka," in Slochower *et al.*, *A Franz Kafka Miscellany.*
59.

The concept of absurdity is earnest of Kafka's religious usage of literary irony and humor. It was Kierkegaard who first pointed out the significance of this concept for theology. We are accustomed to regard a thing as absurd when it violates good sense or reason, and in a sense therefore to dismiss it as either stupid, incredible, or dangerous. Kierkegaard uses the idea of the *absurd* as a qualitative judgment upon the ways of God to man. If we are to keep faith in him, we must wrench the idea of the absurd from its rational context, and, while recognizing an act or whim or wish of God as absurd, resign ourselves to it as another of the things which are beyond man's understanding. Thus resignation to something one cannot comprehend is tantamount to accepting it in an act of faith. This is the clue to the faith of Abraham. The relationship of God to man is essentially paradoxical, when measured by human reason. But when qualified by man's mature acceptance of God's will, paradox no longer exists. Paradox, then, is a characteristic of man's search for faith. As David Swenson puts it, " it is his *reason* as concrete expression for what he initially *is*, in contradistinction to what he strives in faith to *become*. Hence there exists indeed no paradox for faith in its perfection, but for the human individual who is in process of becoming, the paradoxical cannot be avoided without arbitrarily limiting the spiritual process." [35]

There is a superficial resemblance between this notion of the absurd and Freud's discussion of " secondary elaboration " in the dream work. The dreamer, upon awakening, considers some aspects of his dream absurd and unthinkable, and he qualifies his acceptance of them by saying, " Well, it's only a dream after all." The analyst, of course, asks his patient not to regard these dream elements as absurd; on the contrary, he requests that they be considered as important parts of a successful analysis. Both for Freud and for Kierkegaard, man is asked to accept what appears to be contrary to good safe principle. But the resemblance breaks off at this point: the patient is requested to consider the absurd

---

[35] David F. Swenson, *Something about Kierkegaard*, ed. Lillian Marvin Swenson (Minneapolis, 1941), 145. For a modern interpretation of the *absurd*, associated with existentialist reasoning, see Albert Camus, *The Myth of Sisyphus and Other Essays*, translated by Justin O'Brien (New York, 1955), originally published, Paris, 1942. See especially " Hope and the Absurd in the Work of Franz Kafka," pp. 124–38.

seriously because such an attitude will lead to the discovery of its cause, which he can thenceforth reject as absurd. Kierkegaard asks his reader to recognize the absurd so that he may eventually accept it as index to a higher truth.

Such an acceptance causes man great, almost intolerable, anxiety. His ordinary, rational supports are removed from him. The order of his life—such order as his society gives him or forces upon him—becomes meaningless. His reason tells him that such or such a thing is absurd; his groping, fumbling, almost helpless search for faith causes untold anxiety of body and spirit. This idea of anxiety (*Angst*) is explained by Freud as the result of a sudden interruption of instinctual gratification. The anxiety neurosis is a protective device used by the ego to ward off danger which might come as the result of need for repression. " Anxiety is the reaction to a situation of danger; and it is circumvented by the ego's doing something to avoid the situation of retreat from it." [36] Again, psychoanalysis treats the situation as a " disease problem "; a cure will eliminate not only the problem but the anxiety accompanying it. Kierkegaard regards dread, or anxiety, as a necessary emotional constituent of the search for faith. Here too is the lesson of Kafka's writings. Man's way to God is plagued by uncertainty and insecurity. His persistence in the face of absurdity and the experience of dread is by way of becoming an act of faith (*Glaubensakt*). We note that Gregor Samsa suffers debasement and shame in his metamorphosis, which is part of his self-release from the society he knows and understands, the society in which he has assumed a position of dignity. This release involves the acceptance of a horrible external appearance; and the first portion of " Metamorphosis " depicts the dread which this appearance causes him. Joseph K., in *The Trial*, resists almost to the end the demand to give himself up to the horror and strangeness of a mysterious judgment. In the end, however, he goes without much protest. He assents to the pathos and paradox of his death at the hands of two minions of the Court:

> Logic is doubtless unshakable, but it cannot withstand a man who wants to go on living. Where was the Judge whom he had never seen? Where was the High Court, to which he had

[36] *The Problem of Anxiety*, 85–86.

never penetrated? He raised his hands and spread out all his fingers.

But the hands of one of the partners were already at K.'s throat, while the other thrust the knife into his heart and turned it there twice. With failing eyes K. could still see the two of them, cheek leaning against cheek, immediately before his face, watching the final act. " Like a dog! " he said; it was as if he meant the shame of it to outlive him.[37]

Perhaps this interpretation of anxiety in the face of strange and disagreeable surroundings is best demonstrated in another passage of *The Trial*. Joseph K. has come to the Interrogation Chamber on a day when there are no inquiries taking place. He becomes oppressed by the stifling atmosphere and feels faint. The female servant tells him not to worry; such an occurrence is not at all out of the ordinary. The air, " ' Well, on a day when there's a great number of clients to be attended to, and that's almost every day, it's hardly breathable.' " K. must remember also, she says, that " ' all sorts of washings are hung up to dry.' " She assures him that " ' in the end one gets quite used to it.' " K. is himself so overcome by his spell of dizziness, and by the shame of appearing weak before these people, that he cannot answer her. (*Trial*, 84). The two symptoms of anxiety are here demonstrated: a physical repulsion, caused by the unattractiveness of the strange surroundings, and the agony of shame that he should have appeared weak within them. This experience is repeated in K.'s interview with Tintorelli, the portrait painter to whom he has come for advice about his case. The two incidents suggest both the dread felt in the presence of an overpowering circumstance—dizziness is a normal physical reaction to an insupportable circumstance—and the shame felt because of the decline of self-respect and superficial dignity.

The great difference of opinion which Kafka had with psychoanalysis in the matter of religion and ethics can be demonstrated in no better way than by reference to the story of Abraham's trial. Considered from the point of view of social ethics, Abraham's intention must be thought of as murderous. With

[37] Kafka, *The Trial*, 288.

this conclusion Kierkegaard would certainly have agreed. For to slay one's son, if one does not have faith in God's decree—absurd as that decree may appear—is actually to commit murder. It has no spiritual justification and has therefore to be judged in a secular court. The psychoanalyst would dwell upon the absurdity of the notion and would consider Abraham's religious justification of it as an enormous and dangerous illusion. He would probably have committed Abraham to an asylum, as a dangerous incurable, and would be justified in so doing, in terms of his scientific evaluation of motives and behavior.[38] Kafka played whimsically with the theme.[39] He studied Kierkegaard's book carefully during the time when he was composing *The Castle*. In this novel he develops Kierkegaard's thesis most fully in the story of the Barnabas family. Amalia has angrily refused to accept an order from Sortini, which she regards as absurd and loathsome. As a consequence, quite without any deliberate action on the part of Sortini, who has probably forgotten the incident altogether, Amalia and her family lose their position in the Village, are looked down upon, and Amalia is forced to take upon herself the burden of caring for her permaturely aged parents. Amalia's act of refusal is right and reasonable, so K. tells her. That is in accordance with rational standards. Amalia, however, eventually senses the truth that her act was a defiance of the demands of faith —demands which are loathsome and incredible. Kafka is attempting to say here, and elsewhere, that one cannot judge the demands of one's God in terms of rational being. In the acceptance of the irrational one transcends rational ethics and enters into an otherwise inexplicable relationship with God.

[38] American treatment of this theme is to be found in Sherwood Anderson's story " Godliness," in *Winesburg, Ohio*, 55–87. Jesse Bentley tries to offer up his son David as a sacrifice to God, but David escapes. Bentley fails because his faith is anchored in material wishes, and he expects the sacrifice to be rewarded.

[39] See Kafka to Robert Klopstock, in Slochower *et al.*, *A Franz Kafka Miscellany*, 73–74. See also Franz Kafka, " Fragment: Four Sagas Tell About Prometheus," in *Transition*, XXIII (1935), 25, where he discusses four possible versions of the Prometheus story.

iv

Man is somehow suspended between nothingness and infinity. He can measure neither by rational means. His experience of infinity leaves him breathless and incredulous. Within this experience, as a result of it, he appears pathetically comic. Man is, according to Kierkegaard, established upon both an eternal and a finite basis. If he wishes to grasp his relationship with God, he will have to accept the fantastic nature of his reality and forego the pleasures of finite understanding. God manifests himself in strange ways. The trivial may be important, the important trivial. For Kierkegaard, and for Kafka, existence is both comical and pathetic: pathetic because the striving is endless, comical because it is a deliberate distortion and debasement of self. From man's finite point of view, the infinite is incommensurable. Only in the moment of insight (*Innerlichkeit*) can he see the relationship to the eternal, when in this moment of painful comprehension he gains a consciousness of the impotence and pettiness of external reality and when, through these means, the eternal becomes comprehensible. His restless search for this understanding and his numerous hesitations and half-glimpses by the way give rise to the variety of ironic, paradoxical, ambiguous, and comic situations which fill Kafka's pages.

In one sense, Kafka's God is the " father image " multiplied and amplified, his every eccentricity and tyranny exaggerated to give his operations a wider scope. In that sense, Freud might explain, the father-relationship had failed to disappear under the influence of external, social pressures, and it remained to haunt the religious struggles of Kafka's later years. In another, very superficial sense, Kafka's bewilderment and obscurity are simply a picture of the general disintegration of tradition of the age. This, according to Edwin Berry Burgum, is at least one of Kafka's meanings. The inconsistencies of the modern personality, says Burgum, " were locked in permanent contradiction within [Kafka] himself." [40] Such an interpretation might account for the desper-

---

[40] Edwin Berry Burgum, " Franz Kafka and the Bankruptcy of Faith," in *Accent*, III (1943), 163.

ate cry of the country doctor, who falls victim to the merciless ingratitude of a faithless age:

> Naked, exposed to the cold of this unfortunate age, with a terrestrial carriage and supernatural horses, I go wandering on and on, old man that I am. My coat drags behind the carriage; I cannot get hold of it and none of these vacillating blackguards of patients will lift a little finger. Betrayed! Betrayed! once is enough; I was wrong to obey the night bell. . . . It can never be undone.[41]

But the great import of Kafka's writings is not that the age has itself collapsed into a riot of broken traditions, leading to anarchy of spirit; rather the relationship to God—and correspondingly the resolution of all dilemmas—is and always has been that of a finite person to an infinite God. It is a singular and personal relationship, in which no external organization or system can aid more than superficially. The superintendent of the Village thus answers K.'s question about a Control Authority in the castle: " Only a total stranger could ask a question like yours. Is there a Control Authority? There are only control authorities. Frankly it isn't their function to hunt out errors in the vulgar sense, for errors don't happen, as in your case, who can say finally it's an error? " [42]

The nature of the Castle is understood only imperfectly by those in the Village. Documents and papers are piled recklessly in corners and on tables. The officials work hard and long but with a certain eccentric irregularity. The roads leading from the Castle to the Village are known only vaguely, and the officials pass over these roads with distressing irregularity. " ' Now one of them is in fashion, and most carriages go by that, now it's another and everything drives pell-mell there. And what governs this change of fashion has never yet been found out.' " (*Castle*, 278) The officials themselves alter in appearance. Klamm, for example, the official whom K. is anxious to see, has one appearance when he comes into the Village, another when leaving it; " '. . . after having his beer he looks different from what he does before it,

---

[41] Franz Kafka, " The Country Doctor," in *New Directions, 1940*, 442.
[42] Franz Kafka, *The Castle* (New York, 1943) , 85.

when he's awake he's different from when he's asleep, when he's alone he's different from when he talks to people.'" (*Castle*, 228) These alterations of appearance and eccentricities of behavior simply underline the absurdity of attempting to grasp the nature of God through the reason. K., in his restless and erring search for this satisfaction, employs a variety of means, but—because he is at the time limited in his insight—he negects such important matters as answering Momus' questionnaire and listening to the official Buergel, whose droning commentary on Castle Affairs puts him to sleep. At one time Brod asked Kafka if he could promise any hope in such a position. The answer was: "'Much hope for God—infinite hope—but none for ourselves.'"[43] Besides this vagueness of God's nature as man imperfectly views him, the actions of God's will often strike man as repulsive, loathsome, or obscene. Such is Joseph K.'s reaction, for example, when he sees the female servant carried off for the pleasure of one of the Court officials. So long as man's faith is lacking, the peculiar ways of God cause a loathing and are therefore not justifiable in human terms. Once the eternal "Yea" of faith is given, God's ways appear no longer to be peculiar or unpleasant.

The God-man relationship is achieved by an act of faith which goes beyond reason and accepts what would arouse only scorn in the reasonable man. By a recognition of his impotence and a willing suspension of his rational judgment and scorn, man achieves a recognition of divine authority. In *The Trial* and *The Castle*, the heroes (who are in many ways identical) travel the long path toward that knowledge, achieving it only imperfectly, but finding glimpses of it and at least sensing its majesty and omnipotence. Abraham, the model for Kierkegaard and Kafka, had achieved this insight by a remarkable stroke of strategic submission.

The journey to God is difficult and sorrowful. Kafka's heroes employ all means within their power. Each one falls short of the necessary act of faith. It is not wise, for example, to attempt bludgeoning one's way, for that method implies a self-confidence and a scorn for the eternal. Such is at times the attitude of K.,

[43] *Franz Kafka*, 95.

hero of *The Castle*, for he is much too self-confident and regards the struggle too often as a game of wits in which cleverness and shrewdness may win. It is especially improper to employ earthly standards or bourgeois ethics as a means of gaining spiritual ends. Thus Joseph K. all but destroys his case by lecturing to his inquisitor over the injustice of his arrest. The inquisitor listens with great interest to K.'s accusations, but ultimately he loses confidence in this method of handling his case; and a scream from one of the female servants brings the proceedings to an end. Reformers are treated with negligence and boredom. Tintorelli, who has for years painted the portraits of the judges, suggests that the court is not interested in those of their defendants who wish to reform the state of the court. " ' Almost every accused man,' " he says, " ' even quite ordinary people among them, discovered from the earliest stages a passion for suggesting reforms which often wasted time and energy that could have been better employed in other directions. The only sensible thing was to adapt oneself to existing conditions.' " (*Trial*, 153)

The idea of religious reform, of an enlightened religion designed to take out of God's hands the responsibility of punishing man for his evildoing, is criticized by Kafka in the story " In the Penal Colony." The old commander—who, in his multiple role of judge, soldier, builder, chemist, and draughtsman, must be regarded as a portrayal of God—has apparently lost his hold over the colony, and the explorer from a foreign land has successfully induced the commander's one remaining follower to give up the inhumane tortures which were the practice of the earlier government. The torture machine which the old commander had designed is ingenious and cruel. According to the original code, the condemned man is an indifferent matter; he has no right of appeal, nor does he know the precise nature of his sentence. This code has now been completely overruled by the introduction of a humane ethics. But on the stone which covers the grave of the dead commander, there is an inscription, " in quite small letters," which reads: " Here lies the old Commander. His adherents, who may no longer bear a name, have dug this grave for him and erected this stone. There exists a prophecy to the effect that, after a certain number of years the commander will rise from the dead and lead them out of this house to the reconquest of the colony. Believe and wait! " [44]

The story thus presents the human code of morality, characterized as it is by reform and a progressively scientific attitude toward immorality. Superficially the triumph lies with this code; actually the story points to Kafka's eventual preoccupation with the futility of man's attempt to circumvent or even to understand divine justice and wrath.

No stratagem, reasonable or unreasonable, avails in the struggle against the verdict (as in *The Trial*) or for the blessing (as in *The Castle*) of a super-rational power. The path to the God-relationship is uncertain and insecure, and thus the ordinary means at one's disposal—the use of lawyers, advocates, friends of the judges, the " feminine consciousness "—all fall far short of achieving their mark. In his exhaustive and brilliant series of caricatures of worldly professions—so startlingly clear and often so comical that critics have repeatedly considered *The Trial* as a satire of court procedures—Kafka is simply picturing the modern disintegrative approach to salvation through scientific and legal methods. We cannot eliminate from our consciousness the evil of the world simply by setting up courts or professions. The evil is essentially a " misunderstanding " of a law which cannot be grasped by human understanding, or reinterpreted in the interests of humanitarianism. Evil cannot be legislated out of the human soul; nor can it be " cured " by a physician or analyst. Grace cannot be reached through the intercession of sympathetic intermediaries. [45]

[44] Franz Kafka, " In the Penal Colony," in *Partisan Review*, VIII (1941), 158. Cf. Kierkegaard's remarks about the clergymen of his time, *Fear and Trembling*, 34–37.

[45] Kafka's philosophy does not imply an advocacy of fascism, or passively prepare the way for it, as Burgum has suggested ("Franz Kafka and the Bankruptcy of Faith," 161). He regards fascist methods as fully inappropriate as other means. The shift from humanitarianism to totalitarian cruelty does not bring man any nearer salvation. All such methods are earthborn and ineffectual in the face of the one great spiritual—and, by definition, psychological—problem, the personal relationship of each individual to his personal God. The prototype of this relationship is the family relationship, more specifically as outlined in Kafka's " Letter to My Father." For a suggestion regarding the futility of expecting the proletariat to stamp out evil, see the story, " An Old Page," in Slochower *et al.*, *A Franz Kafka Miscellany*, 67–69. For Kafka's opinions of the fascist solution, see " Jackals and Arabs," in *New Directions, 1942*, 408–412.

The only way left is the way taken by Abraham—the unquestioning acceptance of a decree which from all standards but those ascribed to a wrathful and incomprehensible God is bewildering and absurd. Such a way demands of the individual gruesome sacrifices of his mind and spirit, and suggests to some critics at least a masochistic surrender to bodily and spiritual torture. It is true that Kafka admits that a belief is often a disease, when judged by modern medical and therapeutic standards. Kafka felt that an act of faith was so much more profound than bodily well being or social adjustment, that it *appeared* to be a serious disruption of ordinary health of body and spirit. Hence it is that he frequently portrays his heroes in an act of spiritual discovery or search under unhealthful and sometimes horrifying circumstances. It is as though disgust with or scorn of the body were a prerequisite for such a discovery. Health, physical love, while not loathsome, are superficial and disillusioning. Only once does a hero of Kafka have an actual love affair—under circumstances not exactly pleasant or agreeable, and for an end quite beyond itself.[46] In his notebook Kafka once made the statement: " Coitus is a punishment inflicted upon two who find too much happiness in being with each other." Disgust with the body is connected with yearning for death; death is the closest approximation to infinity available to the ordinary mortal. This idea is more than adequately presented in one of Kafka's shorter stories, " The Hunter Gracchus." Gracchus has fallen from a cliff and hurtled to his death below. On the funeral journey, however, the steersman has made a turn in the wrong direction. " ' Thus I, who would live in my own mountains, journey after my death through all the countries of the world.' " This thwarting of the death wish has resulted in an uncomfortable and absurd condition. " '. . . I slipped into my shroud like a girl into her wedding dress. Then the misfortune happened . . . I am here. More than that I do not know. More than that I cannot do. My bark has no rudder,

---

[46] K. and Frieda spend the night together on the floor of the Herrenhof. Sexual intercourse is only another of K.'s devices for achieving his ultimate end. It fails because K. mistakenly assumes that he can approach nearer the castle by lying with one of the women who have been favored by Klamm, an official of the castle. But there is as wide a difference between physical love and spiritual love (not, of course, to be confused with a Platonic love of Ideas) as there is between other earthly affairs and their divine counterpart.

it travels with the wind that blows in the nethermost regions of death.' " [47] The first sign of an awakening consciousness of God is the wish to die. At times this death wish takes the form of a suicidal flight from a sense of guilt—as in " The Sentence." But usually it is the end of the journey toward salvation, as in *The Trial, The Castle,* and " Metamorphosis." [48]

The writings of Franz Kafka are undoubtedly a reflection of modern disintegration, as both Slochower and Burgum have pointed out. They are an aesthetic expression of disgust, a gesture of hopelessness in the face of growing confusion and bureaucratic chaos. By other standards of measurement, biographic and psychoanalytic, they are persistent demonstrations of an anxiety neurosis —a constant flight from anticipated affective danger. Such criticism points to Kafka's relationship with his father—a relationship which, it is said, prevented permanently the normal and successful transition from father image to social and moral conscience. There is much supporting evidence for such an interpretation. But, in his refusal to accept beliefs as simply disease or illusion, Kafka separated himself from his psychoanalytic interpreters. Ultimately his contribution to the thought of our time is the conviction that a belief begins with emotional disturbance, and proceeds to an act of faith by virtue of its acceptance of bodily and spiritual torture and horror. The act of faith culminates in the recognition of God's ways as incomprehensible, absurd, capricious, but just. The attitude which precedes this final acceptance, and which explains much that is mysterious in Kafka's writing, is summed up in the words of Max Brod: " Er hadert nicht mit Gott, nur mit sich selbst." [49]

v

In the mature estimate of Thomas Mann, Freud's work stood out as a storm signal of science against the dangers of nineteenth-century irrationalism. Though he had not always thought thus

[47] Franz Kafka, " The Hunter Gracchus," in *Yisröel: The First Jewish Omnibus,* ed Joseph Leftwich (London, 1933) , 457, 458–59.
[48] Kafka differs from Kierkegaard in a number of ways here. Kierkegaard insists that the " knight of faith " remain within the world and be of the world, enjoying it as no common mortal can.
[49] *Franz Kafka,* 165.

of Freud, Mann ultimately accepted psychoanalysis as a protection against irrational forces. Yet Freud also belongs to the group of nineteenth-century thinkers with whom we have come to associate the anti-intellectualism and irrationalism of our day. Mann has explained this apparent inconsistency for us. The irrationalists think that " every attempt to help the reason to triumph over the instincts—even bad instincts—is a crime against life; for there are no bad instincts, if instinct itself, being chthonic, is sacred." The enthusiasm for the irrational, says Mann, has swept all before it; it is an irresponsible enthusiasm, dividing all things into rational and irrational, instead of into good and evil. Hence instincts destructive and evil are encouraged and praised. " Mindless nature, the folk-soul, hatred, war "—these are the catchwords of the irrationalists.

Psychoanalysis has always held to its therapeutic purpose; ". . . it has preserved in the broader intellectual fields its physicianly character, its human and ethical urge to restore and to reestablish the human element in every distraction and distortion to which it is subject in life." It is not working, " with an interest hostile to reason "; taking advantage of the expert knowledge which it has acquired from " exploring the dark abysses," it is employed for the purpose of combating hostile irrational forces. This is, of course, another in a long series of defenses of Freud which have seemed necessary in the history of his career. Freud is a scientist; upon such a fact is based the merit of his preoccupation with the " daemonic in nature." That he is concerned with the " night side of life " should be commended; but he ought really to be applauded for not assuming that the dark forces of the unconscious are the sole animating motivation of human behavior. " Freud's interest as a scientist in the affective does not degenerate into a glorification of its object at the expense of the intellectual sphere. His anti-rationalism consists in seeing the actual superiority of the impulse over the mind, power for power; not at all in lying down and grovelling before that superiority, or in contempt for mind." [50]

Mann associates Freud with the " romantic, anti-rational "

[50] Thomas Mann, " Freud's Position in the History of Modern Thought," in *Past Masters and Other Papers*, tr. H. T. Lowe-Porter (New York, 1933), 188, 190–91, 193. This essay was originally written in 1928.

tradition in Germany, with that part of German thought which did not flee the responsibilities and consequences of examining man's anti-rational nature. Freud's interest in sex, his so-called " pan-sexualism," has made him an explorer of the unconscious, which " makes him understand life through disease," with the object not of accepting the disease but of curing the patient.[51]

Mann found in the work of Freud a note of hope for the future of human-kind. Mann's acceptance of any body of theory was contingent upon its service in fortifying the spirit and intellect; knowledge of the irrational was important only so far as it gives strength to the human mind. Just when Mann first encountered the theories and practices of psychoanalysis in general is not certain; it is not unreasonable to assume, however, that he was well aware of the discussions and writings of a variety of psychologists some time before he offered his first public tribute to Freud. " One could be influenced in this sphere," he says in a letter, " without any direct contact with his work, because for a long time the air had been filled with the thoughts and results of the psychoanalytic school." [52] The theories of psychoanalysis were therefore quite naturally a part of his penetrating and exhaustive study of the modern mind in *The Magic Mountain*. In fact, the position of the psychoanalyst in the International Sanatorium Berghof is portrayed with great care and much humor. He is Dr. Krokowski, whose lectures on love and disease are no small part of Sanatorium entertainment.

Dr. Krokowski had been pointed out to Hans Castorp when the latter first arrived at Davos: " '. . . devilishly clever article. They mention his activities specially, in the prospectus. He psycho-analyses the patients.' ' He what? Psycho-analyses—how disgusting! ' cried Hans Castorp; and now his hilarity got the better of him. He could not stop. The psycho-analysis had been the finishing touch. He laughed so hard that the tears ran down his cheeks; he put up his hands to his face and rocked with laughter." [53]

[51] *Ibid.*, 196.

[52] Thomas Mann to Frederick J. Hoffman, January 27, 1944.

[53] *The Magic Mountain*, 11. Written from 1912 to 1924. Mann's first reading of the major works of Freud began in 1925. This fact may explain the interesting mixture of Schopenhauerian and psychoanalytic phraseology in Dr. Krokowski's lectures.

It is apparent that Dr. Krokowski is obsessed with a single idea and that his sole concern is to explore its implications: the organic relationship of disease to love. The doctor went about his lectures in a businesslike way, " by adopting a mingled terminology, partly poetic and partly erudite; ruthlessly scientific, yet with a vibrating, singsong delivery, which impressed young Hans Castorp as being unsuitable, but may have been the reason why the ladies looked flushed and the gentlemen flicked their ears to make them hear better." (*Magic Mountain*, 162)

Love and chastity are in perpetual conflict, says the good doctor. Chastity usually wins the struggle. " Love was suppressed, held in darkness and chains, by fear, conventionality, aversion, or a tremulous yearning to be pure." The victory, however, proves to be a pyrrhic one. The suppressed love " would break through the ban of chastity, it would emerge—if in a form so altered as to be unrecognizable." The new form was illness. " ' Symptoms of disease are nothing but a disguised manifestation of the power of love; and all disease is only love transformed.' " (164–65)

This is ironic caricature, not designed so much to discredit psychoanalysis as to comment upon single interpreters and practitioners.

> It seemed that at the end of his lecture Dr. Krokowski was making propaganda for psychoanalysis; with open arms he summoned all and sundry to come unto him. . . . He spoke of secret sufferings, of shame and sorrow, of the redeeming power of the analytic. He advocated the bringing of light into the unconscious mind and explained how the abnormality was metamorphosed into conscious emotion. . . . (167)

For some years before the composition of *The Magic Mountain*, Thomas Mann had been interested in the relationship of the artist to society, and in the problem of genius and disease. The artist seemed a misfit in bourgeois society, and the sources of creation seemed almost directly opposed to social standards. It was part of Mann's debt to Schopenhauer that he recognized in the latter's work the important dependence of the artist upon suffering. From disease the artist derives much of his inspiration, which a healthy man lacks. Indeed, as Dr. Krokowski says to Hans Castorp, there is some serious doubt " ' whether the two conceptions, man and perfect health, were after all consistent one with the other.' " (245)

Each of Mann's earlier tales deals with one of two themes: the artist's painful isolation from bourgeois society, and the persistent function of disease (another mark of separation from the healthy bourgeoisie) in the work of genius. In pursuit of his themes, Mann listened with great interest to two spokesmen of the German Romantic tradition, Schopenhauer and Nietzsche. Nietzsche's effect upon him was to initiate what he called " a period of conservative thinking, from which I graduated at the time of the war; but it made me finally proof against the baleful romantic attraction which can—and today so often does—proceed from an *un*-human valuation of the relation between life and mind." [54] From Nietzsche, Mann derived much that was of interest to his earlier career. The sense of the artist's being unusual, separate from the ordinary run of society, scornful of the reasonable life—this theme, developed to one or another degree of subtlety, combines with Schopenhauer's concept of the artist as an exceptional person, the principal sign of whose vocation is his capacity for suffering. Blind striving, the will to live, dominates the lives of all; it is for the artist, who observes this suffering from a painfully objective point of view, to wrest knowledge from will, and to render permanent his aesthetic comprehension of ideal states. Thus the sharpest perceptions of life and the most beautiful aesthetic conquests of the will have unfortunately forced their creators to suffer isolation from the society of their contemporaries.

Mann was fascinated by the hold which disease and decay apparently had upon life—" the fascination of death, the triumph of extreme disorder over a life founded upon order and consecrated to it. . . ." [55] In part this was a natural result of his interest in all of the varied applications of science to the human body and psyche. *The Magic Mountain* is, after all, a compendium of information about matters in anatomy and medicine. More than that, however, Mann thought to see in a study of disease something of a positive value. For it is disease that causes a shift of attention—

[54] Thomas Mann, *A Sketch of My Life* (Paris, 1930) , 23. At this time (1930) Mann was of course less enthusiastic about Nietzsche than he had formerly been.
[55] *Ibid.*, 43.

provided the disease is not itself stupidly or deliberately willed, as in the case of Christian Buddenbrook—from the superficial level of social observation and "busy-ness" to the inner nature of being. Disease also makes for greater sensitivity, a quality necessary to the full expression of genius. Thus we find that Hans Castorp, an engineer draughtsman in the "Flatlands," becomes, during his prolonged stay at Davos, a student, an intellectual, almost an artist. His conversion has been made possible partly by the suspension of bourgeois time in the Sanatorium, and partly by the disease which directs his attention inward, arouses sensitivities which had remained dormant in his other life. "'What I had in me, as I quite clearly know, was that from long ago, even as a lad, I was familiar with illness and death. . . .'" (*Magic Mountain*, 752).

It is necessary for the artist to go beneath the surface levels of rational life—and rational life is for the most part controlled by social institutions which limit opportunities for spiritual knowledge. Mann, from his reading of Schopenhauer and Nietzsche and his observation of the powerful effect of Wagner's music, participates in the nineteenth-century romantic-irrational revolt against the sanctity of consciousness. It is possible also that this irrationalism was for Mann a fascinating thing, and that he believed the duty of art was to show the most pessimistic conclusions obtainable from it. Further, Mann's acceptance of the exceptional character of the artist, his portrayal of the artist's painful abnormalities, both social and psychological, gave such clear pictures of the artist as neurotic as *Death in Venice*—a story which was immediately claimed by psychoanalysts as a convincing demonstration of the association between the "artistic impulse and the erotic drive." [56]

Mann's career as a writer—varied though it has been—seems remarkably well adapted to interpretation in terms of his association with psychoanalysis. Since he was from the beginning interested in the peculiarities of the aesthetic way of life and suggested an important relationship of genius with disease, it is not unusual to find him more than formally impressed by the philosophies of Schopenhauer and Nietzsche. His visit to Davos in

[56] See Joseph G. Brennan, *Thomas Mann's World* (New York, 1942), 63. Brennan does not claim that this story was directly influenced by psychoanalysis.

1912 and his stay of three weeks suggested eventually to him the possibility of exploring fully the relationship between disease and genius, love and repression, and perhaps a cross-section of all intellectual interests of our century. It is only natural that he should have seen certain quite exciting similarities between psychoanalytic descriptions of neurotic behavior and the general tenor of the stories he had already written. Doctor Krokowski and the theory he explains to Hans Castorp are, however, discussed with a certain ironic reserve. The doctor's theory of underlying motives is not by any means the only one presented in *The Magic Mountain*. Nevertheless, psychoanalysis is ultimately presented with considerable sympathy and understanding; Dr. Krokowski's version of it is a mixture of rhetorical exposition with a poetic caricature of Rémy de Gourmont. It seems that this is the crucial test both for Mann's ultimate position as a man of letters and for his future attitude toward psychoanalysis. It is a matter for pleasant conjecture. Did Mann's experience with psychoanalysis reveal to him certain disadvantages and dangers implicit in the purely anti-rationalistic position? Joseph Brennan has this suggestion:

> *The Magic Mountain* represents Mann's final and complete raising to the level of consciousness the painful roots of his preoccupation with disease and death, exposing them to the play of dialectical movement and all-embracing irony. Not for nothing does the epic novel concern itself with the doctrines of Sigmund Freud. At some time during the composition of the work Mann had experience with psychoanalytic treatment. The novel itself can be conceived as self-administered analysis, in which the author brings to the surface of consciousness the roots of the disease and death concepts, objectifying in a work of art what had for long years weighed on his mind.[57]

The Magic Mountain is a complex work of art. It cannot be said to have had any specific " therapeutic effect " upon its author. The real significance of the work may be summarized as follows: for the first time since the writing of *Buddenbrooks*, Mann was writing a novel on a grand scale. He had fairly well exhausted

[57] Brennan, *Thomas Mann's World*, 68.

the aesthetic possibilities of the philosophies of Schopenhauer and Nietzsche, and it was through the peculiar nature of the setting of *The Magic Mountain* that all of his previous convictions were to be tested and compared with other notions and beliefs. During the twelve years from the inception of the work to its completion (1912–1924), Mann was frequently interrupted—on one occasion, especially, to state his opinion of the relationship of the artist with society. *Betrachtungen Eines Unpolitischen* was published in Berlin in 1918. The impression is strong that Thomas Mann was ready for a reconsideration of his aesthetic principles. He suspected, however, that a simple explanation of the artist's position in terms of his physiological and psychological nature was insufficient justification for his life and work. He was still primarily interested in the artist because of his insight into the irrational wells of man's behavior. Knowledge of the " dark areas " of man's unconscious, plus an understanding of the tension which exists between man's will and the agencies which attempt to control it— these were still the principal distinguishing marks of the aesthetic temperament, as Mann saw it. But it struck him that psychoanalysis was more than an open door to the irrational; it was a science of *control* whereby the irrational might be reformed and shaped to meet the vital needs of twentieth-century man. For one thing, psychoanalysis explained disease and its relationship to genius. Weigand points out that, though Dr. Krokowski is a far less likable person than Behrens, Mann's preference is ultimately for the ideas and theories of the former: ". . . he may be closer to an understanding of the relation obtaining between mind and body than a good physiologist and fine surgeon who is a capital fellow besides." [58] Just as Mann was to become increasingly interested in the larger social implications of his art, he grew more and more convinced of the social importance of psychoanalytic therapy. The narrower social view is given by Settembrini in *The Magic Mountain:*

> " Analysis as an instrument of enlightenment and civilization is good, in so far as it shatters absurd convictions, acts as a solvent upon natural prejudices, and undermines authority;

---

[58] Hermann J. Weigand, *Thomas Mann's Novel, Der Zauberberg* (New York, 1933), 55.

good, in other words, in that it sets free, refines, humanizes, makes slaves ripe for freedom. But it is bad, . . . in so far as it stands in the way of action, cannot shape the vital forces, maims life at its roots. . . ." (*Magic Mountain*, 283) [59]

In Mann's opinion, the virtue and value of psychoanalysis are that it is of and yet not of the " irrationalist drive of his times." It understands man's unconscious, yet does not over-value it, or allow man to disappear within it, or to become a slave to his irrational passions. It is Mann's hope that psychoanalysis will not only contribute new insights to the artist, but will serve reason in the future with a powerful instrument of control over the irrational forces of our day. This is the burden of his extended statement, " Freud's Position in the History of Modern Thought." It is a position which he extends infinitely in his speech given on the occasion of Freud's eightieth birthday, in 1936.[60]

This essay begins by pointing out the tradition of which Freud has always been a part—the line of German romantic philosophy. Freud's great importance to Mann came from his " understanding of disease, a certain affinity with it, outweighed by fundamental health, and an understanding of its productive significance." Freud's interest in the truth had also impressed Mann—primarily because he had given him a method by which " the psychological will to truth " might be studied.

Through his studies of man's unconscious life, Freud had eventually seen the possibility of extending his researches beyond the laboratory into " every field of science and every domain of the intellect." The scientific sanity and thoroughness of psychoanalysis, its laboratory forthrightness and courage, had almost from the beginning allayed Mann's suspicions about it. Its recognition of the importance of disease as a source of knowledge about man suited well his own long established interest in the same ideas. The implications of psychoanalysis for ethics, anthropology,

[59] Mann's treatment of Settembrini is often casually ironic. He is set against Naphta, and for a while against Mynheer Peeperkorn; and though he jealously regards Castorp as his " pupil," it is obvious that Mann believes him a limited person, whose beautiful rhetoric is after all pathetically unable to penetrate the surface of man's spirit on important occasions.

[60] Thomas Mann, " Freud and the Future," in *Freud, Goethe, Wagner* (New York, 1937) , 3–45.

religion, and art gave Mann a true sense of the ultimate significance of Freud's work.

Freud's continuing service to reason made the strongest appeal to Mann and engaged his genuine support. In his *New
Introductory Lectures*, Freud carefully defines and limits the
psychic areas which he calls the ego, the id, and the superego.
The real task of the psychoanalyst of the future, says Freud,

> is to strengthen the ego, to make it more independent of the
> super-ego, to widen its field of vision, and so to extend its
> organization that it can take over new portions of the id.
> Where id was, there shall ego be.
>
>   It is a reclamation work, like the draining of the Zuyder
> Zee.[61]

This essential and yet reasonable role proved very attractive
to Thomas Mann. This is the future of Freudianism: to lay the
cornerstone for " the building of a new anthropology . . . which
shall be the future dwelling of a wiser and freer humanity."
Freud, says Mann, " will be honored as the path-finder towards
a humanism of the future "—a point of view which takes a freer
and bolder attitude toward the irrational, is not frightened by it,
but aware of its possibilities for a more complete and less stupidly
confined life. Once we have removed our unreasonable hatred and
fear of the irrational, we may enjoy " a different relation to the
unconscious which shall be more the artist's, more ironic, and
yet not necessarily irreverent." [62] This optimistic view of the
irrationalism of which Mann was a lifelong student, this hope of
an effective and widespread science of the irrational, is closely
allied with Mann's belief in conservative democracy. He made
precisely the distinction between democracy and Nazism that he
had made between intelligence and willfulness. To fall in love
with the irrational part of the id leads to a submission to an unreasonable reality which takes out of the hands of the individual
the government of both the " pleasure principle " and the basic
emotional or affective drives. From being a subject of merely
aesthetic interest in Mann's early years, the irrational came to

---

[61] *New Introductory Lectures*, 111–12.
[62] " Freud and the Future," 42–43.

offer a challenge to the democracies, and to world government in general. It is not that psychoanalysis at some mysterious time changed Mann's views completely around, or even qualified his enthusiasm for them; Mann's interest in a spiritual stock-taking was coincident with his mature acquaintance with psychoanalysis.

Freud's researches offered Mann an occasion for reviewing the German philosophic tradition, within which he would have liked eventually to see a hopeful union of courageous pessimism and fundamental humanism. Such at least is the intent of a personal statement he has made:

> I was prepared for the Freudian theory chiefly through the philosophy of Schopenhauer, to which it has a deep kinship. In Schopenhauer, I have mostly admired the mixture of pessimism and humanism which is so extremely sympathetic to me, and which, in a changed form, one finds again in Freud. In my first work on Freud which dealt with his position in the history of modern science, I have tried to explain how important and far-reaching this mixture seems to me also in Freud. He is simultaneously a scientist and a believer. He knows well the abyss of the unconscious and the instincts which by far exceed the power and the influence of intellect and reason. But at the same time he fights for what is called progress, i. e., for the expression of reason and free will.[63]

vi

Thomas Mann was one of a few modern writers to take a lively aesthetic interest in Freud's contributions to anthropology. Indeed, it may be said that the Joseph stories—though they are certainly not just one thing—are an aesthetic development of Freud's theories of the racial unconscious. For this statement we have the supporting evidence of Mann's second essay on Freud. It is to Freud that we must accredit a remarkable discovery, which is related to the artist's interpretation of racial and historical legends. It is the idea of the *subjective control* over external events, so that

[63] Thomas Mann to Frederick J. Hoffman, January 27, 1944.

the world as contained within the human soul is more important than the world " happening to " that soul. Thus the idea of God is contained within the soul. This notion of God's residence within the human soul gives history and mythology a subjective cast which only analytic psychology can interpret adequately. Such a startling change in point of view alters history profoundly—changes it from an external reading of documents or records to a reading of the racial unconscious. Hence, says Mann, ". . . when as a novelist I took the step in my subject-matter from the bourgeois and individual to the mythical and typical my personal connection with the analytic field passed into its acute stage." Freudian study of the emotional life of children is at the same time " a penetration into the childhood of mankind, into the primitive and mythical." The repetitive value of the myth, as it appears and reappears, in various guises and disguises, constitutes its true historical importance. The succession of such mythical occurrences causes a suspension of historical time, in favor of a time governed by racial, unconscious rhythms. The artist gains from this idea

> an insight into the higher truth depicted in the actual; a smiling knowledge of the eternal, the ever-being and authentic; a knowledge of the schema in which and according to which the supposed individual lives, unaware, in his naïve belief in himself as unique in space and time, of the extent to which his life is but formula and repetition and his path marked out for him by those who trod it before him.

This is an important extension of Freud's speculations in metapsychology; Mann's interest in it is based upon his own interpretation of infantile regression. He equates it with essential primitivism, which acts as a kind of security for historical truth. The clinical use of regression is, of course, manifestly different; its purpose is to show that the infantile cause of repression, or neurosis, is absurd, and, by so doing, to convince the patient of the futility of carrying it further. To have seized upon the larger implications of a clinical situation requires great imaginative daring. Mann would have us interpret this phenomenon more happily: " to me in all seriousness the happiest, most pleasurable element of what we call education (*Bildung*) , the shaping of the human being, is just this powerful influence of admiration and love, this childish identification with a father-image elected out of profound affinity." [64]

The unity of universal myths and attitudes lies in the unconscious, which insures a continuity of racial memory from one generation to the next. Subsequent legend or history duplicates or repeats, with some slight variation, the points of view, the taboos, even the incidents of the past, if they have been of suffi cient psychological importance. There is, therefore, an unconscious legislative residue, upon which new generations, quite remote from the origins of taboos may draw for the government of their behavior.[65] Thus a race may have its "regression," in much the same way as an individual does. Mann plays upon this theme with admirable subtlety and sympathy in the Joseph tetralogy. The aesthetic use of Freudian anthropology has for its basis three important facts:

(1) The subjective soul wills, not the *nature* of the external world but the *effect* of that world upon it. In a sense, therefore, the soul is " giver of the given."

(2) The recurrence of important spiritual events and types is assured by their residence in the racial unconscious.

(3) Taboos and protections against extreme violence are usually provided in the unconscious memory of consequences of earlier indiscretions, provided circumstances have been severe enough and the emotional disturbance extravagant enough.

In this way Thomas Mann plays with the notion of a mythical id, wherein the ego is shaped by diverse tests, temptations, and defeats. Within the timeless schema of Old Testament story, the pattern can be worked out with infinite attention to psychological detail. Mann sees in the Freudian technique a complete denial of the subject-object separation which so characterized the writers of his time. To identify the outside world with the human soul so that the two are indistinguishable is a practice foreign to the Occidental mind. In the Joseph story he pictures Abraham as

[64] " Freud and the Future," 21–24, 29, 31, 40.
[65] Cf. *Totem and Taboo*, 276.

" in a sense the father of God. He perceived and brought Him forth. . . . God's mighty qualities—and thus God Himself—are indeed something objective, exterior to Abram; but at the same time they are in him and of him as well; the power of his own soul is at moments scarcely to be distinguished from them, it consciously interpenetrates and fuses with them." [66]

Mann also finds in Freud's analysis of the unconscious a suspension of the limitations of time itself and a reassertion of the life of man as a recurrent myth; that is, man is rarely influenced in his behavior by only the present—if indeed the present plays any part at all in determining his conduct—but by the past, or by the myth which is the pattern of the past. Man himself looks upon the chaos of the unconscious with a dread which makes him " cover up his nakedness "; but each time he renounces a pattern of life (each time he surmounts a crisis, or is overcome by it) he dies. " To die: that means actually to lose sight of time, to travel beyond it, to exchange for it eternity and presentness, and therewith for the first time, life." [67] Joseph dies and is reborn twice, and Jacob as well. The myth holds security for such rebirth; it is " the timeless schema, the pious formula into which life flows when it reproduces its traits out of the unconscious." [68]

The Joseph story opens with this latter idea as its theme: time has uneven measure; memory, " resting on oral tradition from generation to generation, was more direct and confiding, it flowed freer, time was a more unified and thus a briefer vista." (*Joseph and His Brothers*, 12) Repetitions of historical incident, which are lived by personalities crucial to the survival of myth, can be explained psychologically:

(1) The unconscious is not necessarily individualized. In primitive times it is synthetic. In individual lives the primitive life is echoed in the life of the child.

(2) Repressions are transmitted, through tradition and taboo. Renunciation is at the very heart of the taboo; [69] the unconscious

---

[66] *Ibid.,* 25–26.
[67] *Joseph and His Brothers* (New York, 1934), 54.
[68] " Freud and the Future," 30.
[69] " The expiation for the violation of a taboo through a renunciation proves

reasserts itself against the same repressions in later ages. In certain ceremonials the unconscious is given ritual recognition—such as the totem feast, the fertility feast. In the latter the taboo against nakedness is temporarily removed.

(3) The taboo is a command of conscience, " the violation of which causes a terrible sense of guilt which is as self-evident as its origin is unknown." [70]

With this belief in " life as myth," Mann begins the story of Jacob, who dominates the first book, appears in it as a powerful background influence, and all but leaves the story in the third of the series. In Jacob's preference for Joseph over the sons of Leah and Bilhah, there is a recurrence of the theme of God-man relationship; it is a preference shown earlier by Abraham and by Isaac. This inconsistency in God's nature is explained time and time again by Mann as due to the intimate relationship of the soul with God. The favored ones of God are in essence the favored ones of the fathers; there is a continuity of preference for the spiritual as opposed to the material. Jacob is encouraged in his preference " by the tradition handed down in his tribe, of God's own intemperateness and majestic caprice in matters of sympathy and preference." (*Joseph and His Brothers,* 84) Hence there is always a struggle between Joseph and his brothers, as there had been between Jacob and Esau, between Isaac and Ishmael. The brothers of Joseph are represented in varying degrees as the symbols of brusque but vigorous materialism, thick-headed and ingenuous. Reuben stands out from them as mediator; though he has sinned against his father, he defends his brother from Leah's sons on many occasions.

The story of Jacob's twenty-five years in the land of Laban provides us with many psychological insights. Jacob symbolizes fertility; his is a sort of unconscious mastery of the fruitfulness of things. Laban's farm therefore prospers: " under [Jacob's] hands the fertility of the flocks increased beyond all known measure." (*Joseph and His Brothers,* 303) [71] Jacob's preference for Rachel

that a renunciation is at the basis of the observance of the taboo." *Totem and Taboo,* 61.

[70] *Ibid.,* 120–21.

[71] Mann's explanation follows: ". . . just as often in the history of the world a damming-up of desires and powers has found its outlet in deeds of the spirit;

over Leah suggests two explanations. It is through Rachel that the " favored one " is to appear; hence the preference is inevitable. Nevertheless, Jacob must do penance for his neglect of the material and the earthly; Leah is substituted by Laban on the wedding night.

As Jacob gets ready to leave the land of Laban, the ever-recurring struggle between the favorite and the rejected takes shape. The sons of Leah are neglected. Their concerns are practical, and they cannot compete in beauty or wisdom with the " favored one." When the second book of the series, *Young Joseph*, opens, we find Joseph and his father together, as we saw them in the Prelude of the first volume. The book opens with a discourse on beauty—which is perhaps " nothing at all but the magic of sex, sex itself become visible." [72] The beauty of Joseph is dual; at the age of seventeen he combines the attractiveness of the male and female. There is also the indefinable attraction that comes with the development of his mind. " He perceived that God had given man understanding in order that he might deal with these sacred matters and make them more consistent. ..." (*Young Joseph*, 15) The quarrel with the brothers continues and is deepened by the obvious preference which Jacob shows for Joseph. Ultimately the course of the brothers' hatred receives positive direction; it leads to the uprising at the well at Dothan.

But in the end, the sons of Leah are to be merely the instrument, or one of the instruments, of Joseph's fate. The robe of many colors that Jacob has given to his favorite is a symbol of life and death. It is the robe in which Rachel has died; and it is to be the immediate cause of Joseph's first spiritual death. " ' Knowest thou not,' " says Joseph in answer to Reuben's inquiry about the robe, " ' that it is in the power of death to change the sex, and that Rachel still liveth for Jacob though in another form? ' " (*Young Joseph*, 127) The story of the first death of Joseph in the valley of Dothan brings together all the tendencies the novel has developed thus far: the preference of the spiritual over the material, the revolt of the material, and the remorse which follows. The second book closes with the picture of Jacob's suffering

so here, by a similar process of transference, they found expression in sympathy and care for the life entrusted to the sufferer." (304)

[72] Thomas Mann, *Young Joseph* (New York, 1935), 4.

over the news of his son's death. He rails at God; he invents and considers little stratagems for circumventing God's purpose. For the brethren the deed brings no comfort; it has all of the characteristics of the violent end-product of a wish-fulfillment, but from it they derive no satisfaction. The pattern has many of the aspects of familial and racial history described by Freud in *Totem*.

The story does not linger over the shattered hopes of Jacob and of the brethren. Joseph is on his way to Egypt. "It was a deep cleavage and abyss that divided his present from his past; it was the grave." He has apparently renounced all of his past life; he changes his name to "Usarsiph"—the "lost Joseph"; his owner is Hequet, "the great midwife," for he has assisted at the rebirth. (*Joseph in Egypt*, I, 6, 31) [73] He is sold in bondage to Potiphar, the favorite of Pharaoh, and he thus begins his "Laban time." For ten years he is to be with the household of Potiphar's estate. Mann's portrayal of the two dwarfs who live on the estate is a masterpiece of ironic characterization. Their antipolar natures set off well the conflict within Joseph's soul. Dudu is the troublemaker, a miniature of Laban, but more spiteful. His principal hope is to destroy Joseph or to drive him out of the household. Slochower calls him an expression of the "primitive pleasure-principle, the Id, with desires that are fundamentally sexual." Bes, on the other hand, is Joseph's guardian and friend; Slochower claims that he "approximates the category of the Super-Ego, the 'warning good conscience.'" [74]

Of Joseph's rise in the house of Potiphar little need be said, for it is already a familiar story: of the favorite one, flourishing "as by a spring," arousing animosity among the less favored, and ultimately falling back into the pit. But to the figure of Mut-em-enet Mann gives much sympathetic attention. Her unsuccessful attempt at seduction is something more than a struggle between evil and chastity. Mann's characterization of Mut is cautious and reserved. Ultimately her actions, through careful explanation, are given a dignity which makes her a tragic figure. She is not by nature a seductress or a wanton, loose woman. "A woman over-

[73] (New York, 1938).
[74] Slochower, *Thomas Mann's Joseph Story*, 44–45. This interesting interpretation has Mann's own approval; see *ibid.*, 45, n. 1.

come as she was, is of course seductive," Mann says; "seductiveness is the exterior and physical shape taken by her affliction; . . ." (*Joseph in Egypt*, II, 372) Her story is rather a study of an excessive sex repression. "The claims of sex . . . Mut's parents passed over," (II, 375) and she herself scarcely notices them until she is attracted to Joseph. When she becomes aware of the danger, she takes steps to avoid it. She begs Potiphar to send Joseph away; and when Potiphar refuses to do so, she accepts his answer as partial justification of what is to follow. Secretly her will has coincided with Potiphar's refusal, and she is glad therefore to prepare for the inevitable. What she now proceeds to do, and the emotional effect which her intriguing has upon her, can only be called the results of intense suffering:

> [Mut's surrender to Joseph] was by its nature nothing else than a violent, terrified outburst concerned to save, in the last or almost the last moment, her fleshly honour and her human womanhood—to save, or rather to secure it, though it meant the abandonment and sacrifice of her spiritual and religious honour, of everything in the realm of the idea on which her life was based. (II, 459–60)

Joseph offends again; this time his arrogant innocence is to make for tragedy and death. The sex drive in Mut is natural; the violence of its exposure is consistent with the strength of its prior repression. Remorse is in this case furiously projected; her instinctual energies finally express themselves in an enraged and bitter accusation against Joseph. Joseph's refusal to yield to Mut's importunate wish is not caused by sexual indifference on his part. The refusal is linked with the religion of Jacob and with Joseph's mission in Egypt. For Joseph this is a struggle between Jacob's God and Atum-Re. He is again "thrown into the pit"; that is, he again dies, in punishment for his arrogance and unthinking egoism.

This elaborate expression of Hebraic story and universal myth follows with artistic freedom the suggestions which Mann found in Freud's speculations about the racial unconscious. The sum total of them is of significance for a fresh and original interpretation of human history.

(1) History is described as a recurrence of myths—personality archetypes, customs, repressions, which constitute the stuff of man. Hence it is not the institutional, but the irrational, not the conscious but the unconscious, that matters.

(2) Life is portrayed as a struggle between the ego and the id; the general result of this struggle is the achievement of a balance between the two.

(3) The life of the individual reflects this larger struggle between taboo and desire.

(4) Punishment is meted out equally for overemphasis upon the spiritual and for reliance upon the material qualities in experience. Thus Jacob is punished by Laban's hoaxing on the wedding night, and Joseph is twice punished. Mut condemns Joseph justly, not for rape but for refusing to satisfy the desire he has aroused in her.

(5) Ultimately, Mann's wish is to show the increasing socialization of the human will, as it alters its purpose through recurring experience. Thus Joseph is used as a symbol of increasing social solidarity and cooperation, in the fourth novel of the series, *Joseph, the Provider*.[75]

The " Freudian hope," expressed in the *New Introductory Lectures*, that the ego will be extended by the future work of psychoanalysis, the energies of the id harnessed to the social good— this is what Mann has in mind, in his fourth novel. We may suggest that Mann intends Joseph as the racial symbol of the ego, which will serve as a prototype of civilization.

One other interesting application of Freudian psychology is to be seen in the union of Biblical story and dream interpretation. Freud's insistence upon wish-fulfillment as the source of most personal dreams may appear to have been disregarded in Mann's analysis of the dreams of Joseph. Though Mann is concerned primarily with the problem of making the biblical story

---

[75] " . . . in Joseph the ego flows back from arrogant absoluteness into the collective, common: and the contrast between artistic and civic tendencies, between isolation and community, between individual and collective, is fabulously neutralized —as, according to our hopes and our will, it must be dissolved in the democracy of the future, the cooperation of free and divergent nations under the equalizing sceptre of justice." Thomas Mann, *The Theme of the Joseph Novels* (Washington, D. C., 1942), 18.

psychologically creditable, he is free to use the analyst's materials with some independence. In the early dreams of Joseph, as well as in those which he interprets for the Pharaoh, God's wish is fulfilled more than that of the dreamer. This is the peculiar quality of these dreams which makes them prophetic. Since, as Mann suggests in " Freud and the Future," the subjective will plays a large role in dictating the nature of events which happen to it, it may not be altogether irregular that the wish-fulfillment is both God's and Joseph's. That Mann was aware of the nature and construction of human dreams, whose wish-fulfillment is obviously of a sexual nature, is brilliantly illustrated by his description of Mut-em-enet's dream at the very beginning of her relationship with Joseph. (*Joseph in Egypt*, II, 390–93) Within the limits of a single dream the story of Mut's seduction of Joseph is told, and the symbolism of the dream suggests a complete fulfillment of her unconscious wish. It is a brilliantly constructed dream pattern, well adjusted to the needs of the narrative, and certainly not in any way a violation of its purpose.

vii

The figures of Thomas Mann and Franz Kafka seem strangely grouped within the same chapter. Kafka's rejection of Freud leads to a personal relationship with a powerful but incomprehensible God, whose irrational caprice demands an act of faith beyond reason and above collective ethics. Mann's acceptance of Freud leads to the development of a hopeful ethical and religious scheme, in which the irrational energies of the id are slowly being brought within the benevolent control of the ego and of all its social and political accessories. Kafka's theology and ethics are intensely personal, deeply rooted in his own experiences, from which they seem to have gained many at least of their external characteristics. At the same time Kafka is more intensely aware—more bitterly aware, one might say—than is Mann of the hopelessness of modern man and of the spiritual disintegration of our time. In such a time as this, neither tradition nor revolution seems to have brought stability; man is thrown back upon his own resources, and he is pitifully inadequate for the task of spiritual reintegration. Mann's first-hand acquaintance with Nazism, on the other hand, forced him to venture a serious reshaping of the relationship of art with morality. He had for some time been teaching the peculiar nature of the artist and pointing out his insight into the unconscious resources of man's behavior and energy. He did not change overnight from an " unpolitical man " to a political lecturer and special pleader. He turned to that form of irrationalism which he thought had most hope for the future of man. This, it seemed to him, is the science of psychoanalysis, especially as it is applied to the study of mythology and primitive religious thought and custom.

Another important difference between the two men can be detected in their separate uses of humor. Kafka's humor is largely *descriptive* comedy, designed to point to the pathetic in man's strivings; Mann's irony is *mediative,* an effort on his part not to take the full responsibility for his character's appearance or acts. Kafka is always deeply involved as a victim of his own irony. Mann's irony is playful but aloof, free from any severe burden of sympathy. The credibility of Kafka's thesis depends upon a permanent breakdown of social controls and a collapse of social morale. His is the position taken by those who mistrust the all-too-human agencies for human betterment. Mann's position, of course, depends for its acceptability upon the immediate fulfillment of what he promised in his political speeches and in the fourth volume of his tetralogy.

Both writers are closely associated with the theories and subject matter of psychoanalysis. Neither accepts psychoanalysis without some aesthetic reserve. Kafka, however, kept his approach to the irrational on purely personal grounds—maintaining that the sole salvation is a personal reconciliation with an all-powerful but indifferent God. In his political philosophy, Mann developed from an individual sense of isolation to the provisional acceptance of a union of democratic souls, who might bring about a healthy set of controls over irrational forces. This interpretation is based, of course, upon the Joseph stories and the addresses of the World War II years. In his last books Mann went back to earlier themes, his irony playing upon a world much more limited in scope but perhaps more deeply penetrating that that of the tetralogy. There is no doubt, however, that in the Joseph novels Mann's social consciousness achieved its greatest aesthetic expression. In the Freudian suggestiveness of the Biblical story—in terms of what Freud thought of as a recurrence in generations of social history of familial complexities—Mann's most incisive commentary upon "the tribe of man" seemed to have emerged gradually from his career as an interpreter of the modern *Geistesgeschichte.*

chapter VIII

THREE AMERICAN VERSIONS
OF PSYCHOANALYSIS

i

At the peak of his career, in the mid-twenties, critics hailed Sherwood Anderson as the " American Freudian," the one American writer who knew his psychology and possessed a rich fund of knowledge and experience to which it could best be applied. Anderson had spoken of the repressed villager, the frustrated American businessman; he appeared to be admirably equipped to portray both, for he himself had had personal knowledge of both types. To the critic of the twenties, the villager or townsman, suffering from the hindering conventionalities of his time and place, and the businessman, deliberately shutting out life so that he might importune the goddess of success, were ideal patients for a psychoanalyst; and a writer who dealt intimately with them must have noticed the remarkable opportunity for the literary use of the new psychology.

This was, at any rate, the nature of Anderson's critical reputation. For one thing, the critics, determined to find influences, were scarcely willing to grant him a native talent, which was founded on personal experience and nurtured by a native sympathy for his subject matter. Was Anderson his own psycho-analyst? Did he proceed utterly unmindful of this influence? In order to answer these questions, it is necessary to determine the antecedent, local influences which affected Anderson's style and attitude. There is no lack of autobiographical material—for, besides the two admittedly autobiographical stories, *A Story Teller's Story* (1924) and *Sherwood Anderson's Memoirs* (1942), there are the two autobiographical novels, *Windy McPherson's Son* (1916) and *Tar* (1926). In these, and in other sources, there is a mass of contradictory material, which has for some time since his death made the biographer's task difficult. We can at best hope only to settle upon certain recurrent themes which, if they are not drawn from life, can at least be regarded as matters with which Anderson's mind was preoccupied.

One of these important themes is Anderson's relationship with his parents. He calls his father a "ruined dandy from the South . . ." who was "made for romance. For him there was no such thing as a fact." [1] He describes his own initiation into the world of letters as a rebirth: "And if you have read Freud you will find it of additional interest that, in my fanciful rebirth, I have retained the very form and substance of my earthly mother while getting an entirely new father, whom I set up—making anything but a hero of him—only to sling mud at him. . . ." [2]

This father is portrayed in Anderson's first published novel as "a confirmed liar and braggart." [3] He describes a pathetic scene in which Windy McPherson offered to blow the bugle for a Fourth-of-July celebration, then, in a critical moment, revealed his utter incompetence with the instrument. In these and many other references to his father. [4] In Anderson's image, the father possessed the same quality of vivid imagination that Sherwood was to exploit in himself, and there is a closer tie between the two men than one would gather from the citations made. In *Memoirs* Anderson devotes a chapter to explaining this am-

---

[1] *A Story Teller's Story* (New York, 1924), 3, 4.

[2] *Ibid.*, 114. His portrait of his mother seemed equally imaginative, for his brothers did not recognize in it any resemblance to the actual mother.

[3] Sherwood Anderson, *Windy McPherson's Son* (New York, 1922), 22. First published, New York, 1916.

[4] Anderson's methods were such that the father of the autobiographical books is as fully colored as is the father-image of the fiction.

biguous relationship. His father was "always showing off"; yet Anderson admits that there was a hidden bond of sympathy and common interest. Among the incidents which reveal this bond to him is a common adventure at a near-by lake: "For the first time I knew that I was the son of my father. He was a story teller as I was to be. It may be that I even laughed a little softly there in the darkness. If I did, I laughed knowing that I would never again be wanting another father." [5] This is a last, considered view, a recognition of the fact that, in the field of literary art, Anderson was himself to demonstrate his father's skill in story telling.

For his mother Anderson felt great sympathy and love. His desire to romanticize her, to show her a heroine who struggled boldly and patiently with poverty and loved silently but sincerely, results in several idealized portraits in his early works.

> It is so wonderfully comforting to think of one's mother as a dark, beautiful and somewhat mysterious woman. . . .
> When she spoke her words were filled with strange wisdom . . . but often she commanded all of us by the strength of her silences. [6]

In his imagination he is always championing her cause against an irresponsible villain, usually some imaginative replica of his father. This devotion to his mother, though it has ample justification in fact, is part of Anderson's rationalization of his life—the "mother image" pursues him through his later years, and the fear that he may be like his father in his treatment of women colors much of his self-criticism.

These are obviously native influences, and he needed no text-book psychology to appreciate their weight or value. Aside from that, Anderson lived his own theory of the imagination, altogether separate from the world of fact. From the childhood which he describes in *Tar*, Anderson is forever shifting from the world of fact to the "larger world of fancy"; standards of honesty and intellectual integrity are presumably rigid in this latter world, though they can not be evaluated by direct reference to the facts of

---

[5] *Sherwood Anderson's Memoirs* (New York, 1942), 49.
[6] Anderson, *A Story Teller's Story*, 7, 8.

the real world. The artist's deliberate entrance into the life of the fancy serves to free him of the restrictions of " Philistia," and secures his work against any tendencies he may have had toward prostituting his talents.

> There are no Puritans in that life. The dry sisters of Philistia do not come in at the door. They cannot breathe in the life of fancy. The Puritan, the reformer who scolds at the Puritans, the dry intellectuals, all who desire to uplift, to remake life on some definite plan conceived within the human brain die of a disease of the lungs. They would do better to stay in the world of fact. . . . (*Story Teller's Story*, 77)

The world of fancy was often the real world—Anderson entertained the idea that the people of his dreams and visions might have more reality than his own physical self and the men and women who populated the ostensible world. His constant reading served apparently to feed his dream mind, or to give him " a background upon which I can construct new dreams." (156) This world of fancy is the half-conscious state of daydream, supplemented by dreams and visions, for the most part elaborated upon by the dreamer. Dreams are for Anderson the most coherent expression of his other world. Dream fragments are the facts of the world of fancy. They are the means by which Anderson flees reality; most often, they are simply wish-fulfillments, with the artist playing a heroic role and gaining in fancy what he has failed to get in actual life.[7] Yet they are not always this; he sometimes reports a dream which one may, with some misgiving, accredit as having actually been experienced:

> Thoughts flitting, an effort to awaken out of dreams, voices heard, voices talking somewhere in the distance, the figures of men and women I have know flashing in and out of darkness.
>
> .   .   .   .
>
> Again the great empty place. I cannot breathe. There is a great black bell without a tongue, swinging silently in dark-

---

[7] Cf. "The Relation of the Poet to Day-Dreaming," 173–83. The writer " creates a world of phantasy which he takes very seriously."

ness. It swings and swings, making a great arch and I await silent and frightened. Now it stops and descends slowly. I am terrified. Can nothing stop the great descending iron bell? It stops and hangs for a moment and now it drops suddenly and I am a prisoner under the great bell.

With a frantic effort I am awake. . . . (189–91)

This follows the pattern of an anxiety dream, with all its distortion and complicated symbolism. Yet Anderson regards the dream as the artist's birthright, an image of the fancy which he may treat as he pleases. He will retreat into it as a means of indirect expression of social criticism; in many respects his trances appear to be deliberately made, though their eventual effect may be genuine enough.

So, in Elyria, as he has pictured the incident in *A Story Teller's Story* and elsewhere, he walks out of his place of business and his home, bound for the adventurous nowhere. To his astonished stenographer he says: " ' My feet are cold and wet and heavy from long wading in a river. Now I shall go walk on dry land. . . .' " (313) [8] This dramatic renunciation of the business world, while it demonstrates a lively imagination, scarcely accords with the facts. According to newspaper dispatches of the time, Anderson was discovered on December 2, 1912, wandering about the streets of Cleveland, and was taken to a near-by hospital, to which his wife came immediately. The case was described as a " nervous breakdown," caused evidently by overwork. While he was still in the hospital, Anderson contemplated writing a book " of the sensations he experienced while he wandered over the country as a nomad. ' It is dangerous, but it will be a good story, and the money will always be welcome,' he said." [9] Upon his return from Cleveland, he spent two more months in Elyria and there made plans for his life in Chicago. The drama of the episode subsides considerably, in the light of these facts. These quotations suggest at best a tenuous relationship between two kinds of experience. He is not willing that these statements be criticized for inaccuracy; often they are imaginative reconstructions of the past,

[8] This incident is described more briefly in *Memoirs*, 194.
[9] Elyria (Ohio) *Evening Telegram*, December 6, 1912. This information was supplied by William Sutton.

only major themes running through them, the details derived from the moment of composition. " When I had been working well," he says in his *Notebook*, " there was a kind of insanity of consciousness. There may be little nerves in the body that, if we could bear having them sensitive enough, would tell us everything about every person we meet." [10] The hidden thoughts are dangerous and had best be glossed over by the fancy. As for the dreams which he is always reporting, " One feels sensuality, wonder, interest, quite naturally—is unashamed, does not try to be logical. . . . As for myself, I leave the fact that I have such dreams to the psychoanalysts." (*Notebooks*, 224)

With the help of Floyd Dell, whom he first met in 1913, Anderson was soon associating with the Chicago intellectuals in their " Greenwich Village." Anderson rarely participated in discussions of ideas, but was always ready to tell a story. (*Memoirs*, 241–43) Nevertheless, he was present when his friends discussed Freud eagerly as a new thing, and he agreed to an amateur analysis:

> Freud had been discovered at the time and all the young intellectuals were busy analyzing each other and everyone they met. Floyd Dell was hot at it. We had gathered in the evening in somebody's rooms. Well, I hadn't read Freud (in fact, I never did read him) and was rather ashamed of my ignorance. . . .
>
> And now [Dell] had begun psyching us. Not Floyd alone but others in the group did it. They psyched me. They psyched men passing in the street. It was a time when it was well for a man to be somewhat guarded in the remarks he made, what he did with his hands. (*Memoirs*, 243) [11]

Anderson had come to Chicago with his mind as yet only vaguely made up about the life of the artist. He was very timid

---

[10] *Sherwood Anderson's Notebook* (New York, 1926), 183.

[11] This amateur psyching ordinarily followed one of two patterns: (1) experiments with word associations, a technique which Freud and Jung recommend as part of the analytic procedure; (2) vague generalizations about a person's " complexes " and " repressions," and popular analysis of " symptomatic acts," following roughly the suggestions given in Freud's *Psychopathology of Everyday Life*, and referring, if the group was well enough read, to parts of the *Three Contributions to a Theory of Sex*.

about admitting that he was interested in writing. Whether or not he had found a parallel in the psychoanalytic approach to human behavior, he denied having actually read Freud or exploited him in his writing. He was in the habit of reading widely, with no more deliberate purpose than to add to his dreams; his reading was unsystematic and diffuse; and he was perhaps jealous of his own originality. It was his habit to search out a man's works, once they had been referred to him, or he had seen some similarity to his own way of thinking. When the critics pointed to a Russian influence, " I began to read the Russians, to find out if the statement, so often made concerning me and my work, could be true." (*Story Tellers' Story*, 48) Sometimes he and his brother would get a copy of a book and read aloud from it; about the work of Gertrude Stein he reports: " My brother had been at some sort of a gathering of literary people on the evening before and someone had read aloud from Miss Stein's new book . . . he bought *Tender Buttons* and he brought it to me, and we sat for a time reading the strange sentences." [12]

Whatever Anderson's reactions were to psychoanalysis, they were scarcely professional. With Dr. Trigant Burrow, the New York psychologist whose work had been approved by both Lawrence and Frank, Anderson held a long discussion of the matter. The argument concerned the ability of any one man successfully to enter into other lives. Burrow ended it by saying: " You think you understand but you don't understand. What you say can't be done can be done." [13] The conversation demonstrates the conflict of two opposing minds concerning a central problem:

> As with the psychiatrist who has kept himself out of the mess and the psychoanalyst who has got himself into it, the result of our differing inquiries seems to me merely to have left us both on conflicting sides of the dilemma. We were both the unconscious instruments of private improvisations. In both, the theme we used owed itself, though unacknowledged, to

---

[12] Sherwood Anderson, Preface to Gertrude Stein's *Geography and Plays* (Boston, 1922), 5.

[13] Trigant Burrow, " Psychoanalytic Improvisations and the Personal Equation," *Psychoanalytic Review*, XIII (1926) 174. Burrow uses the words reported by Anderson in " Seeds," in *The Triumph of the Egg* (New York, 1921), 23. The incident, says Burrow, occurred " ten years ago," in 1916.

the personal equation that secretly actuated our separate positions.[14]

Anderson's opposition to psychoanalysis appears here to be founded upon a personal conviction that the " universal illness " of which he speaks in " Seeds " cannot be remedied by science, though it can be described by the artist. It is another assertion of his independence of the psychologists, and is this time supported by an accurate reference to it by the psychologist in question. In a letter Trigant Burrow has reaffirmed his opinion regarding Anderson's intellectual independence:

> My feeling is that Sherwood Anderson was, like Freud, a genius in his own right. Anderson was a man of amazing intuitive flashes but again, like Freud, the chief source of his material was his own uncanny insight.
>
> I can say very definitely that Anderson did not read Freud, nor did he draw any material from what he knew of Freud through others. Don't you think that all schools like to lay claim to an apt scholar? I think this largely accounts for the psychoanalysts' quite unwarranted adoption of Anderson. Of Anderson I would say that socially he was one of the healthiest men I have ever known. His counter-offensive in " Seeds " amply testifies to this. Indeed on this score many orthodox psychoanalysts might very profitably take a leaf from his book.[15]

There is internal evidence, however slight, that leads us to suspect that Anderson was aware of the intellectual version of Freud and that he did not altogether dismiss it from his mind. The classic reference to Freud in Anderson's writings is the line given to Bruce Dudley: " If there is anything you do not understand in human life, consult the works of Doctor Freud." [16] Nothing further seems to have been done with this reference; it appears to be casual and of little consequence.

Elsewhere, when he deals with such matters as dreams, Anderson submits them to the psychoanalysts for further consideration,

[14] Burrow, *loc. cit.*
[15] Trigant Burrow to Frederick J. Hoffman, October 2, 1942.
[16] *Dark Laughter* (New York, 1925), 230.

but he refuses to label his experience with any of their terms. Occasionally the language appears in his novels. In *Poor White* he refers to Clara Butterworth's vision on the train: " So strong was it that it affected her deeply buried unconscious self and made her terribly afraid." [17] When he describes the dreams of Ben Peeler, Bidwell carpenter, he uses language not dissimilar to that analyst—though there is nothing in this description which Anderson could not have written without the aid of psychoanalysis. Ben's night is taken up with two dreams. In the first, he kills a man, or thinks that he has killed him. Then, " With the inconsistency common to the physical aspect of dreams, the darkness passed away and it was daylight." (206) This is not without some significance, for it indicates a knowledge of the phenomenon of distortion in dreams (as the second dream itself does) and may imply either a deep personal interest in dreams, or a study of Freud's dream-interpretation, or even both.

This is slender evidence indeed for the critics' extravagant claims. Rebecca West, for example, says that Anderson's " excessive preoccupation with the new psychology strikes deeply at the root of his talent." Contrasting his *The Triumph of the Egg* with another American work, Miss West calls Anderson's book infinitely more valuable precisely because its author is saturated with the new psychology, " to an extraordinary degree. It dictates his subjects. His stories are monotonously full of young girls coming back to their home towns with a suit-case and a psychosis, of middle-aged men corked by inhibitions." [18] Reviewing *Winesburg, Ohio*, H. W. Boynton links psychoanalysis with Russian realism as the principal influences upon Anderson: " At worst he seems in this book like a man who has too freely imbibed the doctrine of the psychoanalysts, and fares thereafter with eyes slightly ' set ' along the path of fiction." [19]

In 1931 a volume of essays was published by Regis Michaud, whose task was primarily to oppose the assumptions of psychoanalysis to the inhibitions of Puritanism in American literature.

[17] Sherwood Anderson, *Poor White* (New York, n. d.), 181; first published, New York, 1920.

[18] Rebecca West, " Notes on Novels," in *New Statesman*, XVIII (1922), 564–66. See also " An Exponent of the New Psychology," in *Literary Digest*, LXXIII (1922), 33.

[19] Henry W. Boynton, " All Over the Lot," in *Bookman*, XLIX (1919), 729.

His two chapters on Anderson call him " the Freudian novelist *par excellence.*" [20] Anderson, above all, devoted his literary career to proving and justifying psychoanalytic theory, and to testing it in literary works. The value of *Poor White* " resides in the Freudian sketches aside from the main plot, and in the analysis of the pathological forms of sensibility." *Winesburg* is likewise a " first-rate psychological document . . . entirely in harmony with the most recent contributions of American literature to psychoanalysis." (182) In his enthusiasm for this single preoccupation, Michaud indulges in extremes of commentary; speaking of " The New Englander," he refers to a scene in that story as " literarily beautiful and almost technically Freudian. . . . The tortures of inhibition have rarely been so dramatically and scientifically described." (188–91) Anderson, says Michaud, cooperates with the Freudian psychologist in advocating the release of inhibitions and repressions. He will preach the doctrine, and life will empty the prisons. " It will raise the lid of the ' well ' where the Freudian monsters are asleep, these monsters which the Puritan felt groping within himself, and which he carefully and wisely held in chains." (195–96) [21]

One other example of such criticism comes from the pen of Camille J. McCole, who uses psychoanalysis to prove that Anderson's writings are evil. If we cannot follow Anderson, he says, we shall have to go to Freud for explanation; " One must know the master before he can comprehend the pupil." McCole's method is to argue by analogy, but to confuse the reader so that he is led to believe that the parallel activity actually means direct influence. Anderson commits two of the Freudian fallacies: he looks only " on one side of Main Street and that side the very shady one up which slinks the stream of day-dreamers, perverts, the ' inhibited,' the morally atrophied, the erotics, and the eccentrics that infest his pages." Secondly, Anderson, like Freud, believes that the

[20] Regis Michaud, *The American Novel To-day: a Social and Psychological Study* (Boston, 1931) , 156.

[21] This seemingly apt quotation is derived from John Webster's stream of consciousness, *Many Marriages* (New York, 1923) , 217. But Michaud distorts the reference, and introduces the term " Freudian monsters " of his own accord. It must be admitted, however, that this description of the unconscious " well " resembles closely other metaphors which popularizers or opponents of psychoanalysis used to describe the unconscious.

method of free association, as employed in psychoanalysis, is a good model for the novelist to follow. His characters should "speak freely" and hold nothing back that might be either "shameful or painful." In so following the Freudian method of "telling all," Anderson has violated both good taste and morality. Anderson's preoccupation with sex is not only just *like* Freud's; it is *derived from* psychoanalysis. The cure, for Anderson's patients as well as for Freud's, is to have them give up all restraints, "surrender themselves to the particular impulse or passion which is disturbing their lives. . . ." [22]

These are extreme cases of critical misjudgment. Those who were closest to Anderson during his life in Chicago and New York, either do not refer to Freud at all [23] or suggest moderately that Anderson and Freud are working along parallel lines. [24] There seems little hesitancy, however, in associating the two men; and the temptation to ascribe an actual influence is easily indulged. The reasons for this easy ascription are not obscure. Most important, of course, was the recognition that Freud had contributed to American criticism the term *repression*, which acquired new significance, almost immediately, for the fields of sociology, history, biography, and literary criticism. Anderson was hailed as the leader in the American fight against conventional repression; his novels appeared coincidentally with the beginning of the interest in the new psychology. He dealt with frustration, in many cases with the frustration of normal sex expression. His dedication of

[22] " Sherwood Anderson, Congenital Freudian," *Catholic World*, CXXX (1929), 131, 132, 133. McCole quotes from Eduard Hitschmann, *Freud's Theories of the Neuroses* (New York, 1917), 195, as he acknowledges in a footnote; but the quotations appear to be coming from Anderson, and stand, to the reader, for Anderson's theory of fiction.

[23] See, for example, Robert Morss Lovett, " Sherwood Anderson, American," in *Virginia Quarterly Review*, XVII (1941), 384: " Many of Anderson's stories are concerned with the frustration of human life that comes from isolation, the inability of one being to come near another, to enter into understanding with another."

[24] Among the more moderate critical references to Anderson, one may note John Crowe Ransom's " Freud and Literature," 161; Leo A. Speigel's " The New Jargon: Psychology in Literature," 478 (reference to Bruce's affair in *Dark Laughter*); Maxwell Bodenheim's " Psychoanalysis and American Fiction," 684; Henry Seidel Canby's *Definitions: Essays in Contemporary Criticism*, second series (New York, 1924), 242–48, which links Anderson's *Many Marriages* with the morals of the new age; John Farrar's " Sex Psychology in Modern Fiction," 669; Alyse Gregory's " Sherwood Anderson," in *Dial*, LXXV (1923), 246.

Winesburg, Ohio to his mother is explained on the grounds that she first awoke in him " the hunger to see beneath the surface of lives." Had not the " new wisdom " been here clearly applied to the field of fiction? Anderson's use of dream symbolism, and of the vision appeared also to play a role in influencing his critics. Not the least important, however, was the fact that Anderson hesitated himself to acknowledge any influence; that is, he never committed himself fully, in answer to his critics. Though in many other cases, such as the influence of Gertrude Stein, George Borrow, and James Joyce, he was ready enough to admit influences, and in some cases to embrace his " mentors " enthusiastically, he was oddly silent about Freud and psychoanalysis. The exaggeration of the critics was, therefore, pardonably easy to make.

(1) Anderson's early life in Ohio towns had much to do with his fundamental attitude toward his writing. Certainly he needed no handbook of psychoanalysis as a guide to using his eyes, his ears, or his imagination.

(2) When he came to Chicago for the first time in 1913, anxious to begin a writer's life, he had not as yet heard of psychoanalysis. The ideas in two of his earliest books, *Windy McPherson's Son* (1916) and *Winesburg, Ohio* (1919), so far as we can determine from internal evidence or from a consideration of the facts of Anderson's early " Chicago period," may safely be said to be his own.

(3) In Chicago, with Floyd Dell, the Lucian Carys, and Margaret Andersoin, he participated in literary discussions, and it was here that he first became acquainted with the ideas and terms comprehended under the phrase " the new psychology." He noted the similarity in subject matter, remarked upon the popular habit of " psyching," but claims not to have gone any further than that.

(4) Beginning with *Poor White* (1920), though he did not alter radically his point of view, he noted that his field was also being explored by psychoanalysis, whose researches bore many of the same marks which characterized his fictional approach. *Many Marriages* (1923) and *Dark Laughter* (1925), together with several shorter stories in *The Triumph of the Egg* (1921) and *Horses and Men* (1923), reflect this interest in frustrations and repressions, as they affect families, or unmarried women.

(5) Anderson developed his themes quite independently of Freudian influence, but with such a startling likeness of approach that critics fell into the most excusable error of their times; it seemed an absolute certainty that Anderson should have been influenced directly by Freud.

Throughout all of this Anderson maintains a skeptical attitude toward the new psychology; sometimes the reaction is simply humorous; [25] at other times, as in the case of Trigant Burrow, he becomes actively insistent upon his independent position. That psychoanalysis encouraged hostility to the social sources of repression, especially in America, cannot be denied; but the Freudian deals only with the *individual problem* of neurosis, and has always hesitated to suggest changes in the social system which is in part responsible either for a neurosis or for its imperfect cure. Many writers of the twenties thought otherwise, however; to them psychoanalysis suggested a weapon for fighting the sources of repression, or an excuse for fleeing from them. Further, Anderson's frequent reference to the sex problems of his characters was likely to convince the critics more readily. They hesitated to distinguish between the clinical study of neurosis and the literary study of frustration.

ii

The Andersonian village is examined " from within." Anderson bothers little with the placid and deceptive exteriors of village life, but is concerned primarily with the feelings of those who live within the narrow confines of village society. The energy of the villager has only infrequent opportunity for expression; most often it fails to appear at all, except in violent explosions of emotion, affective orgies, which erupt and disturb mightily the calm surface of appearances.[26] The forces that keep emotional expres-

[25] As, for example: " Only a few weeks ago I dined with a lady who spoke of ' spiral evolution.' My head snapped back. . . . Perhaps I am trying to escape the age of words. I have a dreadful fear of being psychoanalyzed by a psychoanalyst. On some nights I dream of these birds. One has got me cornered on West 8th street in New York. I squirm and squirm but cannot escape. I tore a bed sheet to pieces trying to get away from one. She was a female psychoanalyst, too. . . ." Sherwood Anderson, " Let's Go Somewhere," in *Outlook*, CLI (1929), 247.

[26] As, for example, in the case of Michael McCarthy, who shouts his prayer

sion imprisoned are often the conventions of the village, and the tendency to misunderstand pure for impure motives; not unusually, however, it is the timidity of the villager himself, who permits the curtailment of his emotional life because he is afraid of his strength. Hatred of the conventions or hatred of persons serves to deflect the energies of men from what might be their normal outlets. Escape from boredom, or from a worse fate, disgrace in the eyes of the community, is manifested in little, symptomatic acts—such as Doc Reefy's " paper pills " [27] or Adolph Myers's nervous gestures with his hands [28]—or in symbolic substitutes for actual sensual gratification. The revelation to the Reverend Curtis Hartman, for example, satisfies him because he has observed the hand of God laid on the " immoral " naked form of a woman. For Anderson's villagers the body is fundamentally a medium of expression; no force can effectively silence the body without making it ugly. The desire for wealth has caused Tom Butterworth to neglect the life of the body, makes him a servant of industrial masters; all of his relationships with his wife and daughter are distorted and twisted as a consequence. Clara's " coming of age " temporarily arouses his interest in the body: " As in the days of his courtship of her mother and before the possessive passion in him destroyed his ability to love, he began to feel vaguely that life about him was full of significance." (*Poor White*, 143–44) But this new interest is soon counteracted by suspicion of his daughter's actions; he refuses to allow her any normal outlets for her newly awakened passion, and ships her off to the state university at the earliest opportunity.

Are not these examples evidences of " neurosis through repression "? Not altogether—and in some respects, not at all. For Anderson has another explanation for many of these acts—the

from the jail: " Oh Father! Send down to men a new Christ. . . . Let him go into churches and into courthouses, into cities, and into towns like this, shouting ' Be Ashamed! Be ashamed of your cowardly concern over your snivelling souls! ' " Anderson, *Windy McPherson's Son*.

[27] " In the office he wore also a linen duster with huge pockets into which he continually stuffed scraps of paper. After some weeks the scraps of paper became little hard round balls, and when the pockets were filled he dumped them out upon the floor." Sherwood Anderson, *Winesburg, Ohio* (New York, n.d.), 19.

[28] " The slender expressive fingers, forever active, forever striving to conceal themselves in his pockets or behind his back, came forth and became the piston rods of his machinery of expression." *Ibid.*, 9.

native inarticulateness of the Middle Westerner. The valiant soul of which Anderson speaks [29] will rebel against conformity and defeat it; but the average, all-too-human townsman suppresses the beauty or the yearning in his soul, and appears inarticulate and weak in his community. To Anderson the forces which deprived man of the simple, beautiful life are sometimes social and economic; but it is man's inherent timidity, his unwillingness or his inability to circumvent the laws and restrictions of the " just " which account mainly for his conformity. The life within him is stilled for lack of courage; if it is ever revealed, the realization comes in moments of poignant sorrow, or violent, deathly revolt. Mary Cochran, for example, has hated her father to the day of his death—hated him for what he has done to her mother. Only a moment before he dies of a heart attack does the truth come to her; the wall between him and her has been built solely by his inarticulateness.[30] Not infrequently this inarticulateness arises from an enforced taciturnity regarding matters of sex. Rosalind Wescott confesses to her mother her intention to go to her Chicago lover; her mother breaks a lifelong silence on the subject: love is a male-made fiction, she says; sex is dirty and a sin.[31]

Frustration has two causes: external pressures against an active search for normal happiness—that is, conventionality and " the morality of the average "; and the timidity and weakness of the individual. The plight of May Edgley has been brought about by both of these agents. She is a strict and severe person, the sole hope of a family of village scoundrels. Her studies in the high school, her determination to become respectable against the odds of village opinion, enjoy a temporary success, but eventually she yields to the importunities of Jerome Hadley, and the tongues begin to wag:

---

[29] " Knowing that all about him in the world are men and women striving to fasten upon him their own insanity of conformity, the young and valiant soul will find here a constant demand upon his resources that will be to him a tonic against the insidious poison of association with the weak." Anderson, *Notebook*, 23. This remark was first printed in 1916.

[30] Sherwood Anderson, " Unlighted Lamps," in *The Triumph of the Egg*, 92.

[31] Anderson, " Out of Nowhere into Nothing," in *The Triumph of the Egg*, 260–61. An effective portrait of these small town attitudes is also found in Carl Van Vechten's *The Tattooed Countess: A Romantic Novel with a Happy Ending* (New York, 1924).

There was a very tender delicate thing within her many
people had wanted to kill—that was certain. To kill the
delicate thing within was a passion that obsessed mankind.
All men and women tried to do it. First the man or woman
killed the thing within himself, and then tried to kill it in
others. Men and women were afraid to let the thing live.[32]

The sin had temporarily released her from the respect of her
fellows, but for several reasons it did not point the way to full
happiness. The accusing finger of her society forced her into a
lie—the work of fantasy, which elaborated as elaboration was
needed, until she herself believed and lived it. This projection
of her one sin against conventional morality was absorbed in the
world of fancy, until that world alone existed for her, dictated its
laws, and demanded its own kind of conformity. It was eventually to demand suicide of her. There are psychoanalytic terms for
all of this experience—repression, projection, " defense mechanism," " substitutive gratification "—but they are not needed. Had
a psychoanalyst come upon May Edgley before the coroner was
yet needed, he might have heard her story and interpreted it in
much the same way as Anderson did. For the psychoanalyst the
study of her problem might have led to a cure—a redirection of
interests, or a more wholesome and sensible sublimation of her
instinctive life; for Anderson, the result was tragic death.

Anderson regarded the Puritan world of fact a hard and cruel
master of many of his characters; here too he is speaking of the
phenomenon of repression, as his American contemporaries had
used that term. Anderson considers the conflict one between
nature itself and the world of power, wealth, and religion. The
contrast is symbolized on several occasions by a natural world in
which the character hides from the artificial. In the cornfields
the heroine of " The New Englander " finds the source of life, so
long ignored by her New England world. In answer to an obscure
impulse, she rushes into the cornfield, exposes herself, and, in a
frantic effort to find recompense for thirty-five years of repression,
kisses the cornstalks. This wild, impetuous act is her answer to
the stifling world of the Puritan; it is as though the earth itself

[32] " Unused," in *Horses and Men* (New York, 1923), 76–77.

could serve to point out the folly of excessive inhibition. In his *Memoirs*, Anderson speaks of the cornfield symbol with tenderness and affection: " I could lie on the warm earth under the corn and see the life of insects, hear the soft sound of broad green leaves rubbing across each other as the summer winds blew over the fields. It was a place for lovely thoughts. . . . I even fancied that the rustling leaves of the corn were whispering to me." (33)

Anderson was sympathetically aware of the mute, inglorious midwesterner, and felt that men failed most of all to find adequate sex orientation. The solution of many of the problems posed in his stories (if it can actually be called a solution) lies in sex understanding, just as much of the frustration is discovered in misunderstanding, or mismating. In " The Other Woman," man finds the key to happiness by spending the night before his wedding with a strange woman.[33]

Many Marriages is Anderson's most thorough study of this problem. This novel, one of the first to come from his newly awakened interest in D. H. Lawrence, is indebted to an imperfect understanding of such novels as *Women in Love* much more than to any other source. It is one of the most self-conscious developments of a " thesis," or a documented feeling, that Anderson was ever to be guilty of. In the Preface Anderson says that " If one seek love and go towards it directly, or as directly as one may in the midst of the perplexities of modern life, one is perhaps insane." The thing to do, as his hero decides, is to accept one's insanity. " Nothing either animate or inanimate can be beautiful that is not loved." (27) This need, so strong in him, is almost entirely disregarded by his wife: " She thought, or believed she thought, that even in marriage a man and woman should not be lovers except for the purpose of bringing children into the world." (64) This is the Puritan attitude toward sex—the practical regard for the continuance of the race: " Even when, after long preparation, talk, prayer, and the acquiring of a little wisdom, a kind of abandon is acquired, as one would acquire a new language, one has still achieved something quite foreign to the flowers, the trees, and the life and carrying on of life among what is called the lower animals." It is amazing that life can be perpetuated at

[33] " The Other Woman," in *The Triumph of the Egg*, 33–45.

all under such conditions; it " proves, as nothing else could, the cold determination of nature not to be defeated." (65)

John Webster decides to leave this false world, but before he does he must explain to his wife and daughter the real secret of his revolt. He purchases an image of the virgin, sets it up in his bedroom, and begins his private ritual of the body. Stripping himself, he walks before the image, in a room lighted only by two candles. This is insanity; he will accept it as such: " I accept the notion that I am at present insane and only hope I shall remain so." (86) It is, at any rate, a free surrender to the impulse within himself. Webster tells his daughter the story of his life; he has had " cause to remember " his wife's body, but she has denied the sacred life of the flesh through her own fear of it.

> . . . a thing people called shame, had come between her and the getting of that glad cry past her lips.
>
> .   .   .   .
>
> Outside voices cried " Shame! Shame! " . . . Should one listen to the voices or should one close the ears, close the eyes? (157, 163)

They are living in a world already dead; the only hope for a re-birth lies in a new awakening of the senses, a world unafraid to live intuitively and sensually. There is a constant struggle be-tween the forces of life (the life of the senses and of sex harmony) and the forces of death (rigid conformity to a mechanical social pattern). " There was a deep well within every man and woman and when life came in at the door of that house, that was the body, it reached down and tore the heavy iron lid off the well. Dark hidden things, festering in the well, came out and found expression for themselves, and the miracle was that, expressed, they became often very beautiful." (217)

This study of Webster's conflict and of his solution has an intensity of analysis which does not characterize Anderson's earlier books. This added intensity, though it has not helped his narra-tive style at all, may be said to indicate an attempt on the part of Anderson to understand more fully the problem of frustration which he considered but fragmentarily in *Winesburg, Ohio* and *The Triumph of the Egg.* Unlike *Windy McPherson's Son,* the economic problem is thrown into the background, and the nature of the inner conflict is considered as basically psychological. *Many Marriages* shows Anderson attempting to "intellectualize" his feelings, in the manner of what he at least thought was Lawrence's analysis.

Under Lawrence's influence, Anderson tried to assert a "thesis": that the primitive mind "understood" more fully and more easily the basic secrets of man. Wyndham Lewis has pointed the parallel between Anderson's primitivism and that of Lawrence: the Negresses in *Dark Laughter* "are in the role of the *parrots* in Mr. Lawrence's book." Anderson, Lewis suggests, ". . . is a poor, henpecked, beFreuded, bewildered White, with a brand new ' inferiority complex.' " [34] In *Dark Laughter* Anderson offers a contrast between the embattled, imprisoned white, who has sacrificed almost everything for the dead values of money, power, and social prestige, and the uninhibited Negro consciousness. John Stockton, who has left his Chicago wife and changed his name to Bruce Dudley, meets the wife of his employer; she arranges to escape with him from her husband. In the background the laughter of the Negro servants helps to remind us that Negroes order these matters more gracefully. In this study Anderson reiterates the doctrine of *Many Marriages*: that man (white man, of course) has suffered the life forces to atrophy, and that nature will have its revenge. The ironic chorus of Negresses points to the essential primitiveness and simplicity of Anderson's solution. The figure of Sponge Martin, a kind of imitation of Lawrence's Mellors, represents the ideal triumph over civilization; not at all reconciled with the industrial ingenuity which has threatened his love of craftsmanship, he succeeds in forcing a belligerent compromise upon the enemy. His answer is a vigorous and healthy animalism.[35]

Anderson's themes are primarily bound by his search for the causes of man's frustration. What makes men more decent and moral, than healthy and sensual beings? The figures of *Wines-*

---

[34] Wyndham Lewis, "Paleface," in *Enemy*, II (1927), 61, 65. The reference to Lawrence is to *Mornings in Mexico*, 3-20. The most thorough study of Anderson and Lawrence is in Irving Howe's *Sherwood Anderson* (New York, 1951), 179–96.

[35] Anderson's failure to make this kind of thesis convincing is at least partly testified to in Hemingway's parody of it in *The Torrents of Spring* (New York, 1926).

burg, Ohio, and of *Poor White* are victims of both external restrictions and of their own timidity—a sort of perverted gentleness.
The source of much impotence lies in basic repressions of society—
the business world, industrialism, middle-class decorum. Anderson is anxious to point out that primitive life is unimpeded by
such barriers to happiness. He offers a variety of suggestions to
imprisoned man: the totalitarian, rhythmic discipline preached
by Beaut McGregor in *Marching Men*; simple repudiation, as
practised by John Webster in *Many Marriages* and by Aline Grey
in *Dark Laughter*; the communism of *Beyond Desire*. Fundamentally, Anderson offers no real solution to the problems he
raises.

Anderson himself admits the power of dreams and visions in
the creative life. It is as though he deliberately constructed a
world whose particulars and relationships would be valid only in
the imagination. He is rarely content with simple realism; he
abhors the world of fact—the world of the Puritan, he calls it. His
frame of reference is almost always the psychic center of personal
experience. One may say that the realistic novel seeks to display
the physical causality of events. To supplement this type of realism, in many respects to replace it, postwar writers went to psychology for a new form of characterization and description. Hence,
in the case of the narrative portrait of the village, in place of the
sentimental realism of Eggleston and the drab realistic pessimism
of Ed. Howe, the twenties offered the psychic realism of Sherwood
Anderson. Anderson's characters are real, but in a peculiar sense;
they become real to us only if and when we suspend ordinary
judgment and accept them—not for what they appear—but for
what they think and feel. His method is to approach a character
in terms of his psychic life, and to consider external acts as either
symptomatic or symbolic expressions of it.

The author's critical judgment which ordinarily manifests
itself in selection of judgments stated or implied, is replaced in
Anderson by *sympathy*—that is, in the etymological sense of that
word, a " suffering with." This is especially true, since there is an
autobiographical fragment in almost every one of his creations—
they are creatures both of his imagination and of his temperament.
This preoccupation with the soul of himself, as one critic has put

it, demands recognition of Anderson as a writer whose explorations of the psyche are peculiar to him.[36]

The gentleness and vagueness of Anderson's sympathy are important factors in considering the legitimacy of his village characters as fictional personalities. Violence—and there is much of it in Anderson's novels—is always tempered by the fact that both the act and the actor are at least in part excused by elaborate and advance explanations of the event. Witness the character of Joe Wainsworth, harness-maker of Bidwell. The ultimate succession of acts is demoniac, extravagant. Yet the first of them is preceded by Wainsworth's weeping; the weeping climaxes, as it symbolizes, the defeat of Wainworth's purpose in life. Anderson proceeded originally from a recognition that " something was wrong "; the *bête noire* was not clearly known. It is referred to variously as industrialism, the business mind, the sophistication of the civilized man, the white fear of wholesome impulses.

Were the critics altogether wrong in calling Anderson the " American Freudian "? There is no evidence that he wrote with Freud's works, or a psychoanalytic dictionary, at his elbow. The critics labeled Anderson as they did for this reason: almost any one of his characters could, at a certain stage of his career, have walked into an analyst's office and been justified in asking for treatment. May Edgley, Jesse Bentley, Fred Grey, Bruce Dudley, Hugh McVey, Mrs. Willard—each in his or her own way suffered, not physical, but psychic pain. For each the accepted way of life did not accord well with the inner, psychically motivated wish. In all cases the clinical report and Anderson's narrative report would have had a different conclusion. There is some justification in noting the parallel courses of psychoanalysis and Anderson's fiction, but there seems little evidence to prove that those two courses intersected at any vital points. It is as though Anderson were thrusting upon Freud the burden of clarifying the artist's analysis: " Men who have passed the age of thirty and who have

---

[36] Rachel Smith, " Sherwood Anderson: Some Entirely Arbitrary Reactions," in *Sewanee Review*, XXXVII (1929), 163. Anderson himself admits that his theory of writing is based upon the autobiographical projection of the writer. Cf.: " In every man or woman dwell dozens of men and women, and the highly imaginative will lead fifty lives." Sherwood Anderson, " Some More about the ' New Note,' " in *Little Review*, I (1914), 16.

intelligence understand such things. A German scientist can explain perfectly. If there is anything you do not understand in human life consult the works of Dr. Freud." (*Dark Laughter*, 230) If you have been unable to follow with me into the lives of these characters, Anderson seems to be saying; if they still seem queer to you—if their acts are merely violent and inexplicably so—Dr. Freud has studied these matters calmly and scientifically, and he will aid you. But if you do go to him, you will have failed to understand much of what I wish to say to you.

iii

Waldo Frank occupies a strange position in American criticism. An urgent, tendentious critic, he attempts first to define the grave deficiences of American culture, then to offer his own view of what he calls "organic wholeness." In his three most important contributions to criticism the point of view alternates between cries of despair and echoes of hope. *Our America* (1919) was an explanation of America for European consumption; its dominating tone is pessimism, the *bête noire* the neo-Puritan. *The Re-Discovery of America* (1929) gives the basis upon which Frank's earlier criticism was founded. A collection of essays, ranging from 1925 to 1936 in date of composition, was published in 1937 under the title *In the American Jungle*; here he gives random views of the American chaos, insights into the "mass mind," and suggestions of hope for America's future greatness.

In these books we find both a criticism of American institutions and a reiterated faith in the sources of revival. For Frank, modern industrialism has grown statistically but not organically. American life has been falsely and artificially geared to the wheel of progress. Frank suggests that at the beginning of our history there was a change in the use of emotional energies. The Puritan's denial of life and the pioneer's demand for industrial energy set the pattern of America's peculiar, nationwide repression: the pioneer "must do violence upon himself. Whole departments of his psychic life must be repressed. Categories of desire must be inhibited. Reaches of consciousness must be lopped off. Old, half-forgotten intuitions must be called out from the buried depths of his mind and made the governors of his life." (*Our America*, 18–19)

The source of American ills is a psychic unbalance, the denial of the life of the senses, for a material rather than a spiritual reason. Progress is incompatible with healthy living. The American's progress " was best served by the suppression of Desire." (28) The American has steadily substituted *power* for reality, or confuses the one with the other; this is a form of psychic dishonesty which turns constantly away from the facts of the human organism. It is an evasion of reality—a source of wish-fulfillment as potent and as deluding as the poet's daydream.[37] In the literature of our nation we over-simply life, by reducing it to our own terms. The pioneer, who turned aside his energies and directed them toward the unceasing and one-sided struggle with his environment, did not defeat desire by these means.

> For Desire would not be denied. It sickened and shriveled and grew perverse. It sought expression in neurotic arts, in obversely sensual religions, in sadistic interference with Desire in others. . . . But it *went on*. For it *is* life. And in the birth of each new generation, each new individual, it began once more its healthy journey, strong and fertile and inspired —until the accumulated might of environment and " education " turned it aside. (45–46)

The Puritan denies the God of vengeance—or rather, by identifying himself with Him, thus deprives Him of His striking power—and substitutes a God who is a silent partner in the business world. The Puritan and pioneer are as one, merged and united in character and aim. This is repression on a national scale. Externally, however, the neo-Puritan is doing the work of God. The conventions and censorship of the modern world point ceaselessly to a chaste God, demanding that His followers be discreet and worshipful, above all to attend church on Sundays and to have

---

[37] Cf. " Formulations Regarding the Two Principles in Mental Functioning," 13–21. Frank believes that the " power aim " is the result of rechannelizing the pleasure principle and thus distorting reality. He asks for a recognition of the importance of sources of pleasure—sources which have been distorted and repressed by the power drive.

nothing to do with the naked body or with any of its functions. Apparently his outer observance and worship of a disembodied and despiritualized God is not disturbed by any " revolt of the senses." But, implicit in the more extravagant of his observances one discovers panderings to unsatisfied desire. The Puritan " must not covet woman: so Mr. Sunday gives suggestive discourse upon low-neck gowns, the proximity of bodies in the dance, the theme of ' vampire ' dramas, and the possibilities of unlighted theatres with close seats." (99) [38]

Frank's criticism of the American tradition sets the stage for the battle of the twenties against what has been given such labels as " cultural repression " and " neo-Puritanism." In this metaphoric characterization the American industrial world becomes a monstrous figure, whose striving for material gain has made neurotic. The pattern has been so often sketched, its details so frequently discussed, that it may be well here to pause for a summary: [39] (1) The " body "—the cultural organism, combining primitive and untapped resources and energies; (2) the " desire " —instinctive, normal tendency to effect a balance between pleasure and reality; (3) the " repression "—rechannelizing of natural resources for the single aim of measurable power (such an activity leads to a denial of the senses, intellectualizes and abstracts natural energies by a statistical survey of monetary gain) ; (4) the consequence—sterility of religious principles, their decline to the status of convention and superficial observance; " cultural neurosis " and disguised fulfillment of inhibited wishes.

[38] In a footnote, 99–100, Frank quotes several lines from his contribution to *Seven Arts*, July, 1917: " The success of Billy Sunday is due to the use of what, in pathology, is known as the *conversion-mechanism:*—the channeling of an instinctive desire away from an expression that is forbidden to one that is disguised and not forbidden. It is unsafe to give open leash to sexuality, so turn the passion into the fear of Hell and glut your worry by ' hitting the trail.' . . . And one need only remark the constantly recurring wreath of smiles on the terrier-like countenance of Mr. Sunday to realize what good fun it must be to have this sort of ' religion ' in a materialistic and fun-denying world. The neurotic satisfies himself with a set of distorted symptoms in place of an unfriendly and hard reality. . . ." We need not point out the source of Frank's critical idea here, for the language betrays it.

[39] It will be noticed that the whole procedure is based upon an analogy which assumes a form of humanized anatomy for a state of culture. The culture or historical therapeutist is more comfortable if he can visualize a national " body " on which he can operate. Hence, the transfer of psychoanalytic terms to cultural history is managed by changing a geographic to a physiological entity.

There are obvious differences between Frank's use of psycho-analysis and Freud's ventures into cultural history. Freud stressed a few characteristics which he discovered to be so general as to suggest a form of culture inheritance; he believed that they were a primitive legacy which resided in the unconscious of man, archaic survivals transmitted from one generation to the next.[40] The American attack on Puritanism was a different kind of approach; it alternated from criticism of individual national heroes to general strictures upon the entire national body. The single terms of psychoanalytic techniques were confused with the sociological conception of the mass mind, and these were indifferently associated with a protest against a statistically abstract industrial world. Terms were loosely used, the restrictions of analogy but indifferently observed. The details of a nation's cultural life were subordinated to the needs of a new theory. Psychoanalytic theory was called upon to justify a strongly felt but vaguely determined resentment against the Puritan. He was a repressed and harried creature, whose acts had placed the nation under the black pall of a national repression. Frank was aware of both the economic and the psychic determinants of twentieth-century culture. For him economic exploitation was the end product of the deliberate stifling of cultural health. This repression led to the pitiful weakness of twentieth-century conventions and to neurosis on a national scale.

Waldo Frank was eager to avail himself of the terms and concepts of Freudianism. *Our America* draws upon the vocabulary of the Freudians. The national *malaise* may be symbolized in a single, devastating image which synthesizes both its economic and its psychic causes. But Frank was not simply a destroyer of images. He formulated a positive alternative program, a declaration of "war ... of a new consciousness against the forms and language of a dying culture." [41] All criticism must be philosophically secured against triviality or mere negation: "The roots of culture are philosophical; religious, ethical, aesthetic. There can be no criticism for our modern world until there is a modern philosophical

---

[40] See Herbert Marcuse, *Eros and Civilization* (Boston, 1955). For a study of the specific American ground of this cultural criticism, see especially Solomon Fishman, *The Disinherited of Art* (Berkeley, 1953).

[41] Frank, "For a Declaration of War," in *Salvos*, 14.

synthesis. Without it, the brightest and solemnest discussion is just as impertinent as the dullest." (*Salvos*, 15)

Central to Frank's thesis is his view of nineteenth-century rationalism, which, he insists, helped to break asunder the " matrix within which civilization was born, and . . . the foundations in which it was reared and nurtured." (19) The older sense of organic wholeness was replaced by a series of rationalistic experiments. The modern intellectual is " all mind "; what is worse, he is smug about it and satisfied with a fragmentary security against chaos. " With a religious earnestness, [the intellectuals] fix on whatever element in life is sweetest to their mental habit. They pore over the sentimental or the mechanical or the political man. They deny the existence of what moves beyond their radius and so wall themselves into a smug seclusion." (54)

The alternative is what Frank calls organic wholeness, the " origin and end of all our creative being," [42] a religious state which begins with, and transcends, the personal. Art combines the physical data of the senses with the emotional centers of artistic expression. The artist contributes to this aesthetic unity and keeps it alive by means of his own energies; the " sense of aesthetic form is an unconscious adumbration of our sense of unity with our own body." (*Re-Discovery*, 23) Without such a unity, modern culture is fragmentary. The religion of modern man is not one but many, a succession of illusions and cults, some of them the natural out-growth of business fraternity, others accepted vaguely as theologized protest against such fraternity. Each of these new " Gods and cults of Power " is more than a mere pretense. This condition points to a real need for a resumption of cultural unity. With the pathetic eagerness of the frustrated soul, America has turned to psychoanalysis, and made a cult of it. In this effort the modern intellectual has again mistaken the part for the whole; the jargon of the analytic laboratory is assumed to be a vision of psychic wholeness.

Frank describes Freud as the last of a long line of nineteenth-century Titans, men who strove to replace " the broken synthesis of Catholic Europe." [43] Each of these men sought for an inte-

---

[42] Waldo Frank, *The Re-Discovery of America: in Introduction to a Philosophy of American Life* (New York, 1929) , 19.
[43] Frank, " Sigmund Freud," in *In the American Jungle*, 83. The " Titans "

grating principle to serve as the key to the new unity. Frank admires them but regrets to find that they gave only fragmentary integrations. Freud descends to the " irrational depths of the soul," armed with the principles and method of nineteenth-century science.

> But Freud will not surrender to this phantasmagoric and miasmic world; he will draw forth from its flux, by means of reason, energy for the three-dimensional world of reasonable practice, and this limited world he will insist to be the one reality. It is a struggle between uneven forces, and the con-sequence is a psychological design (called " real ") that is drenched with the passionate and heroic will of its author. (*American Jungle*, 86)

His major criticism of Freud is that the latter overly insists upon the rational. It is the artist's complaint against the scientist. Freud will not allow for the mystical vision in the unconscious; denying one part of the whole and overstressing another, Freud repeats the error of the nineteenth-century " absolutists ":

> in their attempt to exclude a part of man's equipment for finding truth—the one group reason, the other group organic intuition—[the absolutists] are doomed to failure. And in Freud, no less than in Dostoevski, this awareness of limita-tions gives the poignant note of the Titans who are helpless to create a world against the indefeasible God who is the whole. (88)

Frank wants more than a rational view of the unconscious. Jung, he says, " is more logical," since he allows for the " mystic x "; but Jung lacks the intellectual stature of Freud.[44]

This is by no means Frank's final statement. He is disturbed by the social consequences of therapy. Psychoanalysis, as practised by the wealthy, the superficial, and the bored, is a highly expensive

are Schopenhauer, Hegel, Spencer, Comte; Balzac and Dostoevski; Beethoven, Moussorgsky, and Wagner; Delacroix, Ingres, and Cezanne; Marx and Darwin.

[44] Frank's opinion of Jung's intellectual capacity is almost scornful. " As to Jung, I never liked him or read him with much pleasure," he says in a letter. " Although he is more sensitive to the intuitive and creative process than Freud, he lacked it seemed to me Freud's clarity and intellectual integrity." Waldo Frank to Frederick J. Hoffman, November 27, 1942.

game played by the " type of idle woman and parasitic man who are not worth saving at the price of the lengthy effort which the analyst must devote to readjusting them into a morbid world." (*American Jungle*, 89) This is only one of the reasons why Frank finds popular therapy objectionable. In his portrait of Dr. Brill, he enjoys thoroughly the task of lampooning the antics of middle-aged women; Brill's work sets the fashion for popular paranoias and costly complexes:

> They met, in club, in salon, in bed—and " psyched " each other. They discussed. Above all, they confessed. Women roamed about, dreams gushing from their unrouged lips. Young girls wore passionate avowals like posies in their hair, like lurid gems on their breasts. Strong men, inspired by Dream-interpretation, abandoned wife and career, seeking the Mate of a Complex.[45]

Though Frank does not repudiate Freud, he nevertheless believes Freud's contribution to thought is incomplete. Psychoanalysis has performed an inestimable service, a courageous one as well, in revealing the depths and richness of our unconscious life. But mere rational probing and experiments with psychic reclamation omit too many factors which are important for the ultimate, creative reorganization of mankind. In his own development, Frank discovered that Freud was an indispensable aid.

In 1913 or 1914 he first encountered the work of Freud, " and it amazingly corresponded with much of the intuitive thinking I had done for myself, on human motivation." Freud offered a series of conclusions that confirmed him in his own opinions. " Unless Freud had fitted my intuitive sense, I could never have been so helped by him. We are helped, intellectually, and nourished, by those who are apriori close to us. Freud to me is one of the heroes of modern thought; and I am profoundly his debtor." [46] Freudianism had served him when he was first interested in evaluating American culture, and by 1919 Frank used psychoanalytic terms freely, almost without caution, as critical symbols. At the same time, he was dissatisfied with Freud and did not accept him

---

[45] Waldo Frank, " Joyful Wisdom," in *Time Exposures; by Search Light . . .* (New York, 1926) , 97–98.
[46] Waldo Frank to Frederick J. Hoffman, November 27, 1942.

as a mentor or guide, but preferred a therapy which possessed greater educative and social value. In his 1934 revaluation, he considered Freud one of the most important influences upon modern thought but suggested that the future lay beyond the reach of Freudian psychoanalysis. Philosophically, he says, " we are almost in opposite camps." Meanwhile, his criticism of popular psychoanalysis continued as a part of his distaste for the intellectual as such and for the "idle woman and parasitic man." Since his novels are critical doctrines and show the same development observable in his criticism, it is not surprising that they should demonstrate the same attitudes toward psychoanalysis.

iv

In Frank's early novels one observes the materials of the artist, scarcely integrated, just as they appear in his early critical evaluations of American culture. One discovers that Frank is, after all, going beyond his materials, imposing a philosophy of his own upon his ideal hero, a fictional archetype whom he has sought for in vain in his studies of historical and contemporary characters.[47] This ideal man is in some way or other a rebel against the world of statistics and profits. One suggestion for Frank's fictional ideal is in Anderson's *Windy McPherson's Son*—a more tender Sam McPherson, never entirely fooled by the attractions of business gains. In all of this there is a suggestion of Frank's control of his materials; his characters are not mere receptacles of ideas; the *persona* always animates the *idea*. Yet there is much truth in Paul Rosenfeld's criticism: " He approaches his material with the unconfessed wish of making it substantiate his thesis, and forces the protective machinery of a convenient apriorism, a plot or metaphysical formula upon his unconscious life." [48]

David Markand, the most important of these heroes, is the means by which Frank appraises the modern world. His simplicity, naïveté, and deep sincerity make other people uncom-

---

[47] The closest approximation to the "ideal man" in history is Lincoln; among Frank's contemporaries, Alfred Stieglitz.

[48] Paul Rosenfeld, *Men Seen: Twenty-four Modern Authors* (New York, 1925), 105.

fortable in his presence: this is one way of saying that they are uncomfortable in their own inner selves. Such qualities are closely allied with David's unconscious; they are not affected by the hypocrisies the modern world demands of all successful men. David's wide-eyed wonder seems never to have had any single extraneous object to contemplate. David's tender reliance upon his mother is basic to him; he is constantly returning to it in his relationship with others. No Freudian difficulty flaws the glass; it is as though he has escaped all suggestion of perversion or hatred. Frank's reason for giving his hero such simple raiment is to show the source of hatred in others. David's first real struggle is with Tom Rennard; Tom is the rebellious Puritan who, in freeing himself from the grotesque savagery of Protestantism, reverts to its business counterpart: he becomes a busy, shrewd, unscrupulous New York City lawyer. David appears to Tom as the very embodiment of his conscience, torturing and maddening him, and pointing to the peace which Tom has deliberately rejected. *The Dark Mother* is the story of that struggle; and Tom loses in the end, as Frank would have him lose. David is reserved for greater things; Tom turns, embittered, to his world of empty intrigue.

It is clear that David Markand is to pursue his solitary way, affecting other lives as he has Rennard's. The next novel [49] supports his estimate of American life in *The Re-Discovery of America*. The sensitive person of the twentieth century experiments with all forms of religion and faith, seeking a way out of the chaos that lies immediately beneath the surface of American life. There is no single way out of chaos, for within it is the baptism and rebirth which the soul needs. Helen Daindrie's life is intended as a portrait of the timidly brave but ineffectual American who seeks the truth among the surfaces of his culture. She seeks the comforting and sensible unity of science; somehow, the coldness of scientific fact repels her, and she moves within the warm, dark area of David's affections. Here again there is only a partial solution: sex happiness, domestic security, are evasions of the truth. From psychoanalysis she turns to Catholicism, which she finally believes has the unity she has sought. Frank sums up

---

[49] Waldo Frank, *The Death and Birth of David Markand* (New York, 1934).

this search: " ' men have always tried to see the world, at least that part of it they had business with, as a whole. That attempt, you might say, is one aspect of civilization: science is only its latest avatar.' " (*Death and Birth*, 50)

The more earnestly Helen searches, the more remote David seems to her. They are going in different directions, searching for unity in different ways. David again becomes a solitary; and, in an agony of resolution, he cuts himself off from the old world: " ' This is—necessary, even though I don't understand it.' " (88) He returns to the mother; the image of the mother returns to the land and the home to which David goes for refuge. In the remote Massachusetts village, where he had lived his early life, he searches for the answer which will justify his having cut himself off from all his bonds with the outside world. But the greyed, empty, tasteless Puritan spirit of the village drives him out. " ' Let me learn,' " he cries, " ' why I have drawn their hate, how I can draw their love. For we are not separate: it is a lie, our separation, equal in birth.' " His way lies westward and downward—away from the false securities of wealth and of business life. In whatever movement he joins, his simple honesty discovers instantly its flaws. From Kansas he goes to Chicago, is drawn into the turmoil which modern intellectuals make of their frustrations. He breaks away from it, finds a job in the stockyards and lives within another world. But the intellectual world refuses to let him go; he is brought back to be educated, to crib reality from books. He turns to Marxism and the labor movement, and, in the company of two young Communists, roams the country, to learn the " practical truth," which is Communism in action.

In all of this there is implicit a search for physical death; but Frank makes clear that physical death is not the end of David's search. It is negation, and Frank's theory of Wholeness demands an active reintegration of creative forces: " There is a class, hardly born, which struggles with the world to live. By its struggle for life the whole world may be reborn alive again." (528) David's rebirth is inauspicious; he performs a ritual of rebirth, the token of an " awakening will, within the body of death that was still he and the city and the world; the will to overcome itself at last, and be reborn! " (541–42) The pilgrimage of David Markand is a fictional mirror of Frank's theory. Frank has avoided all suggestions for an easy victory over chaos; he treats psychoanalysis as another of the lessons in integration. As in his criticism, Frank has employed Freudian psychology as a means. The story of David Markand demonstrates a close association with Freud's speculations about the life and death instincts.[50] One essential difference lies in Frank's confident expectation of a creative, positive mystic sense in the unconscious; for Freud, this is entirely absent, and the instinctual battle is checked at all times by biological and psychological facts.

The life of David Markand illustrates in fiction the assumptions of Frank's *The Re-Discovery of America.* His other works demonstrate, in one way or another, other features of his knowledge of psychoanalysis. In his first novel [51] as in his first major critical work, *Our America,* Freudian terms are employed more conspicuously than wisely; we have a sense of the young novelist crudely adapting the verbal tools of another craft. His images are frequently harsh, as though color and light were abstract things, best disposed of in abstraction. *The Unwelcome Man* plays freely with terms and concepts; such a passage as the following shows the materials, incompletely mastered, and awkwardly expressed: " Too much passion, and reflection, *thrown up by his unconscious self* like the lava of a volcano, flooded the black slope of Quincy's night. And in his sleep came hectic, vivid dreams—dreams in which a *burst of repressed wishes stormed to realization.* Nor were the wishes good, or gentle, or composed." (*Unwelcome Man,* 78. Italics mine.)

Frank experimented with fictional ideas and styles in the manner of his times. The primitivism of *Dark Laughter* is developed in *Holiday*; the idea of describing the frustration of small lives within a single area is developed in *City Block*. The primitivism of *Holiday* occupies a central place in both the thesis and the plot of the novel. As in Anderson's novel, the lives of the white man are circumscribed by conventional standards, which they honor only in the breach. But in *Holiday* the two opposing forces are brought into a more intimate and more violent focus.

[50] Cf. *Beyond the Pleasure Principle, The Ego and the Id.*
[51] Frank, *The Unwelcome Man* (Boston, 1917) .

The religion of the Negro is genuine; the white preacher " shoots his words like a creature at bay from a recess of fear within him." [52] The heroine echoes the white fear of " Niggertown ": " How can I rest in you when you stand and shout? I am weary with whiteness. To rule, to be civilized and chaste; you do not know what weariness it is. My woman yearns toward me in hunger, I am spent. All the world waves in darkling circles about my white uprightness, I am spent." (*Holiday*, 100) The " shalt not's " of white christianity are feeble substitutes for the Negro " Yea's." The novel's crisis occurs when Negro John Cloud, to whom the heroine is drawn, is falsely accused and is therefore doomed to suffer for his race, to give the whites a holiday from repressions. The impression the novel gives is that of an over-simplified primitivistic drama of two kinds of psychic organization in basic conflict. Its principal motivation is a thesis, with which several elementary psychological ideas are associated.

In the 600-odd pages of *The Bridegroom Cometh* Frank's explicit criticism of popular psychoanalysis is best given. He remarks bitterly that to the intellectuals Freud is nothing but a vague justification of free love and loose living. There is something pathetic in this picture of the stupid, helpless intellectual of the American twenties. The sharp jabs at silly talk continue wherever Frank brings the idle intellectuals together. Mrs. Forbish, who offers Mary Donald a place in her " new School," sums up the empty talk in her casual remark, " I *so* prefer Jung, don't you? he is so much more spiritual." (*Bridegroom*, 498) The figure of Doctor Philip Cariss is exhaustively portrayed. Cariss, the business man's analyst, who cures his patients of their forebodings of financial disaster, is not averse to giving the " pretty, idle woman " what he thinks she wants:

> pretty women, idle women, sex-unhappy women physiologically right, were a good part of his practice and the dramatic realization of the suppressed need of them all . . . to go to bed with the analyst . . . often crystallized their problem and hastened the cure. When they saw what they had done was to go to bed with their dream (the *imago* of the father for

---

[52] Frank, *Holiday* (New York, 1923), 46.

the most part), they were ready to Face Reality (his favorite phrase). Meantime the analyst was nourished . . . and paid for his nourishment at from twenty-five to fifty dollars the session (548–49)

One must distinguish between Frank's respect for Freud and his denunciation of popular Freudianism. Both played an important part in his fiction. Without going directly to Freud for all of his treatment of character, Frank used him more fully and more often than any other of the men we have studied. He is aware even of the minor suggestions which Freud made regarding everyday life—the psychological explanation of forgetting. The successful lawyer of *Summer Never Ends*,[53] Mortimer Crane, renounces business after he has surveyed the wreckage of his personal life. Once his attention has been turned away from the serious business of making money, he forgets the superficial social amenities which had always in the past secured his clients. He forgets to say the appropriate things, and loses one after another of his clientele as a result.

Not the least of Frank's borrowings from Freud is his use of the texture of the dream. Since the dream is perhaps the best means of understanding the unconscious, Frank considers it a legitimate means for revealing the unconscious motivations for the conduct of his fictional people. The dream acts throughout Frank's fiction as a structural device as well. In *Summer Never Ends*, the two dreams which occur to Dagny Petersen on the night after she has first met Crane, represent a summary of the previous action, and an anticipation of subsequent action.[54]

One novel[55] employs vision and dream almost exclusively. John Mark's adventures are an unusual refinement of the Jekyll-Hyde duality. Blameless and successful in his business life, he

---

[53] (New York, 1941).

[54] See *ibid.*, 74–76. In answer to a specific question about this matter, Frank says: "I see no reason why a character's dreams should not be as legitimate material for the artist as his conscious actions, or as a portrayal of his physical traits. I deliberately used dreams, since dreams are, to me, a *part* of the nature of my personae. Doubtless without Freud, I never could have done this with any intelligence.

"Dream to me is less a clue to act-motivation than to general character. . . . It reveals, I think, traits—colors—trends and states of character. . . ." Waldo Frank to Frederick J. Hoffman, November 27, 1942.

[55] *Chalk Face* (New York, 1924).

finds, to his horror, that those who would frustrate his unconscious desires are removed by suicide, murder, or accident, leaving apparently no trace of a culprit or offender visible to the eye of the police. When his fiancée confesses that she cannot decide between him and another man, a telephone message almost immediately announces the death of the rival. His parents oppose an early marriage; they are both killed in an auto accident. Finally, Mark recognizes these deaths, not as mere coincidences, but as the externalization of his unconscious wish. He prepares to face that desire boldly. The dream-vision now takes over entirely. Desire will lead Mark to Death. John tries to best his dream self by coldly evaluating it: " There is revelation in the Dream! Of that I was convinced. Let me explore its strangely shifting realm. But my mind could not enter there, script for action, it pounded at the gate, and it could not enter." (*Chalk Face*, 193) He is convinced now that it is he who has killed his rival, and disposed of his parents, when they would thwart his desire. But he is so changed, so reconciled to his desire, that Mildred is terrified and leaves him.

Waldo Frank's debt to Freud is extensive. We discover it at first in the early works, which, though sincere in intention, are immature in form. Their mass of inadequately assimilated facts are the raw materials which he is to use later in subtler form. In the course of his development several clues suggest that he has not thrown off the influence of Freud: his preoccupation with the unconscious life of his later characters is not merely a deeper study of motivation; for the unconscious of his central character is always the point to which events are referred. What Frank *does* furnish is the creative means of victory over death—the " mystic x " which Freud hesitates to allow. The dream form is utilized in every novel as a means of intensifying characterization, and incidentally as a structural device. His knowledge of dreams is from no popular dream book but from a study of Freud, as he admits. Finally, his criticisms and satires of popular psychoanalysis at no time include the founder of psychoanalysis as an object of ridicule. That he criticized Freud has already been shown; that he respected him and remained indebted to him should be obvious.

v

F. Scott Fitzgerald's *Tender Is the Night* (1934) is interesting not only for what it contains in itself but for the history of its composition. It came at the beginning of what proved to be the second half of his career. Already solidly established as an important writer through the publication in 1925 of *The Great Gatsby* and a popular one since the " early success " of *This Side of Paradise* (1920), Fitzgerald began planning for his most ambitious work in 1925. He spent nine years puzzling over the form it should take, writing preliminary sketches, changing and shifting his characters and scenes. At various times the novel (or its preliminary versions) carried one of these titles: *The Boy Who Killed His Mother, The Melarkey Case, Doctor Diver's Holiday, The Doctor's Holiday, Our Type, World's Fair,* and finally *Tender Is the Night.*

The changes were not all a consequence of Fitzgerald's inability to decide upon a useful form. These were years of extreme trial for the Fitzgeralds. They seemed first of all determined to live up to their reputations; they competed with each other for recognition; and Zelda Fitzgerald began to show the consequences of the pace she had set for herself and for her husband. For the first time in his life, psychiatry became an absorbing and necessary world of discourse. The fortunes of the Fitzgeralds varied as Zelda's health improved or declined. Fitzgerald was forced to judge the world of his fiction from a new point of view. He had already presented that world, with its confusion, its moral chaos, its suggestions of imminent violence, from the perspective of the sensitive artist he occasionally proved he could be. But while his fiction often suggested psychoanalytic situations, easily accessible to the interpretations of analysis, he had seldom considered psychoanalysis itself, either as a frame of reference or as a *modus operandi.* Now, as Zelda's troubles demanded more and more of his time, and he turned to the texts of psychoanalysis from necessity and to satisfy his curiosity, he began to reconsider the plans of his new novel and to give dramatic emphasis to both the science of psychiatry and the lives and work of psychiatrists.[56]

[56] Zelda's first breakdown occurred April 23, 1930. Fitzgerald took her to

Malcolm Cowley, in his excellent editing of the final version of *Tender Is the Night*,[57] suggests three separate developments in its planning and composition. The first, the " Melarkey version " (begun on the Riviera, late summer of 1925) was supposed to feature a young Hollywood technician, Francis Melarkey, who " would fall in love with a woman like Nicole Diver, would go on too many wild parties, would lose control of himself, and would kill his mother in a fit of rage." This plan scarcely resembles the 1934 novel. In the second or " Rosemary version " (written about 1929–1930) Melarkey has disappeared, or has dissolved into three Hollywood characters: Lewellen Kelly, a famous motion-picture director who is taking his wife Nicole to Europe for a vacation; and " Rosemary," who tries to attract his attention in the hope of getting a screen test. In the 1934 novel, Kelly and his wife become Dick and Nicole Diver, the association with Hollywood dropped altogether; Rosemary becomes an accomplished child star, who with her mother is on vacation in Europe as the completed novel begins.

The third and final version, the " Dick Diver version," was begun early in 1932 and became the finished form of the 1934 novel. Here the hero is a promising young psychiatrist. It is obvious that the events of 1930 and 1931 influenced this new development profoundly. Summing up the variations, Cowley suggests that the essential theme of the three versions is that of " an ambitious young American [who] goes to Europe and is ruined by his contact with the leisure class." (337) The leisure

Montreux, Switzerland, for examination; the diagnosis was schizophrenic. At the end of January, 1931, the Fitzgeralds were in the United States when Zelda suffered her second collapse and was taken to Baltimore for treatment. Shortly thereafter she sent to Maxwell Perkins of Scribner's the manuscript of her novel, *Save Me the Waltz*, which she had written in six weeks, mostly during her stay in the hospital. The novel is essentially an attack upon her husband and a self-justification of her own ambition to become a ballet dancer, a plan which Fitzgerald had opposed or at least made difficult of achievement. In December, 1933, she suffered a third breakdown and was returned to the hospital in Baltimore in what appeared to be an incurable state. Throughout these experiences, Fitzgerald was haunted by a sense of guilt; and, although the doctors assured him that the basic cause dated from a time long before he had first met her, he rightly suspected that the years of wildly confused living—in New York, Paris, Hollywood, the Riviera—had much to do with bringing on the several stages of her collapse. See Arthur Mizener, *The Far Side of Paradise* (Boston, 1951), 216 following.

[57] New York, 1951. The following discussion is based upon Cowley's examination of manuscripts at The Princeton University Library.

class was the focus at the beginning, as it continued to be, though with modifications, to the end. The most important change of emphasis came when Fitzgerald decided that the hero-victim-judge should be, not a Hollywood technician or director but a psychiatrist. In this change the novel became a significant addition to the modern evaluation of the social and human comedies. That he thought this to be the most important fact of the novel is evident from a letter to Maxwell Perkins (1938): "[The novel's] great fault is that the *true* beginning—the young psychiatrist in Switzerland—is tacked away in the middle of the book." (Quoted by Cowley, xi) Fitzgerald then proposed taking the section of the 1934 edition which considers Diver's beginnings and his meeting with Nicole Warren and starting the novel with it. The 1934 beginning, which features the point of view of Rosemary Hoyt, would thus be moved back and Dick Diver would gain new prominence as the novel's hero.[58]

At age 26, in the spring of 1917, Dick Diver arrives in Zurich, his entire, promising career ahead of him. It is important to see that he is not just a young psychiatrist, that he has the mark of the Fitzgerald hero upon him. "Dick got up to Zurich on less Achilles' heels than would be required to equip a centipede, but with plenty—the illusions of eternal strength and health, and of the essential goodness of people; illusions of a nation, the lies of generations of frontier mothers who had to croon falsely that there were no wolves outside the cabin door." (307-308)[59] However inexpertly put here, the illusions are strictly needed for the development and collapse of the Fitzgerald hero. He is a man of great promise, charm, earnestness, balanced against a destructive naïveté. *Tender Is the Night* is far more an account of illusions

---

[58] Cowley followed Fitzgerald's wish almost to the letter in the volume prepared for the 1951 edition. See his introduction to that edition for the details. Concerning the *effect* of the changes, Cowley has this to say: "By rearranging the story in chronological order Fitzgerald tied it together. He sacrificed a brilliant beginning and all the element of mystery, but there is no escaping the judgment that he ended with a better constructed and more effective novel." (xiv-xv) There is much to be said for the 1934 arrangement, and it is doubtful that the psychiatric problem is better seen by bringing it up front. In any event, it seems to me that the point of view of Rosemary Hoyt, as it is given in the 1934 version, gives one a more vivid sense of the essential issue of the novel, of which the psychiatry is after all a form of judgment and appraisal rather than its substance.

[59] Page references, given in the text here and following, are to the edition published in *The Portable Fitzgerald* (New York, 1945).

clumsily and pathetically supported than it is a psychiatric appraisal of modern ills. The source of Nicole's illness is in its own way like the source of Dick's ambition. The group of expatriates who are attracted to the Diver world are also in one way or another affected by that combination of naïve hope and neurasthenic despair which characterizes so many of Fitzgerald's personages. The psychiatry is therefore not so much a judgment upon this world as it is an explanation of it. In the life of the Warrens the extreme forms of this confusion are realized. Their basis is wealth—or rather, extraordinary and powerful and wasteful substance, which sponsors and permits indulgences that drive irresponsible persons to disaster. Fitzgerald's analysis of the Warren money involve one in the full range of the novel's meaning; one phase of it is to be found reflected in the image of the 18-year-old movie star, Rosemary Hoyt, and her latest " Daddy's Girl " role:

> There she was—the school girl of a year ago, hair down her back and rippling out stiffly like the solid hair of a tanagra figure; there she was—*so* young and innocent—the product of her mother's loving care; there she was—embodying all the immaturity of the race, cutting a new cardboard paper doll to pass before its empty harlot's mind . . . (250)

The " Daddy's Girl " motif reflects the causes of Nicole Warren's original disorder. Here, in Rosemary's depiction of the " tweetest thing's " vacuous sweetness, we have superficially the criticism of a low level of public taste, but it has also a suggestion of confused morality and basically an ignorance of matters that it is disastrous not to know about the human psychic economy. Another aspect of Fitzgerald's indictment of the American scene (or the Warren phase of it) has to do with the preposterous idea that money confers privilege, mobility, and a beyond-good-and-evil moral advantage. " Baby " Warren, Nicole's older sister, believes in the doctrine: *their* money will buy anything and everything; it will above all purchase a physician-husband for Nicole, and love need not be considered in the arrangement. Fitzgerald portrays this Warren offense as an atrocious violation of moral taste, whose efficiency makes it all the more menacing.

Nicole was the product of much ingenuity and toil. For her sake trains began their run at Chicago and traversed the round belly of the continent to California; chicle factories fumed and link belts grew link by link in factories; men mixed toothpaste in vats and drew mouthwash out of copper hogsheads; girls canned tomatoes quickly in August or worked rudely at the Five-and-Tens on Christmas Eve . . . these were some of the people who gave a tithe to Nicole, and as the whole system swayed and thundered onward it lent a feverish bloom to such processes of hers as wholesale buying, like the flush of a fireman's face holding his post before a spreading blaze. She illustrated very simple principles, containing in herself her own doom, but illustrated them so accurately that there was grace in the procedure, and presently Rosemary would try to imitate it. (233)

This is obviously a " case for the psychoanalyst," but Fitzgerald made it a matter of social case study. The applications of psychoanalysis are imperfect, certainly not strictly accurate; they need to extend beyond the limits of Nicole's illness, to embrace the whole society of a people who for a decade wanted only to be entertained. Specifically, the novel exploits the dramatic possibilities of a transference-love situation. Diver, asked by his friend to help in the case of the wealthy American patient, finds that she has easily fallen in love with him; and, while he is aware of the risks in the situation, is half-inclined to return the love. In a conversation with two colleagues, Diver confesses his perplexity and fear:

Again Franz tried to speak—again Dohmler stopped him with a question directed pointedly at Dick. " Have you thought of going away? "

" I can't go away."

Doctor Dohmler turned to Franz: " Then we can send Miss Warren away."

" As you think best, Professor Dohmler," Dick conceded.

" It's certainly a situation."

Professor Dohmler raised himself like a legless man mounting a pair of crutches.

" But it is a professional situation," he cried quietly.

.   .   .   .   .   .

" I'm half in love with her—the question of marrying her has passed through my mind."

" Tch! Tch! " uttered Franz.

" Wait," Dohmler warned him. Franz refused to wait: " What! And devote half your life to being doctor and nurse and all—never! I know what these cases are. One time in twenty it's finished in the first push—better never see her again! " (335–36)

But Diver does eventually give in, does hope that the " professional situation " can somehow be translated without harm into a personal situation. Throughout " Baby " Warren thinks of her sister's husband as a hired doctor-companion, and in the development of their lives together she is proved to be not too far from right. At any rate, Dick can never settle in his mind which of the two roles he is likely the more to serve. It is only too painfully obvious that she is " using " him, in the manner of a patient's exploiting her doctor's will.

. . . The dualism in his views of her—that of the husband, that of the psychiatrist—was increasingly paralyzing his faculties. In these six years she had several times carried him over the line with her, disarming him by exciting emotional pity or by a flow of wit, fantastic and disassociated, so that only after the episode did he realize with the consciousness of his own relaxation from tension, that she had succeeded in getting a point against his better judgment. (394)

While Nicole " uses " him (drains him of his energies) so that she might advance her cure, the Warren money (administered by the redoubtable " Baby ") gradually triumphs over his struggle for independence. It is not merely a " professional situation " being ruined by deep personal involvement; it is also a destructive circumstance, the harsh, cruel, privileged " rich boy " inevitably crushing out the naïve promise and generous soul of the Fitzgerald hero.

The novel had best be entitled *The Decline and Fall of*

Doctor Diver. Diver absorbs Nicole's illness to himself; as she grows well, he weakens. He had been a man of abundant promise; he becomes slowly, painfully, a " ward " of the Warren money and a parody of his former gracious self. " You used to want to create things," Nicole tells him, near the end. " Now you seem to want to smash them up." (486) The conclusion of the marriage is inevitable. Nicole breaks from her patient role of dependence upon her doctor-husband, begins to view him dispassionately, and is shortly in the arms of another, a younger man, to whom she goes as though upon release from a hospital. Entirely cured, she " cut the cord forever. Then she walked weak in the legs and sobbing coolly, toward the household that was hers at last." (529)

The " case was finished." Doctor Diver is " at liberty." Exhausted, he turns to the Riviera beach that has served so much of the time as the scene of the cure.

> " I must go," he said. As he stood up he swayed a little; he did not feel well any more—his blood raced slow. He raised his right hand and with a papal cross he blessed the beach from the high terrace. . . . (544)

There are several ironies involved. Not the least of these involves Diver's giving in to a " professional situation " and sacrificing himself for love's sake to a person who is more patient than loved one. But other ironies inhere in this. Nicole's illness is after all the result of the Warren situation, caused by the blurring of moral lines that its immensity of wealth and privilege had fostered. The wealth continues to plague Diver; he is victimized again and again by it. In the end his energy of personal will cannot cope with it. Most of all, the novel describes the impotence of a secular art of healing in the face of such odds as are evident from the beginning. Diver's colleagues, inured by a better training and a less generously human though a sounder background, believe in limiting human situations to the terms upon which they might be scientifically treated. This Diver cannot do; or he cannot will so to limit himself. Like many another Fitzgerald hero, he wishes somehow to heal the world by means of good will and an ingratiating smile. His fund of moral capital (his " charm," as Fitzgerald most often terms it) is slowly drained, by the demands of those about him, who are weaker than he and therefore dependent upon him. He inherits this moral good will from his father, the great naïve American moral hero. Diver is therefore both more and less than a scientist; he is a man of generous gifts, who tries to use psychiatry as an instrument of his good will. He cannot be satisfied to work within the limits of professional discretion, but must give of his fund of love. Because his instincts are to do more than " treat " Nicole (he would love her as well), he becomes involved with her and is defeated by her as a psychiatric " case " and by the causes that lie behind the illness.

This pathetic tale is an indication of Fitzgerald's own state of self-realization at the time. The great change in the text of *Tender Is the Night* in the " Dick Diver " version is matched by other reviews of himself and of the 1920s: in the short story, " Babylon Revisited " and in his public confession (in *Esquire*, December, 1934; March and April, 1936) of his own breakdown. There seems to have been something almost frantic about the writing of *Tender Is the Night*, as though he were taking note of his own excesses in the course of describing those of his creatures. The novel is therefore a document of his own declining morale, his own suffering, above all his terrible fright over the spectacle of his descent. Psychiatry was a part of his experience at the time; it became a part of his explanation of the world of the 1920s as he came then to see it. In so doing, he used his knowledge of psychiatry freely, as a layman would who had somehow to know enough about its functioning to comprehend what was happening to him and to the world in which he had always lived.

chapter IX

FURTHER
INTERPRETATIONS

i

No attempt has been made to catalogue the references to Freud or to psychoanalysis in general in the novels of the third and fourth decades of our century. Such an occupation would suggest, what we already know, that scores of writers were acquainted with Freudian theory, but did not see fit to give it a more than passing reference in their books. Writers paid whatever casual acknowledgment they thought necessary of the omnipresence of psychoanalytic theory, practice, and jargon in their world of discourse. The incidental use of terminology in James Huneker's *Painted Veils* is typical; it certainly recognized its intellectual and social sources, but used them eccentrically and with a great sense of aesthetic independence of them. Huneker warns that the modern novel (as of 1919) is beggared by too much " descriptive padding "; the novel might well use a " searching characterization that not only paints your man without but also within." [1] In his portrayal of Mona Milton, and elsewhere in his book, Huneker has occasion to use the jargon of the new psychology; this jargon is

[1] James Huneker, *Painted Veils* (New York, 1930), 146. Written in 1919.

sometimes accidentally derived from Freud. At other times it is linked with the ideas of Nietzsche, in whom Huneker had far more interest. The fact remains that this jargon was common property, as early as 1919, and the use of it was not accompanied by any exact study or application of Freudian theory as such. *Painted Veils* is a complex work, revealing the predispositions of its author, his knowledge of New York and Paris, of Ibsen and Nietzsche, and only incidentally of Freud and other psychoanalysts. When, for example, he was his hero, Ulick Invern, say that music "'is dug out of our subliminal self, brought to the surface of our consciousness by the composer's art,'" (123) he suggests an acquaintance with Freudianism, but the suggestion is of no great consequence.

Huneker's novel is typical of many which in an age of discussion and argument took the place of genuinely creative work. The conventions were, all of them, on the auction block. The new freedoms and their archenemies, the old restrictions, were important matters, and the publishers' lists paid attention to the tremendous interest which they had aroused. Some writers merit a place in a study of this kind for at least three reasons: their intelligent grasp of psychoanalytic theory in most or all of its ramifications; their specific statements, which lend to their employment of that theory a biographical importance; and finally their striking and challenging independence of the scientific restrictions upon an aesthetic use of such materials.

Within the limits of this chapter one may see repeated, with considerable variation, the habits and methods which have already been examined for us above. For Conrad Aiken is in his own way exploiting the researches of the analyst's laboratory, and he contributes a minor *Ulysses*, a psychoanalytic "mystery story" and numerous critical and poetic statements which link readily and decisively with the body of new psychological theory. Ludwig Lewisohn's extensive search for an understanding of contemporary situations, so intensely personal that the dividing line between autobiography and novel is slight, lends a support to Thomas Mann's view of the racial history of mankind. Henry Miller, strange bed-fellow under any circumstances, is comparable to no one whom we have thus far considered—unless it be the surrealists, with whom he has only a superficial similarity. Finally, Dylan Thomas has perhaps most exhaustively explored the varying and eccentric dream-life of modern man, with results not at all similar to those in Joyce's *Finnegans Wake* or Waldo Frank's *Chalk Face.*

ii

Of all American writers, Conrad Aiken has had the most serious interest in Freudianism and in allied psychologies. His approach is that of the artist, independent and critical, but there is no question of his debt to Freud. Aiken found Freud's books rich in suggestions for aesthetics, in his roles of critic and creative artist. In answer to an inquiry sent out by the editors of *New Verse*, he announced that he had been " profoundly " influenced by Freud, " but so has everybody, whether they are aware of it or not. However, I decided very early, I think as early as 1912, that Freud, and his coworkers and rivals and followers, were making the most important contribution of the century to the understanding of man and his consciousness; accordingly I made it my business to learn as much from them as I could." [2]

Aiken had had a casual acquaintance with ordinary medical practice during his childhood in Savannah, Georgia, before the tragic death of his mother and father caused him to be sent to the home of relatives, in New Bedford, Massachusetts. The memory of the double tragedy, the strangeness of this sudden shift of circumstances affected him and gave his writings a quality of introspection that is their most striking characteristic. In his last year at Harvard, Aiken learned from his psychiatrist friend, Doctor G. P. McCouch of Cambridge, " about the subversive doctrines of Professor Sigmund Freud." Aiken was, therefore, " somewhat of a specialist in psychology," or at least an amateur in high standing. [3]

[2] *New Verse*, XI (1934), 13.

[3] Peterson, *The Melody of Chaos*, 48. Peterson's book, in some ways a useful book, was published in 1931 and does not include a survey of Aiken's later work, especially of the novels of the thirties. Aiken puts the date of his first acquaintance with Freudianism at " about 1909 or 1910." This " was the beginning of a lifelong

He was not unaware of the abuses which psychoanalysis might suffer, or of the imperfect grasp which the amateur might have of it. The psychoanalyst plays an ambiguous role in his fiction. With all due respect to the seriousness of studies in the new psychology, Aiken presents a normal resistance against its attempts to resolve all modern dilemmas with the magic of words and the suave, smooth domination of the analyst over the tragic circumstances of the modern soul. Like many another artist of his time, Aiken, captivated by the new vision of the human soul, is reluctant to leave its horrors and fascinations for the cold, clear, reasonable light of the analyst who usually points to the status quo and bids the patient find in it a sensible solution of his problems.

Great Circle, informed as it is with its author's knowledge of the new psychology, portrays with admirable clarity the phenomenon of resistance, that problem that all psychoanalysts face, which varies in degree and strength with the temperament of the patient. Andy Cather, who has thought, dreamed, and analyzed the dangers of cuckoldry, comes finally to the apartment of a friend, who affects some knowledge of psychoanalysis and takes a turn at amateur psyching whenever the opportunity occurs. Aiken's analysis of this meeting must be regarded as half humorous; he is, after all, expressing not his own objections to psychoanalysis so much as the natural, normal reluctance of the freelance intellectual to accept what he considers to be solutions far too simple to match his own estimate of his soul. It is an insult to the richness of my subliminal life, says Andy in effect, to the fascinating complexity and tangle of unconscious motive and desire, to assume that the magic wand and the abracadabra of the analyst will cause all of it to vanish. The analysis, as it proceeds, follows the clinical method exactly—the answers come without hesitation, smoothly, as from a memorized text. Speaking of Andy's failure to find happiness in his married life, Bill gives the approved answers: " In every one of your love affairs, you've tried

friendship with a group of doctors and prospective psychoanalysts, so that to a considerable extent I grew up with and even *in*, the psychoanalytic movement." Letter to Frederick J. Hoffman, January 23, 1944. For a valuable study of Aiken's work in the light of psychoanalytic criticism, see Henry A. Murray, " Conrad Aiken: Poet of Creative Dissolution," *Perspectives, U.S.A.*, no. 5 (Fall, 1953) 27–36; see also *Wake*, no. 11 (1952) 95–106.

to make your sweetheart your mother. That's why they've all been unsuccessful. Why do you want to do it?—that's the question. It won't work. That's why sooner or later you reject or abandon them all, or they abandon you—they have to." [4]

Andy fights self-defensively against his analyst friend and against his apparent attempt to strip his problem of all its rationalized dignity.

> " Resistance, I suppose. Oh, damn you amateur analysts and all your pitiful dirty, abstract jargon. Why can't you say what you mean. Why can't you call a spade a spade. What the hell's the difference between the soul and the subconscious and the unconscious and the will. Or between castration complex and inferiority complex and oedipus complex. Words. Evasions. Vanities on the part of the respective respectable analysts. *Nicht wahr.* For the love of mud, define any one of them for me, so that I'll know absolutely what they mean. Or tell me where they reside in the brain. Have you ever loked at a map of the brain? " (244–45)

Andy wants and deserves the right to suffer in his own way. The analyst not only doesn't want to allow this, but he makes the whole thing appear too simple: " ' You seem to think that merely by driving us back from one set of phrases to another, by a series of historical substitutions, you've settled everything. Childish, by God. Childish.' " (256) The lengthy analysis has discovered the source of Andy's trouble, but it is powerless to remove it, because Andy is fascinated by it, will not give it up. Unconscious forces have a power of their own, against which science does not always prevail. These forces are the motif of tragedy. Suspension of reason makes it impossible for the psychoanalyst to effect a cure. The tragic figure bows before the crushing blow of self-awareness, but, held firmly and fascinated by the dark persuasions of the unconscious, follows them with persistent and irrational obedience to his tragedy. In an important sense, he unconsciously *wishes* the tragedy. The resolution does not come within the neatly limited areas of scientific investigation; the analyst has merely pointed to the source of internal conflict. The subsequent course of that

---

[4] Conrad Aiken, *Great Circle* (New York, 1933), 217.

conflict and its inevitably tragic conclusion are beyond his power to mitigate or prevent.[5]

Aiken was to grant that psychoanalysis had made an important contribution to modern criticism. Look as long as you will at the history of aesthetics, he says, and you must feel distressed at its unsatisfactory and contradictory offerings. In fact, aesthetics has tried always to find beauty in external form. Beauty is not a pattern etched eternally in the skies; it is a *feeling*, a desire, related therefore to man's psychological and biological nature, not a sixth or seventh sense which remains in holy detachment from the corruptions of the body. The only genuine critical question concerns the *source* of that feeling: " Why is it that man so desperately craves the feeling we call beauty, or moral beauty, or aesthetic beauty, that he has developed, developed with religious zeal . . . the activity known as art for the satisfaction of that craving? "

The answer, given by Freud, is that beauty is a pleasurable feeling, " the profound satisfaction we feel when, through the medium of fantasy we escape from imposed limitations into an aggrandized personality and a harmonized universe." [6] Through most of his career, Aiken is haunted by the Freudian explanation of the artist as neurotic. He does not accept it unreservedly; nor does he say that it is the only explanation, for it does omit an important qualitative judgment by which works of art are ultimately evaluated on the basis of their intrinsic merits. The creative process is a conscious one, regulated by the artist's awareness. Ultimately one must leave this all-too-simple explanation of art and grant that the artist must possess both " a fine sensibility " and a knowledge of his craft before he can profit from his peculiar gifts.

[5] The great attention paid to dreams and the analytic situation gives *Great Circle* a prominence among books which use psychoanalysis directly and accurately. In fact, " the publication of Great Circle very nearly made an analyst of me! It brought me the friendship of H.D. and of Winifred Bryher, who were both very close to Freud: they sent him the book, which he is *said* to have called a masterpiece . . . and in consequence they then planned to send *me* to Freud as well. . . . I at last decided myself (somewhat helped to it by Dr. Erich Fromm) that it would all be a mistake anyway. I now greatly regret that I didn't go through with it." Letter to Frederick J. Hoffman, January 23, 1944. Concerning H. D. and Freud, see her recent *Tribute to Freud* (New York, 1956).

[6] Conrad Aiken, " A Basis for Criticism," in *New Republic*, XXXIV (1923), Pt. II, 4.

But, these things admitted, the artist's problem is essentially psychological, and Freud has best and most honestly described his nature. Aiken's interest in this part of Freud's psychology gives substance to the inner conflict of the autobiographical hero of *Blue Voyage*, William Demarest. Demarest tries to explain his position twice—once to Silberstein, a merchant of "chewing sweets" who, of course, doesn't manage to understand much of it, and again in one of several undelivered letters to Cynthia. For Demarest (and in another sense, for Andy Cather) the alternative is offered of indulging or rejecting the neurosis which is the source both of creation and of narcissistic anguish. The psychoanalyst, in calling art a form of neurosis, by implication suggests that the artist abandon it. With this demand Demarest struggles unceasingly, arguing with an analyst whom he has conjured up. All of the terror and complexity with which the creative process is cursed can be eliminated, says the analyst. But he gives up, finally: Demarest has already gone too far. " 'To return to the simple is for you impossible! Misery! You must follow out your neurosis!' " (241)

To grant such a basis for art is humiliating, almost paralyzing. Demarest, in his second letter to Cynthia, has to admit that his career as a writer has fed upon his personal weaknesses; such weaknesses are they that they have also stood firmly in the way of a confident and normal sex life. Should he not give in to these weaknesses? Does not all art at least begin with the act of submission to psychic weakness? Is it not therefore unhealthy and abnormal at its source?

> —I am in process of adjustment to the certainty that I am going to be a failure. I take what refuge I can in a strictly psychological scrutiny of my failure, and endeavor to make out how much this is due to (1) a simple lack of literary power, or genius, or the neurosis that we give that name, and how much to (2) a mistaken assumption as to the necessity for this new literary method. What if—for example—in choosing this literary method, this deliberate indulgence in the prolix and fragmentary, I merely show myself at the mercy of a personal weakness which is not universal, or ever likely to be, but highly idiosyncratic? (290)

The life of the unconscious, of *his* unconscious, has fascinated him, forced him to meet it on his own aesthetic grounds. A work of art, at least so far as he knows the creative process which gives it substance, is the result of a compelling force. That is the sad truth, not only for the artist, but also in some measure for all men. Aiken is not altogether certain about all this, but he is willing to grant the persistent fascination of man's unconscious life, in which are held all of the desires and wishes which reality prevents him from satisfying or realizing.

Of all his works, *Blue Voyage* serves best to demonstrate Aiken's artistic exploration of the unconscious. The novel is in a sense modeled after the *Ulysses* of James Joyce, but it is not a mere imitation of the Irish odyssey. Demarest is, of course, the Stephen Dedalus of *Blue Voyage*, and Silberstein is its Leopold Bloom; the novel is a careful and intimate portrayal of the artist's life. Its pattern follows strictly the descent into Demarest's unconsciousness and the consequent emergence from it into the clear light of self-appraisal. Aiken came to the interior monologue already supported by his thorough acquaintance with psychoanalysis. The exposition of Demarest's mind never suffers from severe obscurity, for the opening chapter states explicitly the time and place, and establishes the external limits which the narrative is to follow. Demarest is on a ship, sailing for England. This situation will of course contribute its share of sights and sounds, and give the study of Demarest's mind some discreet anchor in external circumstance. His attention is further controlled by his all but complete absorption in Cynthia, whom he expects to see in England. After the surprising discovery that Cynthia is on the same boat, and the painful realization that she no longer loves him, the narrative becomes a monologue—Demarest in his cabin, reviewing his life, searching for reasons and explanations he knows but fears to admit to himself. All of chapter four is a revery, which never leaves the approaches to consciousness (for Demarest is awake until the very last). The way back to full and clear consciousness is barred at one point by an extravagant fantasy, in which Demarest quarrels with his censor (in this case, an analyst-friend) about his life and art, and a hallucinatory vision of his shipmates discussing his life calmly but with penetrating sharpness.

No one has expressed so poignantly as Aiken the tragedy of spiritual disintegration in modern man and his consequent help-lessness—" the whole appearance is in reality a chaotic flux, a whirlwind of opposing forces; they and I are in one preposterous stream together, borne helplessly to an unknown destiny. I am myself perhaps only a momentary sparkle on the swift surface of this preposterous stream." [7] This search for personal identity is self-defeating, for it requires a denial of the superficial rational and sensory agencies which ordinarily assure identity. The self, with name attached, has only a temporary hold upon identity, for it dissolves into a thousand uncertainties as it is caught by the flow of unconscious life. The struggle of the " lost people " is pitiful, therefore, more often pathetic than tragic. Often it is given up, and the self submits to the grotesque and gigantic fantasies of dream-life. Of man's dream-life Aiken has full knowl-edge; dreams simple and complex fill the pages of his novels, and are the prime mover of many of his poems. The self, moving as it does from the external world into unconsciousness, moving again " upward from the dark world," obeys reluctantly the im-perious demands of reality. " To move upward like this, . . . surrounded by one's own body, the hand heavy on the heart, the heart beating insistently in the ear, that which a moment ago was the chime of a dream become the rhythm of the pulse, the dis-torted faces and filaments of the dream becoming only the flutter-ing defense of the eyelashes against the square of light from the window." [8]

In dreams one returns with assurance or submission to the origins of life, blotting out willingly the tedious checks and bal-ances of consciousness, dwelling thus in unconsciousness with the simple wishes of the past and present. To submit to the dream is a temptation; but it has its own attendant horrors. The dream path is the path to death. It affords the last full measure of excuse for failing to face reality; submission to the wish for pleasure, organic and unconscious, may ultimately result in the final and total sub-mission which is the unconsciousness of death. The ego thus

---

[7] Conrad Aiken, " Gehenna," in *Among the Lost People* (New York, 1934), 238–39.

[8] Aiken, *Great Circle*, 299–300. Cf. the poem, *The Coming Forth by Day of Osiris Jones* (New York, 1931).

struggles with an impalpable reality but prefers the unreality of unconsciousness. The ego resists with all of its strength the chains of servitude to the reality principle. It yearns for the primitive simplicity of childhood, for the fantasy of the dream-life, for the luxury of unconscious wish-fulfillment.

The great problem of the twentieth century, in Aiken's opinion, is the problem of consciousness—not as the rationalists see it, for they have the most part failed to give any satisfactory answer. If man's consciousness is so much a prey to his unconscious wishes, if the ego loses its identity and the psyche dissolves, then we must certainly revise our interpretation of the total self. How much of that self can legitimately (that is, consistently, with the aims of civilization in mind) be added to or substituted for the older, more superficial notion of self? As the conscious self is ultimately understood in this larger, richer context, its residence in part in the unconscious assumed and admitted, the contribution of Freud to our final understanding of self will have to be granted. " For me," says Aiken, " [Freud] still fits admirably in such philosophic order as I find necessary—a belief in the evolution of consciousness, awareness, as our prime gift and obligation, and a Socratic desire to get on with it at all costs." [9]

iii

The career of Ludwig Lewisohn has in a large sense been a crusade—against stifling moral repressions and stupid modern notions of amoral freedom, and for a wholesome reinstatement of sensible religious and aesthetic standards. The long succession of books, autobiographical fiction and fictional autobiography, is an unceasing campaign, by precept and exemplum, for the sane and intelligent life. Not the least of the moral barriers to such a life has been the American attitude toward sex relationships. On the one hand, says Lewisohn, Americans are taught that there is no such thing as a sex problem in English-speaking countries. The notion of feminine purity assumes that woman is without passion.

[9] Letter to Frederick J. Hoffman, January 23, 1944.

The central weakness of the Anglo-American mind is its "moral illusionism."

Such a deliberate refusal to see man as he is has affected profoundly and unfortunately the habits and attitudes of our countrymen. Such, for example, is the explanation of jazz rhythms: " The choruses of these songs are ugly because they dare not be beautiful, stealthy because they dare not be frank. But in dance and song . . . there is a craving for rhythm—the rhythm of the world that is sex and poetry and freedom." [10] As a result of this excessive repression of a normal and beautiful life, the respectability taboo, American society is subject to periodic explosions, ugly saturnalias, exhausting debauches of the body and spirit, or ferocious and unreasonably bitter wars. World War I, says Lewisohn, cannot be explained away simply. " But its peculiarly unmotivated ferocity, its hectic heat, had in it something unmistakably religious, orgiastic, and hence obscurely sexual. . . . The nation became a lynching party. Its mood expressed itself spontaneously through sex-symbolism." [11]

In America, the dangerous tendency toward excessive repression has had the additional consequence of distorting the normal family relationship. Since woman is sacred and inviolable, legal protections have made man her prisoner. Lewisohn is concerned in several of his books with the question of American divorce laws. *The Case of Mr. Crump,* one of the ugliest books in modern literature, tells the story of a brilliant and sensitive artist, a composer, who has been forced to live in unholy wedlock with a woman twice his age, who will not divorce him and who drives him ultimately to a horrible murder. Men who, driven by the incongruities and hopelessness of their enslavement, flee to the refuge of clandestine affairs, are punished by the publicity of the tabloids, so that their names are on the lips of every indignant shopgirl and soda-clerk. " ' As for me,' " says Anne Crump to her distressed husband, " ' if you want to know it, I would have followed him and the woman in person. I would have seen to it that they hadn't a place to lay their heads, that no one spoke to

---

[10] Lewisohn, *Upstream,* 192.
[11] *Ibid.,* 204. Cf. Freud's " Thoughts for the Times on War and Death," *loc. cit.,* 288–317.

them or gave them a bite of bread or a drink of water and I would have moved heaven and earth and appealed to the decency of all men and women to strip and to beat that vile adultress within an inch of her life! ' " [12]

The problem created by neo-Puritanism is not solved by pseudo-modernism. The original power of love, the " creative Eros," is denied and suppressed by the one, cheapened by the other. All of this polemic leads ultimately to a statement of Lewisohn's position. Upon the intelligent selection by man of his mate rests the hope for all that is valuable in the personal reaches of the human consciousness. Give man a chance to make this all important choice, without hindrance from society, and the good effect upon society should become apparent within a short time. Since a happy, creative marriage is the most genuine source of creative endeavor, society should above all make such a marriage possible. Sex is allied with " a thousand aesthetic and ethical perceptions, preferences, appetences; it reached the mind, the heart, the soul; it required choice, freedom, the exercise of its selectiveness." [13] What are the mutual responsibilities of such a marriage? The modern woman wants an independent life, wants to " realize herself "; at the same time she wants the secure feeling that her husband is faithful to her. These wishes are incompatible. That modern woman has so often sought refuge in feeble and spurious arguments about the duty of women to society and the arts is a symptom of a larger unhappiness in modern society. Revolt and protest against the " old ways," fear of the consequences of their own freedom, dismay over the emptiness of the future—these are negative characteristics, but they are the pitiful handful of justifications for modern thinking.

Lewisohn looks upon the psychoanalyst as the wise man of our century. In default of a priest, he is our confessor; without a religion, we have turned to his theory and practice for something resembling spiritual guidance. The science of psychoanalysis is peculiarly a Jewish science, though its applications are for all men. The Jewish mind and ethics are at the root of psychoanalytic theory and practice. " The spirit of merciful understand-

[12] Ludwig Lewisohn, *The Case of Mr. Crump* (New York, 1930) , 291.
[13] *Don Juan* (New York, 1923) , 270.

ing which has issued in psychoanalysis and kindred substitutions of healing for damnation—that spirit is an integral part of the tradition of Israel." (*Mid-Channel*, 281) Jewish ethics, tested a thousand times by the fire of racial suffering but preserved from madness by a sense of religious unity, comes to us as basic and intrinsic wisdom.

The psychoanalysts of Lewisohn's novels are men of wisdom. The psychoanalyst, if he is not a charlatan, a money-maker, or a bright young man on an opportunistic spree, will heal in incredibly simple ways, by casting aside the shoddy verbalisms which have cluttered up modern thinking and getting back to moral fundamentals. In lieu of a religion in which men might have confidence, the world needs someone to assert simple truths, to give them validity and value. The psychoanalyst supplies this need.

The psychoanalyst is a spiritual guide in many of Lewisohn's novels and a hero in at least one (*The Island Within*). Arthur Levy studies the works of Freud in his college days. He admits finally that diagnostic medicine is somehow inadequate to deal with many modern problems; future medical research must lead in a new direction: "'I mean preventive therapeutics partly through educational direction and partly through psycho-analysis.'" (179–80) But his associates in the Hospital for the Insane scoff at the notion: "Dr. Foster's single scientific observation had been to the effect that as Americans we couldn't possibly go in for that degenerate, dirty Freudian stuff. . . . 'It revolts every decent instinct in one,' Dr. Bryant Foster had remarked." (185) Nevertheless, Arthur is convinced that Freud has pointed out the future direction of medical-ethical practice. His first case is a complete success, and the relieved and happy patient advertises the new analyst as a worker in miracles. Levy begins his career auspiciously. But the hero becomes the instrument of Lewisohn's polemic purpose. Most of his patients, Arthur discovers, are suffering from "a Gentile fixation, the breakdown of a compensatory mechanism that corresponded to no native gift, the terror of an alien law and morality, the problem of the social isolation of Jews who didn't want to be jews." (290) He himself, married to a Gentile girl, is victim; and he is forced to solve his own problem by returning to the Jewish fold.

This singular usage of psychoanalysis is related to another great problem with which Lewisohn is forever concerned, the problem of the Jew in Western civilization.[14] It is also linked with what must be considered his ultimate evaluation of Freudianism. For Lewisohn believes that so far as psychoanalysis is a pure science of behavior, it is helpless in the midst of a social order that has lost its religious and ethical moorings. It can heal individuals; it cannot heal society as a whole. Ultimately, therapy is impotent to correct the imbalance of an amoral society. " If every other generation is to be shell-shocked the Freudian therapeutics have small chance of sanitating the mind of either the individual or the mass." Knowledge and science are not enough; the scientific view leaves the patient at the beginning rather than at the end of his journey toward salvation. Constant spiritual discomfort and dislocation has wounded human society almost beyond redemption. The conventional analyst is quick to recognize the hurt, slow to see the ultimate ethical cause. This is why so many of the analysts in Lewisohn's novels are also Jews; for they add to the effectiveness of scientific discipline, the cultural wisdom and spiritual temperance of the race.

Freud studied this problem seriously in the early stages of his career. To what extent can the analyst go beyond the limits of his science and become a spiritual guide? He condemned Jung for abusing the prerogatives of the scientist beyond belief, but he had eventually to admit that some form of advice was " good, in some cases." Those Catholic clerics who accepted psychoanalysis at all saw in it an excellent improvement upon the confessional. But, they were anxious to point out, the purpose of confession is not to turn the soul free but to call it back to the safe limits of the true faith. In fact, as many modern thinkers have disapproved of Freudian practice because it does not go far enough as have repudiated it for going anywhere at all.

Lewisohn insists upon reaching beyond the limits of the laboratory. There are two reasons for this insistence: his profound confidence in the ethical solidity and purity of the Jewish faith, and his belief in love as a creative force. Both of these convic-

[14] *Trumpet of Jubilee* (New York, London, 1937) is his most complete fictional treatment of this problem.

tions have caused him to read extensively in mythology, the source of all great religions, and in anthropology. Freud's *Totem and Taboo* has helped him immensely in this search.[15] Lewisohn has come to align himself spiritually with the Thomas Mann of the Joseph novels. In an important sense, Lewisohn's belief in a " creative Eros " is the spiritual constant of his search, the residue of his struggle for a better social understanding of the deep meaning of sex. It is this " great mystery of Eros which both your conservatives and your radicals seek to cheapen, the former as sin, the latter as a matter of no importance." (*Stephen Escott*, 216)

iv

The poetry and fiction of Dylan Thomas pay tribute to still another of Freud's contributions to modern aesthetics. In no other single body of work has the aesthetic interest in the dream-life received such exhaustive treatment. One critic refers to Thomas' "assimilation of Joyce, Freud, and the Bible."[16] Of his serious study of Freud we have abundant evidence, and this evidence is supported by a frank avowal of his indebtedness. In a statement concerning this matter, he endorsed Freuds' influence significantly.

> Whatever is hidden should be made naked. To be stripped of darkness is to be clean, to strip of darkness is to make clean. Poetry, recording the stripping of the individual darkness, must inevitably cast light upon what has been hidden for too long and by so doing, make clean the naked exposure. Freud cast light on a little of the darkness he had exposed. Benefiting by the sight of the light and the knowledge of the hidden nakedness, poetry must drag further into the clean nakedness of light more even of the hidden causes than Freud could realize.[17]

The career of Dylan Thomas began conservatively enough. His great mastery of sensory detail, suitable for the most excellent

[15] Ludwig and Edna Lewisohn, *Haven* (New York, 1940), 265.
[16] Francis Scarfe, " The Poetry of Dylan Thomas," in *Horizon*, II (1940), 239.
[17] *New Verse*, XI, 9.

of simple poetic description, betrayed at first no serious preoccupation with the "individual darkness." Progress toward his ultimate mythical awareness of the unconscious and of the dream-life can be observed in his series of autobiographical sketches.[18] By some strange alchemic process, his insight into the unconscious self is linked with a maturing sensitivity to the mystery and charm of sex and a certain paralyzing hesitation to realize it fully. The *Portrait* has its measure of references to a small boy's vulgarities; in fact, these are the common self-conscious acts of schoolboyish scorn for the pomp and circumstance of adult society. In the last of the sketches of the *Portrait*, the direction of his interests is indicated. Physical love is allied with creation in this one respect, that it opens the door to a secret, mysterious, and dark world, the world of "hidden nakedness." It is this world which the artist seems compelled to explore, bring into the light, and creatively re-present. Hence the imagery of this poetic vision of the sexual act is associated closely with Thomas' own theory of poetic imagery: "He and Lou could go down together, one cool body weighted with a boiling stone, on to the falling, blank white, entirely empty sea, and never rise." [19]

Strikingly evident in most of his visions of the "inner darkness" is this image of death: a spiritual anonymity, a blotting out of the single personality in the act of physical and poetic creation. Death stalks his pages; it is linked with life as both are trafficked in the womb:

> A weather in the flesh and bone
> Is damp and dry; the quick and dead
> Move like two ghosts before the eye.[20]

"Death is all metaphors "—a courageous but puzzling slogan, full of the burden of creative grappling with the infinite darkness of unconscious life. This is a poetic view of the unconscious, assuredly. Freud has in fact given the poet his initial opportunity to explore it; he has provided neither the details nor a suggestion of the end of the search.

[18] Dylan Thomas, *Portrait of the Artist as a Young Dog* (Norfolk, Conn., 1940).

[19] Thomas, "One Warm Saturday," in *Portrait of the Artist*, 178.

[20] Thomas, " 2 " in *18 Poems*, in *The World I Breathe* (Norfolk, Conn., 1939), 12.

Three important clues to the poetry and prose both of Dylan Thomas may give some suggestion of his purpose and direction: the theme of death and life, at times a sexual theme, death being simply the expulsion of seminal force; the recurrence of references to the womb as a thing of great physical and spiritual force, ambiguous and obscure though the poet's use of it is; and, finally, the dream symbols for love and lust, scattered and distorted as they are in Thomas' stories, giving them a strange power and beauty.

Of the first it may be said that it has really two meanings, a superficial one and a profound. Death and dying are obviously enough symbols of detumescence, so that it is through such " dying " that life must come. We give of ourselves so that we may receive ourselves in return. The second meaning is the inevitable linkage, organic and spiritual, of life with decay. Some part of that decay may be called simply " frustration "—a forcible suspension of natural or instinctual impulses, which, though it may insure external or sensory continuity, throws both the poet and the lover back upon certain spiritual resources, most of which reside in the unconscious. Psychic decay, caused by fundamental misunderstanding and misuse of the human psyche, renews the poet's need for deeper roots, makes him dissatisfied with the trivial and the traditional.

Thomas' use of the womb as a great mother-symbol is, of course, linked with the notion of life and death. Within the limits of physical generation, the womb is the great and only area in which life is cherished and supported during its period of prenatal helplessness. It is perhaps natural to think of it as a source of renewal when the initial helplessness is duplicated in later social or psychic distress. The womb thus becomes animate and alive, a creative medium in which life and death struggle for domination of the human soul.

The imagery of Thomas' poems and stories is in part derived from these two all-encompassing ideas. But he is also much preoccupied with the dream-life; and some examination of his use of dreams may reward us with a further insight into his work. Within their boundaries one sees the geography of physical love, the dream symbols referring again and again to physical contours given a sexual emphasis. The " map of love," on which dwell the "first beasts of love" is a "square of seas and islands and strange continents with a forest of darkness at each extremity." Here the sea—a persistent image, suggesting birth or a return to the sources of life—is strangely and persistently referred to. We find also the forest and grasses, luxuriant and rich; "the abominations of the swamp, content in the shadow of their own rains and snowings, in the noise of their own sighs, and the pleasures of their own green achings." [21]

The story "The Mouse and the Woman" reveals best the relationship of the artist-creator to this geography and physiography of the unconscious. The poet has created a woman in his dreams; the symbols of the dream are lost; they shift and lose themselves interminably. "And the changes of the details of the dream and the celestial changes, the levers of the trees and the toothed twigs, these were the mechanism of her delirium." He lets the dream control him, gives himself wholly to it. When he awakes, he tries not to think of the dream-creature, the woman. "She is drowned, dead, dead." But she cries for release, "to walk in his dreams no longer." He finally releases her from his dream-consciousness, "gives birth to her." This, then, is a creature of the artist's own willing, "a woman of the devil." "There was nothing to see in her but the ebb and flood of creation, only the transcendant sweep of being and living in the careless fold of flesh from shoulder-bone to elbow." In the world of the artist's imagination real things change places with unreal; the woman changes into ten varying shapes, and finally disappears. He appeals to the image of his father for her return.

> And this is all there was to it; a woman had been born, not out of the womb, but out of the soul and the spinning head. And he who had borne her out of the darkness loved his creation, and she loved him. But this is all there was to it: a miracle befell a man. He fell in love with it, but could not keep it, and the miracle passed And with him dwelt a dog, a mouse, and a dark woman. The woman went away, and the dog died. [22]

The artist has "created" a thing of beauty, but cannot bear

[21] Thomas, "The Map of Love," in *The World I Breathe*, 95, 96.
[22] Thomas, "The Mouse and the Woman," in *The World I Breathe*, 120–38.

its beauty, and covers its nakedness. This lack of courage has caused the beauty to disappear, to return to the "hidden darkness" of the unconscious. It is this darkness which Thomas attempts to bring to the light, for without it we are but half-people. More than that, we are ignorant people, for we do not know of the deep recesses of human experience; we have only simple and superficial explanations of it. Thomas recognized in Freud's researches a brave attempt to reveal what is hidden within us. But he was not satisfied with a psychologist's description of the unconscious; he must *begin* there and, by creative means, "drag further into the clean nakedness of light more even of the hidden causes than Freud could realize."

v

In the course of twentieth-century literary history, it has occurred to few persons simply to accept the fact of chaos and confusion, to do nothing whatsoever about it. It was more the thing to be "disillusioned," to expend much energy upon what George Orwell calls "facile despairs," and to invent new ways of interpreting the course of events, in the hope that it might be directed toward a personally conceived resolution. The negativism of dada sought on the one hand to destroy the temple; the positivism of Van Wyck Brooks, Gorham Munson and James Oppenheim sought simply to redecorate the temple, and perhaps to strengthen its supports.

Henry Miller did neither; he did not wish to destroy civilization; it was destroying itself. He certainly did not care about giving it any direction, for he allied himself with no ism, whether of the intellect or of the heart. The opening editorial of the Paris *Booster*, of which he was one of many editors, expresses well Miller's attitude. The *Booster* "has no fixed policy. It will be eclectic, flexible, alive—serious but gay withal. We will use tact and delicacy when necessary, but only when necessary. In the main the *Booster* will be a contraceptive against the self-destructive spirit of the age. . . . But we are fluid, quixotic, unprincipled. We have no aesthetic canons to preserve or defend." [23]

[23] Editorial, *Booster*, II (1937), 5. The *Booster* had been a commercial maga-

Henry Miller did not set out to explore the manifold areas and dislocations of the modern mind. His task was to accept quite without shame or indignation what he found there, and to represent it in his writings. The great, fluid sentences of his writings, their nonstop syntax and their accumulation of images obscure and obscene, these have alternately the appearance of the grandiose (Rabelaisianism without a critical or satirical purpose) and the disarmingly simple.

> As quietly and naturally as a twig falling into the Mississippi I dropped out of the stream of American life. Everything that happened to me I remember, but I have no desire to recover the past, neither have I any longings or regrets. I am like a man who awakes from a long sleep to find that he is dreaming. A pre-natal condition—the born man living unborn, the unborn man dying born.[24]

Such passivity is implicitly a criticism of the strenuous efforts of modern thinkers to find some kind of rational prop for their civilization. Miller thus belongs to the anti-intellectuals of his day; he admired Lawrence's stand against the intellectualizing of our time. Proust and Joyce, the giants of the present century, have only aggravated the modern disease by probing its sores. " This formidable picture of the world-as-disease which Proust and Joyce have given us is indeed less a picture than a microscopic study which because we see it magnified, prevents us from recognizing it as the world of every day in which we are swimming. Just as the art of psychoanalysis could not have arisen until society was sick enough to call for this peculiar form of therapy, we could not have had a faithful image of our time until there arose in our midst monsters so ridden with disease that their works resemble the disease itself." [25]

Resignation and acceptance—they have ordinarily a religious ring. But Miller's is not the resignation of either the saint or the sinner; it is a " joyous abandonment of the will," a wish to live

zine catering to American tourists in France. It changed amazingly when Miller and Co. took over. Finally, the title was changed to *Delta*.

[24] Henry Miller, Selections from *Black Spring*, in *New Directions, 1937* (Norfolk, Conn., 1937).

[25] Henry Miller, " The Universe of Death," a chapter from an unpublished book, " The World of Lawrence," in *Phoenix*, I (1938), 49.

within the womb of time without disturbing its process. One gets closer to truth as he abandons the will, submitting to the flux of experience. Understanding is not achieved by logically reordering that experience, but by " living blissfully with it, in it, through and by it." [26] The artist who takes such a position is best able to play his proper role. He should not be a part either of the administrative control of society or of the radical opposition to that control. The value of his work is that it is merely " the reflection of the automatism of life in which he is obliged to lie dormant, a sleeper on the back of sleep, waiting for the signal which will announce the moment of birth." [27]

That strange exchange of letters with Michael Fraenkel on the subject of *Hamlet* discusses, among other things, the creative process, the place of an artist in his times. In the opinion of Fraenkel, art is a means of salvation; the artist is delivered from the " aimless movement of biology." [28] Fraenkel criticizes Miller endlessly for what he calls a fear of the intellect, an unwillingness to avail himself of the mind as a source of reconstruction; he calls Miller's writing " physiological writing." Miller, says Fraenkel, is afraid to face " the man in you who stands in the same relation to you as I do, namely, Henry Miller the thinker." (157) To this accusation Miller answers that it is true the intellect is one means of communication, for the clarification and transmission of ideas. But he is not interested in clarity as such. He has been pleased at times to reach " those ice-cold regions of the mind," but the intellect is only a fortunate accident, an interruption in the unconscious flow of man's experience and expression. More than that, intellectualizing brings all things into doubt. To have made a tragic figure of the doubter—so that the modern literary scene presents a succession of two-penny Hamlets who worship their own indecision—is one of the saddest errors of our day. Doubt is not the end-all of thought and expression; it is not even a proper beginning. It is merely one of the aspects of the

[26] Henry Miller, " Reflections on Writing," in *The Wisdom of the Heart* (Norfolk, Conn., 1941) , 23.

[27] Henry Miller, Selections from *The Tropic of Capricorn*, in *New Directions, 1939* (Norfolk, Conn., 1939), 219.

[28] Henry Miller and Michael Fraenkel, *Hamlet* (Santurce, Puerto Rico, 1939) , [I], 46.

human psyche. " I accept Hamlet as phenomenon, just as I accept Jesus Christ, or Krishnamurti. Passing phenomena . . . some more instructive than others." (180)

Hamlet is the archetype of the modern man, whose crippling disease is the " thought disease." The effort to take the law unto oneself, to make oneself the crucial moral center of the universe, so fixed upon the self the burden of responsibility for man's collective sinning that the single self cannot well bear it. From this source comes the " Hamlet-guilt " which plagues the modern mind and, when projected beyond each single self, results in a babel of conscience, moral dictates, and social panaceas. This is the " living death," the refusal to bow before the real. " Living death means the interruption of the current of life, the forestalling of a natural death process. It is a negative way of recognizing that the world is really nothing but a great womb, the place where everything is brought to life." [29] The living death is compounded of fear and stupid optimism; the modern living death is onanistic and paralytic. " It's a sort of Nirvana of the Id, a condition of iceberg without threat of thaw. This loss of contact with reality, which is the schizophrenic motif par excellence, would be excellent if it implied the creation of a new reality, a *poetic* reality. . . . But the prevalent insanity is only the wolf in the cloak of the old masturbative logic." [30]

Such a condition has brought a hurried call for the great spiritual healer of our day; the psychoanalyst, in Miller's opinion, absolves the patient of the moral and psychic responsibility for the world's and his own ills. This is another of the foolish illusions by which modern man avoids both personal responsibility and the truth: " To imagine that we are going to be saved by outside intervention, whether in the shape of an analyst, a dictator, . . . or even God, is sheer folly." [31] As a means of testing the values of psychoanalysis, Miller himself turned analyst in 1936. He objected to Freud for having given to modern fears a scientific sanction; he stands in the way of the patient's view

[29] Henry Miller, " The Enormous Womb," in *Booster*, IV (1938), 21.

[30] Henry Miller, " The Rise of Schizophrenia," in *New English Weekly*, X (1936), 70.

[31] Henry Miller, *The Wisdom of the Heart*, 35.

of reality, prevents him from accepting it. Freud is guilty of "creating a gray realism of scientific hue instead of a Dantesque reality of black and white." [32] Instead of revealing to the patient the chaos of the world, the analyst seeks to cure him of it. This unfortunate circumstance prevents psychoanalysis from being the genuine and important guide it might otherwise have been. The true analyst would "eliminate the doctor as well as the patient, by accepting the disease itself rather than the medicine or the mediator." (*Wisdom of The Heart*, 36)

The important contribution of psychoanalysis is its systematic exploration of the unconscious, its service in making the unconscious a living thing, available to him who wishes to go beneath the surface of his mind. This Miller considers a great addition, a crucial one, to our means of salvation. But he disapproves of the purpose to which Freud's study has been dedicated. The artist will, if he is honest and capable, use this knowledge for another purpose. He will find in the unconscious the real area of actual living and dying, a place where he may hang suspended and passive in the womb of the world. The dream-life is an important avenue of approach. Often between the dream and reality there is "only the thinnest line." He must withdraw, therefore, from the analyst's bright and cheery reality, from the surface of the world, into the unconscious. "For when, by living out his dream logic, he fulfills himself through the destruction of his own ego, he is incarnating for humanity the drama of individual life which to be tasted and experienced, must embrace dissolution." (*Wisdom of the Heart*, 8)

The final act of acceptance is expressed symbolically in terms of the world as womb, in which man may dwell in a sort of pre-

---

[32] Henry Miller, "The Absolute Collective," in *The Wisdom of the Heart*, 80. The impression Miller gives is that though he is fully informed about psychoanalysis, and has had personal experiences as an analyst, he is aware of its limitations and of the general failure of the analyst to rise above the level of commonplace figure: "They are all minor 'artists,' I should say," he writes (I assume he means by "artists," not poets or painters but men who speak and write of problems which may be linked with the materials of art), "and not to be compared, in lasting value with either the poet or the religious figure." In another place in the letter he says, "I think that some of the most egregious nonsense has been written by all the analysts. Their worst trait is their utter humorlessness. None of them, no matter how much they write, will ever have the effect upon the world of a Laotse."

natal security. Such dwelling among the nether regions requires for its adequate description a style and imagery all its own, based partly upon the functions, excretory, digestive, and sexual, references to which have been excluded most discreetly from conventional publications. It is what Fraenkel has called " physiological writing." Miller's point of view steadfastly excludes any possibility for a quick and easy triumph by the intellect over the unconscious sources of chaos. A new world cannot spring full-grown from the mind of any modern Zeus. It must be passively awaited, for implicit in chaos is the haphazard and brutal process by which cosmic gestation takes place. The dark, forbidden processes of the body thus gain spiritual significance by analogy with the world as " an enormous womb." The sexual act is an unconscious process by which forces are released which give life to the world. The " music of the night life," is " Not heights and depths, but ecstasy upside down, inside out, the bottom reaching as far as the top. Abasement not just to the earth, but through the earth, through grass and sod and subterranean stream. . . . Not the cold pricks of conscience, nor the tormenting flagellation of the mind, but bright, cruel blades flashing." (*Wisdom of the Heart*, 195)

Peace is thus achieved by a passive dwelling within the grotesque and obscene chaos of the world's unconscious being. Commenting upon the work of the painter, Hans Reichel, Miller summarized his own attitude toward this nether reality. The great night life of the unconscious is the source of security—not *from* but *with* pain and brutality.

In the absolute night, in the black pain hidden away in the backbone, the substance of things is dissolved until only the essence shines forth. The objects of [Reichel's] love, as they swim up to the light to arrange themselves on his canvases, marry one another in strange mystic unions which are indissoluble. But the real ceremony goes on below, in the dark, according to the inscrutable atomic laws of wedlock. There are no witnesses, no solemn oaths. Phenomenon weds phenomenon in the way that atomic elements marry to make the miraculous substance of living matter. There are polygamous marriages and polyandrous marriages, but no morganatic marriages. There are monstrous unions too, just as in nature, and they are as inviolable, as indissoluble, as the others. Caprice rules, but it is the stern caprice of nature, and so divine.[33]

Miller accepts readily the new opportunity which psycho-analysis affords of viewing a world previously shut off from con-sciousness by both decorum and prudery. But his acceptance im-plicitly condemns the hope of psychoanalysis for a rescue of the world from its neuroses. He is, in brief, allied with no school of thought—not even with the surrealists, who seem to be burrowing in the same mine. For Miller will not grant the surrealist's as-sumption that personal revolution is itself a directing force. The result of all this is a peculiar form of passivity, by which means the artist becomes an organism, his writing secretions and excretions of that organism. Out of the tumult of the unconscious being come the materials for his art. Without a grasp of human tragedy or a sense of protest against the ills of the universe, he is held secure from them by the antisepsis of biological resignation. That this attitude of resignation may eventually become a part of a religious-aesthetic view of the universe is a suggestion made in a number of places in Miller's writings. For the psychoanalyst avoids the larger problem of living by using science " as a crutch "; this problem is met more directly and honestly by the poet and " the religious figure."

[33] Henry Miller, "The Cosmological Eye," in *Transition*, XXVII (1938), 323–24.

chapter X

PRECURSORS
OF FREUD

i

Historically, the attitude toward irrational incentives and acts has at the least been condemnatory, at the most condescending. From the beginning of our tradition the passions, the emotions, the affective qualities in our experiences, have been given credit for stimulating or energizing such overt acts as are considered beautiful, deeply moving, and sometimes tragic. But within a larger social and political framework the works and personality of the artist have been suspect; they have been credited with an unsystematic insight into the deeper sources and resources of human behavior. Art has been on the defensive for the major part of our history. Even the most distinguished of our artists have had to defend or explain themselves in such terms as a rationalized society has furnished them. Although these circumstances have scarcely changed, the simple division of rational-irrational is no longer regarded with the respect afforded it previously. This is both a gratifying and a terrifying change.

Perhaps no one has ever adequately estimated the value of *convenience* as a determinant of our laws. Certainly it is a good standard of measurement. In one sense, convenience is the loyal servant of adjustment: the adjustment of the individual to the social organism, the adjustment of the individual knower to the unknown. Human acts, therefore, and human knowledge have been subjected to the restrictions of individual and social convenience. A strong concept of rational control has developed from this notion of convenience, which seems at all times to insure us against the earthquakes and floods of the human temperament. Control begins with understanding; the more simply and easily the understanding is achieved, the less hazardous the task of control. Communication, therefore, as developed in the history of language and the emergence of simple syntactic forms, is essential to such control. The primary characteristic of such effective communication is that it is reasonable: that is, that one can both anticipate and measure its effects and its referential and relational structures. Rational communication *may* become extremely complex, as the philosopher, for example, attempts to meet the widening areas of the unknown with an enormously subtilized system of rational interpretations.

There is a strong temptation to say that the irrational is a catch-all for all the recalcitrant motives and acts which do not subscribe to, or which actively threaten, the structure of rational communication and institutions. In order to eliminate danger and to make the status quo attractive, the rational mind tries to evade or ignore any demand upon it which interferes with its easy and convenient regulation of human and social reality. The history of science bears out this point eloquently. Science admits change, but ingredients of that change are tested, are themselves subjected to the rational test, before they are permitted to alter in any way the prevailing structure.

The irrational has for the most part been given a grudging recognition. It has consistently been defined in a negative sense— that which is not reasonable, or knowable, or adaptable to rational modes. It is only within the last one hundred years or so that increasing attention to the irrational, new and far-reaching speculations about its nature, texture, and significance, have had a profoundly disturbing effect upon the thinking of man and upon his confidence in his long-established patterns of control. This confidence asserts itself fitfully and spasmodically, but a renunci-ation of it may lead to profound pessimism. If in the minds and hearts of most men these controls have lost their prestige value, pessimism becomes a dominant characteristic of the intellectual elements of a society.

But pessimism is only one of three principal reactions to the loss of rational self-confidence. The second may be considered a variant of hedonism—a condition of balanced tension, of poise, what Kenneth Burke calls a "comic self-consciousness." Implicit in this attitude is a pervasive skepticism about the absolute validity of any truth, an aloofness from extremist attitudes of any kind, and a standard of attention and attitude which con-siders only the immediate and the personal ingredients of ex-perience. This attitude is fundamentally pragmatic in its effect upon the steady and balanced development of a personality. The third of these reactions may be characterized as a mood, or a series of moods, whose principal characteristics are enthusiasm and in-discretion. This reaction is very important for students of our century; at one time or another most of the intellectuals and artists of our time have been blessed, afflicted, or cursed by it. The disintegration of rational structures allowed many intellec-tuals relative or complete freedom to embrace many possible re-interpretations of man, his world, his God, and his fate. Their response to this opportunity has been excessive and illogical; having repudiated traditional rationalism, they may also disap-prove of the logic by which it has been made plausible and effec-tive. They have therefore selected apparently almost at random, from the suggestions made by Schopenhauer, Nietzsche, Bergson, Freud, and others. They have neglected the possible unity and the personal development of each and all of them.

In this pattern of our twentieth century Freud occupies a strange position. He is professedly and avowedly a scientist, but his science deals with the very sources of irrationality. Having reopened the debate on the actual motives of behavior of all types, he has had repeatedly to assert that his discoveries and conjectures do not warrant either ungrounded pessimism or un-restrained irrationality. We should return with renewed con-fidence to the scientific instruments of reason, he tells us; the constructive work of the ego must go on. License and imprudence may set back its work, or nullify it, with dangerous consequences for society and the human soul. Science has dispelled many illusions, Freud says; but the worst illusion of all is that the renunciation of science and of the reason is either good or safe. Our survey of the career of Freudianism in the twentieth century ought by now to have demonstrated to us that Freud's caution has seldom been observed, that he has himself been accused of sponsoring and favoring the very attitude he has condemned. Why have our intellectuals so often neglected or refused to judge Freud on his own terms? The answer brings us to the chief purpose of this chapter: to examine briefly some of the other influences upon twentieth-century attitudes.

ii

Thomas Mann has insisted that at the fountain source of both the Nietzschean and the psychoanalytic temperaments is Schopenhauer's brilliant exposition of the world as Will and Idea:

> Schopenhauer, as psychologist of the will, is the father of all modern psychology. From him the line runs, by way of the psychological radicalism of Nietzsche, straight to Freud and the men who built up his psychology of the unconscious and applied it to the mental sciences. Nietzsche's antisocratism and hostility to mind are nothing but the philosophic affirmation and glorification of Schopenhauer's discovery of the primacy of the will, his pessimistic insight into the secondary and subservient relation of mind to will.[1]

Schopenhauer's description of the world as will by necessity emphasizes the power of instinct, its ceaseless drive to perpetuate itself. It is the will to live, a blind and reckless striving, modified perhaps in its nature in the higher organisms but essentially an irrational force which uses reason merely as an instrument. This will is the key to man's existence, though it is not dependent upon man for its own, but rather relentlessly nullifies man's efforts to

---

[1] Introduction, *The Living Thoughts of Schopenhauer* (New York, 1939), 28.

become independent of it. Manifestations of the will are subject to man's perceptual and conceptual activity, but the will itself is groundless, formless, and relentless. The parts and acts of the human body are the visible expressions, "*the objectification of the will*," [2] the ways in which the will assumes temporary and tentative form. It is folly for us to assume that these forms are the controlling factors in life, or even that they have the limited importance that Kant grants them. Time, space, causality, all a priori knowledge, are outside the world of will as thing in itself. Schopenhauer's objection to Kant is not that he defined the limits of reason but that he underestimated the importance of the reality which lies beyond it. Man is imprisoned in the world of organic striving, and his small efforts to rationalize his existence are so bound and influenced by his will to live that the apparent success of rational controls is neither convincing nor ultimately effective. "For as every body must be regarded as the manifestation of a will, and as will necessarily expresses itself as a struggle, the original condition of every world that is formed into a globe cannot be rest, but motion, a striving forward in boundless space without rest and without end." (69)

It is the fate of the common mortal, "that manifestation of Nature which she produces by the thousand every day," to submit unthinkingly to this condition of restless organic striving. "He can turn his attention to things only so far as they have some relation to his will, however indirect it may be." (77) The genuine condition of our unconscious nature is a "constant striving, without end and without rest." (104) But there is a means of escape from the will—the path of ascesis, which leads to a denial of the will to live. The artist is able to wrench himself free from the will and from all its demands upon the self. "Man now attains to the state of voluntary renunciation, resignation, true indifference, and perfect will-lessness." (124–25) His contemplation of objects and ideas is separated from their residence in the will and from his own struggle for biological preservation. He is thus able to gaze objectively upon things of beauty and in this way to find surcease from the pain of absorption in the will to live. For the rest, all is endless, blind striving. Pleasure is mere absence

[2] *The World as Will and Idea*, in *The Living Thoughts of Schopenhauer*, 50.

of pain and may, if extended, lead to another kind of pain, ennui or boredom. It is natural to say that Schopenhauer is a pessimist, for he has reduced the advantages of reason to the status of mere prisoner of the will; he has granted to a few the prospect of escape from the irrational will, and that at a great sacrifice of the very advantages which men ordinarily seek for themselves. The importance of reason is negligible; by ordinary mortals it is used for organic advantage in the ceaseless competition of organisms for their survival in the flux; the exceptional individual, the genius, replaces it with a Platonic intuition of will-less Ideas.

The measure of difference between Schopenhauer and Nietzsche can be expressed in the alternate phrases: the world as it is and the world as it might be—granting that both are worlds of will. This is the great difference between voluntaristic pessimism and voluntaristic optimism. For Nietzsche condemned Schopenhauer, not for the latter's scorn of reason but for the pall of futility he had thrust upon the strivings of man. To begin with, he agreed with Schopenhauer in the latter's evaluation of reason, but went far beyond him in suggesting the psychological superiority of the will over reason. The notion of consciousness, he says, has far too long been governed by the limits of our endeavor. It is a false simplifying of the problems of knowing and being. Passion and desire are the prime movers of human nature; reason is the instrument of both. Nietzsche regards the complex structure of human desire as evidence not of the will to live but of the will to power. Passions are a force for the assertion of individual importance. When they are frustrated in their drive for satisfaction, they find indirect outlets, such as in elaborate wish-fulfillments or in dreams. Dreams reveal a wealth of evidence of our unconscious life:

> Thus the esthetically sensitive man stands in the same relation to the reality of dreams as the philosopher does to the reality of existence; he is a close and willing observer, for these pictures afford him an interpretation of life, and it is by these processes that he trains himself for life. And it is not only the agreeable and friendly pictures that he experiences in himself with such perfect understanding: but the serious, the troubled, the sad, the gloomy, the sudden re-

straints, the tricks of fate, the uneasy presentiments, in short, the whole Divine Comedy of life, and the Inferno, also pass before him, not like mere shadows on the wall—for in these scenes he lives and suffers—and yet not without that fleeting sensation of appearance.[3]

Nietzsche does not regard all checking of impulses as harmful; nor does he advocate complete release from control. He condemns the control that is the servant of mediocrity. The course of psychological integration must often go on in opposition not only to self-will but also to prevailing dead moralities. " The course of logical thought and reasoning in our modern brain corresponds to a process and struggle of impulses which singly and in themselves are all very illogical and unjust; we experience usually only the result of the struggle, so rapidly does this primitive mechanism now operate in us." [4]

The rationalist has contributed to the greatest mistake of all in the history of philosophy. " Philosophers have assumed that progress lay in becoming more and more conscious, whereas unconscious instinct is the type of perfection, consciousness being rather the sign of some maladjustment." Mind is, or should be, the slave of instinct, though it may so cleverly undermine instinct as to reverse their respective roles. Basically, consciousness, or conscious caution, is an instrument of the timid and the weak. Since they find direct modes of satisfying desires difficult and painful, they resort to cunning and shrewdness, to a narrow intelligence as a means of overcoming their less cautious neighbors and of making their caution a ruling virtue. Thus reason, while originally the servant of instinct, may by degrees free itself from instinct and attempt to dominate it.[5] From the ceaseless struggle of man's will to power with the social barriers to its achievement results man's " bad conscience "; the unconscious becomes increasingly rich and full as man's will is more and more inhibited and frustrated.

The whole inner world, originally as thin as if it had been

---

[3] Friedrich Nietzsche, *The Birth of Tragedy* (New York, n. d.), 169–70. This is the first of Nietzsche's works, written about 1870–1871.

[4] *Joyful Wisdom* (New York, 1924), 157.

[5] George Allen Morgan, *What Nietzsche Means* (Cambridge, 1941), 107, 111.

stretched between two layers of skin, burst apart and expanded proportionately, and obtained depth, breadth, and height, when man's external outlet became *obstructed*. . . . Enmity, cruelty, the delight in persecution, in surprises, change, destruction—the turning all these instincts against their own possessors: this is the origin of the "bad conscience." [6]

Nietzsche argues for such a revaluation of morals as will reinstate the unconscious sources of the individual will to power. The life of reason has almost invariably led to decadence, timidity, and a reduction of all human striving to the level of mediocre security. This way lies stagnation of the human will. The hope of man—indeed, his genuine salvation—lies in the intensification and enrichment of his organic powers, not in their tedious regulation and control. The will-to-power is nothing other than the will to such an enrichment of man's life. But this will-to-power is not a mere brutal, reckless force which smashes all before it. It is precisely that mistake which frightened Schopenhauer from it, says Nietzsche. Greatness lies within the nature of man; it is not measured by the nature of his impact upon history. From level to level of man's achievement, his desires and the means of their satisfaction exist in a state of tension, or balance—a positive and energetic poise which reaches beyond itself and does not rest wearily upon the past. Nietzsche tries to distinguish between psychological and spiritual progress on the one hand and stagnation of the will on the other. Speaking of the genius of Wagner, for example, he says that great energy and passion need to be freed from the narrow constrictions of society and that a genius must recognize the will as a force for good. "From its innermost depths there gushes forth a passionate will which, like a rapid mountain torrent, endeavours to make its way through all paths, ravines, and crevices, in search of light and power. Only a force completely free and pure was strong enough to guide this will to all that is good and beneficial." [7]

The view of the artist and of his role changes in the course of Nietzsche's life. His eloquent championship of the artist in

---

[6] *The Genealogy of Morals* (Edinburgh and London, 1910), 100–101.
[7] *Thoughts Out of Season* (Edinburg and London, 1910), I, 109.

The Birth of Tragedy gave the impression that the artist was the true leader of man, the forerunner of the Superman. Eventually he was to change his mind, but he steadfastly maintained that any just consideration of art must be free from rational restrictions. Kant and Schopenhauer had both erred in associating art with cognition. On the contrary, the real artist, " like the conqueror and the lawgiver, exercises formative will to power," and the appreciation or contemplation of art demands the same qualities of vigor and will which the artist possesses. The artist is possessed, in larger degree than common mortals, of the forces and desires which go to make up the true man of power. " He who approaches these Olympians with another religion in his heart, seeking among them for moral elevation, even for sanctity, for disincarnate spirituality, for charity and benevolence, will soon be forced to turn his back on them, discouraged and disappointed. . . . We hear nothing but the accents of an exuberant, triumphant life, in which all things, whether good or bad, are deified." [8]

The artist is known variously by his expression of life-giving forces and his submission to them. He may give form to the highest desires of man; he may revitalize a society by showing it wherein lies its stagnation. More frequently, however, he submits, not to the will-to-power, but to the prevailing institution or custom, and becomes a mere servant of society. This regrettable fact eventually caused Nietzsche to modify his estimate of the artist. The intellectual of the twentieth century was less likely to note this shift in Nietzsche's thinking, more inclined to link this imagined role with the dynamics of his *The Birth of Tragedy* and *Thus Spake Zarathustra*. This is part of the history of misinterpretation, of which there are many phases, as many as there have been in the case of Freud.

Nietzsche thus joins Schopenhauer in upholding the will as more powerful than reason. But his is a vigorous optimism; rather than sigh at the persistence of mediocre striving in society, he would suggest that the dead elements in society be thrown aside. He appeals to the individual to repudiate restricting and restraining forces and to search for personal progress by means of his will.

[8] *The Birth of Tragedy*, 179–80.

It is an ideal of a spirit who plays innocently (that is to say, involuntarily, out of his superabundance of power) with everything that has hitherto been called holy, good, inviolable, divine; a spirit to whom the highest popular standards would be a mere danger, a decay, an abasement, or at the very least, a relaxation, a blindness, and a temporary forgetfulness of self: the ideal of a humanly superhuman well-being and good-will, which often enough may seem unhuman—when, for example, it confronts all mankind's former seriousness and solemnities as their most lifelike and unconscious parody in gesture, speech, accent, look, morality, and duty—but with which, nevertheless, *great seriousness* perhaps first arises, the first note of interrogation is affixed, the soul's destiny changes, the hour hand moves, the tragedy begins.[9]

Exploration of the sources of man's opposition to reason have taken the form of over-all and systematic studies of man's will, and for the most part the unconscious of man is given a poetic or metaphoric appearance. For both Schopenhauer and Nietzsche, in their arguments against the sufficiency of reason, failed to do more than simple justice to the human desire for careful and compact, comprehensible description. That is why the two most important of Freud's precursors were influential in forming attitudes but contributed little if anything to the anatomy of those attitudes. For the intellectuals of the twentieth century, they were the destroyers of reason, whose arguments simply confirmed a latent suspicion of the weakness of the rational position. In a sense, therefore, their contributions may be regarded as negative.

Another member of the confraternity of influence is Dostoevski; like many of his contemporaries, he has been forced posthumously to subscribe to many and contradictory points of view. Dostoevski's influence upon modern writing has been great; for many writers found in his lengthy expositions of the anti-rational position some supporting evidence for their own views. More than any other writer of his times, he explored the psychological nature of his characters, their " internal world." According to Ernest J. Simmons, Dostoevski, soon after he had been released

[9] *Ecce Homo* (New York, n. d.) 98–99.

from his Siberian prison camp (1854), discovered and read with great interest a book by C. G. Carus, *Psyche: the Development of the Soul.* From it he must have at least derived some suggestions which were to support his point of view: the theory that mental disease is a consequence of a maladjustment between the psyche and its environment; Carus' belief in the intimate relationship between conscious and unconscious life; his notion of the strong magnetic attraction of one personality for another quite different from it; and finally, that " abnormal states of mind may be the gateway to supernormal experiences that are very close to divine. . . ." [10]

For the Russian novelist, man's personality is rarely simple, and certainly his reason leads to superficially and dangerously simple answers to important problems. From the beginning, Dostoevski distrusted the reason, which he regarded either as a clever instrument used for corrupt purposes or the deceptively simple exterior of social doctrines. In all men there is at least a contradiction of impulses; man is neither purely rational nor innocently good. Dostoevski is concerned much of the time with his portrait of the " undergroundling," the impoverished and distorted spirit, whose very insignificance usually breeds evil. Externally his actions appear contradictory; their contradictoriness is motivated and governed by an essentially dual nature, which is alternately kind and brutal, submissive and domineering. In his dreams he achieves the satisfaction of all the desires which his waking life denies him. The worst extension of man's ego is the superficial application of his reason to world betterment, to social welfare. The undergroundling's reason is distasteful to him, for it unceasingly points to the futility of his wishes. Hence he fights the reason and prefers to it the lethe of dreams and wish-fulfillments. Yet his reason is with him in each waking hour and acts constantly to frustrate his will. He is led to believe, therefore, in the qualitative superiority of will over reason.

Dostoevski suggests two substitutes for reason. One of them, he claims, is evil, for it is the brutal expression of the frustrated will on a moral holiday. Murder is its practice, and suicide often its only cure. The other, rare and almost impossible of attain-

---

[10] *Dostoievski: The Making of a Novelist* (London, 1940), 77.

ment, is nevertheless his genuine hope for the salvation of man: simple faith and resignation, a meekness of spirit which turns aside the wrath of both God and man. These qualities are best represented in the figures of Sonya Marmeladova, Prince Myshkin, and Alyosha Karamasov; their theoretical exponents and spiritual exemplars are the monks Tikhon and Zosima. The career of the meek, passive soul is fraught with humiliation and pain. He is a pathetic creature, but he unconsciously exercises a magnetic power over his fellows, and may in fact influence some of them to abandon the tortuous path of downright evil or sinister intelligence. Thus the initial recognition of the evil within himself, if it leads to acceptance rather than defiance, turns unconscious evil into conscious good. Dostoevski's most powerful characters—Stavrogin of *The Possessed*, Raskolnikov of *Crime and Punishment*, and Ivan Karamasov—are at times strangely affected by the attractiveness of this moral attitude, but their wills are far too strong and their pride excessive. Raskolnikov's ultimate submission to Sonya seems a false ending of his career; and Dostoevski's notebooks point to the indecision which preceded his composition of the final chapters in that novel.

The powerful hold which the novels of Dostoevski have had upon the imagination of twentieth-century writers is another indication of their willingness to explore and exploit all suggestions about the irrationality of man. The sum total of nineteenth-century heritage is this emphasis upon the irrational in all its varying manifestations. That man is motivated by something other than his reason, that his reason is a mechanism of restriction and compulsory restraint, is the conclusion many modern writers like to read into the men they admire.

iii

Why should the intellectuals of our time have emphasized what was, after all, only a part of the nineteenth-century heritage? For one thing, they lived in an age of protest, and protest was directed against traditional morality and ethics. There were no great substitute rational structures to replace the old. Again, the prevailing mood, at least until the advent of popular Marxism, was highly personal, a search for personal salvation or for a theoretical support of personal cynicism. The tendency to regard all neatly systematized solutions as suspiciously simple threw the individual back upon subjective resources. The result of all this was to be an overemphasis upon the separate and discrete ego, whose spiritual and intellectual resources lay within itself.

Whatever flattered the self-esteem or strengthened its sense of revolt was welcomed. The egocentrism of modern intellectuals governed their indiscriminate choice of leaders for a highly personal revolt. Nietzsche had stated the terms of the revolt poetically and with great power; Freud had demonstrated the psychic causes of prevailing ills and maladjustments. If one could forget that Nietzsche had qualified his early remarks or refuse to see him whole, he might serve excellently well as a standard-bearer. Similarly, if one were to deny the purpose of Freud's clinical observations, he might well use the raw materials of psychoanalysis for a purpose. This attitude inspired this rather melancholy observation of Thomas Mann, who of all men of our time has studied the philosophers and psychologists of the irrational most thoroughly and well:

> The twentieth century has in its first third taken up a position of reaction against classic rationalism and intellectualism. It has surrendered to admiration of the unconscious, to a glorification of instincts which it thinks is overdue to life. And the bad instincts have accordingly been enjoying a heyday. We have seen instead of pessimistic conviction deliberate malice. Intellectual recognition of bitter truth turns into hatred and contempt for mind itself. Man has greedily flung himself on the side of " life "—that is, on the side of the stronger—for there is no disputing the fact that life has nothing to fear from mind, that not life but knowledge, or rather, mind, is the weaker part and one more needing protection on this earth. Yet the antihumanity of our day is a humane experiment too in its way. It is a one-sided answer to the eternal question as to the nature and destiny of man.[11]

The interpretation of man as an irrational, or at the most as

[11] Introduction, *The Living Thoughts of Schopenhauer*, 29–30.

a weakly rational being, has been a popular determinant of early twentieth-century attitudes. In order to understand these attitudes and the literature to which they gave birth, it is necessary to understand their sources and the modern manner of receiving and altering them. We have already seen that the theories of Freud have been used with varying degrees of understanding and discrimination. Let us summarize one last time the points-of-view in accordance with which the philosophies and psychologies of the irrational have been used in our times.

Suspension of belief in the reason has caused some men to become so absorbed in the manifestations of unconscious life that their perspectives are distorted. Since the boundary line between normal and abnormal has been removed and the distinction between good and evil has been discarded, it is possible to consider the instinctive life as the most important and to neglect the safeguards which protect it against the importunities of external reality. Such an attitude is not by any means uncommon, and it may not argue a complete abdication of responsibility. It may, of course, be an argument for a perpetual moral holiday, on the grounds that restriction of any kind deprives life of its vigor. In another sense, it may be a dark preliminary to a new morality, in which the ego is fully strengthened and the energies of the id ultimately made to contribute to the life of the mind. The surrealists have, of course, begun all of their " campaigns " for a new consciousness by accepting the unconscious as a proving ground for moral and social responsibilities.

Another attitude encouraged by this interest in the irrational is a love of the destruction of the past, with no provisions for moral or social structures in the future. This attitude has generally been adopted only temporarily, and it may be characterized by either exuberant irrationalism (as in the case of the editors of *Blast*, the British magazine published in 1914) or intellectual cynicism. The demonstrations of the former may be thought a symptom of change rather than the establishment of a mode. Nevertheless, its exaltation of life and its disregard of both past and future structure, has been one of the characteristics of the twentieth-century explosion. So, for example, the opening editorial of the *London Aphrodite*, edited by Jack Lindsay and P. R.

Stephensen: " We affirm Life, and for definition quote Nietzsche: Spirit is that life which cuts itself into life. We affirm Beauty, and by that term understand a sensual harmony, a homogeneous ecstasy, which, constructing intellectually yet hates nothing so much as the dry cogs of the objectified and objectifying intellect." [12]

A third response to the overpowering presence of the irrational in modern life is an extension of Dostoevski's doctrine of resignation. Shorn of the latter's nationalism and strengthened by the thought of Kierkegaard, this is the position assumed by Franz Kafka. This position not only assumes the limits of conscious knowledge but also translates the eccentricities and painful irrationalities of the unconscious mind into terms of man's relationship with God. The Freudian analogy is the father-son relationship; it begins from the point at which the attitude of God and his demands upon the human being are inexplicable when judged rationally. Resistance to them is similar to the mind's resistance to what cannot be conveniently catalogued and explained. Spiritual resolution comes as a result of one's reaching the level of the paradoxical and absurd, until the suspension of rational judgment causes it to lose the sense of paradox and absurdity. The eccentricities of the unconscious are effective in two ways in setting up the spiritual minima for such an attitude: in a superficial sense, they are analogous to the impenetrable eccentricity of God's nature; hence they may serve, as they do in Kafka's novels, as symbolic " glimpses " or analyses of the difficulties on the way to salvation. Secondly, they act as a powerful check upon rational morality, pointing to and fostering its weakness and reducing man's confidence in it.

The appeal of the irrational has had other effects. One of the simplest of these is its influence upon the character of the moral revolt. Schopenhauer, Nietzsche, and Freud all recognized the importance of the sex instinct. For Schopenhauer it was the " focus of the will," a powerful organic determinant of the will to live; Nietzsche regarded it as an important expression of the will to power, which the creative artist will possess in abundance

---

[12] " Editorial Manifesto," in *London Aphrodite*, I (1928) , 2. The *Aphrodite* was perhaps the best modern exponent of Nietzsche's position. Cf. Jack Lindsay, " The Modern Consciousness: An Essay Towards an Integration," in *London Aphrodite*, I, 3–24.

in the same measure as he possesses other instinctual strengths. We have already examined Freud's researches in the nature of the sex instinct and its relation to man's psychic life. The prominence of the subjects of sex freedom and extra-marital experiment in the debates of Villagers and others testifies to the great interest these speculations aroused. This was not an irrational attitude, they argued; it is above all the best use of intelligence to rid oneself of Puritan prejudices and Victorian sentimentalities. Modern attitudes toward sex, in and out of literature, derive principally from psychoanalysis. But there are two distinct divisions within their ranks: the sponsorship by Floyd Dell of an intelligent cultural analysis of sex habits and attitudes in modern times is one; the vitalistic sex gospel of D. H. Lawrence is another. The first counsels a greater freedom of sexual choice but does not advocate license; the second considers the sex drive as a ritualistic approach to the deepest and richest experience, but condemns the sexual anarchy of the modernist.

Finally, the psychology of the irrational has, in the opinion of a limited number of modern writers, only emphasized the tremendous task which the mind, or ego, has yet to fulfill. Freud has himself insisted upon this conclusion as the most important which psychoanalysis has to offer. In fact, his reliance upon the ultimate power of the strengthened intellect has been criticized by Theodore Reik, one of his most devoted followers:

> While we cannot but agree with Freud that religion is doomed, that it has run its course, we cannot help doubting the suggestion that men are capable of living without illusions. Education for reality is certainly a consummation most devoutly to be wished; but the most striking attribute of reality is its unpleasantness. . . . The supremacy of the intellect which Freud foresees would never be more than superficial; basically men would still be guided by their instinctual desires. We do not deny the possibility that men will some day be ruled by science. But they will still be men, which is to say, frail, inconstant, more or less unreasonable beings who are the slaves of their instincts and who will never cease to strive after ephemeral pleasure.[13]

---

[13] *From Thirty Years with Freud* (New York, 1940), 130–31.

It is the avowed belief of Freud, of his former pupil Franz Alexander, and of his greatest literary exponent, Thomas Mann, that the psychological appraisal of the unconscious which it has been the pleasure of psychoanalysis to make will ultimately afford us such increased knowledge of human behavior and such strengthened means of control that man will henceforth live both in the increased realization of his basic powers and in the more sober recognition of the necessity of rational controls.

APPENDIXES

appendix I

PSYCHOLOGY AND
LITERATURE*

So many attempts have been made to discuss precisely the relationship of psychology with literature or to suggest the usefulness of psychology to criticism that one needs first of all to see if a new perspective isn't somehow available. I believe we know both the advantage and the limitations of the biographical study of writers; and no one can escape these days the dark presence of Jung's "primordial images." Perhaps we may find our best access to the problem by looking once again at a structure and terminology contributed at the beginning of the century and before by Sigmund Freud and elaborated upon by him in subsequent years.

I refer of course to Freud's definition, description and analysis of the psychic economy. These involve a series of metaphors, as bold a series as was ever advanced by a cautious scientist. Beginning only with the facts of the unconscious and the conscious mind, Freud saw first of all, or suspected, both the tension between the two and what he called the constancy, or balance, of energy that invariably characterized this tension. From these simple beginnings came the terminology with which we are all now fa-

* A paper read at the English Institute, September, 1956; first published in the *Kenyon Review*, Autumn, 1957.

miliar: the id, ego, super-ego; the unconscious, preconscious, conscious; the pleasure principle and the reality principle, and so on.

Described in Freud's own words (*The Ego and the Id*, London, Hogarth Press, 1927), ". . . the ego is that part of the id which has been modified by the direct influence of the external world acting through the Perceptual-Conscious: in a sense it is an extension of the surface-differentiation. Moreover, the ego has the task of bringing the influence of the external world to bear upon the id and its tendencies, and endeavors to substitute the reality-principle for the pleasure-principle which reigns surpeme in the id. In the ego perception plays the part which in the id devolves upon instinct. The ego represents what we call reason and sanity, in contrast to the id which contains the passions." (29–30)

These terms were in the nature of accessory metaphors, introduced as the original insight into psychic tensions required elaboration and its subtleties needed definition. I am aware of the fact that these formulations stem from a desire to assert and affirm the existence of what underlay the conscious, external world, of what we know from having seen or sensed. It is also true that they are the product of a desire to pay a discreet tribute to the language of orthodox science. There is nothing at all unusual or surprising in Freud's characterization of these phenomena; nor was Freud the first to emphasize the need to examine an " unconscious " life or mind. It is perhaps in his admirable and patient *consistency* of attention that the merit of his system lies—as well as in its availability to almost endless fruitful elaboration.

Once we have established that the unconscious is a positive entity, a specific and viable aspect of the psyche, then we may proceed to describe it. We continue to do so, however, by the ingenious method of analyzing causally the aberrancies and obliquities of the conscious mind; and our major instrument in such analysis is language. We must assume a language norm, a norm of linguistic behavior, linked to a kind of systematic logical or rational form. If there are such norms—if they may be maintained without one's retreating too far into abstractions—then it is possible to examine variants, deviations, subterfuges, psychic " jamming," and to explain them as a part of the strategy of the id, as a verbal consequence of the tension resulting from the flow and counter-flow of psychic energy.

Freud's own description of these processes is both precise and illuminating: " By virtue of its relation to the perceptual system, [the ego] arranges the processes of the mind in a temporal order and tests their correspondence with reality. By interposing the process of thinking it secures a postponement of motor discharges and controls the avenues to motility. . . . All the experiences of life that originate from without enrich the ego; the id, however, is another outer world to it, which it strives to bring into subjection to itself. It withdraws libido from the id and transforms the object-cathexes of the id into object-constructions. With the aid of the super-ego, though in a manner that is still obscure to us [1927], it draws upon the experiences of past ages stored in the id." (*The Ego and the Id*, 81–82)

This is what amounts to a psychological analysis of the basic constituents of a literature. In terms of it we may illuminate much of what we discuss in literary criticism as form, texture, metaphor, and symbol. I should like to suggest the following plan for a criticism based upon Freud's initial descriptions of the psychic order. Let us assume that our psychic life may be divided into primary and secondary processes; that these, since they are located differently and react to different kinds of exposure, are in conflict with each other, or more accurately that they cause conflict in the psyche; that basic energies (whether of wish or desire, as Freud maintained, or of some other incentive) are turned back upon themselves, or are permitted only partial expression, or express themselves fully only in extraordinary circumstances; that our understanding of these energies comes from the fact of their being thwarted, controlled, suspended in a state of partial expression; and that, ultimately, the ideal psychic state results from a *balance* of tensions and a *conservation* of psychic energy. A number of important opportunities for the description of our psychic lives occur to us. While the energies are not specifically one thing or another, they may be characterized with a quite satisfactory and useful precision. The push, drive, energy of the id are desire, wish, for pleasure, for specific gratifications; the agency for thwarting the desire is exposed to the reality itself, the external world which indicates its prohibitions by inflicting pain or forcing retreat. An uninhibited drive toward satisfaction of unconscious wishes (or expenditure of libidinal energy) would lead to death. The wish needs instruction in the shock of reality; if the character of inhibition is moderate, the shock will lead to readjustment; if the reality is too suddenly and too brutally enforced, the effect will be a traumatic shock, leading to one of several forms of compulsive behavior. Freud assumes stability in the external world; Hemingway among others did not find it so. But this shock is not limited either to the accidents of uninhibited desire or to the catastrophes of an uncontrolled reality. Repression is in itself a cause of pain; it may, in the interests of protecting the psyche and prolonging life, cause violent dislocations of the psychic system.

However inadequate this may be as a sketch of Freud's superbly exact descriptions, I introduce it here as a preliminary to examining its usefulness as a perspective upon literature. The two have in common what we may call a necessary language—language as the instrument of description becomes in the course of my discussion language as a system of strategies. Language is necessary at first to label and define; next, to put phenomena in order; then to characterize the nature of incentives for labeling and ordering; finally, in the most remarkable of its ranges of use, to effect changes in meaning, to represent situations as more complex than they might be or are or ought to be. In the mind of a person endowed with every resource of language, the phenomena of psychic tension, conflict, drive, repression, are articulated and represented in a discourse at once psychologically just and remarkably subtle. I should like to suggest, therefore, that literature may be viewed and analyzed in terms of the verbal and metaphorical equivalents of the psyche and its behavior. Literature possesses a greater metaphoric freedom than psychology, or perhaps it has the license of its own audacity. But it is actively engaged in providing verbal and metaphoric equivalents of and elaborations upon the simply described behavior of the id, ego, and superego in their dynamic relationships. I can scarcely go on from here, to insist upon exact equivalents; it is perhaps as unwise to find iddities and egocentricities in literature as it is to accept literally biographical peculiarities as definitive explanations of achieved works of art. To locate an author's id, ego, superego, etc., in either characters or lines is to violate the subtlety of their necessary arrangements. My purpose is, instead, to explain the complexities of literary work as the results of symbolic actions which report and reflect on a high level of linguistic articulateness and subtlety the basic tensions, balances, imbalances, repressions, and compensations of psychic energies contained within a system such as Freud has described.

In any application of such a criticism, we can begin with fairly simple definitions. The creative process begins with a relaxation of ego control. There are other examples of such relaxation: drunkenness, forms of schizophrenia, dreams. But the work of the artist differs usually from these in that the regression is deliberate and controlled. The creative artist is *aware* of the regression; one may almost say he *wills* it (there have been cases of poets who have tried to force it by artificial means). The creative mind suspends its work between inspiration and control, or criticism. The artist is aware first of all that he is in a state of suspension; deliberately he has allowed the ego to give in to the flow of energy from the id. As Ernst Kris has put it (*Psychoanalytic Explorations in Art*, N. Y., Int. U. Press, 1952, pp. 253–54) : (with Abraham Kaplan)

> We may speak here of *a shift in psychic level*, consisting in the fluctuation of functional regression and control. When regression goes too far, the symbols become private, perhaps unintelligible even to the reflective self; when, at the other extreme, control is preponderant, the result is described as cold, mechanical, and uninspired.

As Freud has pointed out (in *The Interpretation of Dreams* and elsewhere) , in the unconscious which has been affected by the ego's inhibitions reside the potential strategies for circumventing the ego. Such strategies as condensation, displacement, additive substitutes for negations or for the conditional mode are all a product of the id-ego tension. The verbalization of this tension is available in the preconscious. Of basic interest to literary criticism is the fact that impulse and inhibition are herein *mixed*, that multiple meanings and ambiguities are thus a *result* of the conflict between desire and inhibition. An ambiguity may be said to suggest in language the subtlety of an achieved balance. The *complexity* of the human state resides neither in the fully charged impact of desire upon the ego nor in the ego's use of societal prohibitions to stop the impact (each of these by itself is superficial) —but, rather, in the *product* of the conflict. The ego provides the language of discourse in its relationship with the preconscious (which is largely charged with the oughtness and counter-energy of conscience) ; the id determines the strategies used to mitigate, violate, or circumvent. In a remarkable range of meanings and metaphor, literature records the infinite variety of these exchanges and conflicts.

There are two major considerations relevant to literary criticism: they are the multiplicity of meanings in literature and the element of form. Form is largely a product of the ego; social and moral forms are related to aesthetic forms; or, rather, aesthetic form is an extension of the logic of social and moral forms. That literary forms have great variety is no more remarkable a fact than that form persists through such variety. Experiment in literary form probably comes from a distrust of traditional form; the container no longer satisfactorily orders the thing contained. Thus an attempt to introduce a " qualitative " form, or to insist upon symbolic as distinguished from rational progression comes at least in part from a dissatisfaction with form as not allowing sufficient texture or as overly inhibiting the opportunity of texture. Texture is itself a variant of form: rhythm both encourages and controls freedom of meaning; a rhyme pattern both enhances the quality of word sounds and sets a limit to their frequency.

More specifically, the forms are the special province of the ego; they are the means of inhibition, the ways of containing creative energy, of balancing its tensions and of securing a maximum of discernibility within the range of particulars. The only way of making oneself understood, in short, of communicating, is to contain the charge of psychic energy within a formal pattern that has initially and psychologically been introduced as a way of *preventing* an uninhibited charge of energy. This process may cost much. A slavish obedience to form for form's sake is of course debilitating and unrewarding. But the tension set up by form and texture leads to articulation and then to containment of the basic energy drives that have existed initially inarticulate and without form. Ernst Kris has given us a very interesting discussion of what he calls "stringencies," a term he uses to define external restraints put upon expression in art.

> The level of stringency in works of art—their degree of interpretability—varies markedly from period to period. In some cases ambiguity is fully exploited, and correspondingly great demands are made on the audience; in other cases, there is no more ambiguity than is involved in the work's being aesthetic at all; the demands on the audience are minimal; the interpretations called for are rigidly limited. We may suggest that art is likely to be characterized by low stringency (i. e., high ambiguity and interpretability) where systems of conduct or ideals are in doubt or social values are in process of transition. (*Ibid.*, 262)

This is true especially when those aspects of form which define the thing contained while in the act of containing it no longer serve the ego adequately, whether because they have weakened through an excess of abstraction (the definitions no longer define), or because they have become too arbitrarily fixed (the definitions are too remote from the particulars they are supposed to contain). We may say that any form is the result of a series of accidents. As in any situation where balance serves to make energy intelligible, form in literature is the consequence of the need to compromise with energy by limiting it and allowing it exercise in terms of particular tensions.

Our final discussion of form in literature is by way of transition to its relationship with language and meaning. The major instruments which the ego possesses for the purpose of containing energy are time, space, convention, and logic. The id possesses none of these. They are the means of locating psychic energy within the focus of reality. Each of them is both specific and ambiguous. In simplest terms each arrests energy by shaping it, or shapes it in the act of arresting it. If we could imagine the id with a time sense at all, it would be a future sense—that is, the drive toward total gratification is pure future, and leads, if not inhibited, to death. The ego's function is to arrest future by means of past, to make the present moment a unity of past and future. The result of this process is to slow down the drive toward death; and in consequence, moments are realized and both addition and formal patterns of time are constructed. Similarly, the ego gives spatial concepts to the energy discharge; in the matter of time and space both, the ego localizes, forces the psychic energy into an awareness of *milieu*. Milieu itself is a product of objective temporal and spatial situations. Freud's elaborate discussions of the familial origins and progress of societies should concern us here, but they will have only to be assumed. (See *Totem and Taboo, The Ego and the Id, Moses and Monotheism.* See especially Herbert Marcuse, *Eros and Civilization*, Boston, Beacon Press, 1955). It may be of some interest here to point to the range of psychoanalytic evaluations of milieu. Freud's is hypothetical, but only in the sense of generalizing historically from proven recurrences; a family centered milieu is in Freud's case derived from clinical practices, the interpretation based upon inferences from personal cases. I think that here we may see the source of what we may call "family-centered literature," in which formal controls are defined in terms of manners (for instance, *Buddenbrooks* and *The Magic Mountain*). Jung's milieu, though also an inference from a kind of therapeutic procedure, is nevertheless extremely wide in its range of descriptive implication. Neither conception of milieu is especially noted for its relationship to contemporary social or societal fact, a fact that other analysts are eager to assert. The literary implications of both Freud's and Jung's views are allied with universals, but Freud's universals are at least easier to associate with the particulars at their source. To continue with the discussion of the four terms, convention is a form of the human history of time and space as inhibiting factors. It is the most flexible, the least firm of all the forms of awareness which the ego uses to arrest the progress toward uninhibited gratification. Nevertheless, it may achieve great significance in literature. There is often a close link of social and moral convention with literary form. Convention is the social logic of literary usage. Logic itself is the final restriction imposed upon the psychic energy expressed in the id. There are basic logical principles common to an external world from which the ego draws its reserves of inhibition. These principles are largely either negating or qualifying; that is, they exclude (if this, then not this), or negate (not this), or prescribe (this and not this). Every grammatical detail is an index, a sign, of the inhibition which anticipates form; but as such it may also be a clue to the aesthetic means of articulating psychic balance.

In so arbitrarily stating the formal conditions of inhibition, I have tried to set the stage for the final phase of my discussion. I should maintain that ambiguity, word-play, and what Philip Wheelwright has called " plurisignation " are primarily a part of the process constantly occurring in the psyche which seeks to achieve an articulate balance of tensions between desire and preservation. The id is neither logical nor illogical; it is prelogical until it comes in contact with the ego or the ego with it. After that it acquires the devices of logic but makes them serve its own purposes. The *balance* in literature between the logical and the contradictory, between single and multiple meanings, is the substance of the very lively tension existing and verbalized between energy and form. Freud's description of the dream work is now so well known that I don't need to give it in detail; chapter seven of *The Interpretation of Dreams* is its initial formulation, and there are many explanations of it, by Freud and by others. I should like to infer from them what seems to me a statement important to literary criticism: every ambiguity purposefully introduced into literature is in one way or another a compromise between uninhibited energy and extreme formal inhibition. It is impossible to decide the ideal degree of ambiguity, but one may, I think, assume that the forms of ambiguity reflect both degrees of tension and conditions of balance within the psyche. There are levels, of course, of sophistication. In children there is a fairly free play of wish and inhibition, contained within a limited number of metaphorical possibilities. Alice is after all Lewis Carroll's Alice and not Alice's. James's Maisie assumes the complexities of adulthood by necessity. In a great majority of adults the containment of energy is achieved in a relatively small number of rather abstract, though sentimentally overcharged, figures. The kinds of paradox and irony achieved by Donne, Marvell, Herbert, and others represent a highly endowed sense of the ambiguities residing in such tensions. Indeed, in the case of Donne the figures employed to express them reach a very high level of complexity, the purpose of which is both to individualize desire and to give it a degree of sophistication. The ambiguities resulting may be said to come partly from a genuine appreciation of human corruptibility (both moral and physical), partly from a wish to defend desire by means of defying those who would cynically dismiss it, partly from contemporary religious and metaphysical resources for transcendence. Such paradox is a result of the need both to admit a truth and at the same time to use available forms of transcendence in order to deny it; the admission and the denial are fused. Corruption becomes death, but death is contained within forms so successful in negating physical death that it triumphs over cynicism ("Only our love hath no decay," "The Anniversarie," l. 7). Similarly, the paradox of time and eternity may function within a poem; necessities forced upon us by time are denied by transforming the temporal into aspects of eternity. Yet the limits set by time (by which we narrowly view the corruption of the body as it "matures") are in themselves contained within the image of eternity; indeed, were it not for time, we should not *have* eternity. The complex nature of much religious poetry probably results from the interrelationship in each of us between our sense of physical instability and our desire for immortality; as for the latter, each of us has his own variant of it. Immortality is the ultimate formalization of desire; we continue to desire but come to realize that if we persist we shall die. To wish immortality is to hope for a removal of the reality principle, with a considerable gain in refinement of the pleasure principle. In the poetry of Laforgue and Corbière there is occasionally an attempt to set up ideally foreshortened versions of the id and either to satirize them ("Epitaphe") or to use them ("Locutions des Pierrots") as a means of satirizing, not the fact of ego-control in itself, but the prevailing accepted forms of control. Satire usually protests against the contemporary ways used by the ego to inhibit. In surrealism, and occasionally in the work of Rimbaud, there is an attempt to represent the id pure—or at least to allow the manifest dream content a free display—with the result that the literature describes, not a balance of tension but merely the consequence of a superficial exposure of wish to the idiom of ego.

The greatest range and the finest subtlety of all language exchanges based upon this principle of energy conflict and conservation are found in those types of communication described so brilliantly by Philip Wheelwright, in *The Burning Fountain* (Indiana U. P., 1954), as forms of "expressive language." I should like to use one or two of these, with the apology that I shall shift their context, perhaps even radically, from that of his intention. Mr. Wheelwright defines what he calls the "principle of plurisignation" as meaning "that an expressive symbol tends, on any given occasion of its realization, to carry more than one legitimate reference, in such a way that its proper meaning is a tension between two or more directions of semantic stress." (61) That is, in terms I have chosen to explain it, that the language of the symbol retains the charge and tension of its psychic origins, or of the dynamic shifts and exchanges of the energy which it was before the state was articulated. The many possibilities of stress, of direction, of painful thrust and arrest, are here echoed in the multiplications of meaning within a given image, metaphor, or cluster of images. This symbolic maneuver is accessible to a great variety of strategies: the poet may wish to exploit the irony he sees in his state of acceptance-rejection (that is, he may accept only ostensibly, or reject only ostensibly, but he ironically juxtaposes both acceptance and rejection in his language.) I believe we may say that Eliot both accepts and rejects. He sees as well the pathetic consequences of pure acceptance or of pure rejection. Herein lies the almost too easy irony of some of his poems. The polarities are perhaps too neatly obvious; and the deficiencies of both Prufrock and Sweeney are too much derived from circumstances that forbid transcendence. Eliot's great admiration of Dante seems to me to have come from his recognizing in Dante a means of escaping from the dead ends of Prufrock and Sweeney, as well as from the forbidding milieu responsible for them. The *Paradiso* is prefigured in the *Inferno*; a terrestrial inferno, such as Eliot describes in the early poems, can suggest a purgatory and a heaven only by an act of daring transcendence, an act which of course Eliot attempted. Or the poet may wish to express the tragedy of acceptance which lies in its inevitability (that is, acceptance of control is most unwished for but not in the least uncalled for) ; or he may extend the ambiguity to such an extent that it makes a virtue of transcendence (the effort to create a viable mystic exchange out of a condition of stasis, behavioral or mechanical).

Mr. Wheelwright speaks also of what he calls the " principle of paralogical dimensionality," by which he wishes to suggest " that there are other dimensions or *nodi* of meaning than those of logical universality and existential particularity. . . ." (64) The logical dimension is presumably that which restricts and limits within the strict terms of discernible reality. But, as I see it, this dimension is indispensable as a beginning; one must see what a thing is before he determines the scope and degree of its not being or of its being more. The co-ordinates of reality and desire are first set up, with such dimensional angularity as we are prosaically accustomed to use. The " paralogical dimensionality " of expressive language, as Mr. Wheelwright puts it, is nourished by the dissatisfactions accumulating from this initial effort at compromise. As the dream work refuses to accept either-or, the language of the poet suggests a multiple of meanings from a state of tension. There are several ways in which such a state may be true (effectual, " healthful," conducive of peace) , several in which it may be false. These variants are all contained within the single linguistic or metaphoric representation of a state of balanced tension.

Finally, one must consider the problem of associating the most intricate of literary expressions with Jung's archetypes. The access to myth in recent criticism is at least partly a product of research, or of a quest of mythical surrogates for displaced symbols. The elaborate structure provided by Jung for the purpose of linking individual present with collective past is useful only in that it suggests the extremes to which the imagination may go in generalizing immediate necessities and experiences. But archetypes, beyond the service they perform in cataloguing and arranging, are actually the most inflexible of forms. They may, in fact, arrest the process of articulating psychic tensions and they may oversimplify the results. Whatever one may say by way of crediting

Jung's ingenuity and the vigor of his imagination, the archetypal process, by enlarging and depersonalizing the expressive experience, threatens to destroy both its individuality and its complexity. The appeal to literature and to literary criticism of Jung's archaic forms and residues is, of course, phenomenally great; and it is necessary to explain just what the archetype does to the act of literary creation.

First, the process of verbalizing, of constructing linguistic expressions of any psycho-dynamic state follows along the lines of its own logic. This is not a transcendent logic; it is as complex as the circumstances require and permit. Within the limits seen and set by Freud, transcendence of the actual condition set up by psychic tensions and balances always remains closely associated with them and takes on their quality. Metaphors used to define such states are always individualized according to terms set down by the experiences determined by them.

It follows that the particularities of psychic experiences lend themselves to the act of universalizing. But the universals follow from a commonalty of basic experience, or of basic sources from which the secondary qualities of experience are drawn. To the degree that they may form clusters about a static symbol, they may be called archetypes. The danger is that one will abandon the particular for the archetypical. Once an experience is defined as " shared archetype," its particulars are threatened by dismissal. This indeed is often Jung's therapeutic aim, as I see it.

The advantages of Jung's archetypal portrayal of the collective psyche for literary criticism come primarily from its being available to an almost infinite range of spectacular inference. If poets unconsciously share archetypal interests, and if critics can bring themselves to commune with poets in the sharing, then the lines of tradition, of a discernible past discernibly associated with a felt present, are blurred. There is a great difference between a tradition of the ritual observance of a fixed symbolic and mythical pattern and the direct, knowledgeable, ingenious, overt *use* of myth in modern literature. To explain present literary circumstance by reference to archetypal patterns is to ignore the peculiarities of present practice and need. To say that basically we are linked to the past by archetypal means is to describe falsely the particular nature of our hunger for transcendence. The desire for credible and trustworthy universals is after all, and peculiarly, a feature of our contemporary behavior. It is not that the *desire* is unique, but that its special properties are. In rationally undermining the foundations of our past belief, we have put ourselves in an especially compromising position. We do not submit to any archetypes entirely, but we do love to entertain all of them, as poetic means and as mythical experiences that are half real and half merely " curious."

This peculiarity of our modern circumstance is especially well served by Jung, who serves artists by rescuing them from an unflattering Freudian diagnosis and giving them the role of seer, prophetic bard, guardian of the temple, neighbor of the mystic. Such a characterization makes any analysis of the literary process such as I have sketched impractical and unnecessary. Inspiration is no longer available to psychological explanation, or at least psychological or indeed any other kind of explanation is unnecessary to it. Jung's elaborate system has tried, therefore, to satisfy a great hunger for transcendence. Transcendence, however, is difficult. Jung has tried to make of it a therapeutic necessity, the extreme of psychiatric indulgence. The language of Jung's discourses moves further and further from Freud's cautions; the psychoanalyst becomes priest, " godlike demon," dispenser of positive power, caretaker of archetypes.

To conclude, Freud's meticulously correct choreography of the unconscious maintains the advantages of its discretion. Language in all of its scope of meanings and half-meanings and supermeanings may fit into his remarkable analysis of the psychic economy. The ambiguities of our language are the push-and-pull of our intelligence, alternating between residence in the id and regretful acceptance of the ego. While we may find types of identity with the past, we are not what we were some thousands of years ago; however tempting it is to suggest archetypal identifications, our psychic peculiarities are in the end available only to the sober testimony of systematic investigation. To say otherwise is to ignore both the dilemma and the specific intelligence of our times.

SELECTED
BIBLIOGRAPHY

Adams, Grace. "The Rise and Fall of Psychology," in *Atlantic Monthly*, CLIII (1934), 82–92.

After the Genteel Tradition: American Writers Since 1910, ed. Malcolm Cowley, New York, 1937.

Aiken, Conrad. Answer to Inquiry About the Influence of Freud, in *New Verse*, XI (1934), 13.

———. "A Basis for Criticism," in *New Republic*, XXXIV (1923), Pt. II, 1–6.

———. "Disintegration in Modern Poetry," in *Dial*, LXXVI (1924), 535–40.

———. "Forslin and Freud," in *Reedy's Mirror*, XXVI (1917), 273.

———. *Scepticisms: Notes on Contemporary Poetry*, New York, 1919.

Alexander, Franz. *Fundamentals of Psychoanalysis*, New York, 1948.

Allen, Frederick Lewis. *Only Yesterday: an Informal History of the 1920's*, New York, 1931.

"Analyzing the Psychoanalysts," in *Review of Reviews*, LXXVI (1927), 322–23.

Anderson, Margaret. *My Thirty-Years' War: an Autobiography*, New York, 1930.

Anderson, Sherwood. "Man and His Imagination," in *The Intent of the Artist*, Princeton, 1941.

———. Preface to Gertrude Stein's *Geography and Plays*, Boston, 1922.

———. *Sherwood Anderson's Memoirs*, New York, 1942.

———. *Sherwood Anderson's Notebook*, New York, 1926.

———. *A Story Teller's Story*, New York, 1924.

Auden, W. H. "Psychology and Art To-day," in *Arts To-day*, London, 1935.

Bartlett, Francis H. "The Limitations of Freud," in *Science and Society*, III (1939), 64–105.

Baudouin, C. *Psychoanalyse de l'art*, Paris, 1929.

Beach, Joseph Warren. *The Twentieth Century Novel*, New York, 1932.

Beguin, Albert. "The Night-side of Life," in *Transition*, XXVII (1938), 197–218.

Bell, Clive. "Doctor Freud on Art," in *Nation and Athenaeum*, XXXV (1924), 690–91.

Bergler, E. *The Writer and Psychoanalysis*, New York, 1950.

Blum, W. C. "Impossible Purity," in *Dial*, LXXVIII (1925), 318–23.

Bodenheim, Maxwell. "Psychoanalysis and American Fiction," in *Nation*, CXIV (1922), 683–84.

Bottome, Phyllis. *Alfred Adler: a Biography*, New York, 1939.

Bourne, Randolph. *History of a Literary Radical, and Other Essays*, New York, 1920.

Brennan, Joseph G. *Thomas Mann's World*, New York, 1942.

Brett, Dorothy. *Lawrence and Brett: a Friendship*, Philadelphia, 1933.

Brewster, Dorothy and Angus Burrell. *Modern Fiction*, New York, 1934.

Brewster, Edwin Tenney. "Dreams and Forgetting: New Discoveries in Dream Psychology," in *McClure's Magazine*, XXXIX (1912), 714–19.

Brill, A. A. "The Introduction and Development of Freud's Work in the United States," in *American Journal of Sociology*, XLV (1939), 318–25.

Brod, Max. *Franz Kafka: A Biography*, tr. G. Humphrey Roberts, New York, 1947.

Budgen, Frank. *James Joyce and the Making of Ulysses*, New York, 1934.

Burgum, Edwin Berry. "Franz Kafka and the Bankruptcy of Faith," in *Accent*, III (1943), 153–67.

———. "Ulysses and the Impasse of Individualism," in *Virginia Quarterly Review*, XVII (1941), 561–73.

Burke, Kenneth. *Attitudes Toward History*, New York, 1937.

———. "Freud and the Analysis of Poetry," in *American Journal of Sociology*, XLV (1939), 391–417.

Burrow, Trigant. "Psychoanalytic Improvisations and the Personal Equation," in *Psychoanalytic Review*, XIII (1926), 173–86.

Calas, Nicholas. "The Light of Words," in *Arson*, I (1942), 13–20.

———. "The Meaning of Surrealism," in *New Directions in Prose and Poetry, 1940*, Norfolk, Conn., 1940.

Cargill, Oscar. *Intellectual America: Ideas on the March*, New York, 1941.

Carswell, Catherine. *The Savage Pilgrimage: a Narrative of D. H. Lawrence*, New York, 1932.

Caudwell, Christopher. *Illusion and Reality: a Study of the Sources of Poetry*, London, 1937.

Chesterton, Gilbert K. "The Game of Psychoanalysis," in *Century*, CVI (1923), 34–43.

Cleaton, Irene and Allen. *Books and Battles, 1920–1930*, Boston, 1937.

Colum, Mary. *From These Roots*, New York, 1937.

Corke, Helen. *Lawrence and Apocalypse*, London, 1933.

Cowley, Malcolm. *Exile's Return: a Narrative of Ideas*, New York, 1934.

Daiches, David. *The Novel and the Modern World*, Chicago, 1939.

Dell, Floyd. *The Briary Bush*, New York, 1921.

———. *Homecoming: an Autobiography*, New York, 1933.

———. *Love in the Machine Age*, New York, 1930.

———. *Moon Calf*, New York, 1920.

De Reul, Paul. *L'Oeuvre de D. H. Lawrence*, Paris, 1937.

De Voto, Bernard. "Freud's Influence on Literature," in *Saturday Review of Literature*, XX (1939), 10–11.

———. "The Well-Informed, 1920–1930," in *Forays and Rebuttals*, Boston, 1936.

Dingle, Reginald J. "Psychology and Original Sin," in *Dublin Review*, CC (1937), 134–44.

Dujardin, Eduard. *Les Lauriers sont coupés*, tr. Stuart Gilbert, Norfolk, Conn., 1938.

Eastman, Max. "Exploring the Soul and Healing the Body," in *Everybody's Magazine*, XXXII (1915), 741–50.

Empson, William. *The Seven Types of Ambiguity*, New York, 1931.

Farrar, John. "Sex Psychology in Modern Fiction," in *Independent*, CXVII (1926), 669–70.

Faulkner, William. *As I Lay Dying*, New York, 1930.

———. *The Sound and the Fury*, New York, 1929.

Fite, Warner. "Psycho-analysis and Sex Psychology," in *Nation*, CIII
    (1916), 127–29.
Flores, Angel, ed. *The Kafka Problem*, Norfolk, Conn., 1946.
Frank, Waldo. *In the American Jungle*, New York, 1937.
———. *Our America*. New York, 1919.
———. *The Re-Discovery of America: an Introduction to a Philosophy
    of American Life*, New York, 1929.
———. *Salvos: an Informal Book About Books and Plays*, New York,
    1924.
———. *Time Exposures; by Search Light* . . . , New York, 1926.
Freud, Sigmund. *An Autobiographical Study*, tr. James Strachey,
    London, 1936.
———. *Beyond the Pleasure Principle*, tr. C. J. M. Hubback, London,
    1922.
———. *Civilization and Its Discontents*, tr. Joan Riviere, New York,
    1930.
———. *The Collected Papers of Sigmund Freud*, London, 1924.
    Vol. II:
    "The Dynamics of the Transference," tr. Joan Riviere (1912),
        312–22.
    "The Employment of Dream-Interpretation in Psychoanalysis,"
        tr. Joan Riviere (1912), 305–11.
    "Further Recommendations in the Technique of Psychoanalysis:
        on Beginning the Treatment . . . ," tr. Joan Riviere (1913),
        342–65.
    "Further Recommendations in the Technique of Psychoanalysis:
        Observations on Transference-Love," tr. Joan Riviere (1915),
        377–91.
    "Further Recommendations in the Technique of Psychoanalysis:
        Recollection, Repetition . . . ," tr. Joan Riviere (1914),
        366–76.
    "The Future Prospects of Psychoanalytic Therapy," tr. Joan
        Riviere (1910), 285–96.
    "Observations on 'Wild' Psychoanalysis," tr. John Riviere
        (1910), 297–304.
    "Recommendations for Physicians on the Psychoanalytic Method
        of Treatment," tr. Joan Riviere (1912), 323–33.
    "Turnings in the Ways of Psychoanalytic Therapy," tr. Joan
        Riviere (1919), 392–402.
    Vol. III:
    "The Analysis of a Phobia in a Five-Year-Old Boy," tr. Alix and
        James Strachey (1909), 149–289.

Vol. IV:

"Contributions to the Psychology of Love: A Special Type of Choice of Object Made by Men," tr. Joan Riviere (1910), 192–202.

"Formulations Regarding the Two Principles in Mental Functioning," tr. M. N. Searl (1911), 13–21.

"The Moses of Michelangelo," tr. Alix Strachey (1914), 257–87.

"The Relation of the Poet to Day-Dreaming," tr. I. F. Grant-Duff (1908), 173–83.

"Some Character-types Met with in Psychoanalytic Work," tr. E. Colburn Mayne (1915), 318–44.

"Thoughts for the Times on War and Death," tr. E. Colburn Mayne (1915), 288–317.

"The Unconscious," tr. Cecil M. Baines (1915), 98–136.

———. *The Ego and the Id.* tr. Joan Riviere, London, 1927.

———. *The Future of an Illusion,* tr. W. D. Robson-Scott, New York, 1928.

———. *A General Introduction to Psychoanalysis,* tr. G. Stanley Hall, New York, 1920.

———. *Group Psychology and the Analysis of the Ego,* tr. James Strachey, New York, n. d.

———. *The History of the Psychoanalytic Movement,* tr. A. A. Brill (1916), in *The Basic Writings of Sigmund Freud,* ed. and tr. A. A. Brill, New York, 1938.

———. *The Interpretation of Dreams,* tr. A. A. Brill, New York, 1913.

———. *Leonardo da Vinci: a Psychosexual Study of an Infantile Reminiscence,* tr. A. A. Brill, New York, 1910.

———. *New Introductory Lectures on Psychoanalysis,* tr. W. J. H. Sprott, New York, 1933.

———. "The Origin and Development of Psychoanalysis," tr. Harry W. Chase, in *American Journal of Psychology,* XXI (1910), 181–219.

———. *The Problem of Anxiety,* tr. Henry A. Bunker, New York, 1936.

———. *Psychopathology of Everyday Life,* tr. A. A. Brill (1914), in *The Basic Writings of Sigmund Freud,* tr. and ed. A. A. Brill, New York, 1938.

———. *Three Contributions to a Theory of Sex,* tr. A. A. Brill (1910), in *The Basic Writings of Sigmund Freud,* tr. and ed. A. A. Brill, New York, 1938.

———. *Totem and Taboo,* tr. A. A. Brill, New York, 1927.

————. *Why War?: An International Series of Open Letters*, Paris, 1933.

————. *Wit and Its Relation to the Unconscious*, tr. A. A. Brill, New York, 1916.

Fry, Roger. " The Artist and Psychoanalysis," in *The New Criticism: an Anthology of Modern Aesthetics and Literary Criticism*, ed. E. W. Burgum, New York, 1930.

Gascoyne, David. *A Short Survey of Surrealism*, London, 1935.

Giedion-Welcher, Carola. " Work in Progress: a Linguistic Experiment by James Joyce," tr. Eugene Jolas, in *Transition*, XIX-XX (1930), 174–83.

Gilbert, Stuart. *James Joyce's Ulysses: a Study*, New York, 1934.

Glover, E. *Freud or Jung*, New York, 1950.

Golding, Louis. *James Joyce*, London, 1933.

Gorman, Herbert. *James Joyce*, New York, 1939.

Gray, Ronald. *Kafka's Castle*, Cambridge, 1956.

Gregory, Horace. *Pilgrim of the Apocalypse: a Critical Study of D. H. Lawrence*, New York, 1933.

Hanley, Miles L. *Word Index to James Joyce's Ulysses*, Madison, Wis., 1937.

Hapgood, Hutchins. *A Victorian in the Modern World*, New York, 1939.

Harding, R. E. M. *An Anatomy of Inspiration and an Essay on the Creative Mood*, Cambridge, 1940.

Hatcher, Harlan H. *Creating the Modern American Novel*, New York, 1935.

Hill, Archibald A. " A Philologist Looks at Finnegans Wake," in *Virginia Quarterly Review*, XV (1939), 650–56.

Holt, Edwin B. *The Freudian Wish and Its Place in Ethics*, New York, 1915.

Hook, Sidney. " Marx and Freud, Oil and Water," in *Open Court*, XLII (1928), 20–25.

Huxley, Aldous. *Antic Hay*, London, 1923.

————. " The Farcical History of Richard Greenow," in *Limbo*, London, 1920.

————. " Our Contemporary Hocus-Pocus," in *Forum*, LXXIII (1925), 313–20.

Jacobi, Jolan. *The Psychology of Jung*, tr. K. W. Bash, New Haven, 1943.

Joad, C. E. M. " Psychology in Retreat," in *New Statesman and Nation*, IX (1935), 956–57.

Jolas, Eugene. "The Dream," in *Transition*, XIX-XX (1930), 46–47.

———. *I Have Seen Monsters and Angels*, Paris, 1938.

———. "Inquiry into the Spirit and Language of Night," in *Transition*, XXVII (1938), 233–45.

———. "The King's English Is Dying: Long Live the Great American Language," in *Transition*, XIX-XX (1930), 141–46.

———. "Literature and the New Man," in *Transition*, XIX–XX (1930), 13–22.

———. "My Friend James Joyce," in *Partisan Review*, VIII (1941), 82–93.

———. "Necessity for the New Word," in *Modern Quarterly*, V (1929), 273–75.

———. "Surrealism: Ave atque Vale," in *Fantasy*, VII (1941), 23–30.

———. ed. *Vertical: A Yearbook for Romantic-Mystic Ascensions*, New York, 1941.

Jones, Ernest. *Papers on Psychoanalysis*, Baltimore, 1938.

———. *Hamlet and Oedipus*, New York, 1949.

———. *The Life and Work of Sigmund Freud*, Vol. I: *The Formative Years and the Great Discoveries*, New York, 1953. Vol. II: *Years of Maturity*, New York, 1955.

Jung, Carl G. *Modern Man in Search of a Soul*, New York, 1934.

———. *Two Essays on Analytical Psychology*, London, 1928, New York, 1956.

Kafka, Franz. *Amerika*, tr. Edwin Muir with a Preface by Klaus Mann, Norfolk, Conn., n. d.

———. *The Castle*, tr. Edwin and Willa Muir, with an introduction by Thomas Mann, New York, 1943.

———. *Diaries*, tr., Joseph Kresh and Martin Greenburg; ed., Max Brod. London, 1948, 1949.

———. *The Great Wall of China*, tr. Edwin Muir, London, 1933.

———. *The Penal Colony*, tr. Willa and Edwin Muir, New York, 1948.

———. *The Trial*, tr. Willa and Edwin Muir, New York, 1937.

Kierkegaard, Sören. *Fear and Trembling*, tr. Walter Lowrie, Princeton, 1941.

Klein, David B. "Psychology and Freud: an Historico-critical Appraisal," in *Psychological Review*, XL (1933), 440–56.

Kris, Ernst. *Psychoanalytic Explorations in Art*, New York, 1952.

Kroeber, A. L. "Totem and Taboo in Retrospect," in *American Journal of Sociology*, XLV (1939), 446–51.

Krutch, Joseph Wood. *The Modern Temper*, New York, 1929.

————. *Edgar Allan Poe: A Study in Genius*, New York, 1926.

Landis, Carney. "Psychoanalysis and the Scientific Method," abstract in *Science*, n. s., XCIII (1941), 486.

Lawrence, D. H. *Apocalypse*, New York, 1932.

————. *Fantasia of the Unconscious*, New York, 1930.

————. *The Letters of D. H. Lawrence*, ed. Aldous Huxley, New York, 1932.

————. *Mornings in Mexico*, New York, 1934.

————. *Phoenix: the Posthumous Papers of D. H. Lawrence*, ed. Edward D. McDonald, New York, 1936.

————. *Psychoanalysis and the Unconscious*, London, 1923.

————. *Studies in Classic American Literature*, New York, 1930.

Lawrence, Frieda. *Not I but the Wind . . .* , New York, 1934.

Levin, Harry. *James Joyce: a Critical Introduction*, Norfolk, Conn., 1941.

Lewis, Wyndham. "Paleface," in *Enemy*, II (1927), 3–110.

Lewisohn, Ludwig. *The Island Within*, New York, 1928.

————. *Mid-Channel: an American Chronicle*, New York, 1929.

————. *The Permanent Horizon: A New Search for Old Truths*, New York, 1934.

————. *Stephen Escott*, New York, 1930.

————. *Upstream*, New York, 1922.

Lewisohn, Ludwig and Edna. *Haven*, New York, 1940.

Lhote, André. "The Unconscious in Art," in *Transition*, XXVI (1937), 82–96.

Lindner, Robert, ed. *Explorations in Psychoanalysis*, New York, 1953.

Lindsay, Jack. "The Modern Consciousness: An Essay Towards an Integration," in *London Aphrodite*, I (1928), 3–24.

Lindsay, Jack, and P. R. Stephensen. "Editorial Manifesto," in *London Aphrodite*, I (1928), 2.

Lippmann, Walter. "Freud and the Layman," in *New Republic*, II (1915), Sup. 9–10.

————. *Preface to Politics*, New York and London, 1913.

Luhan, Mabel Dodge. *Lorenzo in Taos*, New York, 1935.

————. *Movers and Shakers*, New York, 1936.

McCole, Camille J. "Sherwood Anderson, Congenital Freudian," in *Catholic World*, CXXX (1929), 129–33.

Macaulay, Rose. *Dangerous Ages*, New York, 1921.

Mann, Thomas. "Freud and the Future," tr. H. T. Lowe-Porter, in *Freud, Goethe, Wagner*, New York, 1937, 3–45.

————. "Freud's Position in the History of Modern Thought," in *Criterion*, XII (1933), 549–70.

——. ed., *The Living Thoughts of Schopenhauer*, New York, 1939.

——. *A Sketch of My Life*, tr. H. T. Lowe-Porter, Paris, 1930.

——. *The Theme of the Joseph Novels*, Washington, D. C., 1942. An address delivered in the Coolidge Auditorium of the Library of Congress, November 17, 1942.

Marcuse, Herbert. *Eros and Civilization*, Boston, 1955.

Menninger, Karl. "Pseudoanalysis: Perils of Freudian Verbalisms," in *Outlook*, CLV (1930), 363–65.

Merrild, Knud. *A Poet and Two Painters: A Memoir of D. H. Lawrence*, London, 1938.

Michaud, Regis. *The American Novel Today: A Social and Psychological Study*, Boston, 1931.

Miller, Henry. "The Rise of Schizophrenia," in *New English Weekly*, X (1936), 69–70.

——. "The Universe of Death," in *Phoenix*, I (1938), 33–64.

——. *The Wisdom of the Heart*, Norfolk, Conn., 1941.

Miller, Henry, and Michael Fraenkel. *Hamlet*, Santurce, Puerto Rico, 1939.

Mordell, Albert. *The Erotic Motive in Literature*, New York, 1919.

Morgan, George Allen. *What Nietzsche Means*, Cambridge, Mass., 1941.

Muller, Herbert J. *Science and Criticism*, New Haven, 1943.

——. "Surrealism: a Dissenting Opinion," in *New Directions in Prose and Poetry, 1940*, Norfolk, Conn., 1940.

Munson, Gorham B. *Waldo Frank: a Study*, New York, 1923.

Murray, Henry. Introduction, *Pierre and the Ambiguities*, New York, 1949.

Murry, John Middleton. *Between Two Worlds: an Autobiography*, London, 1935.

——. "Reminiscences of D. H. Lawrence," in *New Adelphi*, III (1930), 264–75; *Adelphi*, n. s., I (1930), 42–52, 142–52, 195–203 (1931), 322–29, 413–20, 455–61.

——. *Son of Woman: The Story of D. H. Lawrence*, New York, 1931.

Nietzsche, Friedrich. *The Birth of Tragedy*, tr. Clifton P. Fadiman, New York, n. d.

——. *Ecce Homo*, tr. Clifton P. Fadiman, New York, n. d.

Orwell, George. "Inside the Whale," in *New Directions in Prose and Poetry, 1940*, Norfolk, Conn., 1940.

Osborn, Reuben. *Freud and Marx*, New York, n. d.

Parry, Albert. *Garrets and Pretenders: a History of Bohemianism in America*, New York, 1933.

Penton, Brian. " Note on the Form of the Novel," in *London Aphrodite*, VI (1929), 434–44.

Peterson, Houston. *The Melody of Chaos*, New York, 1931.

Prescott, Frederick Clarke. *The Poetic Mind*, New York, 1922.

Prescott, Joseph. " James Joyce: A Study in Words," in *PMLA*, LIV (1939), 304–315.

Ramsay, A. W. " Psychology and Literary Criticism," in *Criterion*, XV (1936), 627–43.

Rank, Otto. *Art and Artist*, tr. C. T. Atkinson, New York, 1932.

Ransom, John Crowe. " Freud and Literature," in *Saturday Review of Literature*, I (1924), 161–62.

Read, Herbert. *Collected Essays in Literary Criticism*, London, 1938.

Reed, Raoul. " Psychoanalysis in Literature," in *Freeman*, V (1922), 490–91.

Reik, Theodor. *From Thirty Years with Freud*, New York, 1940.

Rosenfeld, Paul. *Men Seen: Twenty-four Modern Authors*, New York, 1925.

Sachs, H. *The Creative Unconscious*, Cambridge, 1942.

Santayana, George. " A Long Way Round to Nirvana: or Much Ado about Dying," Review of Freud's *Beyond the Pleasure Principle*, in *Dial*, LXXV (1923), 435–42.

Scarfe, Francis. " The Poetry of Dylan Thomas," in *Horizon*, II (1940), 226–39.

Schlauch, Margaret. " The Language of James Joyce," in *Science and Society*, III (1939), 482–97.

Schroeder, Theodore. " Deterministic Presupposition of Psychoanalysis," in *Open Court*, XLI (1927), 90–102.

Simmons, Ernest J. *Dostoievski: The Making of a Novelist*, London, 1940.

Sinclair, May. *The Life and Death of Harriet Frean*, New York, 1922.

Slochower, Harry. " Freud and Marx in Contemporary Literature," in *Sewanee Review*, XLIX (1941), 315–24.

———, et al. *A Franz Kafka Miscellany*, New York, 1940.

Spencer, Theodore. " ' Stephen Hero ': the Unpublished Manuscript of James Joyce's ' A Portrait of the Artist as a Young Man,' " in *Southern Review*, VII (1941), 174–86.

Spender, Stephen. *The Destructive Element: a Study of Modern Writers and Beliefs*, Boston, 1935.

Spiegel, Leo A. " The New Jargon: Psychology in Literature," in *Sewanee Review*, XL (1932), 476–91.

Stuart, Michael. " Mr. Joyce's Word-Creatures," in *Symposium*, II (1931), 459–67.

Sullivan, Mark. *Our Times: the United States, 1900–1925*, New York, 1932. 4 vols.

Swenson, David F. *Something about Kierkegaard*, ed. Lillian Marvin Swenson, Minneapolis, 1941.

Tauber, Herbert. *Franz Kafka: An Interpretation of His Works*, tr., G. Humphrey Roberts and Roger Senhouse, London, 1948.

T., E. *D. H. Lawrence: A Personal Record*, London, 1935.

Thomas, Dylan. Answer to Inquiry about Freud's Influence, *New Verse*, XI (1934), 9.

Thurber, James. *Let Your Mind Alone*, New York, 1937.

Thurber, James, and E. B. White. *Is Sex Necessary?* New York, 1929.

Tindall, William York. *D. H. Lawrence and Susan His Cow*, New York, 1939.

Tridon, André. *Easy Lessons in Psychoanalysis*, New York, 1922.

———. *Psychoanalysis: Its History, Theory, and Practice*, New York, 1923.

Trilling, Lionel. *Freud and the Crisis of Our Culture*, Boston, 1955.

———. "The Legacy of Sigmund Freud; II: Literary and Aesthetic," in *Kenyon Review*, II (1940), 162–68.

Van Vechten, Carl. *Peter Whiffle: His Life and Works*, New York, 1922.

Vivas, Eliseo. "The Legacy of Sigmund Freud: Philosophical," in *Kenyon Review*, II (1940), 173–85.

Ware, Caroline F. *Greenwich Village, 1920–1930: A Comment on American Civilization in the Post-War Years*, Boston, 1935.

Weigand, Hermann J. *Thomas Mann's Novel, Der Zauberberg*, New York, 1933.

West, Rebecca. *The Strange Necessity*, Garden City, New York, 1928.

Wickham, Harvey. *The Impuritans . . .*, New York, 1929.

Wilson, Edmund. "The Dream of H. C. Earwicker," in *The Wound and the Bow: Seven Studies in Literature*, Boston, 1941.

———. "The Historical Interpretation of Literature," in *The Intent of The Critic*, ed. Donald A. Stauffer, Princeton, 1941.

———. "James Joyce," in *Axel's Castle: a Study in the Imaginative Literature of 1870–1930*, New York, 1931.

Wittels, Fritz. "Revision of a Biography," in *American Journal of Psychology*, XLV (1933), 745–49.

———. *Sigmund Freud: His Personality, His Teaching, and His School*, tr. Eden and Cedar Paul, New York, 1924.

INDEX

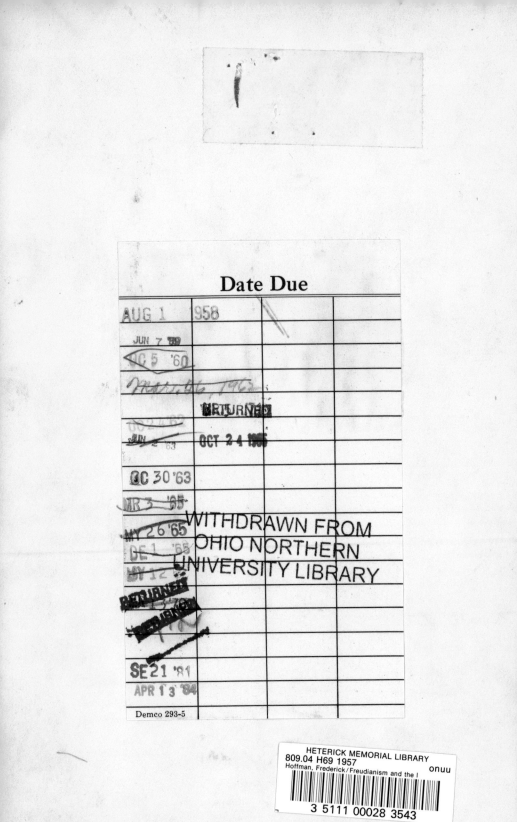

Date Due

AUG 1 1958			
JUN 7 '59			
OC 5 '60			
	RETURNED		
JUN 2 '63	OCT 24 1966		
OC 30 '63			
MR 3 '65			
MY 26 '65	WITHDRAWN FROM		
DE 1 '65	OHIO NORTHERN		
MY 12	UNIVERSITY LIBRARY		
RETURNED			
SE 21 '81			
APR 1 3 '84			

Demco 293-5

HETERICK MEMORIAL LIBRARY
809.04 H69 1957   onuu
Hoffman, Frederick / Freudianism and the l

3 5111 00028 3543